# NORMANDY

# NORMANDY

## THE LANDINGS
## TO THE LIBERATION OF PARIS

## Olivier Wieviorka

Translated by
M. B. DeBevoise

*The Belknap Press of
Harvard University Press*
CAMBRIDGE, MASSACHUSETTS
LONDON, ENGLAND
2008

Originally published as *Histoire du débarquement en Normandie:
Des origines à la libération de Paris, 1941–1944*
© Éditions du Seuil, janvier 2007

LIBRARY OF CONGRESS CATALOGING-IN-PUBLICATION DATA

Wieviorka, Olivier, 1960–
[Histoire du débarquement en Normandie. English]
Normandy: the landings to the liberation of Paris / Olivier Wieviorka ;
translated by M. B. DeBevoise.
p.   cm.
Includes bibliographical references and index.
ISBN 978-0-674-02838-8 (alk. paper)
1. World War, 1939–1945—Campaigns—France—Normandy.   I. Title.
D756.5.N6W5313 2008
940.54′21421—dc22      2007052152

*For Pascale and Sophie*

# Contents

# Abbreviations and Code Names

*Military, Governmental, and Other Entities*

| | |
|---|---|
| AEAF | American Expeditionary Air Forces |
| AEF | Allied Expeditionary Forces |
| AFH | Allied Force Headquarters (Algiers) |
| AGWAR | American Government War [Department] |
| AMGOT | Allied Military Government of Occupied Territory |
| ANCXF | Allied Naval Command Expeditionary Force |
| AP | Associated Press |
| BBC | British Broadcasting Corporation |
| BCOS | British Chiefs of Staff |
| BCRA | Bureau Central de Renseignements et d'Action [Central Bureau of Information and Action] |
| CBS | Columbia Broadcasting System |
| CCS | Combined Chiefs of Staff |
| CFLN | Comité Français de la Libération Nationale [French Committee of National Liberation, subsequently renamed GPRF] |
| CNR | Conseil National de la Résistance [National Resistance Council] |
| COMAC | Commission d'Action Militaire [Military Action Commission of the CNR] |
| COPP | Combined Operations Pilotage Parties |

| | |
|---|---|
| COSSAC | Chief of staff to the Supreme Allied Commander (designate) [and his staff] |
| ETO | European theater of operations |
| FFI | Forces Françaises de l'Intérieur [French Forces of the Interior] |
| FFL | Forces Françaises Libres [Free French Forces] |
| FHW | Fremde Heere West [Foreign Armies West] |
| FLAK | Fliegerabwehrkanonen [Antiaircraft guns] |
| FTP | Francs-Tireurs et Partisans Français [French Partisan Irregular Riflemen] |
| FUSAG | First United States Army Group |
| GPRF | Gouvernement Provisoire de la République Française [Provisional Government of the French Republic] |
| IGS | Imperial General Staff |
| JCS | Joint Chiefs of Staff |
| LCS | London Controlling Section |
| MI5 | British Counterintelligence Service |
| MI6 | British Foreign Intelligence Service |
| MMLA | Mission Militaire de Liaison Administrative [Military Administrative Liaison Mission] |
| NKVD | Narodny Komissariat Vnutrennikh Del [People's Commissariat for Internal Affairs] |
| OB West | Oberbefehlshaber West des Heeres [Army Field Command in the West] |
| OKH | Oberkommando des Heeres [Army High Command] |
| OKW | Oberkommando der Wehrmacht [High Command of the Armed Forces] |
| OPD | Operations Plans Division |
| OSS | Office of Strategic Services |
| OWI | Office of War Information |
| PCF | Parti Communiste Français [French Communist Party] |
| RAF | Royal Air Force |
| SAS | Special Air Service |
| SD | Sicherheitsdienst [Security Service of the SS] |
| SFHQ | Special Forces Headquarters |

| | |
|---|---|
| SGS | Secretary, general staff |
| SHAEF | Supreme Headquarters, Allied Expeditionary Force |
| SiPo | Sicherheitspolizei [Security Police of the SS] |
| SIS | Secret Intelligence Service |
| SOE | Special Operations Executive |
| SOS | Services of Supply |
| SS | Schutzstaffel [Protection Squad] |
| USAF | United States Air Force |
| USFET | U.S. Forces European Theater |
| USSR | Union of Soviet Socialist Republics |
| USSTAF | United States Strategic Air Forces |
| WPD | War Plans Division |

*Landing Craft and Vehicles*

| | |
|---|---|
| AVRE | Armoured vehicle Royal Engineer |
| LCA | Landing craft, assault |
| LCF | Landing craft, flak |
| LCG | Landing craft, gun |
| LCI | Landing craft, infantry |
| LCI (L) | Landing craft, infantry (large) |
| LCM | Landing craft, mechanized |
| LCT | Landing craft, tank |
| LCVP | Landing craft, vehicle, personnel ("Higgins Boats") |
| LSD | Landing ship, dock |
| LSE | Landing ship, emergency [repair] |
| LSH | Landing ship, hospital |
| LSI | Landing ship, infantry |
| LSI (H) | Landing ship, infantry (hospital) |
| LST | Landing ship, tank |

*Meetings of Allied Political and Military Leaders*

| | |
|---|---|
| ARCADIA | Washington (22 December 1941–14 January 1942) |
| EUREKA | Teheran (28 November–1 December 1943) |
| QUADRANT | Quebec City (14–24 August 1943) |
| RATTLE | Largs, Scotland (28 June–1 July 1943) |

| | |
|---|---|
| SEXTANT | Cairo (22–26 November 1943) |
| SYMBOL | Casablanca (14–24 January 1943) |
| THUNDERCLAP | London (7–8 April 1944) |
| TRIDENT | Washington (12–25 May 1943) |

*Military and Paramilitary Operations*

| | |
|---|---|
| ANVIL | Allied invasion of Provence (August 1944), renamed DRAGOON at the last moment |
| AVALANCHE | Allied invasion of southern Italy (September 1943) |
| BAGRATION | Final Soviet offensive, launched 22 June 1944 |
| BARBAROSSA | German invasion of the Soviet Union, launched 22 June 1941 |
| BLEU, VERT, VIOLET, TORTUE | Operations carried out by the French Resistance in support of OVERLORD (June 1944) |
| BLUECOAT | British assault on Vire (July–August 1944) |
| BOLERO | Buildup of OVERLORD forces in Great Britain |
| BUCCANEER | Plan for Allied attack on the Andaman Islands, Bay of Bengal (canceled) |
| CHASTITY | Plan to build an artificial harbor in Quiberon Bay, Brittany (never implemented) |
| CITADEL | German offensive against Kursk, July 1943 |
| COBRA | American breakout from the Cotentin Peninsula (late July 1944) |
| CROSSBOW | Allied precision-bombing campaign against V-weapon installations, 1943–1944 |
| DRAGOON | New name for ANVIL, adopted in deference to Churchill |
| EPSOM | Montgomery's third attempt to take Caen (late June 1944) |
| GOODWOOD | British breakout attempt at Caen (July 1944) |
| HUSKY | Allied invasion of Sicily (July 1943) |
| NEPTUNE | The 6 June 1944 landings in Normandy |
| OVERLORD | The Allied invasion of northwestern Europe |
| POINTBLANK | Strategic bombing campaign against Germany, 1943–1944 |
| SLEDGEHAMMER | Allied contingency plan for emergency invasion of France in autumn 1942 (never acted upon) |
| SPRING | First Canadian attack on Falaise (late July 1944) |

| | |
|---|---|
| TORCH | Allied invasion of French North Africa (November 1942) |
| TOTALIZE | Second Canadian attack on Falaise (early August 1944) |
| TRACTABLE | Anglo-Canadian thrust to close the Falaise pocket (mid-August 1944) |

*Normandy Training Exercises*

| | |
|---|---|
| DUCK I–III | January–February 1944 |
| FABIUS I–VI | 23 April–7 May 1944 |
| KRUSCHEN/ | April–July 1943 |
| FILIBUSTER/ | |
| JANTZEN | |
| ROUNDABOUT I–VI | Winter 1943–1944 |
| TIGER | 22–30 April 1944 |

*Allied Disinformation Plans and Operations*

| | |
|---|---|
| BODYGUARD | The overall plan for the various deception operations aimed at misleading the Germans about Allied intentions in northwestern Europe in 1944 |
| COCKADE | A campaign under the aegis of Plan JAEL, comprising several operations aimed at misleading the Germans about Allied intentions in northwestern Europe in 1943 |
| FORTITUDE NORTH | Series of operations meant to keep German Scandinavian forces in place, in anticipation of Allied invasion of Norway |
| FORTITUDE SOUTH | Series of operations meant to persuade Germans that the main Allied invasion would occur in the Pas de Calais, rather than Normandy |
| GLIMMER | Simulated D-Day landing on the Pas de Calais |
| JAEL | Original code name for Plan BODYGUARD (changed December 1943) |
| OAKFIELD | Allied operations in the Mediterranean (1943–44) |
| QUICKSILVER | Threatened invasion of the Pas de Calais by the U.S. First Army under Patton |
| ROYAL FLUSH | Diplomatic pressure on neutral countries to support Allied stratagems |
| SHINGLE | Allied landings in northern Italy (1944) |

| | |
|---|---|
| STARKEY, TINDALL, WADHAM | Deception schemes devised in the summer of 1943 to persuade the Germans of imminent large-scale Allied landings in the Pas de Calais, Norway, and Brittany, respectively |
| TARBRUSH | Final COPP raids in May 1944 on the Pas de Calais |
| TAXABLE | Simulated D-Day landing on Cape Antifer |
| VENDETTA | Invasion of the French Mediterranean coast between Sète and Narbonne |
| ZEPPELIN | Successor to OAKFIELD |

# Illustrations

# NORMANDY

# INTRODUCTION

## *Return to France*

THE NORMANDY LANDING OF 6 JUNE 1944 unquestionably ranks among the greatest events in modern history. In marking the end of one phase of the war in Europe, it announced the advent of another, radically different state of affairs. Months of frantic waiting, nervous speculation, and intense preparation came to a close: the campaign that was to contribute to the defeat of the Third Reich had at last begun. By the evening of D-Day, the face of battle had changed irrevocably: what had come before was now set apart from what would come after. And yet nothing had been decided—a fact that is obscured if this day is considered the symbolic epilogue to the war in the West, in the aftermath of which the Allied campaign amounted to no more than the execution of a series of secondary missions. But this longest and most exhausting of days had to support the weight of myth. Eager to magnify the importance of a monumental event still further, soldiers and historians alike have often preferred its heroic charms to the harsh realities of the day, in relegating to the margins of silence everything that contradicts the legend. Already more than fifty years ago, however, the British military historian Basil H. Liddell Hart complained that there had been "too much glorification of the campaign and too little objective investigation."[1]

A first element of legend has to do with numbers. The colossal scale of the resources mobilized quite naturally captured the popular imagination. Insisting on the numerical superiority of the Anglo-American forces arrayed against the Germans, some observers concluded in retrospect that the Allies' relative advantages in men and matériel made victory inevitable. It was assumed that America's industrial wealth assured the Allies not only of overwhelming firepower but of an uninterrupted stream of reinforcements as well. In this view, the Allied command could therefore afford the luxury of tactical and strategic errors: the "arsenal of democracy," whatever its shortcomings, guaranteed the defeat of the enemy.[2] History had not yet been written on the morning of 6 June 1944, however, and it needs to be kept in mind that any such sense of inevitability corresponds neither to the thinking of officials at the time nor to a careful examination of events since. "It would be unwise to assume we can defeat Germany simply by outproducing her," General Leonard T. Gerow, head of the U.S. War Plans Division, advised the undersecretary of defense, John J. McCloy, in the fall of 1941. "Wars are won by sound strategy implemented by well-trained forces which are adequately and effectively equipped."[3]

The myth of D-Day also extends to the political and moral significance of the invasion, portrayed both before and afterward as the decisive episode in an epochal struggle between good and evil, right and wrong, democratic and totalitarian systems of government. "You are about to embark upon the Great Crusade, toward which we have striven these many months," General Dwight D. Eisenhower exhorted the troops in his proclamation that day: "The eyes of the world are upon you. The hopes and prayers of liberty-loving people everywhere march with you."[4] These words seemed so pertinent that Eisenhower's publishers gave them a prominent place in their edition of his war memoirs, significantly entitled *Crusade in Europe*.[5] And indeed the landing did lead to the destruction of Nazism—a regime that incarnated absolute barbarism, as Auschwitz and Buchenwald enduringly testify—while reestablishing the rule of law and freedom, at least in Western Europe. Until the fall of the Berlin Wall, as we now know, Eastern Europe was to suffer a less happy fate.

Must Operation OVERLORD therefore be seen as a holy war, and its soldiers as modern crusaders? The curiously naive view that the Allies fought only for principles, sacrificing their national interests on the altar of morality, suggests that the three Allied powers, led by the United States, were uninterested in the geopolitical consequences of a German defeat—that they were concerned only to save the peoples of Europe from the Nazi plague and to reinstate democratic values and regimes. The story line follows a familiar arc: none of the young men who landed "wanted to be part of another war. They wanted to be throwing baseballs, not hand grenades, shooting .22s at rabbits, not M-1s at other young men. But when the test came, when freedom had to be fought for or abandoned, they fought. They were soldiers of democracy. They were the men of D-Day, and to them we owe our freedom."[6] No country owed more to them than did France, delivered from the Hitlerian yoke by the willingness of Great Britain and the United States to sacrifice their blood and treasure on its behalf. But if the land of Washington paid back, handsomely and with interest, the debt incurred to Lafayette, the land of Rochambeau showed scant gratitude. "Sacrifice: They Died for France but France Has Forgotten," read a headline in the *New York Post* in February 2003—a moment of some turbulence in Franco-American relations.[7]

What is more, in fighting for principles, the United States made a grievous error, according to this premise, as much through gullibility as through an excess of idealism. Obsessed by the necessity of vanquishing Nazi Germany militarily, Franklin Roosevelt subordinated diplomacy to strategy—clearing the way in a single stroke for the seizure of Eastern Europe by the Soviet Union, despite the entreaties of Winston Churchill. Not long after the war, General Omar Bradley, the former commander of the American First Army, bluntly noted in his memoirs: "At times during that war we forgot that wars are fought for the resolution of political conflicts, and in the ground campaign for Europe we sometimes overlooked political considerations of vast importance. Today, after several years of cold war, we are intensely aware that a military effort cannot be separated from political objectives."[8] This assessment was to be echoed by a great many later writers, among them the French historian Georges-Henri Soutou:

> For Roosevelt the chief priority was the struggle against the Axis, out of a purely military concern with maximizing efficiency and systematically excluding political considerations from the planning of the war (there was no question, for example, of conducting operations in such a way as to limit the advance of the Red Army in Europe, as the English sometimes thought of doing). A lesser priority was the establishment of international institutions. . . . Thinking about the geopolitical facts of the postwar period came later: it is clear, in particular, that the Soviet factor was not carefully considered in Washington, in any case less so than in London by Churchill and the British cabinet.[9]

However successful it may have been in strictly military terms, the Normandy invasion led to a diplomatic Munich, owing to Roosevelt's credulous attachment to a peculiarly American set of ideals.

Whether exalting the humanitarian generosity of the Western powers or lamenting the shortsightedness of the American president, such a view of the matter neglects to take into account an essential element, namely, that Normandy had less to do with opposing ideologies than with opposing armies. Before the meaning and consequences of the confrontation can be worked out, we need to recapture the essence of it. And the essence of Normandy was war. This means looking closely not only at the facts of the military situation—the terrain, the orders of battle, and so on—but also at the combat conditions and the state of mind of the soldiers, from the generals on down to the enlisted men. It also means frankly acknowledging the sheer violence of the campaign that followed. This was hardly forgotten by the combatants themselves, who were long to be marked by the ordeals they endured in the summer of 1944; but the violence has frequently been downplayed by historians seeking to glorify the exploits of the Allied soldiers. The romanticized picture of young British and American men ready to sacrifice their lives in the name of democracy cannot withstand the evidence of the archives. Little can be found there to support General Frederick E. Morgan's view that "even after years of tedious waiting and frustration, after years of bombardment and defeat, there was no doubt whatever that when the time should come to lead them across the water to France they would jump to it in a big way."[10]

We need to recognize that the war, by its cruelty, managed to provoke fear and disgust in a good many of those who were called upon to wage it. "For the past fifty years," observes the American historian Paul Fussell, himself a veteran, "the Allied War has been sanitized and romanticized almost beyond recognition by the sentimental, the loony patriotic, the ignorant, and the bloodthirsty. . . . What is missing from all the high-minded wartime moments is any awareness of the mind of the troops in the field. They were neither high- nor particularly low-minded. They were not -minded at all."[11] Ralph Ingersoll, an American journalist and publisher who served as a staff officer in the planning section of General Bradley's field headquarters, noted just after the war that "the average GI never learned what the war was all about from one end to the other, or really knew why he was fighting in Europe or for what. In his own mind, I think that to the end he fought simply to get it over with, and to get home. He fought to kill men who were trying to kill him. He also fought because he was told to fight—and because there was no respectable way out of fighting."[12] Timothy Corsellis, a young enlisted man in the Royal Air Force, gave voice to a cynical sense of resignation that many soldiers no doubt shared:

> We sat together as we sat at peace
> Bound by no ideal of service
> But by a common interest in pornography
>     and a desire to outdrink one another.[13]

Rediscovering the war obliges us, then, to reexamine its violence—whether administered or endured—and to challenge the legend that the Allied soldiers fearlessly stormed the shores of Normandy under a hail of enemy fire, ready to die for the cause of democracy.[14] Calling attention to incidents of desertion, cowardice, and fear forces us, too, to inquire into the nature of the bond that unites citizens to a democracy. Liberal regimes, undermined between the wars by the political, economic, and social crisis that immediately succeeded the Great War, and then by the Wall Street crash of 1929, cut a pale figure in contrast to the vigor that totalitarian regimes—whether Italian, German, or Soviet—embodied in many minds. The French right-wing polemicist Pierre Drieu la Rochelle was not alone in contrasting the virility of the kingdoms of the new man with the decadence of democracies worn out by routine, sapped by pacifism, discredited by scandals. The democracies seemed incapable of competing with the renewed might of Germany, even of Italy; indeed, many civilian and military leaders feared that France and Great Britain could scarcely hope to stand up to the Third Reich and its allies on the battlefield.

It is in this context that Eisenhower's glowing tribute to the Western powers in the aftermath of the war is to be understood: "Victory in the Mediterranean and European campaigns gave the lie to all who preached, or in our time shall preach, that the democracies are decadent, afraid to fight, unable to match the productivity of regimented economies, unwilling to sacrifice in a common cause."[15] A hasty judgment, perhaps, or so it may seem in retrospect. Mobilization for war in both Great Britain and the United States was not without its problems. The fact that many soldiers themselves doubted the declared war aims of their governments invites a degree of skepticism regarding the effectiveness of official British and American propaganda. Nor did the American war economy function as smoothly as is generally supposed. Eisenhower, in order to have the necessary number of landing ships at his disposal, had to delay D-Day by a month in order to give the builders more time. British armaments production was inadequate, with the result that equipping the United Kingdom's forces depended on American assistance. To cite only one example among many, two-thirds of British armored brigades and divisions in the Normandy theater were supplied with tanks made in the United States, domestic manufacturers having failed to meet the demands of their army with regard either to quality or quantity.[16] And not everyone wholeheartedly answered the call to service, either in the factories at home or on the beaches of Normandy. The price that men and women, civilians and soldiers, bosses and workers were willing to pay on behalf of their country and the cause of democracy varied by individual, class, and nation.

But rediscovering the war in France must not lead us to neglect what we have known since the time of Clausewitz, namely, that the essence of war itself is politics. And yet his celebrated formula "War is the continuation of politics by other means," has sometimes been forgotten by writers on the Normandy invasion who have concentrated mainly on military and strategic questions, to the exclusion of its diplomatic aspects. In much the same way, authors who are chiefly concerned with the political and diplomatic dimensions of the landing have tended to ignore its economic elements, and vice versa.[17] The specialization of historical writing in the United States, Canada, and Great Britain has served only to mask how closely and profoundly related to one another all these things are. The very choice of France as the theater of operations, for example, cannot be understood without taking into account a whole web of interconnected considerations: notwithstanding that the decision was readily justified on logistical grounds (the proximity of the Norman coast to England and the density of local transport and communication networks left no other option), it also furthered Anglo-American geopolitical interests in laying claim to the most prosperous part of Europe at the expense of the Soviets (France and Germany, quite obviously, were a more attractive prize than the Balkans).[18] Winston Churchill, in arguing for a peripheral strategy by which the invasion of northwestern Europe would be launched across the Mediterranean, rather than the English Channel, sought to spare his country the heavy losses of human life that a frontal assault on the well-defended coastline of northern France seemed to make unavoidable. History, it must be said, was on his side. Amphibious operations—always hazardous, since arrival from the sea places attacking forces at a considerable disadvantage—had often led to disaster. The memory of Gallipoli in 1915 was still fresh in the minds of British strategists.

Yet even if Churchill cannot be reproached for counseling caution, his real reason for wanting to protect the lives of as many of his men as possible was connected also with a desire to maintain the influence of the

United Kingdom in a region where British commercial and other interests had long been established. Conversely, the cross-Channel option
finally decided upon by Washington, and imposed on London without
any great concern for British sensibilities, could be justified on military
as well as logistical grounds as a way to end the war as quickly as possible by attacking the enemy at its strongest point. But this decision, in addition to signaling the end of British hegemony in the Mediterranean,
meant accepting the expansion of Soviet influence there.

Nor was the enemy camp immune to such calculations. In early July
1944 General Rommel argued that Germany should attempt to negotiate
a settlement either with Russia, on the one hand, or with Britain and
America, on the other. While favoring an approach to the Western powers, he cautioned that it was in any case "high time for the politicians
to act as long as we hold any kind of trump."[19] There can be no doubt
that considerations of this sort weighed on the course of action pursued
by the German commanders, not least of all Rommel himself, after the
landing.

I shall begin by considering Operation OVERLORD from the military perspective. Because the Normandy landing was first and foremost an armed
operation directed against the Third Reich, strategy, tactics, and the
fighting itself must be placed at the heart of the narrative, so that the campaign from 6 June 1944 until the liberation of Paris on 25 August can be
seen as a coherent whole. The highly complex motivations of the actors
in these events can scarcely be ignored, not least because victory was
to give rise to interminable controversies, exacerbated by national passions.[20] American historians' vigorous criticism of the conduct of operations by Field Marshal Montgomery, for example, prompted their British
counterparts to come at once to the defense of the hero of El Alamein.[21]
Yet this rivalry must not be allowed to divert our attention from other aspects of the campaign in France, particularly the role played by the
French Resistance and the way in which the fighting was experienced by
civilians and soldiers alike.

The landing itself was not as bloody an affair as it has often been made
.out to be. By the evening of 6 June, Allied casualties amounted to some

4,900 men, or about 2.8 percent of the troops that disembarked—hardly the slaughter that the general staff had anticipated. But the battle of Normandy, waged on farmland whose hedgerows—the infamous *bocage*—created formidable obstacles for both sides, was to take a heavy toll, not only in lives lost, but also on the lives of the survivors, many of whom experienced profound and lasting psychiatric trauma. Readily euphemized in the generals' memoirs (though not in their reports from the field), and frequently passed over in silence by many of the soldiers themselves, the grueling psychological ordeal of the Normandy campaign posed uncomfortable moral dilemmas for the Allied high command, which wrestled with the question whether men who cracked under the strain should be treated as medical patients needing to be hospitalized or as cowards deserving to be brought before courts-martial. Military discipline was further undermined not only by desertion, but also by the many thefts and rapes that were committed in the course of the campaign. These forms of misconduct need to be taken into account, and their effects upon the civilian population investigated, for soldiers were not the only ones to suffer the violence of war. The people of Normandy—bombarded by Allied planes and ships, caught in the fighting and exposed to the brutalities of the soldiery—also paid heavy tribute to Mars. In Lower Normandy, where operations were responsible for some 14,000 civilian deaths during the summer of 1944, the population harbored mixed feelings toward its liberators, who were the object of both gratitude and resentment.[22] "The French population did not seem in any way pleased to see us arrive as a victorious country to liberate France," Field Marshal Sir Alan Brooke observed. "They had been quite content as they were, and we were bringing war and desolation to the country."[23] However much heroism the Allies and civilians may have shown—and much of it was indeed genuine—we will be able to free ourselves from the hold of the misleading commonplaces mobilized by legend only if these less glorious realities are given their rightful place in the story of the Normandy campaign.

Nor can economic and logistical aspects be neglected, for to a large extent they determined the outcome of the operation. This depended, of course, on the Allies' ability to field enough troops and matériel—guns, tanks, planes, battleships, and so on; but it was no less important to be able to transport them to the theater of operations just when they were needed. Indeed, the strategy on both sides proceeded from the assumption that forces sufficiently large to crush the adversary could be brought into position at the very outset. The crucial role of economic planning and logistical support has nonetheless sometimes been overstated. American industry, despite its undoubted efficiency from 1943 onward, was not in fact an instrument perfectly adapted to waging war, capable of "answering every need."[24] And although the logistics experts at Supreme Headquarters, Allied Expeditionary Force (SHAEF) are properly credited with accomplishing wondrous feats, not all of their projects achieved what was expected of them. The two artificial ports that were constructed off the Atlantic coast, for example, are usually considered to have been decisive in channeling the flow of reinforcements needed to sustain the Allied drive inland from the Normandy beaches. But in fact the Arromanches harbor—the only one left in place following the great storm of 19–22 June 1944—handled only a third of British tonnage alone between D-Day and mid-October.[25] Here, again, the myth stands in need of some qualification.

The landing in Normandy invites us to reflect not only on the shared purposes that united the Allies, but also on the political and strategic differences that divided London, Moscow, and Washington in varying and changeable ways as the war went on. Although it is true that the coalition held together until the defeat of Germany, Eisenhower's idyllic picture of unselfish cooperation ("Governments and their subsidiary economic, political, and military organizations had combined into one great effort in which no major difficulty could be traced to diverging national interest")[26] bears little relation to the day-to-day reality of disagreements and rivalry. Churchill, Stalin, and Roosevelt were all concerned first and foremost with shaping the contours of the postwar world. Roosevelt, in particular, far from subordinating American diplomacy to near-term military objectives, acted very much as a statesman, rather than merely the commander of his nation's armies, in developing a novel and encompassing conception of the international system.[27] Indeed, it is not too much to say that "if there was a Cold War, it is because the allies of the anti-Hitlerian coalition were mutually prevented from realizing the incompatible war aims that they had defined for themselves before 1945."[28] The fact that OVERLORD was designed not to satisfy a simple military purpose, but to prepare the way for achieving a set of geopolitical goals, explains in part the treatment reserved by the White House for Charles de Gaulle, who was kept in ignorance of the planning for the liberation of France for reasons that went far beyond Roosevelt's personal dislike for him.[29]

In undertaking to write a brief but comprehensive history of the Normandy landing, I gladly acknowledge my debt to the many fine American, Canadian, and British historians who have gone before me. At the same time, I have not omitted to conduct my own research on both sides of the Atlantic, at the Public Record Office in Great Britain, the National Archives and Records Administration and the Eisenhower Library in the United States, and the Ministry of Foreign Affairs in France. Piece by piece, the elements drawn from these collections form both the foreground and background of a portrait that conceals neither the difficulties nor the failures of a titanic enterprise. By acknowledging imperfections and the vagaries of chance we are able to gauge the true price of victory and to recognize the young British, American, and Canadian soldiers who dashed forward onto the beaches of Normandy in the dawn of 6 June 1944 not as demigods, but as human beings. Is this not the most honest homage that can be paid them?

# 1

# ALLIES, NOT FRIENDS

I T SEEMS OBVIOUS TO US TODAY that the Allies had to regain a
foothold on the European Continent in order to vanquish Germany—
and that to do this, they would have chosen France as their landing site.
For history and memory have conspired to cast Normandy as the result
of implacable necessity, now consecrated by the transformation of its
beaches into a place of pilgrimage where former combatants, friends,
and family come together to celebrate D-Day. Yet Operation OVERLORD,
launched in the dawn of 6 June 1944, was by no means a foregone conclusion. For almost two years the prospect of a cross-Channel expedition had aroused fierce debate among American, British, and Soviet leaders, each defending geopolitical positions so difficult to reconcile that
a final decision was repeatedly delayed. It was not until 13 April 1943
that Frederick Morgan, a British general, was officially charged with
drawing up plans for an invasion. But these were no more than preliminary sketches. It was not until the Teheran Conference in late November
1943 that OVERLORD was approved; Eisenhower was named supreme
commander of the expeditionary force the following week, on 6 December 1943. His arrival in London well after Christmas left the Allies
scarcely five months, from January to May 1944, to plan an enterprise
whose complexity no one underestimated. Complicating matters further
was the fact that each of the Allied powers wished to conduct the war in
its own way.

## EARLY DISAGREEMENTS

Until 1943, Great Britain looked out into a darkening world. Under the firm leadership of Winston Churchill, prime minister since 10 May 1940, it had managed to withstand the German blitzkrieg, repatriating a part of its expeditionary force at Dunkirk, prevailing over the Luftwaffe during the Battle of Britain, and confronting the bombardment of London and Coventry with the unshakeable determination of a resolute people. Yet despite the protection afforded by the North Sea and a long coastline against Nazi invasion, the U-boats of the Kriegsmarine threatened British sources of supply. Abroad, in East Asia, the outposts of the empire had proved incapable of resisting Japanese assault: Hong Kong fell on 24 December 1941; Malaysia, Singapore, and Burma were conquered in the following months. In North Africa, Rommel conducted a lightning campaign, seizing the stronghold of Tobruk on 14 June 1942 and threatening Alexandria. Although Field Marshal Bernard Law Montgomery did succeed in inflicting a severe defeat on the Afrika Korps at El Alamein on 3 November 1942, this victory—the only real success achieved in two years by British arms alone—could not mask the extent of their reverses.

Great Britain had no choice but to adopt a defensive posture, while avoiding direct engagement—a strategy that, again with the notable exception of El Alamein, had so far ended in crushing defeat, in France as in Crete, at Dieppe as at Tobruk.[1] Its aim was to hold rather than to conquer. Churchill hoped to overcome the enemy through a war of attrition, using the ships of the Royal Navy to impose a blockade of German ports and the bombers of the Royal Air Force to conduct nighttime raids inside the country. In this way he could buy time to rebuild British ground forces, too weak to be sent over to the Continent and in any case incapable of holding their own against the armies of the Reich.

From the time of the coalition against Louis XIV, assembled by Churchill's ancestor the Duke of Marlborough, to the First World War, London had historically preferred to pursue a peripheral strategy, attacking the enemy's weak points rather than launching a frontal assault, always costly and frequently useless. As the biographer of his illustrious forebear and champion of the disastrous Dardanelles expedition as First Lord of the Admiralty during the First World War, Churchill had absorbed the lessons of military history.[2]

The limitations of this approach nonetheless very quickly made themselves felt. In condemning Great Britain to disperse its forces throughout the Mediterranean, Africa, and the Middle East, where they were forced to fight for positions of relatively little strategic interest, indirection led on to a series of failures between 1940 and 1942.[3] Already it was clear that the fate of the Reich would be played out on the plains of Continental Europe and not in the Egyptian sands.[4] A war of delay conspicuously failed to answer the central question, namely, how to defeat Germany in the shortest possible time. British planners had not in fact ruled out the possibility of an invasion: in 1940, following the retreat from Dunkirk, Churchill created a Combined Operations Staff for the purpose of planning a grand amphibious assault and testing landing craft and other equipment; in the meantime it was charged with carrying out commando raids on occupied Europe. But the landing was delayed indefinitely, in the hope that the collapse of Germany could be achieved by other means.[5] Haunted by the memory of the First World War and the offensives of Passchendaele, as deadly as they were futile, Churchill preferred to wait until Germany had been bled dry before throwing his troops into an assault on Western Europe. In view of German industrial potential, the moment when the German armies would no longer be capable of counterattacking might yet be many years away.

The Soviet Union, for obvious reasons, did not enjoy the same freedom of maneuver. Surprised by the German attack of 22 June 1941, it had only narrowly escaped defeat: in the first eighteen days, the Wehrmacht marched 275 miles toward the east; in the first six months of the campaign, it took the Baltic countries and a large part of Ukraine, captured 3,350,000 Soviet soldiers and officers, and seized control of the industrial heart of the country with more than 40 percent of its population.[6] The Red Army managed to halt this advance in the fall of 1941 and stop the German forces before the gates of Moscow and Leningrad, only to face new offensives in the spring and summer of 1942 that ended in the loss of the Crimea and a part of the Caucasus and carried Hitler's armies to the banks of the Don and the Volga. Miraculously, Stalin succeeded in stabilizing the situation by the end of 1942, adopting the scorched-earth strategy that Kutuzov had employed during the war against Napoleon. By laying waste to their own land and dismantling its factories, the Russians avoided the fall both of Moscow and of Leningrad, cradle of the Revolution. None of this, however, guaranteed victory. Stalin, in his first telegram to Churchill on 18 July 1941, emphasized the urgent need to open a second front: by forcing the Germans to fight on two fronts, an Allied landing would have the strategic advantage of easing the military burden on the Red Army in the East. But the operation carried diplomatic implications as well, for it would affirm wholehearted Anglo-American commitment to the war, thereby protecting the Soviets against the risk of a separate peace uniting London, Berlin, and Washington against Moscow. Stalin nonetheless felt he could compromise if he had to, so long as Great Britain and the United States agreed to deliver the civilian and military supplies that the Soviet Union desperately needed.

The United States displayed surprising firmness on the question of a second front. Having entered the war following the attack on Pearl Harbor on 7 December 1941, the Americans had no alternative but to designate Japan as their principal adversary. Yet from 1941 onward Washington made it clear that its main objective was Germany, and this despite the reservations of the American people. As late as February 1943, 53 percent of the country still felt that Japan remained the primary enemy of the United States, with only 34 percent naming the Third Reich.[7]

This paradoxical state of affairs was due less to the arguments of the diplomats in the State Department than to those of the planners in the War Department, for whom Germany represented the logical target: once it had been defeated, Japan could not carry on the struggle alone. This analysis, which recommended an offensive war against Germany and a defensive one against Japan, in order to vanquish the more formidable adversary as quickly as possible, carried on an already venerable tradition. In the American Civil War, experience had taught the Union generals the wisdom of mounting a frontal assault against the enemy, attacking the Confederate Army head-on, over the whole of the front, rather than trying to turn its flank by means of enveloping maneuvers. Pershing had successfully pursued the same course of action in 1917–1918.[8] The War Department therefore saw little reason to innovate with respect to military doctrine. Moreover, the "Germany first" option presented the advantage, from the point of view of the army, of strengthening the position of the infantry. An overriding commitment to the Pacific theater would have favored the U.S. Navy, which had taken charge of the logistics of amphibious operations in its campaign against Japan. But in 1942 the American fleet, not yet recovered from the disaster of Pearl Harbor, had no means of realizing its ambition of assuming by itself the primary burden of a world war. Paradoxically, the stunning victory at Midway, on 4 June 1942, deprived it of its chief argument, for it could no longer be claimed that the Empire of the Rising Sun constituted a mortal danger to the United States.[9] Furthermore, any hegemonic designs on the part of the navy would have been fiercely contested by the army, resolved to defend its preeminence at all costs. From the army's point of view, a second front presented the ideal solution to an equation with several unknowns, by making it possible to conquer Germany as quickly as possible, contain the navy's aspirations to dominance, and consolidate the alliance by keeping the Soviet Union in the war and allaying British fears through the assurance that having subordinated the war against Japan to the defeat of the Reich, the United States could be counted on to stand by Great Britain's side until victory in Europe had been achieved.[10]

The idea of an invasion of northwestern Europe, first advanced in August 1941 by Lieutenant Colonel Edwin E. Schwein of the Army's Intelligence Division as a way of aiding the Soviet Union, was not slow in gaining support. On 28 February 1942, the new head of the War Plans Division, General Dwight D. Eisenhower, sent General George C. Marshall, Jr., the U.S. Army Chief of Staff, a memorandum insisting on the necessity of a landing. On 27 March, this same unit—now called the Operations Plans Division (OPD)—submitted a more precise proposal, subsequently known as the Marshall memorandum, that called for troops to be transported to the United Kingdom at a deliberate but gradually intensifying pace (hence the code name BOLERO, by analogy with the slow-building crescendo of Ravel's work), with a landing scheduled for the spring of 1943 (Operation ROUNDUP). In the event that Germany showed signs of weakening or that the Soviet Union appeared to be on the verge of collapse, a less ambitious approach (SLEDGEHAMMER) was to be considered. On 1 April 1942, the president gave his approval to this plan.[11]

Until then Roosevelt had not been deaf to arguments in favor of a peripheral war of attrition. His military chiefs grumbled, suspecting the president of having fallen under the pernicious influence of Great Britain in general and of Winston Churchill in particular. In the spring of 1942, however, Roosevelt removed all grounds for doubt. By endorsing the Marshall memorandum, and thereby ruling out the Pacific option, he brought the full weight of his office to bear in favor of a landing in northwestern Europe. It now remained for the United States to find a way to overcome the reluctance of Great Britain and to restrain the impatience of the Soviet Union—in a word, to establish a consensus about the nature of the operation, its date, and its location. The great conferences that took place between 1941 and 1943 were meant to serve exactly this purpose, by laying the groundwork for an undertaking the like of which had never before been contemplated.

## SUMMIT CONFERENCES (ACT I)

In early 1941 the British and the Americans met in Washington to work out the terms of their wartime collaboration. At talks lasting from 29 January until 27 March, the general staffs reached agreement on several main principles. Germany having been designated the major adversary, as the "predominant member of the Axis Powers," the Allies resolved that "the principal United States military effort" should be concentrated in the Atlantic and Europe.[12] The two powers also agreed to exchange military embassies for the purpose of facilitating cooperation. In the economic sphere this was to take place within the framework of a lend-lease arrangement, formalized by an act of Congress and signed by Roosevelt on 11 March, whereby America undertook to provide the United Kingdom with aid, equipment, and arms in exchange for overseas military bases. At a time when the United States remained untouched by the conflict, it was probably impossible to do more than this. Great Britain nonetheless received assurances that in the event of an expansion of the war it could rely on the continuing support of its former colony.

The attack on Pearl Harbor dramatically altered the situation. Allied from now on against a common enemy, Churchill and Roosevelt met to discuss the conduct of the war in more concrete terms at a second conference in Washington (code-named ARCADIA), which lasted from 22 December 1941 until 14 January 1942. The prime minister came away from it with three guarantees: Germany remained, in spite of Japan's treachery, the chief adversary; American military production would not be reserved exclusively for U.S. forces;[13] and a unified structure of command would be created. To the Combined Chiefs of Staff (CCS), which had its seat in the American capital and was endowed with considerable authority, fell the task of drawing up operations, supervising planning, and submitting recommendations for the approval of the coalition's political leaders. The CCS did not, strictly speaking, constitute a single command structure, since power was shared equally between representatives of the two countries; nor did it include the Soviets, though they too were now involved in the struggle against the Nazi armies (a sign that the war in the East remained separate from the war in the West at this point). Nonetheless, by making it possible to harmonize the strategies of the two Western powers while taking a common approach to resources and supplies, this system represented a considerable advance over the situation during the First World War, when no comparable apparatus was available to Germany's adversaries.

Just the same, there were areas of disagreement. Whereas the American chief of staff, General Marshall, urged that a direct assault be mounted against Germany, Churchill argued in favor of an operation in French North Africa once the Libyan campaign had been concluded. To the great dismay of the American military delegation, Roosevelt lent an attentive ear to the British proposition (code-named GYMNAST), and the project was approved. A North African operation had several undeniable advantages. In strategic and economic terms, it would have avoided the need for convoys transporting men and equipment to the Middle East to make a long and costly detour around the Cape of Good Hope. The

Allies had already sent a million men, six thousand airplanes, and forty-five hundred tanks by this route in the two years between June 1940 and June 1942; according to British estimates, control of North Africa could be expected to save a million tons of freight per year.[14] Moreover, a campaign would have the effect of strengthening morale, by giving large numbers of soldiers stationed in Great Britain and the United States something to do other than idly mark time in their barracks. Finally, on the political level, GYMNAST would serve to distract American public opinion from the Pacific theater, where the news remained grim.[15] In promising the Allies an easy success, it would place the Democratic Party in a good position to win the midterm elections, scheduled for 3 November 1942.

In the meantime, the president's military advisers had begun to draw up plans for a second front in Europe. They argued that the peripheral strategy supported by the British would do nothing to hasten the defeat of the Reich: by drawing men and equipment to the Mediterranean theater, it delayed the buildup of forces that would be needed to launch a major offensive in northern France. Above all, it risked angering the Soviets, who now bore the burden of the war almost alone.

### BETWEEN EAST AND WEST

By unleashing Operation BARBAROSSA against the USSR on 22 June 1941, Adolf Hitler did the Allies a great favor. A power that until then had been, if not an enemy by virtue of the Nazi-Soviet pact, at the very least an unlikely partner had now suddenly by a decree of the Führer become a de facto member of the group of powerful forces ranged against the Axis. The same evening, while recalling his hostility to Bolshevism, Winston Churchill vowed to give "to Russia and to the Russian people all possible aid."[16] On 12 July, the Soviet minister of foreign affairs, Vyacheslav Molotov, and the British ambassador, Sir Stafford Cripps, signed a declaration of mutual assistance in Moscow. Roosevelt, for his part, dispatched his personal representative and adviser, Harry Hopkins, to assure Stalin of American support—and to gauge both the willingness and the ability of the Soviets to fight following the severe setbacks sustained in the first weeks of the German offensive. In September 1941, an

Anglo-American mission led by W. Averell Harriman, Roosevelt's personal envoy, and Lord Beaverbrook, minister of supply in Churchill's cabinet, laid the foundations for economic cooperation with Moscow.

None of this dispelled the mutual mistrust among the new partners. While the anticommunism that flourished between the wars in Great Britain and the United States had left its mark in both countries, its effects should not be overestimated. An October 1941 poll revealed that 51.4 percent of Americans approved of the assistance granted the Soviet Union, and only 13 percent opposed it.[17] The sense that a Russian defeat was probable was widely shared, however, even at the highest levels of the American government. Great Britain, fearing that any aid given to Moscow by the United States would be deducted from its share, did its best to restrain American generosity.[18] Stalin, for his part, placed little confidence in the Western powers, whom he suspected of being more than happy to stand aside and allow Nazis and Bolsheviks to slaughter each other. Quarrels over territorial claims further complicated the situation. Should the Western powers recognize the Soviet occupation of the Baltic states, annexed in 1940 as a consequence of the Nazi-Soviet pact? Which boundaries were to be accepted in the case of Poland, divided up by the Reich and the USSR at the beginning of the war? A dramatic change in the fortunes of the Red Army would strengthen Russia's bargaining position.

It is hardly surprising, then, that the demand for a second front should have remained at the top of the Soviet diplomatic agenda in the years following BARBAROSSA. Stalin first invoked the risk of a Soviet collapse and then brandished the threat of a separate peace. In a telegram of 23 July 1942 addressed to Churchill, he expressed regret that the question of a second front was "not being treated with the seriousness it deserve[d]." He continued, "I must state in the most emphatic manner that the Soviet government cannot acquiesce in the postponement of a second front in Europe until 1943."[19] Stalin also conducted a vigorous campaign in the press. His order of the day for 23 February 1942, widely reported in the West, displayed unusual moderation: "The Red Army's aim is to drive out the German occupants from our country and liberate Soviet soil from the German fascist invaders. It is very likely that the war for liberation of the Soviet land will result in ousting or destroying Hitler's clique. But it would be ridiculous to identify Hitler's clique with the German people and the German state. History shows that Hitlers come and go, but the German people and the German state remain."[20] By suggesting that it was enough simply to expel the German armies from Soviet territory, Stalin raised the possibility of a separate peace—an unsubtle way of ratcheting up the pressure on Great Britain and the United States. Moscow rallied popular support in the Allied countries as well. In May 1942 a demonstration in favor of a second front attracted some fifty thousand people in Trafalgar Square.[21] On the diplomatic front, in July 1943, the Soviet Union recalled its ambassadors to London and Washington, Ivan Maisky and Maxim Litvinov—a step that aroused perplexity within the Nazi leadership. "The Führer does not understand," Joseph Goebbels noted in his diary of 10 August 1943, "why the two Jews Maisky and Litvinov have been recalled from the Anglo-American capitals by Stalin. He must have an ulterior motive. In any case, Stalin is subjecting the Anglo-Americans to enormous blackmail. He wants to force them to open a second front."[22] This, it must be said, was not badly judged. But was it merely posturing on the part of the Soviet dictator, or was he genuinely angry because a promise had not been kept?

Although he had demanded a second front two years earlier, in 1941, Stalin was aware that for the time being the Allies were wholly incapable of opening one. The matter assumed a more complex aspect with Molotov's visit to Washington in the spring of 1942. On 30 May the foreign minister asked if the United States could "undertake such offensive action as would draw off 40 German divisions which would be, to tell the truth, distinctly second-rate outfits. . . . He requested a straight answer. The President then put to General Marshall the query whether developments were clear enough so that we could say to Mr. Stalin that we were preparing a second front. 'Yes,' replied the General. The President then authorized Mr. Molotov to inform Mr. Stalin that we expect the formation of a second front this year."[23] Armed with this assurance, the Soviet foreign minister was fully justified in citing the president's pledge in the months that followed as grounds for claiming his due. And yet negotiations followed a more tortuous course, the result in part of the duplicity practiced on both sides.

Soviet diplomacy aimed at two parallel objectives: recognition by London and Washington of its 1940 boundaries and a commitment to invade Europe. On 7 May 1942, Churchill asked whether Roosevelt would agree to sign an accord on boundaries—a measure supported by the British foreign secretary, Anthony Eden, but one that the White House found unappealing.[24] Two weeks later, Molotov, still in London, where he had begun his tour of the Western capitals, found his hopes dashed. Churchill balked at making any territorial guarantees, noting also that the Allies had no means whatever for opening a second front. From the American ambassador to London, John B. Winant, Molotov knew that the United States would not budge on the boundary question but was prepared to keep an open mind on the questions of a landing, lend-lease, and the possibility of postwar assistance. Reasoning that it was better to have the promise in hand of a second front than the illusion of a slapdash treaty, he therefore refrained from raising the matter of boundaries during his meetings in Washington.[25] And although he did succeed in obtaining a guarantee from the president, as we have seen, the British Chiefs of Staff had in the meantime come to the conclusion that launching Operation SLEDGEHAMMER was an impossibility. When Molotov came back through London, he discovered that the promise of a landing had been rendered null and void, the Allies having neither the intention nor the ability to make good on it—as Moscow was well aware.

"It is unlikely that the English will organize a second front this year," Molotov confided to the Bulgarian Communist leader Georgi Dimitrov on his return to Moscow.[26] The Soviets nonetheless had Roosevelt's guarantee, which gave them a certain amount of leverage. "For the next two years," the Australian war correspondent and historian Chester Wilmot observed, "the assurance [Roosevelt] had given lay uneasily on his conscience and left him at a moral disadvantage in his dealings with Stalin."[27] It also allowed Russian propaganda to attribute the Red Army's reverses to the shortfall in Allied aid—an excuse that hardly ever went unmentioned. In his report celebrating the twenty-fifth anniversary of the October Revolution, for example, Stalin noted that the "main reason behind the Germans' tactical success at our front this year is the absence of the Second Front in Europe, which enables them to send all their free reserves to our front and ensure great numerical superiority in the southwestern direction."[28] The British, for their part, having declined to enter into a treaty that would have tied their hands, found themselves in trouble with the Poles. The Americans, by contrast, proved their goodwill without having to yield on the territorial question, thus strengthening Soviet resolve at little cost to themselves.[29] According to Charles E. Bohlen, then a high-ranking Soviet expert at the State Department, the president felt that "encouragement, even when based on false premises, would stiffen the Soviet will."[30] "I am especially anxious," Roosevelt told Churchill, "that Molotov shall carry back some real results of his mission and give a favorable report to Stalin. I am inclined to believe that the Russians are a bit down in the mouth at present."[31] Molotov's trip had produced a fool's bargain with which, paradoxically, all the partners were satisfied.

The first six months of 1942 therefore ended in confusion. Roosevelt had placed himself in the impossible position of indulging Churchill's Mediterranean schemes, while promising Stalin a second front in Western Europe. Far from clarifying its policy in the months that followed, the United States persisted in trying to marry the Russian carp with the British rabbit—a strategy that in exchange for only very modest results threatened to gravely compromise plans for a landing.

## OPERATION TORCH AND ITS AFTERMATH

The American military chiefs took a dim view of all this. Even if the ill-considered promises made by Roosevelt to the Soviets in no way committed them, they were alarmed by the Mediterranean option—all the more because Churchill had announced his intention to come back to Washington to plead his case at the end of June 1942. General Marshall, seconded by Admiral Ernest J. King, proposed on 10 July that the Pacific theater be granted primacy, overturning the "Germany first" option that the general staff had successfully lobbied for the previous year. Was this a ploy to turn Roosevelt against Churchill?[32] Perhaps. But there could have been another reason for the about-face: between the North African Scylla and the Pacific Charybdis, Marshall may have been driven to choose what he considered, sensibly enough, to be the lesser evil—war against Japan.[33] Be that as it may, the tactic backfired. The president firmly dismissed the Pacific option and on 25 July, against the advice of his military staff and in the absence of an agreement with the British regarding SLEDGEHAMMER, settled on the North African landing plan, Operation GYMNAST (renamed TORCH the day before). This change of course had now to be justified to the Soviets, for it ran counter to the promise made to Molotov two months earlier.

Churchill took charge of this chore. After leaving London on 1 August, he went to Moscow via Cairo, arriving on 12 August. The talks were difficult, with the Russian leader masterfully blowing hot and cold for hours on end. Charmed by Churchill's image of the Mediterranean as the "soft underbelly" of the Axis powers, Stalin showed some sympathy on the first day, even demanding that the attack in North Africa "be launched at the earliest possible moment."[34] By the next day he had changed his mind: "It is easy to grasp that the refusal of the Government of Great Britain to create a second front in 1942 in Europe inflicts a moral blow to the whole of the Soviet public opinion, which calculates on the creation of a second front, and that it complicates the situation of the Red Army at the front and prejudices the plan of the Soviet Command."[35] He insinuated further that the British army was guilty of cowardice, a suggestion that incurred Churchill's wrath.[36] And yet on the final day of the talks, 15 August, the British prime minister was to be surprised by Stalin's enthusiastic defense of TORCH and the warmth of his reception, so much so that the two men sat up drinking until 2:30 in the morning and parted on friendly terms.[37] With Russia's agreement now in hand, the operation was launched on 8 November 1942. Probably Stalin had no choice but to put on a brave face—while making it clear to Churchill that he was not fooled by his maneuvering.

The advantages of TORCH, as we have seen, were that it promised to strengthen Allied control over the Mediterranean, reduce the cost of maritime shipping, raise the troops' morale, and compensate the Soviets for the postponement of a second front in northwestern Europe, while at the same time—or so it was hoped—putting French forces back into the war. But there were serious drawbacks to the plan as well. By diverting troops and equipment to Algeria and Morocco, it delayed the assembling in Great Britain of the expeditionary force that was to carry out the invasion. Allied projections furthermore assumed that Soviet forces would be able to withstand the Nazi onslaught, a proposition that was still uncertain in 1942—defended by the British but doubted by the Americans. Most of all, the plan offered the temptation of substituting other options in the Mediterranean, which would soon be within reach, for a landing in Western Europe.

These concerns were hardly imaginary. In the ten months following TORCH, a substantial reduction in the number of American troops dispatched to the United Kingdom did in fact compromise BOLERO's chances of success. Two-thirds of the sixteen divisions embarking from American ports in 1942 were sent to the Pacific, and by January 1944 the number of troops engaged in battle against the Japanese was almost half again as large as the number fighting in the Mediterranean theater.[38] Whereas 168,000 American soldiers had been stationed in the United Kingdom at the end of 1942, only 59,000 were based there at the end of March 1943.[39] From a strictly statistical point of view, at least, the "Germany first" option had clearly been replaced by a "Japan first" strategy. By any reckoning, however, the British desire to use North Africa as a base for attacking the soft underbelly of the Axis—Italy and the Balkans—was to have serious consequences for the invasion of Normandy. "For TORCH," Lieutenant General Omar N. Bradley later observed, "the Allies were to pay a high price. Not only did it force us to cancel ROUNDUP [the landing in northwestern Europe] for the following year, but it delayed the ultimate cross-Channel attack until 1944. For with this diversion to the Mediterranean, the Allies had branched off on a siding in their strategic offensive. . . . Although ROUNDUP had not yet been formally abandoned, the diversion of Allied resources to North Africa had precluded the likelihood of a successful Channel invasion in 1943."[40]

Indeed, Churchill and Roosevelt, at their conference in Casablanca between 14 and 24 January 1943, agreed that a landing could not be achieved that year. Their military chiefs instead recommended intensifying the submarine and bombing campaigns against the Reich. Moreover, the large number of troops now stationed in North Africa created a certain impetus for extending the Allied land offensive to Sicily, the nearest theater of operations—a gambit that would help placate the Soviets, who were already beginning to suspect a weakening of the determination to insist on Germany's "unconditional surrender."

This ultimatum, which Roosevelt issued at Casablanca without consulting Churchill, was meant to accomplish several purposes. It showed Moscow that the British and American governments did not wish to conclude a separate peace—a modest but nonetheless real compensation for the postponement of a cross-Channel invasion. The ultimatum was intended also to remove the possibility of a postwar revival of German militarism by preventing the German command from claiming, as it had after the First World War, that it had been "stabbed in the back." In the wake of the uproar surrounding the "Darlan deal" of 22 November 1942, by the terms of which the Allies recognized the commander of Vichy's armed forces in Algiers, Admiral François Darlan, as high commissioner for North and West Africa in exchange for a promise to attack the Germans, Roosevelt's declaration also sent a signal that the time for compromise was now past: the Allies openly refused to negotiate with the Axis governments. Germany, a great Continental power, suddenly found itself deprived of the ability to determine its own fate in the event of defeat.

Some authors have suggested that the requirement of unconditional surrender had the effect of prolonging the war. "By doing this," argued Chester Wilmot, "the Anglo-Saxon powers denied themselves any freedom of diplomatic manoeuvre and denied the German people any avenue of escape from Hitler. . . . After Casablanca, Goebbels had delivered into his hands a propaganda weapon of incalculable power. The Nazis were now able to command conviction when they said to the Nation: 'It is you, as well as we, that they want to destroy.'"[41] As General Alfred Jodl, chief of the operations staff of the High Command of the Armed Forces (Oberkommando der Wehrmacht, or OKW), emphasized, "The elements for negotiation, as they existed in previous wars, where one could say, We have lost, we lay down our arms, we hand over a province—these elements no longer exist."[42] But this reading probably assigns too much importance to the American statement of resolve. For the tenacious resistance of the German people had a variety of sources: "Adequate provision of fresh supplies, the unexpected repercussions of the bombing and the Allied demand for capitulation, the fear of Red Asiatics on the one side and of the police on the other, and so on"—not to mention the prospect of victory, a flickering flame after 1942, yet far from extinguished even in the spring of 1945, when many citizens yet clung to the belief that fortune would ultimately favor the Nazi armies.[43] "In Hamburg in early April 1945, in spite of everything the city had endured, opinion surveys picked up confident remarks. There were no indications anywhere that a strike, much less surrender, was contemplated by anyone, and into March 1945 hope persisted for a 'good end to the war.'"[44]

Despite his contentious relations with the leaders of the anti-Vichy forces, Generals Charles de Gaulle and Henri Giraud, Roosevelt was pleased with the outcome of the Casablanca Conference. He had not traveled abroad since assuming the presidency eleven years earlier, but he now took time to tour Morocco, where he was greeted with magnificent (indeed royal) hospitality. Relations between the United States and the United Kingdom had been cordial, justifying the code name given to the conference (SYMBOL), which was meant to emphasize the convergence in the views of the two great powers. From Churchill's point of view, at least, the conference was a complete success, for he had gotten his way on everything. Not only did he obtain authorization to negotiate with Turkey over the terms of its entry into the war, but he gained approval for Italy as the next theater of operations, thus once again putting off the disagreeable prospect of a cross-Channel attack. Although General Morgan had been appointed chief of staff to the supreme Allied commander (COSSAC), charged with making preparations for a landing, no date had been agreed on. American planners were under no illusions. "We came, we listened, and we were conquered," Lieutenant General Albert C.

Wedemeyer noted with dismay.[45] Once again the Americans had given their support to a strategy urged on them by Great Britain.

## Summit Conferences (Act II)

With the two great Anglo-American conferences that followed in the spring and summer of 1943—TRIDENT at Washington (12–25 May) and QUADRANT at Quebec City (14–24 August)—the plans for an invasion of northwestern Europe finally took shape.

In Washington, the two powers baptized the nascent operation OVER-LORD, intending by this name to indicate the full importance that they attached to the operation. What is more, they finally set a target date: 1 May 1944. Twenty-nine divisions were to be committed to the enterprise, including five in the first wave, a figure which meant that seven divisions had to be redeployed to Great Britain from the Mediterranean. The possibility of pursuing operations in Italy after Sicily was not ruled out in principle, but since any such plan would have to receive the approval of the CCS, the United States could reasonably hope to turn away unwelcome proposals.

The Washington Conference had produced a consensus (or at least so the participants believed). London committed itself firmly to a landing in Normandy, which would force the British to shorten their sails in the Mediterranean. But this outcome could not fail to disappoint the Soviets, who had been counting on an invasion before the end of 1943. Stalin reacted angrily to the news, accusing the Allies of bad faith, sending acrimonious telegrams, and recalling his ambassadors, Maisky and Litvinov.[46] "There was now an atmosphere alarmingly reminiscent of that which had preceded the Molotov-Ribbentrop Pact of August 1939, and the fears of a separate Russo-German armistice were revived. The Roosevelt-Stalin meeting was postponed indefinitely."[47] Washington nonetheless remained optimistic—an attitude that was soon to be undermined by the Quebec Conference, however, which went back on some of the decisions taken three months earlier.

Appearances can be misleading. At the August meeting, by confirming the target date of 1 May 1944 and agreeing to support the scheduled landing in Normandy by means of a complementary operation in the South of France (ANVIL), the United States and Britain had appeared to establish the primacy of OVERLORD.[48] Not only did they give their blessing to the plan that had been drawn up by General Morgan within the framework of COSSAC, while suggesting substantial modifications, but the British gave further proof of their goodwill by accepting the principle of an American commander in chief and subordinating operations in Italy to the requirements of the cross-Channel assault. At the same time the British introduced a number of qualifications that cast doubt on the plan's viability. Churchill attached two conditions for launching the operation: the Luftwaffe's capabilities had first to be substantially diminished, and the number of mobile German columns (as opposed to the static garrison divisions responsible for coastal defense) reduced to fewer than a dozen.[49] This was a cunning move, in furtherance of the prime minister's favored strategy of attrition, for it tied the landing in Normandy the following year to circumstances that could not at present be foreseen. On the one hand, Churchill had done nothing more than restate the technical conditions laid down by General Morgan. On the other, however, by transposing these reservations from the logistical to the political sphere, he recast the terms of the bargain. Rather than plan OVERLORD independently of the state of German defenses, Churchill took them into account and, by means of this gambit, prohibited the launching of the operation if enemy preparedness passed a certain threshold, while reserving the right to modify the plans as necessary in response to changing circumstances. For the British, "success depended not on the absolute strength of the united forces available for OVERLORD, but on the relative strength of those forces vis-à-vis the Germans opposed to them."[50] In other words, a substantial strengthening of enemy defenses would not cause the plans to be modified; it threatened to cancel the operation altogether.

The compromise arrived at in Quebec therefore left the question of OVERLORD's viability unanswered. Though the attack was still scheduled for 1 May 1944, it did not enjoy the overriding priority that the American planners demanded. In the meantime, the commitment to a Mediterranean campaign was reconfirmed, with the further expectation that Allied forces would reach Rome before a landing took place in Normandy. The scale of this campaign was unchanged for the time being, because the CCS had refused to allot additional troops to the Italian theater.[51] Yet nothing decided at the Quebec Conference prevented the Allies from exploiting any fresh opportunities that might arise on the peninsula and revising strategy accordingly. The Americans stood firm: "If present conditions justify our principal effort in the Mediterranean . . . , conditions have not so changed as to justify on sound military grounds the renunciation of the *Trident* concept. We must not jeopardize our sound over-all strategy simply to exploit local successes in a generally accepted secondary theater, the Mediterranean, where logistical and terrain difficulties preclude decisive and final operations designed to reach the heart of Germany."[52] Whether they could resist the pressures of their ally, however, remained to be seen.

If the Washington and Quebec Conferences had narrowed the range of possibilities, by settling upon OVERLORD as the principal operation for 1944, it still had scant basis in reality: a commander with overall responsibility for the landing had yet to be named; cooperation with the Soviets remained little more than a promise; and the British continued to lobby for the Mediterranean option. In a private conversation in early June 1943 Eisenhower later recounted, "Brooke [Field Marshal Sir Alan Brooke] told me that he would be glad to reconsider the cross-Channel project, even to the extent of eliminating that bold concept from accepted Allied strategy."[53] In Brooke's mind, it was "all so clear and palpable that the policy we must pursue is to complete the elimination of Italy, profit from the situation by occupying as much of Italy as we require to improve bombing facilities of Southern Germany, and to force a withdrawal of German forces from Russia, [the] Balkans, and France. If we pin Germany in Italy she cannot find enough forces to meet all her commitments."[54] When the chief of the Imperial General Staff wrote these lines, on 6 August 1943, the Quebec Conference was about to be convened— for the purpose, at least in theory, of confirming the priority attached to OVERLORD. The Americans therefore had every reason to feel uneasy, if not actually annoyed with their partner.

From the spring of 1942 onward, Roosevelt, encouraged by his military advisers, had clearly expressed his support for a landing in northwestern Europe. The repeated postponement of this operation, notwithstanding its declared importance, raises the question why the United States, through the summer of 1943, nonetheless preferred to align itself with the strategic interests of Great Britain rather than to impose its own will. It needs to be kept in mind, first of all, that between 1940 and 1942 the Americans were relatively poorly equipped to conduct effective diplomacy. By contrast, the United Kingdom, heir to a vast empire stretching across five continents, had long been in the habit of negotiating on an international basis with the most diverse partners. They "had a large body of internationally educated, politically informed soldiers and civilians to draw from in putting together a team to deal with us," remarked one American observer. "They were used to dealing with foreigners, and to getting their way with them—foreigners in their own Empire, such as Canadians and Australians, and foreigners of other nationalities. They had a hundred years of experience behind them. We had almost literally none at all."[55] This deficit was all the more pronounced because the isolationist policy of the interwar period had removed the United States still further from European problems. In keeping with the constitutional principle of civilian control over the military, Roosevelt assigned to the War Department the task of working out the technical details of a policy that had already been settled upon at the White House. Having served for eight years early in his career as undersecretary of the navy (1913–1921), he took an occasional interest in naval strategy but for the most part refrained from directly intervening in military matters, about which he could in any case make little claim to expertise. If Admiral King went to the Oval Office once a week, sometimes more, General Marshall sometimes went a month without meeting with the president.[56] Similarly, the secretary of state, Cordell Hull, was never invited to discuss military strategy.[57] The two spheres remained quite separate: the diplomats concerned themselves with the "what," the military men with the "how."

Presenting a united front in negotiations with the British was additionally complicated by the fact that each of the three armed services, jealous of its independence from the others, looked to defend its own interests. The chiefs of staff, lacking internal political departments, were not accustomed to weighing the diplomatic consequences of their plans.[58] Until

TRIDENT, then, the Americans were poorly prepared for the great conferences. They hardly imagined that Great Britain might try to fool them, rather naively taking its good faith and understanding for granted—thus the tribute that virtue pays to vice, as it may now seem. The disappointment of Casablanca in January 1943 nonetheless prompted Washington to react. In April a new agency, the Joint War Plans Committee, was given responsibility for developing plans that would serve as a basis for decision making by the Joint Chiefs of Staff (JCS) and as a guide for theater commanders. Coordination among planners in the White House, the State Department, and the armed forces was improved as well, a sign that the general staff was now resolved to incorporate a political dimension into military decision making.[59] The realization that precious time had nonetheless been lost further strengthened Great Britain's hand.

For Winston Churchill held other trump cards. As both prime minister and defense minister, he could dictate military policy, and all the more readily given that he had direct authority over the heads of the services. Although his own chief of staff and military secretary to the War Cabinet, General Sir Hastings L. Ismay, usually represented him at the meetings of the British Chiefs of Staff (BCOS), Churchill sometimes sat in on them personally.[60] He seldom failed to take full advantage of his position, by intervening in strategic decisions both large and small and working out in advance of negotiations a single line of argument that all British representatives could unanimously defend. Furthermore, British forces still outnumbered American forces in 1942. It was therefore difficult, if not actually impossible, to impose on London an operation that it rejected and for which it would have to supply the bulk of the troops. Finally, the British prided themselves on their excellent intelligence services, an area in which the Americans were sorely deficient: "With a monopoly on intelligence, the British could, in the beginning, arrange to get almost any answer they wanted to a military equation—by the weight they chose to put on the equation's most important variable: the enemy's capabilities and intentions."[61] All these things combined to confer supremacy on Great Britain between 1941 and the middle of 1943, and they explain why the United States, being unable to oppose its wishes, acceded to them. Yet in the end Washington's patience ran out. The Teheran Conference represented a sharp setback for Churchill. It was there that Roosevelt administered the most painful rebuke imaginable, by siding with Stalinist Russia against Great Britain.

## TEHERAN

Prefaced by the military discussions conducted during the Third Moscow Conference of 18 October–1 November 1943 and then by the talks between China, Great Britain, and the United States held in Cairo (codenamed SEXTANT) from 22 to 26 November, the meeting that took place at Teheran (EUREKA) between 28 November and 1 December marked a turning point. There in the Iranian capital Churchill, Stalin, and Roosevelt finally took concrete decisions that directly influenced the fate of Operation OVERLORD. This renewed sense of purpose was due to the course of events in the war itself, but also to the growing place of postwar planning in the calculations of the Big Three.[62]

From the military point of view, the outlook in November 1943 had brightened noticeably. In the East, having turned back the Germans first at Stalingrad in February and then at Kursk in July, the Red Army suddenly found itself in a position to go on the offensive. Whereas for two years Moscow's dire predicament had led it to plead with its partners for the opening of a second front in the West, now it felt confident of victory. "By the end of 1943," recalled Marshal Georgii K. Zhukov, "we had finally overcome our grave situation and means of war, firmly held the strategic initiative and, generally speaking, no longer needed a second front in Europe so much as we had during the earlier two grim years. However, desirous of seeing the speediest possible defeat of Nazi Germany and the earliest possible termination of the war we all looked forward to the Second Front being opened in the immediate future."[63] The British and the Americans, not immediately suspecting the strategic importance of Stalingrad, continued to weigh the implications of the reversals sustained by the Germans in the course of 1943.[64] The prospect that a collapse of the Reich would open the door to westward Soviet expansion, redrawing the map of Europe, alarmed Anglo-American strategists. "On the one hand," noted Ivan Maisky, the Soviet ambassador to London, "the British government would like to push back the opening of the second front to a later date, in order to await the moment when the Red Army will have done the main part of the work and broken the back of the German military machine. . . . But on another hand, if the English (and the Americans), while awaiting 'comfortable conditions,' delay the opening of the second front in the West too long, they risk missing the right moment and letting the Red Army enter Berlin before the Allies. The English and the Americans are very afraid."[65] Hence the dilemma that haunted the Western leaders: whether to treat the Soviets as allies or as rivals.

From 1941 onward, after looking to both the near and the medium term, Roosevelt had clearly opted for the first alternative. For the immediate future, the burden of the war was to fall mainly on the Soviet Union. The United States sought therefore, to the fullest extent possible, to grant the Red Army the material assistance it needed, first to counter the assaults of the Wehrmacht and then, once Germany had been defeated, to join forces with the West against Japan. The possibility had not been excluded that Russia might become a major power after the war, in which case the assistance given it during the war would lay the groundwork for a regime of international cooperation that promised to serve both American interests (by opening the Soviet market to American-made products) and the cause of peace (by integrating the USSR, via the United Nations, into the international community).[66] The Canadian lieutenant general E. L. M. Burns emphasized in a memorandum addressed to Roosevelt's adviser Harry Hopkins, "We not only need Russia as a powerful fighting ally in order to defeat Germany but eventually we will also need her in a similar role to defeat Japan. And finally, we need her as a real friend and customer in the post-war world."[67] Roosevelt's own instinct in dealing with Stalin was to play things relatively straight. Disregarding the recommendation of a 23 January 1943 report by his Operations Plans Division ("The United States should continue to furnish lend-lease supplies to Russia to the full extent of our capacity, provided—and provided only—that Russia cooperates with us and takes us into her confidence"), Roosevelt refused to use lend-lease as a means of forcing the Kremlin to compromise—and all the more resolutely because economic blackmail had failed during the 1930s.[68] Furthermore, he forbade military intelligence to carry out espionage missions by means of convoys and planes bringing aid to Russia. In October the head of the U.S. Military Mission to Moscow, General John R. Deane, was expressly instructed by General Marshall "to avoid seeking information about the Russians."[69] The British had no such scruples, however. The Kremlin complained, for example, that "some of the officers at Arkhangelsk were not dealing with problems of delivery to the Soviet Union, being rather specialists of the British intelligence services."[70]

Witnesses to these events, later seconded by historians, have accused Roosevelt—not altogether fairly—of naïveté. It needs to be recalled, first, that the president declined to let Stalin in on the secret of the atomic bomb (though, of course, until the Potsdam Conference in July 1945 the Americans had no assurance whatever of being able to use it). From the point of view of the United States, an invasion of Normandy offered only advantages. By helping the Soviet Union and hastening the end of the war, OVERLORD strengthened mutual trust between East and West. In the event that the Third Reich were to collapse, the United States, now firmly anchored in Europe, would be in a position to prevent Soviet domination of the Continent, something that American planners had begun to fear as early as the spring of 1943.[71] In November of the same year, Roosevelt announced that "there would definitely be a race for Berlin" and added, "We may have to put United States divisions into Berlin as soon as possible."[72] By aiding the USSR, while at the same time limiting its westward expansion, the second front was a way of striking a compromise and creating a new balance of power.[73] Roosevelt's strategy was the product of a lucid geopolitical vision in which idealistic impulses supplemented tough-mindedness with consistency: Washington distrusted the Soviet Union no less than London did, but it preferred to confront the Russians in Western Europe rather than in the Balkans. The temptation to compare Roosevelt's presumed innocence unfavorably with the stark realism of his successor should be resisted, if only because the policy of force pursued by Truman prevented neither the expansion of Soviet control in Eastern Europe nor the extension of Communist rule to much of East Asia.

Great Britain, by contrast, in urging that the assault on Germany be mounted from bases in the Mediterranean theater, had embraced a plainly unrealistic policy. In North Africa, Allied troops struggled to secure control of Tunisia, where the German expeditionary force surrendered only on 13 May 1943—six months after the launching of Operation TORCH. Nor was the Italian campaign free of difficulties. Although the landing in Sicily (HUSKY) on 9–10 July was followed fairly rapidly by conquest of the island, the Germans nonetheless succeeded in evacuating the bulk of their forces, amounting to some 50,000 soldiers. The overthrow of Mussolini on 25 July and then the signing by Italy of a secret armistice with the Allies on 3 September, formally (and most inopportunely) announced by the Americans five days later, precipitated a disaster. That same day, 8 September, Anglo-American troops landed in the south of the boot and at Salerno. But far from being warmly received by their new allies, they were met with a barrage of fire from German forces dispatched to the front by Hitler. By the end of 1943, the Allies had managed to gain control of southern Italy, but the north long eluded their grasp, the Gustav Line firmly barring the way until the fall of Rome on 5 June 1944. In Greece, notwithstanding the modest aid given by the British on the Dodecanese islands of Leros, Kos, and Samos in the eastern Aegean, Italian insurgents were ruthlessly suppressed by German garrisons on Rhodes and Cephalonia.[74]

In the end, the strategy favored by Churchill yielded little in the way of results. Italy remained partly under the control of the Reich and, far from falling like a ripe fruit, turned out to be a trap for the Allied troops. The reverse was true as well, however, for by the beginning of 1944 twenty-two German divisions were fighting in Italy, as opposed to six in July 1943. The ruse of drawing German forces away from the eastern front, in order to relieve the pressure on the Soviets and reduce the number of troops available for the defense of northwestern Europe, had therefore worked—but not entirely, since between April and December 1943 Berlin transferred twenty-seven divisions from the West to the East.[75] In October eleven Allied divisions faced only nine German divisions in Italy.[76] Even allowing for the growth in German strength by the end of the year, this ratio was to increase in the spring of 1944. On 11 May, on the eve of the fourth battle at Monte Cassino, twenty-nine Allied divisions were ranged against twenty-two German divisions (or twenty-three, according to some sources).[77] So it is open to question who had trapped whom. The Allies in any case ended up having to commit many more troops to the Italian campaign than had been anticipated. Moreover, the attempt to gain control of the Greek islands had turned to catastrophe, causing thousands of deaths, while doing nothing to weaken German positions there. To make matters worse, the Mediterranean theater ended up taxing the resources allocated to OVERLORD, just as Allied strategists had feared. At the end of 1943, 768,274 American troops were stationed in the British Isles—whereas the general staff had made provision for the deployment of 1,026,000 men. By contrast, 597,658 men were fighting in Italy, when there ought to have been only 432,700.[78] Rather than face the facts, Churchill demanded that still more forces be allotted to this theater of operations. He elaborated various plans aimed at drawing Turkey into the war, mounting more substantial operations in the Dodecanese, and achieving a breakthrough in Italy, where, once the Pisa-Rimini line had been reached, one part of the advancing force would pivot to the west, crossing from there over the border into France, and the other eastward toward the Balkans.

This option presented grave disadvantages. The conquest of Italy risked draining away valuable troops in exchange for results that were neither substantial nor certain, and which in any case could be obtained only at the expense of OVERLORD. A war in the Balkans posed the additional problem of how to transport men and equipment over geographically forbidding terrain: driving northward into Austria, for example, meant having to cross the Alps. Moreover, any attempt to persuade Turkey to abandon its neutrality and enter the war on the side of the Allies threatened to revive the quarrel over the Bosporus and the Dardanelles, needlessly turning Moscow and Ankara against each other—although the Soviets, in October 1943, had welcomed the initiative.[79] Whereas the proposed landing in Normandy urged by the Americans elegantly resolved the terms of a complex equation, Churchill's strategy complicated matters to no apparent purpose. It swallowed up large numbers of troops, without guaranteeing that Nazi Germany would be defeated in the end—

for "if Anglo-American strength had been concentrated in Southern and Southeastern Europe, what eventually would have stopped the Russians from marching into the Ruhr and Saar and even to Normandy?"[80] And by inaugurating an era of suspicion toward Moscow, the British plan promised to multiply the potential for conflict with an ally that was still shouldering the principal burden of the war, and this at a time when victory over Germany and Japan was still far from being achieved.

These strategic disagreements, which it had been possible to paper over at the Washington and Quebec Conferences through a series of hard-fought compromises, were now forcefully expressed at Teheran. The inability of the British and Americans to coordinate their approach to the negotiations had the effect of making Stalin the referee of the matters in dispute.[81] Roosevelt, sailing out on the battleship *Iowa,* began at once to make meticulous preparations for the talks, with the assistance of some sixty military planners who were firmly resolved not to let themselves be lured into accepting a Mediterranean strategy. In Cairo, the president declined to meet privately with Churchill, a show of defiance that he repeated on his arrival in the Iranian capital.

To Stalin, however, he was prepared to show every courtesy. Roosevelt agreed to take up residence at the Russian Embassy, the site of the conference—supposedly for reasons of security, which was in the event enforced with no concern for subtlety; indeed "the President and his party were never permitted to forget it, for the servants who made their beds and cleaned their rooms were all members of the highly efficient NKVD, the secret police, and expressive bulges were plainly discernible in the hip pockets under their neat, white coats."[82] Roosevelt, for his part, seems not to have suspected "that the building was, inevitably, bugged and that every word uttered by himself and his delegation would be recorded, transcribed, and regularly reported to Stalin"[83]—unless, of course, he had knowingly acquiesced in this arrangement, in order to prove to his Soviet hosts that he had nothing to hide. However this may be, and as his son, Elliott Roosevelt, wryly remarked, "certainly the Russians did everything possible to make Father's stay in their Embassy pleasant."[84]

Once seated at the negotiating table, the Soviets and Americans promptly joined forces against the British. From the very first meeting, on 28 November, Stalin emphasized that he considered OVERLORD the principal operation of 1944. He stated that "he would even prefer to assume a defensive rôle in Italy and forego the capture of Rome for the present if this would admit the invasion of Southern France by, say, ten divisions. Two months later, 'Overlord' would follow, and the two invasions could then join hands."[85] A campaign in the Aegean or the Balkans, by contrast, seemed to him a waste of time. Thanks to his intelligence services, Stalin knew that Roosevelt intended to do his utmost to reach an agreement with Russia—even if it meant offending Churchill[86]—and therefore did not hesitate to speak bluntly. The next day Stalin rather abruptly asked who would command the operation. On being told that a commanding officer had not yet been chosen, he hardened his tone and demanded that his interlocutors agree to do three things immediately: fix a date for the landing in Normandy; organize an operation in the South of France; and name a commander.[87] "Marshal Stalin said he desired it to be understood that he did not presume to take part in the selection of a commander for OVERLORD but merely wanted to know who this officer would be and felt strongly that he should be appointed as soon as possible and be given responsibility for preparation for OVERLORD as well as the executive command of the operation. . . . The Soviets believe that until such a commander has been appointed, no success from OVERLORD can be expected in the matter of organization for this operation."[88] In this way, as General Sergei Shtemenko observed,

the Soviet delegation literally compelled the British delegation to acknowledge that Operation Overlord should be the Allies' main effort, that it should begin not later than May of the following year, and that it must definitively be carried out on the territory of Northern France. . . . The operations in the Mediterranean were regarded by the Soviet Supreme Command as secondary, since the enemy was using relatively small forces there and this theater was a long way from Germany. As for the Italian theatre, the Soviet delegation considered it very important for securing free passage of Allied shipping in the Mediterranean but quite unsuitable for striking directly at the Reich, since the Alps stood in the way. Nor were the Balkans, which Churchill viewed with greater eagerness, suitable for an invasion of Germany.[89]

In his memoirs Churchill explained that he was trying to save the vestiges of his Mediterranean strategy: "I was willing to do everything in the power of His Majesty's Government to begin 'Overlord' at the earliest possible moment, but I did not consider that the very great possibilities in the Mediterranean should be ruthlessly sacrificed and cast aside as if they were of no value, merely to save a month or so in the launching of 'Overlord.' There was a large British army in the Mediterranean, and I could not agree that it should stand idle for nearly six months."[90] This argument left Stalin completely unmoved. He now redoubled his efforts to draw Churchill out. "Before we separated, Stalin looked at me across the table and said: 'I wish to propose a very direct question to the Prime Minister about "Overlord." Do the Prime Minister and the British Staff really believe in "Overlord"?' I replied, 'Provided the conditions previously stated for "Overlord" are established when the time comes, it will be our stern duty to hurl across the Channel against the Germans every sinew of our strength.'"[91] Plainly, the Russian line of attack had been prepared in advance, for General Kliment Voroshilov immediately confronted his British counterpart with the same question. After praising the Americans' determination, Voroshilov "wished to know if General Brooke also considered the operation of first importance. He wished to ask both Allies whether they think that OVERLORD must be carried out or whether they considered that it may be possible to replace it by some other suitable operation when Turkey has entered the war."[92]

In the face of this humiliation, which somewhat dampened an otherwise warm celebration of his sixty-ninth birthday, Churchill was obliged to contemplate, not without a certain bitterness, the United Kingdom's sudden loss of influence. A noticeable change had come over the prime minister during the past several days:

> For Churchill, the Teheran Conference was not only the turning point of the war but a watershed in his life. . . . Suddenly, in the middle of the conference, he aged from hour to hour, becoming

long winded, forgetful, erratic. . . . His behaviour [afterward] became somewhat incoherent and unpredictable, somewhat "hand-to-mouth." He was still—or once more—brimming with energy and ideas, still vigorous and eloquent, still capable of great decisions and actions, but his decisions tended to be precipitate and his actions off-the-cuff. They were no longer based on a grand design. That had been wrecked, and its disappointed author was no longer quite the man he had been three years earlier. He was still the same person, but older, more irascible, and less self-controlled.[93]

Teheran therefore marked a turning point. The conference had led to the enshrinement of OVERLORD, still scheduled for the month of May and from that point on irrevocable. The Mediterranean remained a secondary theater of operations, one that would no longer pose a threat to the success of the landing. It should be emphasized that political factors were no less decisive than military factors for arriving at this decision. The invasion plan consolidated the alliance, not only by supplying a plausible strategy for conquering Germany, but also in holding out the possibility of cooperation with the Soviet Union after the war, while at the same time blocking any attempt at belligerent expansion into Western Europe. From then on, the second front was thus the cornerstone of mutual understanding among the Allies—only now the mission was to help Russia prevail, not to rescue it from defeat.[94] In this respect, the crucial move was to subordinate the special relationship between London and Washington to a new alignment of interests between Washington and Moscow. Roosevelt was perfectly aware of the risk involved. "The biggest thing," Roosevelt confided to his son, was "making it clear to Stalin that the United States and Great Britain were not allied in one common bloc against the Soviet Union. I think we've got rid of that idea, once and for all. I hope so. The one thing that could upset the applecart, after the war, is if the world is divided again, Russia against England and us. That's our big job now, and it'll be our big job tomorrow: making sure that we continue to act as referee, as intermediary between Russia and England."[95]

By establishing a dialogue with Moscow, Washington sought to supplant London as the chief arbiter of East-West relations and free itself at last from British tutelage in the geopolitical sphere. "And in doing that, it was clear, the United States had become world leader. No longer was our foreign policy simply tailing after Britain's."[96]

# 2

# PREPARING FOR WAR

FOR THE INVASION AGREED UPON at the Teheran Conference to have any chance of succeeding, the British and Americans had to find a way to mobilize immense resources—human, economic, and military. They had gotten off to a very slow start. If the Soviet Union has often been criticized, and rightly so, for its unpreparedness on the eve of Operation BARBAROSSA, the United States on the eve of Pearl Harbor stood exposed to the same charge. It was to be many months before American industry and the nation's armed forces were able to provide planners with the men and matériel they counted on, a situation whose urgency was compounded by the severe shortages from which Great Britain suffered.

## ECONOMIC MOBILIZATION

It is quite true that the United States registered spectacular performances for the war as a whole. Between 1940 and 1943, military production grew by 800 percent. Gross National Product (GNP) rose from $88.6 to $135 billion between 1939 and 1945 (in constant dollars).[1] And between 1942 and 1945 U.S. factories produced some 170,000 airplanes, 90,000 tanks, 65,000 landing craft, 1,200 battleships, and 320,000 pieces of artillery.[2] In 1944 American production was double that of Germany, Italy, and Japan combined. By furnishing 60 percent of Allied munitions, for example, the United States was indeed the arsenal of democracy (and of Soviet totalitarianism, one might be tempted to add).[3]

American mobilization on behalf of the Allied effort occurred only belatedly, however, for Roosevelt had long hesitated to place the country on a war footing. Already in 1939 Bernard Baruch, a leading financier and a member of Roosevelt's New Deal Brain Trust, had urged that the United States begin preparing for the coming conflict. But the White House resisted calls to build up stocks of raw materials and refused to revive the War Industries Board, which had administered military production during the First World War. Although the president did finally create the Office of Production Management on 7 January 1941, and then on 28 August 1941 the Supplies Priorities and Allocation Board, he was wary of assigning them precise functions, looking instead to protect his own powers by encouraging personal rivalries and overlapping spheres of authority. On 15 January 1942, in the wake of Pearl Harbor, the War Production Board was established under the direction of Donald Nelson, with responsibility for economic mobilization of the country on a national scale. The board's powers were in principle executive, but in practice they met with resistance from the various offices and boards of the armed forces, particularly since Nelson was painfully lacking in charisma and leadership qualities. The creation of the Office of War Mobilization in May 1943 added yet another layer of bureaucracy to an already labyrinthine system, although its head, James F. Byrnes, managed to earn a reputation for himself as an extremely efficient administrator.[4] Unlike Great Britain, the United States did not have at its disposal a single agency of government with undisputed authority for planning and coordinating war production.

An additional obstacle to wartime mobilization was the government's reluctance to call up citizens for military duty. The Selective Training and Service Act of 16 September 1940 was due to the initiative of Congress, not the White House. Nor did Roosevelt make alternative forms of service obligatory for women. This circumstance explains the relatively restricted role they played in the war economy: whereas in Germany women accounted for more than 51 percent of the labor force in the spring of 1944, in the United States it was 35.7 percent. And although the number of women actively employed in the war effort rose from 11.3 to 17 million between 1940 and 1944, only one American woman in three was working outside the home in 1944.

Not only did the United States avoid committing itself to the "total war" waged by Nazi Germany and the Soviet Union, it was unwilling even to match the sacrifices of Great Britain. Civilian consumption of goods and services in the United States rose by 12 percent between 1939 and 1944, whereas in the United Kingdom it fell by 22 percent.[5] Rationing did not begin until the spring of 1942, and then only on a limited basis. To mobilize the nation's resources, Roosevelt preferred to rely on market mechanisms (wage increases, for example) rather than coercive measures enforced by governmental authority. Although the country's security was at stake, he sought as far as possible to minimize the demands made on the American people—for reasons combining noble sentiments with possibly less lofty motives.

Despite the urgency of the conflict, the cycles of political life followed their usual course, as they had done during the Civil War and World War I. In addition to the presidential campaigns of 1940 and 1944, midterm elections were held on schedule in the fall of 1942. Roosevelt was anxious not to give the Republicans any openings by alienating public opinion. Unlike Churchill, however, he declined to campaign on a platform of national unity as a way of disarming the opposition. Two great issues divided Americans prior to Pearl Harbor: the ongoing reforms of the New Deal and the conflict in Europe. In 1935, 70 percent of those polled felt that American intervention in World War I had been an error; in 1940, only 12 percent of Americans favored a declaration of war against Germany in support of Great Britain, in spite of its dire predicament. Politically, large-scale military and industrial mobilization was out of the question. The ingrained individualism of American society, together with mistrust among business elites of New Deal reforms, left Roosevelt no choice but to cultivate the goodwill of workers and captains of industry alike. In the absence of a centrally administered war economy, military production is estimated to have fallen short of theoretically maximum levels by 10–20 percent.[6] Forced though he was to rely on moral suasion, Roosevelt showed remarkable restraint about using his office as a bully pulpit. Because he was determined above all to avoid confrontation, and therefore reluctant to force business interests to accept a policy they opposed (co-opting them instead by hiring prominent executives as dollar-a-year managers of agencies created to meet problems on an ad hoc basis), he had no alternative but to trade reduced economic efficiency for political gains in the form of popular support for the war effort.

In the United Kingdom, the problems of production appeared in a very different light. Even before the First World War, British industry had showed signs of weakness, aggravated by the crisis of the interwar years, despite the government's attempts to combat it. Mechanization and standardization lagged—the result of declining levels of investment and the resolve of trade unions to preserve traditional manufacturing skills. Unlike their counterparts in Germany and the United States, for example, British shipyards refused to construct vessels using prefabricated elements. Obsolete machinery stood in the way of innovation; managers, many of them self-made men, were skeptical of the new techniques devised by university-trained engineers; unions feared that increased labor flexibility would threaten standards of workmanship. Thus, for example, the Boilermakers' Society successfully insisted that pneumatic riveting be monitored by a corps of supervisors—doubling, rather than reducing, the number of workers needed.[7] Coal production declined, from 231 to 192 million tons between 1939 and 1944; mine owners, having underinvested during the 1930s, avoided mechanizing their operations during the war out of a fear of nationalization and a desire to reserve the best seams for postwar production. Worker absenteeism grew: a more vigilant regime of health inspection in the workplace led sick miners to stay home; at the same time, they were no longer willing to go down into the mines, fearing that their failing strength might imperil others—not unreasonably, since between 1943 and 1945 one miner in four was the victim of a serious accident.[8] Psychological and economic circumstances therefore conspired to slow the advance of productivity, which on a per capita basis and for industry as a whole in the United Kingdom grew at half the rate of that of Germany over the course of the war.

Shortfalls in production threatened the vitality of sectors that were essential to the war effort. The Royal Air Force was luckier than other branches of the military: it took delivery of 7,940 aircraft in 1939, 20,094 in 1941, 26,263 in 1943, and 26,461 in 1944. Modernization of the aeronautical industry was nonetheless handicapped by the promotion of inexperienced men to managerial positions and the relatively small scale of production. Factories employed between 3,000 and 15,000 workers, as opposed to between 20,000 and 40,000 in the United States. Until the advent of the Meteor jet fighter, the British had to content themselves with gradually increasing production of aircraft designed during the 1930s—notably the Spitfire and the Mosquito—at the expense of genuine innovation.[9]

Tank production, on the other hand, was less efficient. The Churchill, specifications for which were issued during the summer of 1940, was found to be unsuited for service in the Middle East the following year, and its principal defects were not corrected until 1943. The Cromwell, designed in early 1941, was more satisfactory from a technical point of view, but there were too few of this type, and British manufacturers were unable to increase output during the course of the war. Low levels of investment in research and development, outmoded assembly methods, inadequate advance planning—all these things combined to slow a rate of production that was modest to begin with. In its best year, 1942, the United Kingdom brought out only 8,611 tanks and self-propelled guns, whereas Germany, at the zenith of its production in 1944, brought out 22,100. That same year, British output declined to barely 5,000 guns and armored vehicles.

Great Britain was therefore forced to rely on lend-lease aid. The United States was hardly ungenerous, giving some 9 billion dollars of goods in 1943 and 10.4 billion in 1944, mainly food products and military equipment.[10] American manufacturers supplied roughly 20 percent of the weapons used by British forces during the entire war, and a higher proportion in 1943–1944 than in 1940–1942.[11] Two-thirds of His Majesty's armored brigades and divisions were equipped with Sherman tanks in the Normandy campaign. Left to its own devices, the United Kingdom would have found itself grossly outmatched by an enemy whose war production continued to increase until July 1944.

Indeed, the achievement of the British economy in supplying even

four-fifths of its military arsenal exceeded all expectations, especially because vulnerability to the U-boat warfare waged by the Kriegsmarine
forced it to reduce its reliance on trade within the empire and with the
United States: between 1939 and 1944, imports of raw materials fell from
22 to 12 million tons, and those of foodstuffs from 29 to 10 million tons.[12]
Improved agricultural efficiency and mandatory rationing jointly caused
food consumption to decline from a base of 100 in 1938 to 88.2 in 1944,
whereas in the United States it grew by about 8 percent during the same
period.[13]

It is worth noting that economic dependence was not entirely one-
sided. Material assistance flowed from Great Britain to the United States
as well in the form of "reverse lend-lease," or mutual aid, as the British
called it. In the spring of 1944, British factories supplied the U.S. Army
with 1,100 aircraft, several hundred gliders, and 10,600 airplane wheels.
The American Quartermaster Corps fulfilled some 63 percent of its orders in Great Britain, the Corps of Engineers 58 percent, and the air
forces 21 percent. The total value of goods and services provided by the
British as of 30 June 1944 by way of mutual aid amounted to more than a
billion dollars—not including another billion in worldwide shipping services and buildings constructed for the use of the U.S. Army.[14] To be
sure, this assistance did not come close to matching the extraordinary
sums that Washington made available to London under the terms of the
Lend-Lease Act; but it does show that, far from sponging off a wealthy
protector, the United Kingdom tried to the best of its means and ability
to contribute to the common war effort.

The obstacles in Great Britain to economic mobilization were partly
due, then, to the worldwide depression of the 1930s and the power of
trade unions at home. But there was a deeper historical reason as well:
the British economy, having been integrated into an open international
trading system since the eighteenth century, could not suddenly revert to
autarky. Given these constraints, and notwithstanding the advantages of
hindsight, it may be unreasonable to expect that Great Britain's performance should have been more robust than it was.[15]

Be that as it may, even a cursory examination of the performance of the

Allied war economies challenges simplistic views about the planning of the invasion. Far from being able to draw on a bottomless pool of resources that permitted every possible extravagance, logistics experts on both sides of the Atlantic were forced to take into account the limits of productive capacity. Indeed, there was no guarantee at the close of the Teheran Conference that the equipment and supplies necessary for OVER-LORD would be available five months later. By repeatedly putting off a final decision, the heads of the coalition ensured that the initial and indispensable stages of planning for the operation would amount to little more than an abstract exercise. "It was an unpreparedness that went far beyond the fact that we had but a single infantry division on hand," the American officer Ralph Ingersoll later recalled, "and that a division which had never even practiced getting in and out of landing craft because in all England there seemed to be no beaches that could be spared to play with. The unpreparedness began with the somnolent inertia of everyone concerned, from the British generals and their staffs to the civilian agencies preoccupied with raising and rationing food, distributing manpower and requisitioning land and buildings."[16] This inertia weighed heavily on the project—all the more so because the American, British, and Canadian armies at the end of 1943 displayed serious flaws.

## THE ARMED FORCES

The rise of expansionist powers in both Europe and East Asia during the 1930s ought to have led the United States to prepare itself militarily for a conflict that was, if not probable in the near term, at least foreseeable. When General Marshall assumed his duties in July 1939, the American army was still a minor and underequipped force, having only 20,000 officers and 174,000 men under arms, with an additional 200,000 ready to be called up from the National Guard units of the individual states. As a result of the Burke-Wadsworth Act of September 1940 (imposing the first peacetime draft in American history), the federalization of the National Guard, and increased Congressional funding for the military, the number of enlisted men rose in short order to some 500,000.[17] Yet this increase failed to meet the urgency of the situation, in part because the army's need for manpower now entered into competition with the requirements of industrial mobilization.

The exceptional availability of large numbers of soldiers—a selective draft had been instituted only once before in the United States, during the First World War—led planners in the War Department to think in terms of ideal scale: in principle, there were enough young men to win the war without diverting labor resources from the industrial sector. This simple calculation turned out to be overly optimistic, however. On the assumption that Germany and its allies had fielded some 400 divisions, it would be necessary to double that figure in order to be sure of victory. Taking into account Great Britain's 100 divisions, the United States faced the daunting prospect of raising 700 divisions and 28 million men in order to protect against the possibility of British capitulation or Soviet collapse, or both.[18] For a country of 135 million people, unable to call up more than 10 percent of its population for service in the armed forces, this was plainly impossible. In January 1943 the War Department presented the White House with a range of alternatives, including a maximum figure of 334 divisions and 10.5 million men; in the end, the president opted for the minimum estimate of 100 divisions and 8,028,000 men.[19] This figure was later revised downward in view of mounting Soviet resistance and of the aerial supremacy over the Reich that had been achieved in the meantime. In June 1943 the Committee on the Revision of the Military Program recommended mobilizing 88 divisions and 7,657,000 men. These numbers were subsequently rounded up to 90 divisions and 8,300,000 men, a target that ultimately was met. On 8 May 1945 the United States deployed 89 divisions in the various theaters of operation (including two units that were not activated)—a rather modest force if one considers that on the same date the Red Army numbered roughly 400 divisions and that the Germans, over the course of the war, deployed on average 300 divisions. Of this total, ground combat forces represented a relatively minor, though stable, component: on 31 December 1942 they numbered 1,917,000 men; on 31 March 1945, 2,041,000. At the end of the war, then, not quite a quarter of the men mobilized were

fighting on land, the others serving in the navy and air force, and in substantial numbers as infantry support troops.[20]

Notwithstanding its preference for maintaining divisions at their full
complement, the War Department took a cautious approach to the management of human resources. Rather than multiply the number of units,
Marshall had deliberately provided for ample reserves of reinforcements—
something that partly explains the discrepancy on paper between Soviet
and American forces. But other measures suggest that manpower was not
mobilized as fully as it might have been, particularly in order to avoid
damaging the morale of families with draft-age sons. Until November
1942 the armed services limited recruitment to men twenty-one years of
age or older; thereafter, the lower age limit remained fixed at eighteen.
This circumspection, however understandable it may have been in human (and political) terms, significantly restricted the options available to
war planners.

American military capabilities were hampered further by an attachment to outmoded ways. It was not until July 1940 that Marshall agreed
to create the Armored Force, under the leadership of Brigadier General
Adna R. Chaffee, Jr.[21] The formation of a tank corps ran up against resistance within the army, an institution proud of its heritage. As late as the
interwar period, the horse still conferred social status upon officers, who
had difficulty renouncing an animal that symbolized the heroism of the
nineteenth-century wars against the Indians and the Mexicans.[22] American strategy, heir to a dual and conflicting legacy, was no less problematic. Whereas the Indian Wars had been based on mobility, the Civil War
had demonstrated the advantages of brute force. Ideally, it would have
been possible to follow the Wehrmacht's example of combining power
and rapid maneuver, as Chaffee recommended, but practical considerations interfered. In the end, the arguments of Lieutenant General Lesley
J. McNair—commander of U.S. ground forces beginning in March 1942
and by virtue of his former position as chief of staff of general headquarters a central figure in planning for a European war—prevailed, and
concentrated power was subordinated to mobility. Unlike Germany, the
United States relied on motorized infantry and equipped armored divi-

sions with self-propelled artillery that increased their maneuverability. In September 1943, however, these units had on average only 263 tanks each—a complement that was all the more modest since the tanks themselves were poorly armed by comparison with their German counterparts: the Sherman carried only a 75 mm gun, whereas the Tiger was equipped with an 88 mm. No less than in the glorious days of the cavalry, U.S. strategists laid emphasis on the tactical missions of pursuit and exploitation, rather than organizing armored forces into autonomous units capable of making their own decisions. As a result, the planners missed an opportunity to implement the novel conception of mechanized warfare pioneered by General Heinz Guderian's Panzer Corps, whose devastating campaign in May–June 1940 was responsible for the greatest misfortune ever to befall French arms.[23] By the end of the war the United States had at its disposal fully sixteen armored divisions; because the debate over power and mobility had not yet been decisively settled, however, the advantage of exceptional force was compromised by a curious form of strategic schizophrenia on the eve of the Normandy landing.

In many respects, the infantry—mobile and equipped with its own artillery—remained the backbone of the American armies, and the brunt of the offensive effort rested on it. American strategists, contemplating the lessons of World War I, had concluded that breakthrough capacity depended on both firepower (to neutralize the enemy) and maneuverability (to conquer terrain).[24] In this scheme, the chief purpose of armored vehicles—the Sherman tank especially—was to open up breaches in the adversary's defenses large enough to permit the penetration of foot soldiers.[25] But how capable were these soldiers? Nothing on the eve of the invasion gave grounds for confidence. The system of recruitment, based in large part on voluntary enlistment in specific service branches (navy, marines, airborne force, and so on), caused the infantry to be filled by default with the weakest conscripts—weakest in every respect. In the second half of 1943, 46 percent of the 713,854 white GIs (African-Americans were seldom assigned to combat units) served in the ground forces; but only 24 percent of these infantry recruits were ranked among the most highly qualified, as opposed to 64 percent judged to be among the least qualified.

Few wished to serve in the army. A survey taken in the second half of 1943 revealed that, if the choice were theirs, 76 percent of the airmen would sign up for another tour of duty, whereas only 11 percent of the infantry were willing to stay on. The main reason, of course, had to do with the much greater risks they faced on the battlefield. In the North African theater alone, the army accounted for 80 percent of the casualties, two-thirds of which involved combat soldiers. There were other reasons as well. The army paid less well than the air force; army service carried less prestige and offered fewer professional qualifications that would help men find civilian employment after the war.[26] General headquarters was aware of these problems and took steps in early August 1943 to correct them, with only very limited success. The fact of the matter is that the major role in the fighting to come was assigned to the very branch of the American forces that was least equipped to carry it out.

An army that had ambivalent feelings about the war to begin with was additionally vulnerable. To be sure, many soldiers subscribed to the Allies' declared objectives: 66 percent of the airmen questioned in 1942 believed that the United States ought to continue fighting until democratic freedoms could be guaranteed to all the peoples of the earth.[27] Similarly, 52 percent of the enlisted soldiers endorsed the "Germany first" principle; only 12 percent thought that Japan should be defeated before the Allies took on the Reich.[28] The principle of unconditional surrender enjoyed broad support as well: more than 70 percent of the soldiers and officers questioned thought that the enemy should be crushed. Only 15 percent of the sample expressed a preference for entering into peace talks.[29] Finally, a majority of soldiers (66 percent) and officers (59 percent) said that they understood the reasons for the war.[30]

This apparent determination to prevail failed to conceal a deeper skepticism, however. Only 38 percent of the soldiers in Tunisia and Sicily said that they "never [had] doubts" about the need to go to war; 31 percent confessed to "sometimes" having doubts, and 9 percent had them "very often."[31] In March 1944, 38 percent of the officers serving in Europe affirmed their resolve to carry on the fight, but the majority of those interviewed were more hesitant, wondering "only once in a great while" (22 percent), "sometimes" (29 percent), or "very often" (11 percent)

whether the war was really necessary. Similarly, the commitment to unconditional surrender waned over time. In the same March 1944 survey
33 percent of the officers expressed the view that if the Reich were to
propose an end to hostilities, the offer should be given serious consideration; 17 percent felt that it should be accepted at once.[32]

These reservations had nothing to do with the weariness that inevitably accompanied a long and bloody conflict, for the struggle against Japan aroused fewer doubts: only 16 percent of the officers serving in the
South Pacific thought "sometimes" or "very often" that the war was not
worth waging—by comparison with 40 percent of their fellow officers
serving in Europe. Seventy-seven percent rejected the very idea of a Japanese peace offer; only 45 percent of the officers serving in Europe adopted
an equally firm attitude toward Germany.[33] Whereas 70 percent of the
veterans of the Tunisian and Sicilian campaigns wished to see the Nazi
leaders punished after the war, though not the Reich destroyed (only 18
percent), the proportions were reversed in the case of Japan: 64 percent
called for its annihilation, but only 23 percent felt that its leadership
should be brought to account and the population as a whole shown le-
niency.[34] These numbers suggest a harmony of opinion between the army
and the American people, 53 percent of whom in February 1943 considered that Japan was indeed the principal adversary, with only 34 percent
naming the Third Reich.

Despite the urgings of government propaganda, then, American soldiers did not show the same hostility toward Germany that they felt toward Japan—a belligerence that was fueled in large part by revelations of
atrocities committed by Japanese soldiers, notably at Bataan.[35] It is not
that they were mistaken about the quality of their adversary: 77 percent of
the U.S. infantrymen in Tunisia and Sicily reckoned that the fighting that
lay ahead would be difficult and likely to result in heavy losses; only 5
percent expressed the opposite view. The crucial point is that the Americans did not regard the Germans as ignorant beasts. This should perhaps
not come as a surprise, since Germans constituted the largest ethnic
group in the United States. Indeed, 66 percent of the American soldiers
who had seen combat in the Mediterranean in late 1943 claimed never to
have heard of inhuman practices committed by the enemy: to the con-

trary, the Germans had behaved honorably on the whole.[36] Air force crews shared this view:

> Actually, very little hate for the Germans can be found [among airmen]. The attitude generally seemed to be one of respect for a worthy adversary. Stories about Germans picking Americans out of the Channel who had ditched near the Dutch coast were much more frequent than stories of machine-gunning parachutists. . . . The attitude toward the enemy seemed to be one of intense rivalry, very much like the attitude towards an opposing college football team just before a big game. . . . However it would be an exaggeration to say that any large part of the motivation to keep fighting comes from an adequate knowledge and understanding of what we are fighting for.[37]

Demonization of the adversary is, of course, a powerful stimulant to combat. American troops, feeling on the whole neither hatred nor contempt for the Germans, found themselves in a delicate position. Divided over the justice of the cause they claimed to serve and considering that the men of the Wehrmacht were no different than other men, Americans displayed little eagerness for fighting—something that did not go unnoticed by their officers. "The 'will to fight' is most important," noted Lieutenant Colonel Samuel Sandler, director of the Consultation Service at Camp Lee in Virginia. "About 50 percent didn't have it, I found in my induction work." Major Calvin Dreher, a psychiatrist attached to the Fifth Army, concurred: "I found a lot of men who didn't care to fight. *We are fighting a war with a poorly indoctrinated army.*"[38] A summary report in the fall of 1945 concluded, "There is general agreement that American soldiers' motivation was less than that of the troops of most other large nations involved in the war. The American fought mainly because he had to."[39] Indeed, the chief question in the minds of 43 percent of the American soldiers preparing for the invasion of Normandy was "How long will it be before we can go home?" Only 17 percent wondered about the nature of the fighting to come, in particular the place and date of the landing.[40]

It is hard to provide a fully satisfying explanation for the failure of the U.S. Army to galvanize its troops for action in Normandy. Nonetheless, several points are worth bearing in mind. First, official war propaganda had to contend with widespread public skepticism. Americans had ambivalent memories of the First World War, and many people felt that the government had shown a disregard for basic civil rights, in recklessly inflaming passions, simplifying difficult problems to the point of caricature, and arousing futile hopes. Determined not to repeat these mistakes, Roosevelt proceeded cautiously, contenting himself with the creation of a few agencies—notably the Office of War Information (OWI) in June 1942[41]—that for want of any well-defined purpose accomplished little. Indeed, the OWI's budget for lectures and motivational films was reduced in 1943, with the result that diffusion of the government's message was left largely to private initiative, particularly in the form of volunteer groups such as the Hollywood Writers' Mobilization and the Writers' War Board. By and large, however, the presentations given by the army were well received by the troops. In the European theater of operations (ETO), 79 percent of the talks were judged "very useful" or "fairly useful."[42] Some units, especially the heavy-bomber crews of the Eighth Air Force, made additional efforts to keep themselves informed: 40 percent of these men read British newspapers three to four times a week, and more than 90 percent read *Stars and Stripes,* the daily paper published by the U.S. military.[43] Even so, as the American cultural and literary historian Paul Fussell observed, "the puzzlement of the participants about what was going on contrasts notably with the clarity of purpose felt, at least in the early stages, by those who fought in the Great War." In the minds of most American servicemen, the United States "was pursuing the war solely to defend itself from the monsters who had bombed Pearl Harbor without warning." Many soldiers, knowing what their fathers had endured in the First World War, felt they had a good idea of what awaited them in France this time around—not something they could look forward to with pleasure: "Among those fighting there was an unromantic and demoralizing sense that it had all been gone through before." To be sure, the seriousness of the present conflict was in no way underestimated, but the heroic aura of the earlier war had dissipated: "Even the air war had lost most of the chivalric magic attending it in 1914–1918, and the use of the air as a medium and conduit for the German V-weapons quite thoroughly completed its deromanticizing."[44] Casting the struggle in a valiant and inspirational light was therefore in many ways an impossible mission, and the reluctance of soldiers to hurl themselves selflessly into battle was a consequence in large part of the difficulty of disguising the sinister realities of modern warfare.

Differing perceptions of the relative burden the war placed on soldiers and civilians further aggravated the problem of military morale. A study of soldiers stationed in the United States, done by the Research Branch of the U.S. Army in December 1942, had underestimated this divide. More than half (55 percent) of the troops questioned felt that most civilians took the war seriously; 81 percent said that "almost all" or "many" supported the armed forces. Yet beneath this near unanimity of opinion lay muffled resentments. For although 73 percent of the soldiers agreed that farmers strongly supported the war effort, 54 percent thought that "workers in companies making war materials 'could do more'"—a feeling shared by 62 percent with respect to the owners of such firms, and by 86 percent with respect to union leaders.[45] More than a year later, in April 1944, this socially polarized sense of dissatisfaction was felt keenly by many soldiers overseas, airmen not excluded:

For a Group Commander [it was difficult] to develop strong morale in his group and to get them to identify closely with the American people's struggle to provide world freedom when the stories from the States are principally concerned with strikes, black markets, the difficulties of getting home from a winter vacation in Florida, salaries of $65 a week for boys just going out of high-school, the problem of getting gasoline for pleasure driving, and the annoyance of having to use rationing points in buying food. . . . It was reported by practically all the commanders in [the European and North African] theaters that one of the principal sources of motivation in keeping the aircrew men flying and fighting was the desire to get their immediate job done and get back to the United States.[46]

Could it have been otherwise? For most people at home, a conflict be-ing waged on the other side of the Atlantic, against an enemy that had not attacked them, did not seem to constitute a war of national defense. Nor could American soldiers be expected to display the same passion for their cause as the German troops, who were strongly indoctrinated and who in 1944 were fighting for the survival of their homeland—as the Nazi leadership itself observed: "As far as the war in Europe is concerned," Goebbels noted in his diary in early March of that year, "the Americans are very skeptical. They know very well that the war in Europe will bring them nothing and that, for them, the [real] war is taking place instead in the Pacific. This is why, for example, the Americans are fighting so badly on the Italian battlefield. They would like to go home as soon as pos-sible."[47]

In the months leading up to the landing in Normandy, then, the psy-chological mobilization of the American people was far from complete. Unlike the Soviet general staff, American planners could neither count on a virtually inexhaustible supply of manpower nor deceive themselves about the motivation of their soldiers, particularly in the case of the in-fantry. This sobering prospect was further complicated by serious short-comings in the armies of Great Britain and Canada.

Great Britain began to mobilize young men twenty and twenty-one years of age by decree in May 1939. Nonetheless, it was not until the declara-tion of war against Germany on 3 September of that year that Parliament authorized conscription. By year's end, British forces numbered 1.5 mil-lion men—the majority of them in the army—supported by 43,000 female auxiliaries.[48] Although the country had not been caught off guard, rear-mament having begun in 1935, no one imagined that this effort would be nearly enough. Indeed, attempts to strengthen military capability en-countered severe obstacles.

Because human resources were far more limited than in the United States, His Majesty's government found itself obliged to enlarge the pool of potential recruits. By 1941, the authorities were calling up young men nineteen years of age. More drastic measures followed shortly. In Decem-ber of the same year, the National Service Act was amended to broaden military eligibility for men aged eighteen to fifty-one; citizens of both sexes aged eighteen to sixty were subject to national service, and single women between the ages of twenty and thirty were being called upon to serve either in the armed forces or in industry.[49] By June 1944 the British armed forces numbered 4.5 million men and 450,000 female auxiliaries, or slightly more than 10 percent of a population of 47.7 million. Reluctantly, Churchill had elected not to enforce conscription in Ulster, for fear of swelling the ranks of the Irish Republican Army and infuriating the Irish community in America.

The need to balance military needs and industrial requirements forced a number of painful choices, as the manpower crisis of 1942 was to reveal. Troop levels, low to begin with, were to be reduced still further as the war went on. Sluggish demographic growth during the interwar period had reduced the pool of fresh recruits from which the army could draw in 1939, and the losses sustained subsequently as a result of the campaigns in the Middle East, Asia, and Italy had now drained it dry. The prospect of having to field a large force for the invasion of France explains in part Churchill's preference for a war of attrition that would delay the landing as long as possible. "In the long race of history, the British horse was in. . . . The cynics felt that, from 1942 on, the British were spending Russian lives and American dollars and getting a profitable banker's percentage on both. So what's the hurry?"[50] The shortage of manpower also explains the cautious strategy that was to be pursued by Montgomery in Normandy. Better than anyone, the commander in chief of the Twenty-first Army Group knew that his losses—unlike those of the Americans—would never be recouped.

The morale of British troops toward the end of 1943 was doubtful as well, though it had been improved by recent successes in North Africa and Italy and by the delivery of new weapons (Cromwell tanks and Bofors guns).[51] "Confidence—in the quality of weapons, equipment, and training, in the ability of the High Command, and in the outcome of the war—is strong in all the ranks," noted one report. News of the appointment of Eisenhower, an American, and Tedder and Montgomery, both British, as the top commanders of OVERLORD, was favorably received. Nor did the prospect of an imminent invasion appear to arouse any great apprehension. "Evidence of this is shown by the spirit in which the ban on privilege leave has been accepted, the high confidence placed in leaders, training, and equipment, and, that the imminence of offensive operations on the Continent was observed to be generally anticipated with enthusiasm by those who expected to take an immediate active part and by others whose duties were to sustain the expeditionary force."[52]

Nonetheless, the men were mistrustful of the grand ideals for which they were supposed to be fighting. "All the available evidence suggests that the mainspring of the soldier's morale (particularly the soldier who is serving 'for the duration') is his home—which he thinks of as including not only his present home but also the home he hopes to return to after the war. This rather than any abstract ideal, is what he is fighting for, and his hopes and fears about it influence his will to serve more deeply than do victories or defeats."[53] A May 1944 report on morale in the army observed: "The course of the war, revealing in ever darker colors the innate beastliness of the Boche, has not in any way weakened the average British soldier's desire to exterminate the Nazi and all his work. But the longer the war goes on, the more do the conditions of life of his family and dependents, things which in the first flush of enthusiasm in the early stages of a war are relegated well to the background, matter."[54] Chief among the worries, real or imagined, were infidelity on the part of a wife or girlfriend, and more generally the plight of loved ones tested by the hardships of the war—not the least of which, for many, was the loss of a home because of enemy bombing. Requests for leave on account of family or matrimonial problems rose, from 21,791 between November 1943 and January 1944 to 25,598 from February to April of 1944, as did unauthorized absences.[55] Being absent without leave (AWOL) was by far the most frequent grounds for cases brought before courts-martial, 1,488 of which were adjudicated in 1939–1940, 13,936 in 1942–1943, and 14,167 in 1943–1944. That the majority of such incidents occurred in Great Britain and not, apart from the period of 1944–1945, in cross-Channel theaters of operation probably reflects soldiers' desire to be reunited with friends and family, if only briefly.[56]

Altogether natural anxieties of this kind were accompanied by ambivalence about the future. Enlisted men looked for assurances that the postwar period would, if not open the gates to earthly paradise, at least justify hopes of a better future. The War Office concluded that the ordinary soldier "doesn't want Utopia, and if he is satisfied that his needs are really being considered sympathetically by those in authority he will care little about 'plans.'"[57] A subsequent report on morale qualified the judgment somewhat, noting that the average Tommy "is not pre-occupied with political theories, but he is intensely interested in 'post-war planning' insofar as it affects his home, his job, and the prospects of his family."[58] By itself, then, a resolve to defeat Nazi Germany was not sufficient to motivate soldiers who were mainly worried about the future. In this respect, at least, they were no different from their countrymen at home.

To sustain civilian morale, the government held out the prospect of a benevolent welfare state, whose main outlines were sketched in the Beveridge Report on Social Insurance and Allied Services, published in November 1942.[59] Civilians, no less than soldiers, thought more readily about the aftermath of the war than about the war itself and meant to do everything in their power to stay alive, so that they might enjoy the fruits of the new dispensation. The fighting men, for their part, were worn out by a conflict that in 1944 was entering its sixth year—having carried many of them from the troubled waters of Dunkirk to the burning sands of El Alamein and the mudflats of Anzio and Nettuno. Enthusiasm for combat had diminished: the more unmistakably victory loomed on the horizon, the greater the soldiers' interest in proceeding with caution, in hopes of making it back home in one piece. The generals, for their part, could no longer count on the unquestioning devotion of men whose sense of duty had been eroded, as the Normandy campaign would show. Nor, finally, should the effects of the pacifism of the interwar years period be underestimated. "The trouble with our British lads," Montgomery confided to General Brooke, "is that they are not killers by nature."[60]

Class differences between soldiers and officers played a significant role as well. In the United States, sons of good family had never been attracted by the prospects of a military career: General George S. Patton, a child of privilege who went on to marry a wealthy heiress, was very much the exception rather than the rule. In Great Britain, by contrast, the upper classes had long been in the habit of sending their sons to military academies. In 1939, 84 percent of the cadets at Sandhurst came from public schools.[61] The need to expand officer recruitment during the war in order to train a rapidly growing army did not, at least initially, encroach on the aristocratic sense of entitlement: "What does your father do? Do you hunt? Which pack do you hunt with?"—these were the sort of questions that aspiring officers were likely to be asked at the outset of hostilities.[62] As the war went on, and with the introduction of psychological testing, recruitment acquired a more scientific basis. But the social divide between enlisted men and their leaders was no less great than before. Not a few of those who survived Dunkirk felt that they had been abandoned by their superiors. Many had a hard time accepting orders from senior officers, themselves survivors of the Great War. All these things conspired to give rise to an

> attitude of antagonism to an impersonal "they," variously identified with "the war office," "the authorities," and (by the rank and file) with "the officers," or even, "the Army" generally, which militates against solidarity, co-operation and esprit de corps [in the Army as a whole]. It makes the soldier think of the Army as an institution of which he is not fully a member, administered by those who do not in any real sense lead or represent him. . . . More men are driven to the extreme Left by lack of consideration on the part of their superiors than are lured in that direction by politically-minded comrades, and the potential creator of class-feeling and disaffection is more often to be found in the officers mess than in the barrack room.[63]

Indeed, many officers showed "a lamentable degree of ignorance" about the effects of fighting on the men under their command.[64] The traditional culture of deference, solidly rooted until quite recently, no longer served to inspire in British troops the sense of boldness and daring needed to launch an assault on the beaches of Normandy.

On the eve of its declaration of war against the Third Reich, on 7 September 1939, Canada's military capability was modest, to say the least.

Until 1938 it had no tanks, and the following year its armed forces numbered only 4,500 soldiers, 1,800 sailors, and 3,100 airmen.[65] To remedy
these deficiencies, Ottawa instituted a limited system of conscription in
1940: men between the ages of twenty-one and forty-five were required to
perform national service, overseas duty being reserved solely for volunteers. A referendum in April 1942 overturned this restriction, but the government did not make use of its new authority until November 1944.
Even so, by the spring of 1944 a force of 405,834 men had been raised for
combat outside Canada, on a wholly voluntary basis.[66]

Far from attracting the dregs of society, the Canadian military managed
to recruit men who were well integrated into the life of their communi-
ties. Of those who volunteered during the first three months of the war,
89 percent had left jobs—a sign that they did not regard enlistment as a
way of escaping unemployment. Though poorly educated on the whole
(a third had not finished elementary school, and only an eighth had completed high school), they had nonetheless enlisted in full cognizance of
the situation facing them. Many felt a strong sense of attachment to Great
Britain and, believing that the war against Nazi Germany would be long
and difficult, wanted to offer their assistance in defeating a regime whose
ideology they thought constituted a threat to the values of the free
world.[67] Others, however, were considered lacking in patriotic fervor.[68]

The Canadian army suffered from two main problems. On the one
hand, its officers were inexperienced and did a poor job of training the
troops, a defect that was to be revealed in the Italian campaign. On
the other hand, owing to the refusal of General Andrew McNaughton, the
Canadian commander in Europe, to commit his forces to secondary
theaters of operation, the soldiers remained inactive for long periods.
McNaughton emphasized two points in particular in his letter to President Roosevelt of 9 March 1942: "First, that in the present period it was
desired to contribute as well as we could to the security of the United
Kingdom, which we considered to be under-insured, and to the maintenance of our foothold for an eventual attack on the Continent of Europe;
secondly that we never lost sight of the fact that we were part of an important strategical reserve, which sooner or later there would be an opportunity to employ against Hitler, and even in the meanwhile its very

presence in England would continue to tie down German Divisions perhaps of greater total strength."[69] This policy was reconsidered in July 1943, when Ottawa agreed to dispatch the First Infantry Division and the First Armored Brigade to Italy. In the meantime, the 180,000 men stationed in Great Britain as of 31 December 1941 had remained idle, succumbing to boredom and alcoholism, which gave rise in turn to friction with the local population.[70] The desire to see action, frustrated for so many months, explains why the Canadians demanded to be in the front lines during the disastrous raid on Dieppe on 19 August 1942. "For this army of volunteers, many of them enlisted in 1939 in the hope and expectation of early fighting, the many disappointments and the long inaction were an exacting and difficult experience. The years in England were in fact as severe a test of morale as has been faced by any Army in this generation."[71] The experience was to leave its mark on the Canadian campaign in France.

Despite their massive presence, the Allied forces assembled on the eve of the invasion of Normandy were far from invincible. Even their numbers were smaller than might have been expected, the Americans having avoided thoroughgoing conscription, the British having been held back by demographic constraints, and the Canadians having chosen a regime of voluntary enlistment. The troops themselves were not fully convinced of the urgency of their mission. American soldiers, though they harbored a fierce hatred toward Japan, did not share the grand ideals of their leaders and wanted to be done with the war as soon as possible, in order to go home; the British, desirous though they were of conquering the Reich, were also—perhaps primarily—concerned about what the future held in store for them after the war; and the Canadians, sluggish from four long years of inactivity, brought even less experience to the battlefield than their neighbors to the south. None of these drawbacks were likely to be counteracted by official propaganda, which in any case was powerless to strengthen a shaky military capability.

# 3

# PLANNING FOR D-DAY

A FTER MONTHS OF DISAGREEING over grand strategy, while at the same time preparing both their armies and their peoples for the decisive campaign in the West, the Allies reached the decision to launch OVERLORD only in the late fall of 1943. The long delay handicapped the planning of the operation all the more seriously, as they continued to differ over how best to proceed.

## PRELIMINARY SCHEMES

At the Casablanca Conference in January 1943, while failing to agree on the ways and means of invading Normandy, the Americans and British had named General Frederick Morgan chief of staff to the Allied supreme commander. Formally invested in his office some six weeks later, on 12 March 1943, Morgan was charged with making preliminary preparations for the operation in advance of the appointment of a commanding officer. Morgan's background suited him for the job. In October 1942 he had been placed at the head of First Corps of the British Army, assisting Eisenhower in the planning and execution of Operation TORCH. Without being in any strict sense expert in amphibious ("combined") operations, he did nonetheless have real experience in this domain.

On assuming his new duties at Norfolk House in St. James Square, London, Morgan set to work at once, notwithstanding that his instructions from the Combined Chiefs of Staff were exceptionally vague. In the first place, no specific objectives were mentioned. Morgan was directed simply to anticipate the destruction of the Wehrmacht's forces in northwestern Europe. Was he therefore to contemplate laying waste to Germany? Overthrowing the Nazi regime? Creating a new political order? On this matter, as on many others, his instructions were silent. The failure of the Allied high command to identify and order its priorities obliged COSSAC to devise three broad scenarios: diversionary operations in the West aimed at relieving the Soviets in case the Red Army were to collapse; a precipitate return to the Continent in the event that Hitler's government should suddenly disintegrate; a large-scale landing to take place in 1944 somewhere along the Channel coast of France or its Atlantic coast. Not only were Morgan and his staff unable to guess which scheme would ultimately be accorded priority, but they did not have enough time to proceed with the planning of all three missions simultaneously. The problem was still more intractable because their ignorance with regard to strategic objectives prevented them from estimating how many men and how much matériel would be required. Finally, on 25 May 1943 the CCS informed Morgan that twenty-nine divisions were to be allocated for the purpose of launching an assault by sea and air, and directed him to draw up a plan of action on that basis.[1] In effect, then, the planners were forced to work backward, defining objectives as a function of a given force level. The CCS also indicated that a "lodgment area" would need to be secured from which operations could subsequently be launched against the Reich. Finally, it set a date for the invasion: 1 May 1944.

In addition to the endless squabbling among the people at sea, land, and air headquarters, Morgan and his staff had to contend with the tensions produced by collaboration between nations whose military staffs did not wholly trust each other: the Americans doubted the British commitment to OVERLORD; the British felt that the Americans failed to understand their arguments.[2] Deprived of any effective authority, Morgan was all the more unable to settle disagreements because he lacked the access to resources that the operational theater commanders enjoyed as a consequence of their greater prestige.

Little by little, however, the atmosphere improved. Morgan succeeded in creating a genuine esprit de corps, in large part by urging his men not to think of themselves as planners: "The term 'Planning Staff' has come to have a most sinister meaning—it implies the production of nothing but paper. What we must contrive to do somehow is to produce not only paper; but action. . . . We differ from the ordinary planning staff in that we are . . . the embryo of the future Supreme Headquarters Staff."[3]

The men who had come from America, by contrast, quickly accustomed themselves to life in the English capital—to the point of appearing not Johnny-come-latelies, but "Johnnies-Come-Much-Too-Long-Ago. They were bedded down in London and each seemed to come complete, equipped with an American uniform of British cloth, cut for him by a London tailor, a working vocabulary of British military initials, a pretty British girl driver, cards to night clubs, a favourite pub and a well-developed feeling towards his British opposite number."[4] Humor went some way toward easing tensions, however. One staffer was much admired for producing a clever parody that played on the passwords and jargon current at COSSAC headquarters: OVERLORD became "Operation OVERBOARD," for example, and the security stamps "American Secret" and "British Most Secret" now appeared as "American Stupid" and "British Most Stupid." Unavoidably, a send-up of this sort contained a great deal of revealing detail, and measures were taken to restrict its circulation to Norfolk House. A few weeks later, however, a representative of the *Pointer,* the cadets' newspaper at West Point, having obtained a copy by unknown means, approached a member of the British army staff in Washington for permission to publish the piece for the edification of future American officers. The staff officer, "quick to perceive a distinct aroma of rat," alerted General Morgan in London, and as a result not only was the *"Pointer . . .* deprived of a notable contribution, but what might have proved a serious leak of priceless information was effectively stopped."[5]

In the meantime, progress had nonetheless been made. During June and July the burden of research was divided and shared, the Americans studying the Normandy option and the British the Pas de Calais alternative. A conference (code-named RATTLE) at Largs, in Scotland, convened between 28 June and 1 July 1943 by Admiral Lord Louis Mountbatten, chief of Combined Operations, made it possible to clarify the choices facing the Allies in a relaxed and friendly working atmosphere. It was on this occasion that the British planners were won over at last to the idea of invading northwestern Europe, and that Normandy was selected as the landing site. It was also decided to examine the possibility of building artificial harbors, to avoid having to capture existing ports that were firmly held by the Germans.[6] Now that these preliminaries had been settled, Morgan was in a position to present a complete and coherent plan at the Quebec Conference in August.

The fundamental idea was to establish a base of operations that could accommodate between sixteen and thirty divisions. Once the troops had been safely brought ashore, this encampment would serve as the launching point for a series of ground offensives. During the first two weeks following D-Day, the Allied armies were to pivot north and west in order to take the Cotentin Peninsula and its great port at Cherbourg, while at the same time consolidating their hold on the area around Caen, where air bases were to be established. At that point it would be necessary to choose between two options: moving south from Cherbourg into Brittany, with a view to capturing its Atlantic ports (particularly Brest), or turning eastward in order to seize Le Havre and Rouen. Fearing that the Germans would be able to form a sufficiently strong line of defense along the Seine to arrest the Allied advance, Morgan had advised against the second option.[7]

In either case several conditions had to be satisfied. First, the Allies must enjoy mastery of the skies, which meant that the German fighter force would have to be reduced. Second, German ground forces on D-Day must not exceed twelve divisions of the first rank, not counting garrison troops, Luftwaffe units, and training detachments. Finally, it was vital that the Wehrmacht not be able to transfer more than fifteen divisions from the eastern to the western front in the two months following the landing. Assuming that all these aims could be achieved, the invasion would begin with a brief aerial bombardment, after which three Allied divisions would launch a coordinated assault from the Normandy beaches, followed the same day by an equal number of armored brigades. At the same time, airborne forces would seize Caen, with commandos simultaneously taking control of key bridges and coastal defenses.

The main thrust of this plan was approved, including the choice of the landing area. Morgan and his staff had ruled out the Pas de Calais, which, although it offered a shorter cross-Channel route for Allied ships and planes, suffered from three crippling disadvantages: its coastline was powerfully fortified; its hinterland constituted the pivotal defensive area of the German fighter command; and the comparatively limited opportunities for breaking out from a beachhead would make it necessary to seize Antwerp quickly, as well as Le Havre and the riparian ports of the lower Seine. In the vicinity of Caen, by contrast, stretched vast beaches, sheltered by the prevailing winds and equipped with good exit routes for evacuating men and matériel. Farther inland the terrain lent itself to the rapid establishment of air bases as well as the marshaling of troops and equipment. Finally, the enemy defenses along this part of the coast were relatively weak. There was, however, one significant drawback: the absence of a deepwater port. Morgan suggested that reinforcements could be brought ashore onto the beaches directly or, where this could not be done, landed by using improvised forms of anchorage. Minor problems were also resolved in due course. In November 1943 the areas along the southwest English coast were selected from which the troops were to set out on the great crusade, the first wave of U.S. forces embarking to the west of Poole and reinforcements leaving from Southampton, Portland, and Plymouth—ports the American troops had already passed through on their arrival in the United Kingdom.[8] Accordingly, and in order to avoid unfortunate entanglements crossing the Channel, the Americans were to land in Normandy to the west, and the British and the Canadians to the east.

Not all of Morgan's recommendations survived closer scrutiny. Not only did an assault relying on three divisions lack the necessary force, but the relatively narrow front that was initially contemplated carried with it the risk that beaches flooded with men and equipment would become fatally congested. It was furthermore decided that the paratroop and airborne forces, restricted to taking Caen and controlling a few key sites, played too limited a role. And although the possibility was not excluded that the navy might be assigned the mission of bombarding coastal defenses, the strategists gathered at RATTLE avoided taking a clear-cut position out of concern that uncontrolled artillery fire might threaten the safety of disembarking troops.[9] These weaknesses were not the product of analytical failures on the part of the planners; they were due instead to the inadequacy of the resources that had been allocated to them. It is quite true, of course, that Morgan had six divisions at his disposal for the first wave, but the ships available to him could carry only three. And although provision had been made for two airborne divisions and five to six parachute regiments, the 632 aircraft assigned to OVERLORD could transport only two-thirds of an airborne division.[10] The scale of inadequacy in this case becomes clear when one considers that the parachute troops of the American 101st Airborne Division alone mobilized 432 planes of the Ninth Troop Carrier Command on the night of 5–6 June, and that airborne operations in their totality required 1,298 aircraft.[11] Even at the time it was plain that COSSAC had nowhere near the resources it needed.

General Montgomery, in particular, cast a skeptical eye on the proposed operation. Morgan, he observed, "had to work on information supplied by the Combined Chiefs of Staff as to forces which would be available; he had no alternative. And he had no experienced operational commander to guide and help him. The more I examined the proposed tactical plan of 21 Army Group, based on Morgan's outline plan, the more I disliked it." These retrospective criticisms were intensified by the resentment that Montgomery felt toward a man who embraced the cause of the Americans during the Normandy campaign, to the point that "Morgan and those around him . . . lost no opportunity of trying to persuade Eisenhower that I was defensively minded."[12]

Morgan himself was aware of the weaknesses of his plan. In August 1943 he recommended broadening the assault to include the east coast of the Cotentin Peninsula. "The Prime Minister also enquired if the assault would include an attack on the inside of the Cotentin Peninsula and was informed by General Marshall that 'present plans would not provide for such an operation, but that if more landing craft could be made available there was a possibility that this landing would be included in the initial assault.'"[13] The Allied supreme commander later came to the defense of his chief of staff. "My ideas were supported by General Morgan personally," Eisenhower recalled, "but he had been compelled to develop his plan on the basis of a fixed number of ships, landing craft, and other resources. Consequently he had no recourse except to work out an attack along a three-division front, whereas I insisted upon five."[14] Morgan, in other words, was the victim of arbitrary decrees handed down by the CCS. Despite its evident defects, most of them remedied in the ensuing months, his plan was approved in its main lines at the Quebec Conference as a rough blueprint for OVERLORD.

## THE COMMANDERS

The planners' task was not made any easier by the Allied leaders' failure to specify precisely the rights and obligations of each party to this great undertaking. The operational commands were apportioned among British and American generals. As for the supreme command, Washington's view was that by virtue of America's greater contribution to the war effort that privilege should be awarded to an American—a demand the White House was now prepared to insist on in order to forestall any backsliding on the part of the British. Before the Quebec Conference, Henry Stimson, the secretary of war, took the unusual step of writing a solemn letter to Roosevelt that read, in part:

> Though [Churchill and Brooke] have rendered lip service to the operation, their hearts are not in it and it will require more independence, more faith, and more vigor than it is reasonable to expect we can find in any British commander to overcome the natural difficulties of such an operation carried on in such an atmosphere of [Churchill's] government. . . .
>
> I believe therefore that the time has come for you to decide that your government must assume the responsibility of leadership in this great final movement of the European war which is now confronting us. We cannot afford to confer again and close with a lip tribute to Bolero which we have tried twice and failed

to carry out. . . . Nearly two years ago the British offered us this command. I think that now it should be accepted—if necessary, insisted on.[15]

Churchill graciously acceded to American wishes—although he had already in June, and then again in July, promised the post to General Brooke, who was bitterly disappointed at being passed over.[16]

The supreme commander being an American, the three adjunct posts fell to the British. All the land forces came under the authority of the Twenty-first Army Group, the direction of which had initially been confided to General Sir Bernard Paget on 15 July 1943. But Paget, a former director general of the Home Guard respected for his ability to train soldiers, had no experience of combat, and he was replaced by General Montgomery five months later, on 25 December 1943. At the Quebec Conference, the CCS put Air Marshal Sir Trafford Leigh-Mallory in charge of the air forces and Admiral Sir Charles Little at the head of the navy (Little was replaced by Admiral Sir Bertram Ramsay in October 1943), while reserving several prominent subordinate positions for Americans. General Bradley received the command of the First U.S. Army, as well as of the future First United States Army Group (FUSAG). At the end of 1943, Rear Admiral Alan G. Kirk was named commander of the American naval force at Normandy, with Major (later Lieutenant) General John C. H. Lee serving as head of the Services of Supply (SOS). Finally, in January 1944 General George S. Patton was notified that he had been placed in charge of the Third U.S. Army.

But it was not until the first week of December that the Allied supreme commander was named. Early on, Roosevelt had thought of George Marshall. The U.S. Army chief of staff possessed the requisite organizational abilities, having managed in the space of several years to create, from very modest materials, an impressive military machine. Nor were his diplomatic talents inconsiderable, for he had to referee disputes among the three service branches while at the same time working, as a member of the Combined Chiefs of Staff, to promote military cooperation between Great Britain and the United States. In the eyes of the president, Marshall deserved to be rewarded for his years of service in the Washington bureaucracy with an unprecedented operational command that would attach to his name the only glory that truly mattered to a military man: the glory won on the field of battle. Yet Marshall's nomination was by no means assured. For were he to leave the CCS, this body would lose its best advocate of OVERLORD—a luxury that the United States could ill afford in the face of British maneuvering; if, however, he continued to sit on the CCS while assuming the operational command of the landing, he would be answerable only to himself; and if, finally, he were to be replaced by Eisenhower, both on the CCS and as head of the army general staff, Marshall would find himself placed under the orders of his former subordinate. King, Pershing, Arnold, and Leahy argued for keeping Marshall in Washington; Stimson and Hopkins for his transfer abroad.[17] The military bureaucracy weighed in as well. Both the *Army and Navy Journal* and the *Army and Navy Register* pointedly suggested that politicians were seeking to rid themselves of this great American by removing him from the capital.[18] There was some question whether appointment as supreme commander of OVERLORD amounted in this case to a promotion or a demotion. Some Republican newspapers, fearing Marshall's departure, complained that assignment to London would constitute shabby treatment, in forcing him to accept a lower post than the one he already occupied; others claimed that his fellow chiefs of staff, out of jealousy, had done everything they could to prevent the elevation of a rival.[19] In the end, Roosevelt decided to keep Marshall at his side in Washington, famously telling him, "I feel I could not sleep at night with you out of the country."[20] These words have frequently been recalled as evidence of the trust that Roosevelt placed in him. Yet the suddenness with which the news was announced to Marshall should not be forgotten: it was while taking dictation from the president of a telegram informing Stalin of Eisenhower's appointment that Marshall realized the post would not be his.[21]

On 6 December 1943, then, the supreme command was entrusted to General Eisenhower. The appointment was not made public until almost three weeks later, however, during a presidential radio address on 24 December. After coming back to the United States to enjoy a well-deserved rest and to meet with Roosevelt and Marshall, Eisenhower returned to

London on 14 January 1944 "to undertake the organization of the mightiest fighting force that the two Western Allies could muster."[22]

Was the man up to the job? Then fifty-four years of age, a graduate of West Point, Dwight David Eisenhower had steadily advanced through all the stages of a brilliant career as a staff officer, attracting particular notice for his performance in the Philippines between 1935 and 1938. Later, as head of the War Plans Division and then, starting in June 1942, as commander of the European theater of operations (in which capacity he was in charge of the forces stationed in Great Britain), he had supervised Operation TORCH and directed the Tunisian, Sicilian, and Italian campaigns. A peerless logistician, he had also demonstrated real diplomatic ability as de facto proconsul in North Africa, managing the Allies' tense relations with Generals Giraud and de Gaulle—experience that was to prove exceedingly useful in 1944. Affable and cordial, a man who liked to be liked, who inspired confidence in others and knew how to get them to work together as a team, he had an easy manner with the troops despite his inflexible insistence on military discipline and courtesy. Late to bed and early to rise, he kept himself going with endless cups of coffee and an unbroken succession of cigarettes (four packs a day), finding distraction from time to time by indulging a lifelong love of pulp Westerns. In short, Eisenhower was neither a patrician nor an intellectual, but his simplicity and modesty served him well in dealing with men whose egos were larger than his own—de Gaulle and Montgomery, to name but two.[23] The only reproach that could be made against him was that he had never seen battle. "I would not class Ike as a great soldier in the true sense of the word," Montgomery later remarked, though not ungenerously. "He might have become one if he had ever had the experience of exercising direct command of a division, corps and army—which unfortunately for him did not come his way. But he was a great Supreme Commander—a military statesman."[24] This opinion should be borne in mind because what was needed above all, in the direction of OVERLORD, was a logistician rather than a warrior. Eisenhower, as it turned out, was indeed the right man at the right place at the right time.

Once back in London in mid-January, he took steps at once to transform COSSAC into the Supreme Headquarters, Allied Expeditionary

Force. Initially occupying the London offices of its predecessor, at Norfolk House, SHAEF moved in March to Bushey Park (code name Widewing), near Kingston-on-Thames, some ten miles outside the capital.[25] It is true that Eisenhower was anxious to protect his planners against London's many temptations, preferring instead to impose an austere discipline, "since it was [his] experience that a city did not provide the best atmosphere for a staff to work in."[26] Relocation to the suburbs provoked complaints. "Staff officers get entrenched in comfortable living quarters and some like the leisurely luncheon afforded by the London clubs," Captain Harry C. Butcher, Eisenhower's aide-de-camp, observed. "To remove themselves from easy access to club life seems a hardship and consequently there is much pulling against the new."[27] But in fact the move was the result of a misunderstanding: the Allied Supreme Command was meant to be established at Bushey Heath, to take advantage of the proximity of air headquarters, located at Stanmore.[28] When the confusion between the two sites was discovered, it was too late: workers had already begun refitting the premises, which on 6 June 1944 housed some 750 officers and 6,000 men. Communication between SHAEF and air force planners suffered from the distance between them, subsequently aggravated by the transfer of the land and sea headquarters to Portsmouth.[29] In May 1944 Montgomery, alarmed by the lack of coordination, directed his assistant, Lieutenant General Sir Miles Dempsey, to bring the air and land staffs closer together—a result that was to be achieved only in Normandy.[30]

In the meantime, Eisenhower set about assembling his team. He kept on as chief of staff his countryman Lieutenant General Walter Bedell Smith, whose Prussian appearance and harsh manner terrified subordinates. On 17 February 1944, Eisenhower arranged for Air Chief Marshal Sir Arthur Tedder, whose judgment he valued and who enjoyed the confidence of Air Chief Marshal Sir Charles Portal, chief of staff of the Royal Air Force, to be posted to his staff. A sizable number of commands nevertheless remained to be filled: one army group, three armies, twelve army corps, and fifty divisions were awaiting assignment of chief officers.[31] Eisenhower, exploiting his impressive network of personal contacts, named fellow West Point cadets (such as Major General J. Lawton Collins) and officers he knew from the Philippines (Major General Troy H. Middleton), while relying also on the sensible advice of Bradley (a classmate at West Point) and Bedell Smith (a former colleague from War Department days). By February 1944 the Allied supreme commander had at his disposal a close-knit and efficient group of assistants, each going out of his way to preach harmony: "When [any two staff members] meet, the thought must be: 'How can I help this chap?'" Montgomery sternly insisted. "Each must give the other mutual aid, and not criticism. If I hear any criticism by anyone I will immediately remove him."[32] Eisenhower himself, though he did not mind hearing someone called a son of a bitch, was prepared to severely punish any American officer referring to a "British son of a bitch."[33]

A few false notes intruded, however. While accepting that the top command should be given to Eisenhower, London tried surreptitiously to reassert control over the Italian theater—much more important, to its way of thinking, than Normandy. Roosevelt was not fooled. Although the principle of an American chief had been ratified at the Quebec Conference, he wondered in November 1943 if it would not actually be preferable to name Eisenhower commander in chief for Mediterranean operations: "The President agreed that it would be satisfactory if General Eisenhower became commander in chief of the Mediterranean. However, there might be some danger should [Field Marshal Sir Harold] Alexander take over the Mediterranean command and then be dominated by the Prime Minister."[34] Eisenhower's promotion concealed an additional British calculation: "We were pushing Eisenhower up into the stratosphere and rarified atmosphere of a Supreme Commander, where he would be free to devote his time to the political and inter-allied problems," General Brooke noted in his diaries, "whilst we inserted under him one of our own commanders to deal with the military situations and to restore the necessary drive and co-ordination which had been so seriously lacking of late!"[35] Eisenhower, distracted by diplomatic questions, was in the habit of giving considerable latitude to his British assistants, who were free to regulate the strategic tempo as they liked. This arrangement, it should be noted, had worked perfectly well in North Africa. There, absorbed by the intrigues in Algiers, Eisenhower had left day-to-day responsibility for conducting the war to General Alexander. "It was confidently expected by London that [Eisenhower] would repeat his Mediterranean performance, stick to politics and leave the management of the war in the field to those with more experience while reaping the appropriate rewards and elevations in the public's eyes."[36] The Anglo-American partnership celebrated on the newsreels was therefore something rather different from the one at Bushey Park.

Tensions were further sharpened by disagreements over staffing at lower levels. In assembling their teams for the invasion of Normandy, Eisenhower and Bedell Smith not unnaturally looked to draw from the Mediterranean pool of candidates—to the great vexation of the British, who stood to be deprived of their best men. "I had to put Bedell-Smith in his place," Brooke noted in his diaries, "and inform him that I was responsible for the distribution of the staff on all fronts, and could be relied on to take their various requirements into account."[37] As a result, Eisenhower got neither General Alexander (whom he preferred to Montgomery) nor Brigadier General Lucian K. Truscott, Jr. (an American officer whose services he had requested in January).[38]

Interservice relations were additionally complicated by personal frictions among the top commanders themselves. The British airmen cordially detested Leigh-Mallory, who, following the Battle of Britain, had connived to supplant its true heroes, Air Marshal Sir Hugh C. T. Dowding and Air Marshal Sir Keith Park. Indeed, it was owing to Leigh-Mallory's pessimism and indecisiveness, and above all his reluctance to commit forces, that Eisenhower appointed Tedder, who took a more favorable view of Anglo-American cooperation and who was held in higher esteem by his subordinates.[39] Montgomery, for his part, resented Patton for spoiling his triumphal march through Sicily by entering Messina first.[40] Nor did Montgomery have any greater liking for Tedder, whose offer of air support for the pursuit of Rommel's forces after El Alamein he judged improper.[41] Although Montgomery himself incontestably possessed great skills as a leader—among them a remarkable ability to galvanize his troops, meticulous preparation of offensive plans, and a knack for spotting able subordinates—he could be nitpicking, overly cautious, and mean to the point of pettiness; more troublingly, he did not always find it easy to be truthful, which complicated matters during the crisis of July 1944.[42] Closer in outlook to the commanders of the First World War than to those of the second, he showed a lack of interest in logistical questions—which did not prevent him from constantly demanding more supplies and equipment. "It takes no great leap of the imagination to see Marshall or Eisenhower or Bradley or MacArthur running a major corporation," one historian has remarked. "The same couldn't be said of Montgomery or Patton."[43] And yet logistics played an essential role in modern warfare. For all these reasons, the Americans reacted to Montgomery's appointment rather coolly, even if they came to think better of him later on. "Although [the American chiefs of staff] had utmost respect for his demonstrated qualities as a superb soldier, they considered him a commander of the 'down to the last shoelace' school, and they feared that he would delay and postpone to such an extent that the one opportunity favorable as to weather for this enormous and complex operation would be lost."[44] After the war, Bradley was among those who praised Montgomery: "For the thin, bony, ascetic face that stared from an unmilitary turtle-neck sweater had, in little over a year, become a symbol of victory in the eyes of the Allied world. Nothing becomes a general more than success in battle, and Montgomery wore success with such chipper faith in the arms of Britain that he was cherished by a British people wearied of valorous setbacks."[45]

Not all of Eisenhower's lieutenants were so highly respected, however. General John C. H. Lee, deputy commander of U.S. Forces in the European theater (from January 1944) as well as head of the Services of Supply, is usually depicted as a figure of caricature. It is not hard to see why. Arrogant and immensely full of himself, Lee quickly earned the nickname (inspired by his initials) "Jesus Christ Himself."[46] He traveled in his own train, insisted on being shown every sign of official respect, and tended to distribute equipment on the basis of favoritism rather than logistical need. Not surprisingly, he was almost universally disliked.

A few subordinates were an inexhaustible source of trouble, none more than General George S. Patton. Impetuous and hotheaded though Patton surely was, he hardly resembled the loutish figure of popular legend. At West Point, where his statue stands near the library, it is said that he never came near a book—a manifestly unjust charge to bring against a man who read widely, thought deeply, and wrote well about the art of war.[47] Yet his explosive temper frequently created problems for the Allied supreme commander, whose meteoric career had aroused his jealousy (Eisenhower's own initials, Patton used to say, stood for "Divine Destiny"). On a visit to a hospital during the Sicilian campaign in August 1943, Patton slapped a soldier, accusing him of shirking his duty. "'It's my nerves,' the soldier said, and began to cry. 'Your nerves, hell,' Patton shouted. 'You are just a god-damned coward, you yellow son of a bitch. You're a disgrace to the Army and you are going back to the front to fight, although that's too good for you. You ought to be lined up against a wall and be shot. In fact, I ought to shoot you myself right now, goddamn you.'"[48] The affair was hushed up by Eisenhower; but once revealed by the journalist Drew Pearson, it caused an outcry and cost Patton an operational command after Sicily. On 25 April 1944 Patton made another gaffe. Invited to say a few words at the opening of a Welcome Club for American servicemen at Knutsford, Cheshire, he reluctantly accepted. Warming to the theme of Allied unity, he went on to stress its importance, "since it is the evident destiny of the British and Americans to rule the world, [and] the better we know each other the better job we will do."[49] Needless to say, this sentiment was not welcomed in Moscow, Pretoria, Algiers, or Ottawa. Eisenhower was furious and issued a stinging reprimand. On 30 April he cabled Marshall to say that he was prepared to relieve Patton of his command—but then thought better of it the next day. In a private meeting, Eisenhower informed Patton that he would continue as head of the Third Army. "Few generals could surpass Patton as a field commander," Bradley observed. "But he had only one enemy he could not vanquish and that was his own quick tongue. It was this unhappy talent of Patton's for highly quotable crisis that caused me to tighten the screws on press censorship at the time he joined my command."[50]

The need to massage injured egos, calm personal animosities, and otherwise deal with unforeseeable accidents and blunders—combined with the fact that the missions of the various operational commands were far from settled—complicated Eisenhower's task still further.

## Jurisdictional Quarrels

In theory, the roles of the top officers at Allied headquarters were clearly demarcated. Overall responsibility for coordinating the planning of OVER-LORD and supervising its execution lay with the Allied supreme commander. The heads of the three branches of the invasion force—Ramsay (navy), Montgomery (army), Leigh-Mallory (air force)—were to prepare the plans for their respective domains and then to see that they were carried out.[51] Almost two months separated Eisenhower's official appointment (on 24 December 1943) and the directive (of 12 February 1944) specifying his powers. In the meantime, London sought to increase the power of the three chief subordinates—all of them British—while Washington demanded that the directive be drafted in sufficiently vague terms to grant broad latitude to the supreme commander. General Morgan, by dint of great effort, managed to limit the text to an enumeration of the forces at Eisenhower's disposal, while reserving for himself the right to draw up his own instructions to the operational chiefs.[52] The directive therefore provided that Eisenhower would "exercise command generally in accordance with the diagram given," which indeed placed the three branches under his direct authority.[53]

The British Bomber Command and the U.S. Strategic Air Forces stationed in Europe escaped the Allied supreme commander's control, however. Their respective heads, Air Marshal Sir Arthur T. ("Bomber") Harris and General Carl A. ("Tooey") Spaatz, argued vigorously in favor of continuing the air campaign against Germany—a strategy that in their view was itself sufficient to bring Germany swiftly to its knees—while resisting the idea that their bombers should be diverted for the purpose of attacking more modest objectives in France, much less acting in support of ground troops. Churchill, for his part, sought to assure the freedom of maneuver of the Bomber Command, now the only autonomous military arm of the Allied coalition. In that case Eisenhower would be able to count only on the aircraft attached to the British Tactical Air Force and the American Tactical Air Force (Ninth USAF)—to his mind, an unjustifiable restriction of the supreme commander's authority. On 29 February 1944 an initial compromise was reached that entrusted the command of the air

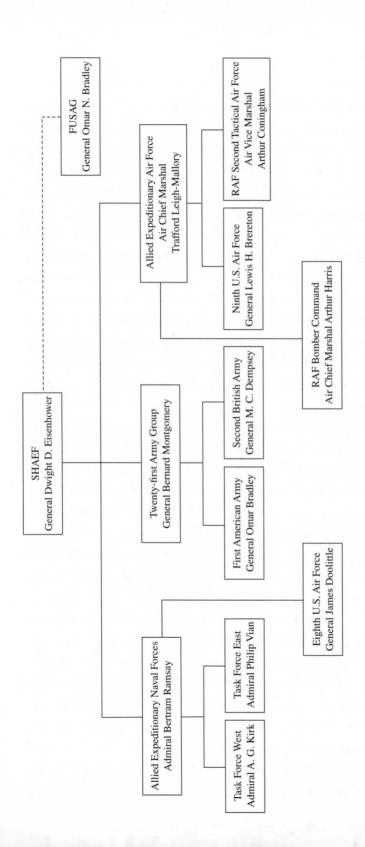

1. Allied Command for Operation OVERLORD

forces to Tedder—Eisenhower's assistant—on two conditions: the CCS could set specific missions for the bombers; and the British reserved for themselves the right to intervene in case the security of their islands was threatened. By the terms of this understanding, as the British Chiefs of Staff interpreted it, Eisenhower received only "supervision" of aerial operations and not "command" over them. The more the supreme commander thought about the arrangement, the less he liked it. "It was desirable that for the preparatory stages of the assault," Eisenhower later recalled more calmly, "and for proper support during the critical early stages of the land operations—until we had established ourselves so firmly that the danger of defeat was eliminated—all air forces in Britain, excepting only the Coastal Command, should come under my control."[54] At the time, he expressed both irritation and surprise that the British seemed to have hardly any confidence in Leigh-Mallory—though they themselves had nominated him.[55] Under the circumstances, he felt that he had no alternative but to resign if the command of the strategic air forces were denied him. In a handwritten note to the BCOS dated 22 March, he indicated that the term "direction" might supply the basis for an acceptable compromise. On 7 April the CCS settled the matter: "The USA Strategic Air Force and British Bomber Command will operate under the *direction* of the Supreme Commander, in conformity with agreements between him and the Chief of the Air Staff as approved by the Combined Chiefs of Staff."[56] This was only a partial victory, perhaps, given that the stronger term "command" was abandoned; but still Eisenhower had won effective control over both the strategic and tactical air forces.

Matters were equally uncertain from the naval point of view. As of 1 April 1944, Admiral Ramsay exercised operational command over the naval forces—American battleships included—but his authority over the U.S. Navy remained largely theoretical. And as for the American ground forces, it was agreed that once they had reached a certain size they were no longer to fall under the control of the Twenty-first Army Group, now coming under the authority of the First U.S. Army Group, which had been created (though in name only) in October 1943. Nonetheless no date for the transfer of jurisdiction had been set. In the meantime, noted a SHAEF directive of 21 March, "the Commander in Chief 21st Army Group will be responsible for the command of all ground forces engaged in the operation until such time as the Supreme Commander allocates an area of responsibility to the commanding general First US Army Group."[57] Until the summer of 1944, then, FUSAG was no more than a notional entity. "FUSAG was hardly in existence a month before the mention of its name in London was as good for a laugh as a mention of the Brooklyn Dodgers in a Manhattan review—for FUSAG had no troops, no mission and, as far as anyone could see, no future."[58] Finally, on 1 August the Twelfth Army Group—the successor to FUSAG—was constituted the operational umbrella for all the American armies in Normandy, dispossessing Montgomery of the integrated command of the Allied ground forces. Forewarning did nothing to diminish his wrath when the moment came.

Despite all these difficulties, Eisenhower managed to make the complex machinery of the Allied high command function fairly smoothly; at the very least, SHAEF's work was animated by a degree of harmony that the Germans were incapable of forging for themselves within the Axis. And although various crises were to weaken interallied cooperation in the months ahead, none posed a serious threat to it. By ensuring that the American-British coalition stayed intact until victory was achieved, Eisenhower succeeded in creating what Foch had first attempted on a far smaller scale during the First World War, namely, a general staff drawn from the military command of two countries and equipped with broad prerogatives for planning and execution. This remarkable achievement counted for a great deal in the Allies' ultimate triumph.

## THE FINAL PLAN

The plan presented by General Morgan at the Quebec Conference in August 1943 was, as we have seen, understood to be provisional and in many respects imperfect. Steps were taken at once to amend it, even before the appointment of an Allied supreme commander. On 10 December 1943 Ramsay, Leigh-Mallory, Paget, and Montgomery began to prepare a new version, and not quite three months later the draft plan for NEP-

TUNE—the code name for the landing itself—was finished. Its main points were then communicated to the subordinate units, with each staff subsequently elaborating its own instructions in a cascade that started at the level of the armies and ended at the level of the regiment.[59]

The narrowness of the front envisaged by Morgan had raised objections at the very outset. "By D plus 12," Montgomery wrote to Churchill in a memorandum dated 1 January 1944, "a total of twelve divisions have been landed on the same beaches as were used for the initial landing. This would lead to the most appalling confusion on the beaches and the smooth development of the land battle would be made extremely difficult, if not impossible. Further divisions come pouring in, all over the same beaches . . . [so] the confusion instead of getting better, would rapidly get worse. . . . [The] initial landings must be made on the widest possible front."[60] Eisenhower shared this view, and immediately upon assuming his duties directed that planning for the operation be based on a first wave of five divisions.[61] The front would therefore extend westward as far as the east coast of the Cotentin Peninsula, with an additional British division being committed near Ouistreham in the east, north of Caen. The idea was to sow confusion among the enemy by striking at many places at once. By increasing the number of beaches, and therefore the number of exit routes, it would be possible not only to move troops rapidly inland, but also to take the deepwater port of Cherbourg as quickly as possible.[62] Finally, in order to support the ground troops at the moment of the landing itself, when they would be the most vulnerable to enemy fire, paratroop and airborne forces were to take up positions behind the beaches well before dawn. On 1 February 1944, the CCS gave its approval to the revised plan.

At the Quebec Conference the previous summer, over British objections, the United States and the Soviet Union had won acceptance for the principle of a diversionary operation, known as ANVIL, to be conducted in the South of France. The agreement was subsequently ratified at the Cairo and Teheran Conferences, and Eisenhower, as commander in chief of the Mediterranean theater, was charged with planning the operation in conjunction with COSSAC.[63] Whereas the Allied leaders conceived of ANVIL as a simple ruse to distract the Germans, Eisenhower called for a genuine offensive engagement involving two to three divisions.[64] "'OVER-LORD' and 'ANVIL' must be viewed as one whole," he explained to Marshall in late January 1944.[65] The difficulty was that a Mediterranean landing would divert resources, both men and ships, to the detriment not only of Normandy but of the Italian theater as well—a consideration that had led Montgomery and the British Chiefs of Staff earlier the same month to demand that it be canceled. They advanced two principal reasons. "First, we wanted the landing-craft for Overlord," Montgomery recalled in his memoirs, "and second, it weakened the Italian front at the very time when progress there had a good chance of reaching Vienna before the Russians (failure to do this was to have far-reaching effects in the cold war that broke out towards the end of 1945)."[66] In mid-February 1944, he renewed his appeal, arguing against the withdrawal of divisions from Italy and their reassignment to OVERLORD.[67] Yet Eisenhower refused to give in. A landing in Provence held out the prospect of protecting the southeastern flank of the Normandy contingent by drawing off German troops stationed in the South of France, while at the same time gaining possession of Marseilles, a port of major importance. The operation had in any case already been promised to Stalin, and it could only strengthen good relations among the Big Three. It would also make effective use of the forces of the Corps expéditionnaire français in Italy, which could be expected to fight with redoubled energies for the liberation of its homeland.[68] Finally, although this argument was not explicitly made, ANVIL constituted the surest means of assuring the priority of OVERLORD, by preventing the Italian theater from absorbing surplus resources. In short, as Eisenhower was later at pains to emphasize, "the complementary attack against southern France had long been considered—by General Marshall and me, at least—as an integral and necessary feature of the main invasion across the channel."[69]

The supreme commander stuck to his guns, turning aside the call of the British chiefs on 17 January 1944 for ANVIL's cancellation and rejecting Montgomery's subsequent petition, with the support of the American chiefs of staff at their meeting with Roosevelt on 21 February. In the face of continuing opposition from London, which insisted that the Italian offensive be allowed to go on, a compromise was worked out three days later: Italy would still have priority, but preparations for ANVIL would go forward. In the event that the operation should be canceled, however, the troops would then be reassigned to OVERLORD and not, as the British hoped, to the Italian theater. A month later, on 21 March, Eisenhower reluctantly consented to the decoupling of ANVIL and OVERLORD, consoling himself with the expectation that this step represented only a postponement, rather than the annulment, of the operation in southern France. In addition, the Americans agreed to the unprecedented step of withdrawing twenty-six landing ships, tank (LSTs) and forty landing craft, infantry (LCIs) from the Pacific theater—but with the express understanding that these vessels were to be allocated to ANVIL. At this point, on 12 April, Churchill intervened. In order to draw away the maximum number of German divisions from northwestern Europe, he proposed that the highest priority be attached to linking up the Allied units already operating in Italy with the expeditionary force that had been precariously landed at Anzio almost three months earlier, on 22 January. Only once they had successfully joined forces, he felt, could ANVIL be reconsidered with respect to the new perspectives opened up on the Italian peninsula.[70] A week later, on 18 April, the CCS arrived at a delicate compromise: General Sir Henry Maitland Wilson was charged with launching a grand offensive in Italy as soon as possible, while developing ANVIL as a subsidiary operation, either with a view to supporting the operations there or to exploiting any opportunities that might present themselves in the South of France, or indeed elsewhere.[71] The Americans, for their part, would wait to assess the outcome of the Anzio expedition and the offensive aimed at Rome that was to be launched in May, before withdrawing battleships from the Pacific theater and transferring them to the Mediterranean.

It must be said that this delaying tactic resolved nothing from the strategic point of view and, what is more, angered the British, who were instructed to push on toward Rome without any assurance of receiving the supplementary resources they sought. "At last all our troubles about Anvil . . . are over," an embittered Brooke noted. "We have got the Americans to agree, but have lost the additional landing craft they were prepared to provide. History will never forgive them for bargaining equipment against strategy and for trying to blackmail us into agreeing with them by holding the pistol of withdrawing craft at our heads."[72] Eisenhower was no less resentful. Nonetheless, he remained hopeful that the landing in Normandy would yet be supported, in more or less short order, by a landing in Provence.

With regard to the invasion of Normandy itself, Supreme Headquarters substantially modified the draft COSSAC plan in one key respect. It was now anticipated that air power would play an essential role, with Allied planes pounding any German defenses that might "interfere with the approach of the Naval Forces."[73] Aware that such a campaign, if undertaken prematurely, was likely to arouse enemy suspicions, the Allies chose to err on the side of caution: between mid-April and 5 June, only 10 percent of the designated bomb load would be devoted to the destruction of coastal defenses; and of this amount, only a third would be directed at the invasion area.[74] With the bulk of the aerial bombardment scheduled for the night of 5–6 June, there was no guarantee that the first line of German defenses would be disabled. To offset this danger, the Allies looked to the navy to wipe out gun batteries and other fortified installations—some twenty targets in all, notably in La Pernelle, Houlgate, and Ozeville.[75] To further increase the chances of success, additional resources were committed. At the Cairo Conference, the British had agreed to furnish all of the vessels required for naval bombardment. It soon became apparent that the number initially contemplated would not suffice. Belatedly but not unwillingly, Admiral King agreed on 15 April to detach three battleships, two cruisers, and twenty-two destroyers from his fleet.[76] In all, the Allies brought on line thirty-six cruisers and battleships, as well as 164 destroyers responsible for destroying enemy artillery in addition to protecting the landing fleet.[77] Finally, to further strengthen the firepower of the attacking forces, some of the landing craft would be armed as well.

On 7 April Montgomery convened a meeting (code-named THUNDERCLAP) of the senior commanders at his old school in London, Saint Paul's, now home to Twenty-first Army Headquarters, for the purpose of reviewing the major phases of the operation. The proceedings opened with a ban on smoking (Montgomery was legendarily allergic to tobacco) that was soon lifted, however, after the ten-minute pause following the first part. "There was a ripple of laughter in the audience," General Bradley later recalled, "for both the Prime Minister and Eisenhower were to join us."[78]

The plan in its present form was intended to carry out the instructions given by the CCS in its directive of 12 February 1944: "You will enter the continent of Europe and, in conjunction with the other United Nations, undertake operations aimed at the heart of Germany and the destruction of her armed forces. The date for entering the Continent is the month of May 1944. After adequate channel ports have been secured, exploitation will be directed towards securing an area that will facilitate both ground and air operations against the enemy."[79]

The expeditionary force therefore had three objectives: first, to establish a logistical base near the beachhead for marshaling men and matériel, while at the same time gaining control of open areas on which air bases could be established, thereby obviating the need for costly return flights across the Channel to the United Kingdom; next, to move out from this stronghold to destroy the German army—in the best case, west of the Rhine; finally, to launch an offensive toward the Saar and the Ruhr. For if Berlin constituted the ultimate target, it was located "too far east to be the objective of a campaign in the west,"[80] whereas within the Saar and the Ruhr "lay much of Germany's warmaking power."[81] Capturing these regions was tantamount to victory, as Goebbels recognized in September 1944: "If we lose the Ruhr, we will be able to continue the war for a few more months, but with no chance of carrying on with it over the long term."[82]

On D-Day, five divisions were to mount an assault along a front roughly fifty miles in length, stretching from the east coast of the Cotentin Peninsula to the northern outskirts of Caen. Five landing sectors were marked off, from west to east: Utah and Omaha (reserved for the American forces), and Gold, Juno, and Sword (for the British and Canadian forces). Three airborne divisions were to support the ground forces, with parachute troops from the American 101st Airborne Division being assigned the task of protecting the exit routes from Utah Beach; the Eighty-second Airborne intervening to the west of Coutances;[83] and the bulk of the British Sixth Airborne taking the Bénouville-Ranville bridge over the Orne, securing the Orne-Dives area, destroying the Merville battery, and slowing any German attack from the east and southeast.[84] The balance of the force, in addition to paratroops, was to be transported by gliders landing among the hedgerows of the Norman farm country.

This version aroused the misgivings of Leigh-Mallory. In a note of 23 April, the air chief marshal enumerated those points that, in his view, violated the most elementary rules of sound military practice: the parachute troops would be jumping into immediate contact with the enemy, not keeping at a safe distance; the gliders would be landing on forbidding terrain; the unarmed Dakotas transporting the parachute troops would be vulnerable to enemy fire; deployment of forces on such a scale over a period of several hours would make it impossible to achieve tactical surprise; finally, the landing forces would be entering an area under bombardment by planes and naval artillery.[85] Prophesying a massacre, Leigh-Mallory had no intention of giving his blessing to this operation. Bradley describes the pointed exchange that followed:

"Very well, sir," I replied, "if you insist on cutting out the airborne attack, then I must ask that we eliminate the Utah assault. I am not going to land on that beach without making sure that we've got the exits behind it."

Leigh-Mallory stared briefly across the table. "Then let me make it clear," he said, "that if you insist upon this airborne operation, you'll do it in spite of my opposition."

With that he squared himself in his chair, turned to Montgomery, and added, "If General Bradley insists upon going ahead he will have to accept full responsibility for the operation. I don't believe it will work."

"That's perfectly agreeable to me," I answered. "I'm in the habit of accepting responsibility for my operations."[86]

At the end of May, the reinforcement of German defenses to the south of Cherbourg brought about a modification in the plan. The Eighty-second Airborne would no longer jump to the west of Coutances, but closer to the 101st, in order to control the important crossroads of Sainte-Mère-Église. Leigh-Mallory remained unconvinced. Estimating that only 50 percent of the airborne troops would be capable of fighting, he emphasized the risk of attempting a seaborne landing with so little support behind enemy lines. He pointed out furthermore that the gliders would approach their destinations at low altitude, offering a perfect target for German antiaircraft artillery (FLAK); that three hours would elapse between the first and the last glider landing, long enough to set off an alert among the defenders; and that the scattered drops of parachutists and other troops would prevent them from joining up to form cohesive units capable of taking out the enemy's coastal defenses.[87] Once again, Leigh-Mallory predicted a slaughter, with losses of about 70 percent for the gliders. His warning, coming only a week before the landing was to take place, sowed doubts in the mind of the Allied supreme commander. "I realized, of course, that if I deliberately disregarded the advice of my technical expert on the subject, and his predictions should prove accurate, then I would carry to my grave the unbearable burden of a conscience justly accusing me of the stupid, blind sacrifice of thousands of the flower of our youth," Eisenhower later wrote in his memoirs. "Outweighing any personal burden, however, was the possibility that if he were right the effect of the disaster would be far more than local: it would likely spread to the entire force."[88] Canceling the airborne operation, on the other hand, meant abandoning the landing at Utah Beach, a practical impossibility at this point. Eisenhower therefore decided to allow the American airborne operations to go forward.[89]

The revised invasion plan, finally, underscored the importance of Caen, which was to fall on the first day. The Norman capital commanded the access to a vast plain favorable to the maneuver of armored columns and to the installation of air bases; more important still, it lay on either side of the Orne, which the Allies could not avoid crossing if they were to carry out the planned offensive.

In the first twenty days, then, the Allied forces were assigned the mission of securing a lodgment area, the British consolidating the eastern flank while the Americans, to the west, went up the Cotentin with the aim of seizing Cherbourg. Bradley's U.S. First Army would then pivot and turn southward toward the Breton peninsula, in order to capture its ports, control of which was crucial from the logistical point of view. After thirty-five days (D + 35), the entire Allied force would be ranged along a line running from Deauville to north of Le Mans. By D + 90, it would have reached the Seine, the Canadians meanwhile liberating first Rouen and then Le Havre.

The revised plan was laid out with great ceremony during a second meeting at St. Paul's School, on 15 May 1944, where the bitter cold obliged the participants—among them King George VI, Churchill, and the South African Prime Minister and British Field Marshal Jan Smuts—to keep their overcoats on. Eisenhower made it clear that frank criticism was welcome. The three chief field commanders presented their respective scenarios. Montgomery, in charge of ground operations, made a particularly strong impression, affirming that he did not doubt the success of OVERLORD. Churchill, in Eisenhower's account, was less sanguine. "'Gentlemen, [he declared], I am hardening toward this enterprise,' meaning that, though he had long doubted its feasibility and had previously advocated its further postponement in favor of operations elsewhere, he had finally, at this late date, come to believe with the rest of us that this was the true course of action in order to achieve victory."[90] Whether or not Eisenhower was mistaken in interpreting the prime minister's puzzling locution as evidence of a fundamental and longstanding opposition to OVERLORD, only very recently overcome, Churchill's remarks filled the American ranks with a sense of dismay that the king's lackluster speech did nothing to dispel.[91]

## THE DAY AND THE HOUR

The plan finally devised by the strategists—most of them British—was not one of startling originality. But the constraints weighing on the operation considerably reduced the margin for maneuver. With regard to the site of the landing, they left no choice but to proceed by process of elimination. The same was true for the date and hour of the landing.

Each service branch laid down its own conditions. The navy insisted that the surface winds be lower than force 3 (eight to twelve miles per hour) near the shore, while accepting winds up to force 5 (nineteen to twenty-four miles per hour) on the open sea. Additionally, visibility greater than three miles was needed, to allow an armada comprising thousands of ships to approach shore without incident. The air force, for its part, required a cloud ceiling of at least 1,000 feet for its fighters, and for medium bombers a ceiling of 4,500 feet and visibility greater than or equal to three miles; for the parachutists, the winds must be not too strong (less than twenty miles per hour) and the skies not too bright (but also not dimmer than when lit by a half-moon). From the point of view of the army, finally, conditions could not be too wet, for terrain saturated by rains would pose obvious problems for the advance of vehicles; clouds should cover not more than three-tenths of the sky and should lie above 3,000 feet, and visibility should be greater than three miles.

If one took all these requirements into account, it followed that D-Day must fall between one day before and four days after a new or a full moon. The statistical probability that the relevant conditions would be satisfied was 24 to 1 in May, 13 to 1 in June, and 50 to 1 in July.[92] The need to allow the air forces enough time to destroy enemy supply lines and defenses ruled out the month of May. Consequently, the CCS agreed at the end of January to push back the anticipated date of the invasion from 1 May to 1 June—this at the request of Eisenhower, who wished to take full advantage of the delay to add to the number of landing ships available to him. And since the army needed "all the summer weather that [it] could get for the European campaign," July was eliminated, because it allowed too little time to break out from the lodgment area.[93] That left only the month of June. Three favorable dates—the fifth, the sixth, and the seventh—presented themselves. If none of these turned out to be suitable, it would be necessary to postpone the operation by fourteen or twenty-eight days.

The choice of the hour posed a cruel dilemma. A nighttime landing offered the advantage of protecting the approach of the fleet and limiting the impact of enemy artillery, forced to rely on radio-location instruments. Darkness, on the other hand, would handicap the bombers and make maneuver more difficult for the naval forces. The planners elected to split the difference. In choosing dawn, they hoped to give adequate cover for the approach of the convoys, while at the same time ensuring sufficient light for air and naval bombardment, which in turn would improve the chances that the ground forces could safely be brought ashore.[94]

There remained the question whether to attempt the landing at high tide or low tide. The first option had the advantage of limiting the distance that the attackers would have to traverse under enemy fire. Otherwise, weighed down by their kit, the men risked sinking into the wet sands exposed by the receding waters, which would make them easy targets.[95] Aerial photos taken on 20 February revealed that the Germans were installing a variety of mines and obstacles that would be concealed at high tide, portending disaster in the event that large numbers of landing craft were blown up or became impaled. Once again a compromise was struck. It was agreed that the troops would come ashore when the tide had risen to half its height; they would thus be spared a long, unprotected assault, and some of the obstructions would still be visible. "Eventually by trial and error," Bradley recalled,

we learned that 30 minutes would be required to blow paths through a belt of underwater obstructions. The engineers could dynamite those obstacles in water up to two feet deep. And since the tide rose at a rate of a foot every 15 minutes, two feet would allow them 30 minutes.

With that, the answer fell into place. We would assault when a rising tide reached the obstacle line and give the engineers 30 minutes to clear it before the water became too deep. Successive assault waves would then ride the rising tide nearer the sea wall through gaps in the obstacle belt.[96]

Scarcely three weeks before D-Day, then, the invasion plan had been worked out down to the last detail. A little after midnight the British airborne troops were to be dropped between the Orne and the Dives, followed shortly by the two American airborne divisions landing in the Cotentin. Heavy and medium bombers would begin the assault on the German batteries. Forty-five minutes before H-Hour, the naval forces would unleash a massive round of artillery fire aimed at completing the destruction of the enemy defenses. The landing proper would begin at 6:30 A.M. in the American sector and, because of local differences in the tide table, at 7:45 A.M. in the Anglo-Canadian sector.

The final plan benefited from lessons learned in the other theaters of operation. The fiasco of Dieppe had underscored the importance of strong artillery support—something the navy could provide—as well as the need for marshaling troops in compact formations and providing them with adequate air cover. Sicily had shown the necessity of achieving mastery of the skies in order to protect the fleet—a conclusion that Salerno had confirmed in its own way, for only the dominance of the Royal Air Force (RAF) and the U.S. Air Force (USAF) had prevented the Germans from bringing up reinforcements. Salerno had also shown that units should maneuver in close proximity to one another, in order to forestall breaches from opening up, through which the enemy could escape, and had demonstrated the value of naval bombardment (whereas the air force had dropped some 3,000 tons of bombs, sea-based artillery had fired 11,000 tons of shells and achieved a greater degree of accuracy as well). Anzio, for its part, had shown that a small port could handle large quantities of both troops and equipment. The landings in North Africa, by contrast, were less instructive: the coast was virtually undefended, and no account needed to be taken of tides. Moreover, because all the operations in the Mediterranean had taken place at night, no useful precedent could be consulted for attempting a dawn landing. Nor did the OVERLORD planners look to the American experience in the Pacific theater, in part because communications between the Pacific and Europe were inadequate, but mainly because the physical and strategic situations were fundamentally different.

From the strategic point of view, at least, the plan presented little that was novel. By proposing to bring overwhelming force to bear directly on the enemy, as we have seen, the Allied high command adopted a line of attack that had its roots in the American Civil War almost a century earlier.[97] The success of the landing therefore depended on achieving a relation of forces favorable to the attackers. This in turn placed the decisive burden on logistical ingenuity: preventing the Germans from bringing up reinforcements to consolidate coastal defenses implied a corresponding effort to strengthen Allied positions still more effectively. The Germans were under no illusion about what the situation required. "Whoever has the organizational power to solve the problem of movement," Hitler had predicted more than a year before D-Day, "will be victor in this war."[98] For the Allies, solving this problem did not turn out to be easy.

# 4

# LOGISTICS, TRAINING, REHEARSALS

THE ALLIED VICTORY IN GENERAL and the outcome of the invasion in particular were, in the last analysis, a wager on numbers. If the Allies were to defeat the Reich, they had to find a way to transport enough troops and equipment across the Channel, while at the same time slowing the delivery of German reinforcements to the front. This requirement had two distinct but complementary aspects. On the one hand, it implied a logistical need to plan complex transfers of men and matériel from the United States and the Mediterranean to Great Britain, which meant in turn that the Allies had to have a sufficient number of ships at their disposal. On the other hand, restricting the number of German forces in Normandy to the degree possible meant that they had to be lured away toward other theaters of operations. A variety of options presented themselves. The Allies attempted to exploit the possibilities that the conflict had opened up, both in the east and in the south, while making extensive use of methods of disinformation aimed at deceiving the enemy about the site of the landing itself.

## SHIPS AND LANDING CRAFT

Despite the weaknesses of the British economy and the incomplete mobilization of the American economy, the Allies were in fact capable of furnishing Supreme Headquarters with what it needed, except in one crucial respect. Operation NEPTUNE called for the majority of troops to be transported most of the way across the Channel by ship and then, once they were within a few miles of the coast, transferred to landing craft that would bring them ashore. In effect, this meant doubling the number of vessels required, with the result that a total of 4,266 boats were mobilized during the operation.[1] This figure included tank landing ships (LSTs), capable of transporting sixty armored vehicles and 3,000 men; infantry landing ships (LSIs), which, depending on their size, could accommodate between six and fifteen boats and from 400 to 2,000 men; and smaller infantry landing craft (LCIs), carrying between 102 and 260 men. Assembling this spectacular armada turned out to be an unexpectedly formidable challenge. The difficulty had to do as much with producing the necessary number of landing craft and ships as with moving them into battle position in time. Until January 1944 the size of the expeditionary force that the navy would have to transport was unknown. Simply increasing the force from three to five divisions obliged the planners to redo their calculations and find one additional hospital landing ship (LSH), six large infantry landing ships (LSI [Large]), one hospital/infantry landing ship (LSI [H]), seventy-two LCIs, forty-seven LSTs, and 144 tank landing craft (LCTs)—all in the shortest time possible. The last vessels to reach the staging area had to arrive, at the latest, twenty days before the launching of OVERLORD.[2]

In the matter of production, the British had a head start on the Americans, having begun to manufacture landing craft after the First World War. A mechanized landing craft had been constructed in 1920, followed by the prototype of the assault landing craft (LCA) in 1938. In June 1940 Winston Churchill ordered the design of a vessel that could transport three forty-ton tanks. The first LCTs were delivered in November 1940, while the much larger LST—based on the design of an oil tanker—was being tested.[3] Washington, meanwhile, considering amphibious operations too risky, hesitated to give its approval. The Marshall memorandum, in making the case for a landing in Europe, nevertheless had the consequence of pushing the White House to increase production. On 4 April 1942 Roosevelt moved up the construction of ships for a landing in France from tenth to second place on the list of the U.S. Navy's priorities. But less than a year later, the shift of the center of gravity toward the

Mediterranean theater made him reconsider, and by January 1943 the landing craft and ships had fallen back from second to twelfth place—a demotion due also to the priority that the White House now attached to conducting the antisubmarine campaign in the Atlantic and supplying the British Isles.[4] Since building destroyers and merchant ships involved many of the same components (steel and engines, in particular), this decision was problematic. The production of landing craft was affected still more adversely because the backlog of orders at the main naval shipyards caused contracts to be reassigned to small boat manufacturers, such as Andrew Jackson Higgins's firm in New Orleans, or to large industrial concerns having no experience in naval construction, such as the Chicago Bridge and Iron Company. As a result, production on a mass scale began only in the spring of 1942.

Knowing that sooner or later it would have to wage a Continental war in order to defeat Germany, Great Britain did not share its ally's reluctance to plan along these lines. Considerable obstacles nonetheless stood in the way of production. As in the United States, hard choices had to be made, forcing the Admiralty to forgo the launching of new merchant ships and battleships. In March 1944 the British Chiefs of Staff summarized what had to be done "if full British participation in operations agreed at 'Sextant' is to materialize. Approval in principle has recently been given by the War Cabinet to build 80 ships of this type [LST]; 45 in the United Kingdom at the expense of warship and merchant ship production, and the remaining 35 in Canada. . . . Broadly speaking, each LST built in a merchant ship berth represents a loss of 5,000 tons gross. Thus, the building of 15 LST[s] will amount to a total loss of 75,000 tons gross of shipping in 1944–45 (i.e., the equivalent of about 10 standard type freighters)."[5] Mass production also faced resistance, as we have seen, from trade unions determined to protect the privileges of skilled labor. In the event, LCTs were manufactured in the Royal Navy's shipyards, which were not subject to union pay scales. Awarding the contract to commercial shipyards would have meant having to pay labor at a higher rate, not only for LCTs, but henceforth for every type of ship built by private-sector firms throughout the United Kingdom, which, according to the Admiralty, would cause productivity to fall by 10 percent.[6] Similarly, the authorities were reluctant to antagonize metalworkers by mandating soldering (rather than riveting) and the use of prefabricated elements.[7] A final source of complication was that the Germans targeted some manufacturers for bombardment. On the night of 22–23 February 1944, for example, the industrial plant of David Paxman and Co. in Colchester, Essex, which supplied an essential component of the landing craft engines, was destroyed.[8]

All these reasons taken together help explain the inadequacy of British and American production. In August 1943 the American chiefs of staff, emphasizing that "the provision of landing craft still constitutes a bottleneck in the conduct of military operations and will continue to do [so] for some time," sounded the alarm.[9] At the Teheran Conference, as Churchill later recalled, General Marshall declared that "the problem confronting the Western Allies in Europe was not one of troops or material, but ships and landing-craft and getting airfields close enough to the scene of operations. Landing-craft were particularly short, and the most vital need was for the L. S. T.s, which carried forty tanks apiece. So far as 'Overlord' was concerned, the flow of troops and supplies was proceeding according to schedule. The variable and questionable factor in almost every one of the problems facing the Allies was landing-craft."[10] For Eisenhower, the question was of paramount concern. He told his aide-de-camp, Harry Butcher, that when the time came to bury him, "his coffin should be in the shape of a landing craft, as they [were] practically killing him with worry."[11]

The Allied leaders tried to compensate for these shortcomings by every means possible. First and foremost, they sought to increase output through gains in productivity. Whereas the first tank carrier manufactured at the Seneca, Illinois, plant of the Chicago Bridge and Iron Company had required 875,000 man-hours over a period of six months, the last LST required only 270,000 hours over four months. The plant operated twenty-four hours a day, and employees sometimes worked seventy-hour weeks. Wages were good, overtime was paid (not always the case elsewhere in the United States), and housing built by local and regional authorities was available for relocated workers. The LSTs were launched with great fanfare at ceremonies that were both formal and convivial, and government propaganda praised the blue-collar contribution to the war effort. Higgins Industries in New Orleans, whose eponymous "Higgins Boats" (LCVPs) ferried a great many of the infantry platoons and jeeps ashore in Normandy, offered a comparable schedule of benefits that included day care, housing, and schools in addition to attractive wages. What is more, and exceptionally for the time in the Deep South, it recruited women and blacks to a trade that until then had been open only to white males.[12]

In both the United States and Great Britain, certain lines of production had to be discontinued. In August 1943 Admiral King was looking into "the possibility of increasing the production of landing craft by stopping production of 110 foot submarine-chasers and slowing up the production of destroyer escorts. The steps he was examining might produce an increase of 25 per cent in the landing craft program, but this must not, however, be taken as a firm figure."[13] On 8 September, the American chiefs of staff approved the idea, and contemplated raising the proportion to 35 percent despite the higher costs involved.[14] Increasing production of landing craft by 25 percent meant depriving the invasion force of either 125 M4 Medium Tanks, sixty-five destroyers, thirty-five Liberty ships, or twenty-six T2 oil tankers, and required 260,078 extra tons of steel; it also placed great demands on production capacity at Pontiac and General Motors plants, which jointly would have to supply a total of 5,500 diesel engines a month. If this target could not be met, the planners suggested reallocating 1,913 engines intended for British Valentine tanks, 3,397 for Soviet tanks, and 194 for electric generators to be used by the engineering corps.[15] Great Britain was forced to resort to similar trade-offs. To construct seventy-five additional LCTs, it delayed completion of one aircraft carrier, four destroyers, and fourteen frigates, meanwhile hiring some seventy thousand unskilled workers—a sign that it had managed to allay the hostility of the unions.[16] At Eisenhower's request, as we have seen, the date for the landing had been pushed back from 1 May to 1 June to gain a month's production time, which made it possible to enlarge the fleet by an additional ninety-six British LCTs.[17]

In spite of all these measures, production remained insufficient. Each partner looked to the other to shoulder the burden. In May 1943, noting with apprehension that only thirty-five LCTs, gun-equipped landing craft (LCGs), and antiaircraft support vessels (LCFs) could be constructed in Great Britain each month, the British government suggested "request[ing] the USA to provide by 1 April 1944 at least the following . . . : 122 LST, 6 LSE, 125 LCT, 280 LCM, 140 LCI."[18] Two months later, observing that "the planned production of all types of landing ships and crafts in America was prodigious," Lord Mountbatten again urged that "in view of our requirements for replacements and for possible expansion to meet the needs of future strategy, we should ask for some share of this production."[19] The Americans were reluctant, and even considered reducing their monthly production of vessels from fifty-five to forty. London then issued a grave warning. "We had however made it clear to them," Churchill reminded the War Cabinet in May 1944, "that if they reduced the program, the result might well be a limitation on the contribution that we could make in the Far East in 1945."[20] Yet no amount of American industry and goodwill alone could solve the problem. Because the LCTs were not equipped to cross the Atlantic, they had to be broken up into sections, loaded onto cargo ships, and then reassembled on their arrival in the United Kingdom.[21] The crossing itself took some six weeks.

By March 1944 worries began to mount. "American production of L. S. T.s is now running very much behind schedule," a British War Cabinet memorandum noted. "In February, for instance, they only produced 18 against a programme of 37."[22] What was more, the interval between the placement of an order and its fulfillment was very long, in Great Britain reaching eighteen months for landing craft.[23] Rather than count, therefore, on an increasingly doubtful increase in supply, whose effects would not in any case make themselves felt until after the landing, the planners looked for ways to diminish demand.

Anticipated rates of loss constituted a first variable of adjustment. The number of vessels that could be expected to be sunk or lost owing to mechanical failure, wear, or damage from enemy bombardment during the landing operation depended on the total number required to bring reinforcements ashore. Turnaround time, reckoned at two to three days for an LST, remained an unknown.[24] At the Quebec Conference in August 1943 the planners had assumed that 50 percent of the landing craft were liable to be lost, but this proportion, subsequently considered overly pessimistic, was reduced in October 1943 to 25 percent for LCAs and support ships, and the rate of 50 percent retained for LCIs, LCTs, and LCMs.[25] The Royal Navy later reduced it further, estimating the "serviceability" (or survival rate) of LCTs at 85 percent and 90 percent for LSTs.[26] These were still relatively low estimates, based on the navy's experience in the Mediterranean; a bolder forecast would have made it possible to reduce overall demand by three LSTs and thirty LCTs.[27] The Americans showed greater confidence, in that they after some debate assumed a survival rate of 90 percent for the LCTs and 95 percent for the LSTs, which saved seven LSTs.[28] The import of these calculations was hardly trivial. According to the most optimistic assumptions, it would be possible to transport 188,895 men and 21,275 vehicles—figures that in February 1944 were to be reduced by more cautious analysts to 155,980 men and 17,844 vehicles.[29] Events proved the optimists right: the survival rate turned out to be 99.3 percent for the American ships and 97.6 percent for the British ships, a performance as exceptional as it was unforeseeable.[30]

Next, the plan for loading the ships was modified as well. Considering that the men would not need to have all their equipment for the initial assault, Bedell Smith suggested reducing the number of vehicles per division from 3,000 to 1,450. Together with the elimination of 1,050 other pieces of equipment, this reduction made it possible to carry more men during the first waves.[31]

Finally, the planners reconfigured the allocation of the naval fleet among the various theaters of operations. At the Cairo Conference, the Americans agreed to cancel the planned operation (code-named BUCCANEER) against the Andaman Islands, thereby allowing 26 additional LSTs, 24 large LCIs, and 64 LCTs to be assigned to the Normandy landing.[32] The Italian theater was also tapped. Eisenhower's decision on 21 March 1944 to postpone the ANVIL landing in Provence freed up 26 LSTs and 40 large LCIs, which were scheduled to reach the United Kingdom by 30 April.[33] These reallocations met with strong resistance from the British. Churchill tried by every means possible to keep ships in the Mediterranean theater, to the point of recommending that British production be increased. "It would therefore be very valuable," he urged, "if we could say to [the Americans] that certain landing craft could be left in the Mediterranean without detriment to 'Overlord' because we had managed to arrange for 75 more L. C. T.s to be built here by 1st May, 1944."[34] Admiral King, for his part, controlled the forces at his disposal in the Pacific theater with an iron hand. Although on 1 May 1944 the U.S. Navy had 409 LSTs, 687 LCTs, and 478 LCIs, it transferred only 188, 279, and 124 of them, respectively, to OVERLORD, a sign that the "Germany first" option was not entirely supported by the navy.[35]

Even so, blame for the operation's logistical complications lay less with the American admiralty than with Allied political leaders, whose hesitation over diverting equipment and munitions from the Italian theater and indecision in the face of other mutually contradictory choices obliged the planners not to put all their money on one horse. "You can't imagine the difficulties here in planning," one SHAEF strategist complained. "It is enough to drive you mad with this uncertainty and these changes. When you have to sit down and figure the balance of divisions, the loading table and everything of that sort and you don't know what kind of craft you are going to load them in or whether you are going to have as many as you think you are going to have, it is enough to drive a man insane."[36] Fighting a war on many fronts, like the unforeseen possibilities this opened up in various places, worked to limit the political priority that in theory at least had been granted to the landing in Normandy.[37] By a singular reversal of fortune, Great Britain ended up bearing the brunt of the additional burden imposed by procrastination. Whereas the United States supplied 81 percent of the LSTs, 66 percent of the LCTs wound up being produced in the United Kingdom.

In any case, production did not count for everything. Of the 233 LSTs and 835 LCTs that were to cross the Channel on 6 June 1944, only 50 and 40, respectively, were in place by April—numbers that put the planners into a cold sweat.[38] Despite their own equivocations, the politicians refused to budge. "How it is that the plans of two great empires Britain and the United States should be so hamstrung and limited by a hundred or two of these particular vessels," Churchill fumed, "will never be understood by history."[39] The prime minister's impotent rage merely underscored how acute the problems posed by the landing ships would continue to be until the last minute—almost to the point of determining grand strategy.

## THE MULBERRIES

The need to capture ports in order to be able to offload the necessary reinforcements for the campaign in Normandy constituted a categorical imperative for Allied strategy. The Americans resolved to seize Cherbourg at once, and then move on to take control of several coastal cities in Brittany. Although Nantes and Saint-Nazaire were initially selected, it was decided in April 1944 to lay siege to Quiberon (Operation CHASTITY), which offered more than a mile and a half of beach, four small ports, and anchorage for two hundred Liberty ships.[40] In view of the destruction that the enemy could be expected to inflict on Cherbourg, and the inherently unpredictable advance of the Allied forces southward to Quiberon, these places would not be ready to receive troops and cargo for several weeks. A provisional solution therefore imposed itself, since in choosing Normandy the Allies had, as a practical matter, given up on the idea of taking ports that the Germans were prepared to defend to the last man, the disastrous consequences of which Dieppe had already amply demonstrated.

At the RATTLE Conference in June 1943, the chief of the naval planning staff, Commodore John Hughes-Hallet—picking up on an idea thrown out by Churchill in May 1942—suggested that the construction of artificial installations be investigated. Protected by breakwaters, these would provide safe harbor for both small craft, which could ferry supplies to the beaches, and larger vessels, which could unload directly onto trucks waiting on floating piers.[41] In July the War Office charged a team of engineers and other specialists with responsibility for working out various solutions to the problem. Its report was sufficiently convincing for Roosevelt and Churchill to give their approval on 15 August 1943, at the meeting in Quebec, to the construction of two artificial ports. By October 1943 specifications for the overall architecture were ready.[42] To break the waves in the Channel, a line of 113 large buoys known as Bombardons

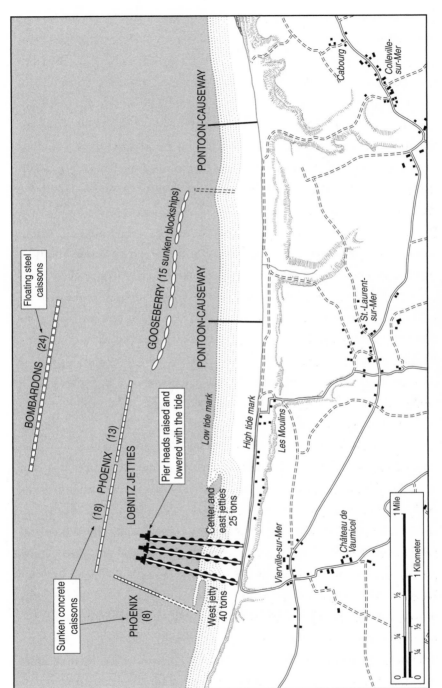

1. Plan for Mulberry A (Omaha Beach)

was to be anchored at a depth of eighteen meters. In the shelter of this line two ports would be constructed, Mulberry A (at Saint-Laurent) serving the American forces, and Mulberry B (at Arromanches) the British.[43] Enormous hollow floating caissons of concrete about six stories high, called Phoenixes, formed an inner wall protected by the line of Bombardons. Towed across the Channel, 149 Phoenixes (weighing, depending on their size, between 1,672 and 6,300 tons) were sunk on their arrival, in a matter of fifteen minutes. In the interval, temporary small-craft anchorages called Gooseberries were created before each of the five beaches, by sinking some sixty decommissioned vessels (or "blockships") behind the Bombardons. Since the blockships—unlike the Phoenixes—could be moved into position under their own power, it would be possible to organize five sheltered zones immediately (Varreville, Saint-Laurent, Arromanches, Courseulles, and Ouistreham), with the Gooseberries at Saint-Laurent and Arromanches serving as the base for construction of the Mulberries. Finally, a system of floating piers composed of prefabricated Lobnitz and Whale elements would allow the ships to be unloaded more easily than with stationary jetties, since the treadway—a pontoon sixty meters long by eighteen meters wide tethered to concrete piles—would rise and fall with the tide.[44]

The job of manufacturing and transporting these various elements across the Channel fell to Great Britain. Work on the Phoenixes began at the end of October 1943, but in the first two months it encountered worrisome delays: of the 15,000 workers needed for the project, fewer than half were on-site by 1 December.[45] Similar delays affected the Whale and Lobnitz components. Given the congestion of the naval shipyards, however, it was difficult to move faster. The planners had no choice but to reduce the scale originally contemplated, settling instead for ninety-three Bombardons and 146 Phoenixes, and to augment the labor force by calling on the 108th Naval Combat Battalion. Finally, and perhaps most important, they devised an ingenious method of production. Rather than use the slipways of the naval shipyards, clogged for the moment with vessels under construction, they dug great basins next to the Thames in which the steel reinforcing beams could be assembled and the concrete poured on dry land. Excavating machinery was then used to dig a trench between the basins and the river. Once a basin had filled up with water, the partly finished Phoenix was floated down the Thames. Constructing forty-eight Phoenixes according to this procedure made it possible to satisfy production quotas in May.[46]

The planners' relief was short-lived, however, for almost at once a new problem arose. Two hundred tugboats were needed, of which 164 were to be dedicated solely to the transport of the Phoenixes.[47] Dozens of caissons had to be brought to the Portland peninsula from Poole, Southampton, and Bromborough in addition to those floated along the Thames—a gargantuan task in itself.[48] In the event, only 158 tugs could be found, and of this number only 125 were immediately available. Again, the planners had no alternative but to push back the opening of the Mulberries from D + 14 to D + 21 (or from 20 June to 27 June), though in fact they were partly operational before this date.[49]

The anticipated advantage of these installations—namely, that they would free the Allies from the need to take ports staunchly defended by the Germans—came at a price: construction swallowed up thirty thousand tons of steel and more than three hundred thousand cubic meters of concrete, with the total cost coming to the staggering sum of 20 million pounds (approximately $80 million in 1945 dollars).[50] In the end, was it worth going to so much trouble and expense? The answer turned out to be equivocal, to say the least.

## BOLERO

The transport of American troops and equipment from the United States to Great Britain—Operation BOLERO—was to be carried out in accordance with the terms of the Marshall memorandum and the ensuing staff discussions held in London in April 1942. The campaigns in North Africa and Italy, however, in siphoning off most of the troops in the months that followed, justified the War Department's fears. To be sure, the overall statistics came very close to meeting expectations: on 31 December 1943, 1,416,485 men were serving overseas, of a projected force of 1,510,700. The forces stationed in the United Kingdom were kept to a strict minimum. By March 1943 only 59,000 Americans had reached

Great Britain. And although U.S. troop strength there did increase sharply, reaching 768,274 by the end of the year 1943, this number was still far from the 1,026,768 assumed by the planners. On the same date, 31 December 1943, U.S. soldiers fighting in the Mediterranean totaled 597,658, exceeding the allotted contingent by 165,000.[51] Moreover, of the 119 air groups deployed outside the United States (out of a total of 262), only 39 were stationed in northwestern Europe, with 37 assigned to the Mediterranean and the rest divided between the Middle Eastern and the Pacific theaters. American strategists therefore faced a twofold problem: the bulk of the air forces, at the start of 1944, were still based in the United States; and the minority deployed outside the American continent could not be assigned to OVERLORD, since they were not in the United Kingdom. This situation threatened the very viability of the cross-Channel operation.

In the summer and fall of 1943, however, in the wake of the Washington and Teheran Conferences, BOLERO received a decisive impetus whose effects were to make themselves felt early in the new year. The American forces stationed in Great Britain more than doubled, rising from almost 775,000 to 1,527,000 men between December 1943 and May 1944, so that by 31 May Great Britain was home to twenty combat divisions and 102 air groups. During this period two American divisions arrived each month and more than six million tons of equipment and supplies were unloaded in British ports (40 percent of the total tonnage received since January 1942).[52] Ninety-five percent of the American forces made the crossing by sea, most in convoys (59 percent); two transatlantic liners, the *Queen Mary* and *Queen Elizabeth,* between them brought over a quarter of the troops. Refitted to carry some 15,000 soldiers each (having originally been designed for only 2,000 passengers, in luxurious accommodations), the ocean liners offered the advantage of speed: in making the crossing in five to six days, as against the two weeks needed for Liberty ships, they reduced the turnaround time and limited the risks still posed by the submarine fleet of the German navy.[53]

Vital though it was to the success of OVERLORD, the accelerating tempo of BOLERO gave rise to new problems. Chief among these was the difficulty Great Britain faced in absorbing such enormous quantities of men and matériel. A medium-sized convoy docking in the United Kingdom in

March 1944 comprised 42 freighters carrying 1,500 wheeled vehicles, 2,000 crated vehicles, 200 planes and gliders, and 50,000 tons of supplies. Its unloading required 100 special trains and 18,000–20,000 vehicles. In all, 9,225 special trains were assigned to this Sisyphean task in the first half of 1944—hence the choking burden on rail and road lines anticipated by the Ministry of War Transport in January 1944, which feared that "the country's transport would not be able to continue to move the present load as well as the additional traffic arising from 'Overlord.'"[54] This congestion obliged freighters to wait their turn out at sea—a waste of resources that the Allies could ill afford, given the shortage of shipping capacity.[55]

Initially, the British limited the entry of American troops to their shores, admitting only 132,000 men in May and 125,700 in June of 1944, whereas the United States was prepared to send 151,000 and 152,000 in these two months, respectively. To reduce congestion in British ports, the Allies also used a "type-loading" system: vessels already loaded in the United States with cargo intended for the European theater could be held in British waters until they were needed in Normandy, where they could then be unloaded en bloc—thus lowering handling costs—or else serve as floating warehouses from which stores could be taken as required, on a piecemeal basis. This clever expedient, by means of which some two hundred vessels between May and July were able to bypass British ports, nonetheless had the disadvantage of tying up scarce resources, while at the same time offering a choice target for Admiral Doenitz's torpedoes. It was therefore necessary to resort to more drastic measures. To ensure the success of the landing, the British agreed to tighten their belts yet another notch and reduce imports of civilian goods by five hundred thousand tons.[56]

## BRITS AND YANKEES

The most noticeable consequence of Operation BOLERO was that it obliged the British to put up the three million Americans who passed through the United Kingdom between January 1942 and May 1945 en route to the North African, Italian, and French theaters. The length of their guests' stay varied from a few weeks to several months—or more, as in the case of the Twenty-ninth Infantry Division, which lived in Southwest England for almost a year and a half before embarking for Omaha Beach.[57] This proved to be a trying experience on all sides.

First, there was the question of lodging. Bases and barracks were needed for the 1.5 million soldiers and airmen who were stationed in England on 5 June 1944. The British government reconverted existing installations (the old Tidworth barracks, for example, near Salisbury, were assigned to the Twenty-ninth Infantry Division) and built new ones (the famous Nissen huts). The construction of airfields and training grounds, which diverted scarce resources and occasionally provoked disputes with farmers determined to retain ownership of their land, was accomplished with somewhat greater difficulty.

Moreover, the arrival of so many foreign soldiers destabilized the demographic balance of the country. Disembarking in the west of the United Kingdom (on the river Clyde near Glasgow, the river Mersey in Liverpool, and the Bristol Channel), they were lodged in the southwest of England, substantially altering the ratio between outsiders and natives. Suffolk counted one American for every six local residents, and Wiltshire one American for every two.[58] Overcrowding led to social conflict and to a dramatic increase in motor traffic. Whereas twenty thousand American vehicles were in circulation in summer of 1943, there were more than one hundred thousand in March of the following year, causing an increase in accidents that was attributed by the British to "dangerous driving."[59] In fact, only a sixth of the twenty-four thousand accidents occurring after July 1943 involved excessive speed; most of them were due to the narrowness of English roads, to which American drivers were unaccustomed.

There were other sources of friction as well. Stereotypes died hard. Many of the Americans thought of Great Britain as a waning power, populated by snobs who showed little interest in fighting—this despite the massive evidence to the contrary provided by the Battle of Britain. In March 1942 only 40.2 percent of GIs interviewed felt that Great Britain was doing its part to support the war effort, slightly more than the 38.3 percent expressing a contrary view.[60] This unfavorable opinion was slow to be dispelled. In the second half of the same year, only 5 percent of the enlisted men considered that Great Britain was doing everything it could to achieve victory (48 percent ranked the United States ahead of Great Britain for martial valor; indeed, 30 percent placed the Soviet Union, and 9 percent China, ahead of Great Britain).[61] Moreover, 40 percent of the 15,000 men questioned in the ten months preceding September 1942 acknowledged mistrusting their British counterparts and having a low opinion of their fighting abilities.[62] The arrival of General Bradley's First Army therefore came at a time when, as its commander noted diplomatically, "the relations between US soldiers and British soldiers as well as between US soldiers and British civilians had not progressed to a satisfactory point."[63] The British, for their part, regarded their former colony as a kingdom of corruption where basic freedoms—particularly the right of labor to organize—were not always guaranteed, and looked down on its people for their selfish obsession with material comforts.[64]

Such perceptions as these drove a wedge between the two allies, creating a gap that at least initially was bound to grow wider on their closer acquaintance. Though they were fighting for the same cause, GIs and Tommies drew unequal lots. At the beginning of 1944 the American soldier received a daily ration of 340 grams of meat, sausage, and bacon—half again as much as that of his British counterpart and three times greater than that of a civilian; his pay was three times what a British soldier received; he paraded in three different uniforms and had access to seemingly unlimited supplies of scarce goods—chocolate, cigarettes, and nylon stockings. The American military tried to disguise the difference in salaries by paying the men twice a month and, in the hope of reducing ostentatious displays of spending, urged GIs to purchase American products sold in the barracks and encouraged them to save (Eisenhower was able to announce triumphantly in July 1944 that 75 percent of the soldiers' pay was spent in these ways). The British authorities, for their part, increased salaries by 20 percent in August 1942—a praiseworthy measure, but one that only marginally narrowed the gap between the two armies.[65]

In the eyes of local women the advantages enjoyed by American soldiers conferred incomparable prestige—an additional source of tension. For these young men, English girls were not like the ones they knew back home. "The GIs who every night saw a film in which the hero waited forever to get from an American 'bombshell' what a foreign woman was ready to offer them for a bit of courtship, a bar of chocolate, or an invitation to dinner, could not help but use the sexual availability of women [in England] to take their revenge on the feminine myth that held sway in their own country at that time."[66] From the urgency of desire to sexual harassment was but a small step, which many soldiers took. And for many young women, wartime multiplied opportunities for being in the company of young men. Teenage girls who had been evacuated from cities ravaged by bombardment, and left to their own devices while their mothers were working, were easy prey. Adult women, bored with jobs in the factories, found in casual sexual encounters a welcome diversion from the drabness of their lives, which were all the lonelier since English males had become a vanishing species, whether they had been stationed away from home or sent to fight overseas. Considering, too, that some marriages had been entered into too hastily as the storm clouds gathered over Europe in the late 1930s, it is not surprising that the war should have favored adultery—a state of affairs reflected not only in the explosive rise in divorces between 1939 and 1945, from 8,357 to 25,789, but also in the stable and substantial proportion of illegitimate births (13.7 percent in 1940 and 12.3 percent in 1944).[67]

From the Tommies' point of view, then, the GIs were indeed "overpaid, oversexed, and over here." Yet one should not make too much of this. Many—perhaps most—encounters were social rather than sexual, and the majority of Americans conducted themselves with decency, even where they were lodged in private homes (as one hundred thousand of them were in 1944). In homes that had lost men of the family, the foreign guests played the role of brother or father by default, bringing a masculine presence to lives that had been cruelly deprived of it.

The racial question constituted an additional stumbling block. Both in principle and in practice, the American military pursued a discriminatory policy. Although blacks accounted for 10 percent of the American population in 1940, they made up only a very small fraction of the land and sea forces (1.5 percent of the army, 2.3 percent of the navy) and until January 1941 were excluded from the air force. Beginning in January 1940, the

Department of War had sought to increase troop strength by encouraging the recruitment of African-Americans (a way, too, of attracting the black vote in the upcoming presidential election). Three years later, at the end of 1942, blacks formed 7.4 percent of the army. But racist practices persisted. Blacks did not have the right to command white units: officers of color were almost invisible (in August 1942 there were 817, or 0.35 percent of black troops); and segregation continued to be the order of the day, with the result that black and white soldiers frequented separate social centers, cinemas, and exercise facilities.[68]

Imposed from the top down, this apartheid was largely supported by those at the bottom. In the air force, 56 percent of the white ground crews (37 percent among Northerners, 66 percent among Southerners) were hostile to the idea of working with a team that included blacks.[69] Many enlisted men from the North acknowledged "a strong prejudice" against the idea of sharing facilities with soldiers of color, a distaste that was still more manifest among Southerners.[70] Blacks, by contrast, were only moderately offended by this animosity: 45 percent felt that segregation in clubs and other settings was a positive thing—as against 85 percent of whites.[71] All in all, "second-class citizens were regarded as second-class soldiers."[72]

The United States tried, not altogether successfully, to enlist the help of Great Britain in maintaining this racist system on its soil. Whatever their fundamental reasons for opposing American policy may have been, the British refused to enforce racial distinctions in the public sphere, so long as individuals behaved in a respectable fashion. They did find it difficult, however, to countenance sexual relations between blacks and whites, perhaps because violent incidents (brawls and especially rapes) reinvigorated old imperialist prejudices and aroused subliminal fears of genetic contamination through intimate contact with an inferior race. Nonetheless, as a practical matter, the institution of segregation represented a luxury that an overcrowded host country could ill afford. At a time of strict rationing, the duplication of barracks, pubs, and sporting grounds struck authorities as a wholly unjustifiable waste of resources. At the same time, however, the British government found it difficult to oppose the wishes of its powerful ally outright. Evasive action was therefore required. First, it asked for—and received—assurances that blacks would not exceed 10 percent of the total number of forces stationed in Great Britain. Next, it prohibited all official discrimination, as the home secretary explained on 4 September 1942: "The policy of His Majesty's Government is to assure that no discriminatory act toward troops of color will be due to any British authority whatever. The Secretary would be grateful to the police not to apply discriminatory measures to the owners of public houses, restaurants, and other public places. If such measures are taken by the American authorities themselves, the British police are in no case to compel respect for or otherwise be party to the enforcement of these measures."[73]

In the event, the British relaxed their application of this policy, to avoid giving embarrassment to the Americans. Military regulations were cited in forbidding English women who wished to meet black American soldiers from setting foot on bases and in barracks. Blacks were also left out of social events that brought Brits and Yankees together for sports or drinks. Separate pubs and dance halls were assigned to black and white servicemen, or otherwise set aside for them. The Americans in turn adopted a more moderate position. Eisenhower, in lifting censorship, gave the press permission to raise the question of race by showing that the British held more tolerant views. Mixed units were created within the military police, and officers were directed to treat blacks fairly. It must be admitted, however, that such orders were apt to be ignored in an army in which Southern officers had formed 30 percent of the total during the interwar period.

In the face of these humiliations, blacks turned their back on the military. Fifty-four percent of men with fewer than three months' service declared themselves proud of their unit, but this feeling declined over time. At the end of one year of enlistment, the proportion fell to 31 percent. In 1943 only 27 percent of black servicemen thought that they were more useful to the country as soldiers than as workers, a sentiment that was shared by 40 percent of their white counterparts.[74]

Insults and brutal attacks did not improve morale. "When one or several blacks entered a dance hall frequented exclusively by whites, the band sometimes found itself ordered to stop playing until the blacks had left the premises, of their own accord or by force." Nor was it unknown for drunken white GIs to organize "nigger hunts." But violence was not the monopoly of whites. African-Americans, in addition to responding in kind to physical aggression, were given to provocations of their own. "Aware that the [English] had taken up their cause, if only in order to express their growing antipathy toward the 'invaders,' blacks are described in various [official] documents as having 'adopted a perpetually mocking attitude in the presence of their fellow [white] soldiers' where the latter found themselves in a minority in a public place frequented by English clients." Moreover, blacks were implicated in one-third of the 121 rape cases that occurred in Great Britain, though they accounted for only a tenth of the troops. Whether this figure reflects a higher level of criminal behavior or greater severity on the part of racist American military courts is, of course, difficult to determine.[75] Even so, the incidence of rapes committed by black troops was a troubling reality, and one that was to be repeated in Normandy in the summer of 1944. Commanding officers, many of them inexperienced, found it difficult to curb misbehavior and occasionally imposed severe penalties that had the effect of increasing blacks' feelings of dissatisfaction with the military, which gave rise in turn to fresh episodes of violence. This vicious circle probably could have been avoided if the fighting abilities of the black soldier had been recognized and valued. With very rare exceptions, such as the all-black Ninety-second ("Buffalo Soldier") Division, which fought bravely in Italy, African-Americans were assigned to support units rather than to combat units. As a result, the U.S. military did little to help resolve the racial question, which was to pose itself in far more acute form in the aftermath of the Second World War.

In the meantime, aware that cultural differences threatened to divide armies that nonetheless had to fight side by side, both sides redoubled their efforts to bring their men closer together. GIs, equipped with a pocket guide to Great Britain, were invited to talks and films (such as *Welcome to Britain* and *Know Your Ally: Britain*) aimed at acquainting them with British ways and customs. To promote goodwill between the two countries, meetings of all sorts were encouraged. American officers, acting in concert with the mayors of the towns where their units were stationed, sponsored Christmas trees for local children. British families invited American soldiers on leave to join them for Sunday dinner (the guests being instructed by their superiors to bring their own food, in order not to further reduce their hosts' meager rations); sporting competitions between American and British units were organized; and beginning in 1943 units exchanged personnel for two-week periods so that both officers and men could have a firsthand sense of the training and everyday routine of their companions-in-arms. In the case of the First U.S. Army, these exchanges involved 915 officers and 4,726 men.[76]

This last initiative in particular seems to have borne fruit. If many Americans had a low opinion of the British at the outset, living and working together led them to revise their judgment. In April–May 1943, 86 percent of the officers and 81 percent of the men interviewed thought that their British counterparts showed the utmost will to fight, with only 13 percent and 16 percent, respectively, expressing a contrary view. Moreover, 71 percent of the officers and 61 percent of the men now objected to the idea that Great Britain was more interested in controlling the world than in constructing a new democratic order.[77] This change in attitude was largely the result of relationships forged over time with the local population. Whereas 63 percent of the men who were present in the United Kingdom for fewer than three months professed to like the British (22 percent admitted to occasionally being irritated by them, and 15 percent to detesting them), the proportion of those positively disposed rose to 78 percent among soldiers present for more than a year (with only 7 percent persisting in their antipathy).[78] "Comments indicate that exchange of personnel between British and American Armies for short periods is having a favorable effect, and bringing about a better understanding between the two forces," a U.S. Army report on troop morale noted with satisfaction in February 1944.[79] The same observers reported two months later that "the preponderance of favorable comments continues. The American soldier particularly admires the British for the manner in which they have accepted any privations incidental to war. The soldier seems surprised when he is accepted and treated well in British homes. The general tenor of all these reports has been a steady improvement in Anglo-American relations."[80] The British reaction was still more positive: "With US troops the problem is, as usual, a lack of relations rather than bad relations. The two Armies do not mix, largely because the British soldier does not like to accept hospitality which he cannot afford to return. . . . The system of exchanging parties of a dozen or so for about a fortnight, which has now been in operation for two or three months, is proving an unqualified success."[81]

On the eve of the landing, then, the clouds of mutual misunderstanding seemed to have been chased away. A happy omen—assuming that the troops had been properly trained to withstand the ordeal that awaited them.

## BATTLE READINESS

Defeating the enemy in Normandy would require that troops be not only prepared for battle but also capable of undertaking specific missions aimed at destroying German coastal defenses. The soldier's basic education had therefore to be supplemented by special training that took into account the peculiar circumstances of the landing itself. Although the British army had real experience of war, having been deployed since September 1939, some units—such as the Third Infantry Division, charged with leading the assault on Sword Beach—had hardly fought since Dunkirk; others, like the Fifteenth (Scottish) Division, had been confined to coastal surveillance at home.[82] The U.S. forces, for their part, were mostly inexperienced. The North African campaign had demonstrated the weakness of American infantry. Poorly trained, careless, undisciplined, they were reluctant to engage the enemy, with the result that in hilly terrain they often presented an easy target. The disaster of the Kasserine Pass in Tunisia, in February 1943, had fatally revealed these defects, which the high command hastened to remedy. The shortage of facilities in Great Britain meant that basic training had to take place mainly in the United States, the soldiers receiving equipment and provisions only once they had crossed the ocean. Typically, a conscript reported first to a training center (Fort Bragg in North Carolina, for example), where he was given his orders and a uniform. He was then sent to another camp where, in addition to military discipline and courtesy, the basic elements of soldiering were taught. He completed his training overseas in the unit to which he had been assigned.[83]

The inadequacy of this apprenticeship is clear in retrospect. Enlisted men often faced a wait of four to five months before joining their units, which undermined morale, weakened discipline, compromised fitness, and interrupted training. In Normandy, where initially they were sent to replacement depots behind the lines, they found themselves mixed together with the wounded, victims of battle fatigue, and misfits—a frightening and demoralizing experience for many new recruits.[84] Above all, the men found it difficult to endure the nitpicking discipline of narrow-minded noncommissioned officers. A great many felt strongly that they were unprepared for what lay in store: in one division, 91 percent of the officers and 57 percent of the enlisted men interviewed in March 1943 demanded more training;[85] in March 1944, 30 percent of the men in another division likewise felt that their training was not sufficiently rigorous.[86] In April of that year, on the eve of the landing, 37 percent of the men of the Fourth Infantry Division deplored the importance attached to marching; 12 percent wanted more realistic combat training; 8 percent called for gunnery practice with real ammunition; 7 percent requested instruction in reading maps.[87] Two months earlier, a poll of twelve thousand soldiers serving in five divisions of the First U.S. Army revealed a deep sense of ambivalence: 65 percent of the men felt ready to face battle, but only 28 percent wanted to leave for the front immediately; 50 percent thought they had received sufficient training, but only 35 percent felt they were in good physical condition.[88]

Field commanders also sought to toughen the men for the tasks they would have to perform on the shores of Normandy. TORCH had disclosed a number of weaknesses (poor coordination among units, breakdowns in authority, deficiencies in amphibious technique, and so on) that had to be corrected at once, and indeed the operations in Sicily were conducted more successfully. On the British side, three English divisions and three Canadian divisions began training in Scotland for amphibious operations in the spring and summer of 1943 by means of a series of specific exercises: KRUSCHEN, aimed at taking fortified batteries; FILIBUSTER, at mounting an assault on a port; and JANTZEN, at maintaining control of a beachhead.[89] The Americans, meanwhile, constructed a center at Ilfracombe on the Devonshire coast, where beginning in September men were trained in disembarking and seizing fortified positions. Land was subsequently acquired at Slapton Sands, near Dartmouth, and assigned to the First Army in December.[90] Among the various exercises conducted there, DUCK I (4–6 January 1944) concentrated on interservice cooperation in the loading and unloading of LCTs as well as the organization of men and equipment on the beaches. FABIUS I–VI (23 April–7 May) brought together all the forces that were to launch an assault in the area of Caen-Isigny. The first four exercises were intended to familiarize the troops with the procedures for assembling, embarking, and crossing the Channel, and then for disembarking and readying the beaches to receive reinforcements; the fifth was devoted to training the teams responsible for the assembly and embarkation of support troops; and the sixth and final exercise was given over to reviewing the elaborate procedures involved in bringing reinforcements ashore.[91] TIGER (22–30 April) was a dress rehearsal for the landing at Utah Beach. Of the nine days of exercises, six were taken up preparing for assembly and embarkation.[92] Toward the end, disaster struck. At 2:20 in the morning of 28 April, German motor torpedo boats operating under cover of night slipped through a screen of British destroyers and succeeded in sinking two LSTs and heavily damaging another. Some 638 men perished by drowning or died from explosions; 300 were wounded.[93] The bodies were fished out of the waters in the course of a long search, but not all the dead could be accounted for. Intense fears arose among the Allied leaders that under interrogation captured officers with knowledge of NEPTUNE might reveal the secret of the landing. "Their bodies were secretly bulldozed into a mass grave on the Devon farm of Mr. Nolan Tope while the wounded were quarantined at the hospitals and threatened with court-martial if they talked. At the critiques following the exercise . . . the British, some of whom believed the American troops to be quite hopeless, tactfully kept silent."[94] The casualties appear to have been discreetly added to the tally of aggregate Allied losses sustained during the invasion five weeks later. By a cruel irony, TIGER claimed more victims than the actual operations conducted on Utah on 6 June.

The exercises, taken as a whole, revealed grave shortcomings. JANTZEN had been so disappointing that a series of supplementary training exercises was scheduled during the winter of 1943–44 at Gullane, on the Firth of Forth, so that cargo ships could be unloaded more efficiently (ROUND-ABOUT I–VI).[95] DUCK I revealed flawed coordination between the army and the navy, violations of security rules, and overloading of troops and vehicles. DUCK II and III (February 1944) brought scarcely any improvement. Traffic control, interservice coordination, and boarding procedures remained weak points. The failure of landing craft to arrive on schedule caused bottlenecks, with the consequence that troops did not always disembark at their designated locations.[96] By contrast, the procedures for assembling the men, loading the ships, and filling up DUKWs (small amphibious landing vehicles, better known as Ducks) with munitions for the immediate resupply of certain units were executed satisfactorily.

Still, there was no denying that the American forces had so far failed to exhibit the drive and determination that would be required. Harry Butcher, a Navy officer, noted in late April:

> I am concerned over the absence of toughness and alertness of young officers whom I saw on this trip [the TIGER exercise]. They seem to regard the war as one grand maneuver in which they are having a happy time. Many seem as green as growing corn. How will they act in battle and how will they look in three months' time?
>
> A good many of the full colonels also gave me a pain. They are fat, gray and oldish. Most of them wear the Rainbow Ribbon of the last war and are still fighting it. . . .
>
> On the Navy's side, our crews are also green, but they seem to know how to handle their boats, yet when I dictate this, I recall that in plain daylight, with a smooth sea with our LCI standing still, she nearly had her stern carried away by a landing craft fitted out as an antiaircraft ship. We were missed only by inches—in clear daylight.[97]

In short, as Ralph Ingersoll observed, "With each amphibious maneuver, through the winter and early spring, we seemed to get worse at it instead of better."[98] More worrisome still, training maneuvers had not dealt with certain aspects of OVERLORD that were nonetheless crucial. "As a result of our inability to get together with air in England," General Bradley later recalled, "we went into France almost totally untrained in air-ground co-operation."[99] On the eve of D-Day, then, the Allied high command had very real reasons for anxiety.

# 5

# STRATEGIES AND STRATAGEMS

THE BATTLE OF NORMANDY was in part a wager on numbers, as we have just seen. The Allies had not only to transport troops and equipment and supplies across the Channel in immense quantities—a task that fell to the logistics experts—but also to prevent the Germans from transferring additional forces to the Norman front. To achieve this result, the Allies counted on three things: a bombing campaign, aimed at crippling the rail network, that would cut off Normandy from the rest of France and prohibit the enemy from bringing up reinforcements; the Soviet promise to unleash a summer offensive in tandem with OVERLORD that would keep the bulk of the German troops in the East; and finally, a campaign of disinformation that would mislead the Germans about where the landing would take place.

## BOMBING

The idea of placing the strategic air forces in the service of OVERLORD was repugnant to the chiefs of the British Bomber Command and the U.S. Strategic Air Forces (USSTAF). Generals Harris and Spaatz felt strongly that in bringing airpower to bear against targets inside Germany they would dramatically hasten the end of the war, if not actually bring it about by themselves. At Casablanca, Churchill and Roosevelt resolved to intensify and above all to coordinate raids on Germany, in order to destroy its military-industrial network by a "continual and sustained" aerial assault. It was not until the late spring of 1943, however, that the strategic bombing campaign was finalized in the form of Operation POINTBLANK. In May, having identified nineteen industrial complexes as being vulnerable to air attack, the American general staff targeted six key industrial sectors: submarine construction, aircraft manufacture, ball bearings, oil, synthetic rubber, and military transport vehicles. These targets were distributed over seventy-six precise objectives, the destruction of which would eliminate 89 percent of German submarine manufacturing capacity, 65 percent of its bomber production, 76 percent of its ball bearing output, 48 percent of its refineries, and 50 percent of its synthetic rubber production. By attacking the Reich, the Combined Chiefs of Staff aimed primarily to force the Luftwaffe to fight in the skies above its own country, rather than elsewhere; and by seeking to engage the German fighter plane force in particular, they gave priority to protecting the landing in Normandy, rather than to achieving victory solely by aerial assault on the cities and industries of the Reich.[1]

Approved during the Washington Conference in late May 1943, POINT-BLANK nonetheless yielded uneven results. German antiaircraft artillery remained a powerful deterrent, and the Luftwaffe showed itself to be a formidable adversary in defending its territory. Poor weather, as well as the remote location of the Reich's aircraft factories, beyond the reach of the planes of the U.S. Air Force, further complicated the Allies' task. The American raids against Ratisbonne in August 1943 and Schweinfurt in August and October of 1943, in which more than 15 percent of the 376 B-17s engaged were lost, were a sobering reminder of the risks of this strategy.[2] As a result, concentrated attacks against the Reich were interrupted between November 1943 and February 1944.

On 13 February 1944 a new directive thoroughly revised the air plan, placing greater emphasis on the destruction of the German air force without, however, setting precise targets. In the meantime, the Americans had improved the protection of their bomber squadrons. By arming fighter planes with fuel tanks under the belly and the wings, they provided the bombers with a powerful escort that could now ward off enemy attacks over longer distances.[3] In July 1943, tanks carrying an additional seventy-five gallons increased the range of the P-47 Thunderbolt by 100 miles; by March 1944 the P-51 Mustang was able to fly to Prague or Berlin—a range of about 1,500 miles. The U.S. Air Force also modified its tactics: if a third of its fighters remained dedicated to the protection of the bomber fleet in January 1944, two-thirds were now assigned the mission of taking out the German fighter force.[4] The British, for their part, had not abandoned General Harris's program of bombing German cities, with the objective of sapping the morale of the civilian population.

From Eisenhower's point of view none of these measures promised OVERLORD the air support it would need. He turned to Solly Zuckerman, a distinguished zoologist who by virtue of his wartime work at Combined Operations Headquarters, and later for the campaigns in North Africa and Sicily, had become an expert on aerial warfare strategy. Extrapolating from data for the period of March through December 1943, Zuckerman calculated that it would be impossible by means of strategic bombing to achieve a reduction in German industrial production greater than 7 percent.[5] The Allies' experience in Italy, however, suggested that a methodical campaign against the French rail network would disrupt enemy logistics at relatively little cost. This strategy, formulated in January 1944 and known thereafter as the Transportation Plan, could not fail to appeal to a commander in chief who was anxious to prevent the Reich from promptly dispatching reinforcements to the Normandy theater. Predictably, the plan was bitterly opposed by General Spaatz, who on 5 March urged that an offensive be launched against Germany's petroleum installations (the "Oil Plan"). The destruction of fourteen synthetic oil factories supplying 80 percent of German needs, Spaatz argued, would cause the enemy war machine to grind to a halt.

On the night of 6–7 March 1944, however, acting on the recommendation of the chief of staff of the RAF, Air Chief Marshal Sir Charles Portal, the British launched an experimental attack against the railway depot at Trappes, southwest of Paris.[6] The results surpassed all expectation: the locomotive shed was destroyed, and the marshaling yards were extensively damaged (indeed repairs had not yet been completed by the end of April). Eisenhower therefore decided to throw his weight behind the Transportation Plan. At the next bombing policy conference, on 25 March, Spaatz restated his objections, but they did not alter the fact that, even assuming the bombers were to reach their targets in a network of widely dispersed oil fields (many of them in Romania), refineries, and depots, the Oil Plan could bring results only in six months' time—well after the launching of OVERLORD. Moreover, the heads of the strategic air forces had promised so many miracles over the course of the war that their predictions were now largely discredited.[7] On 31 March, putting the best face on the matter, Spaatz agreed that operations against the Luftwaffe and the rail network should henceforth be favored, but in return for this concession he received permission to attack certain petroleum objectives. Nonetheless, thanks to the support of Tedder, Portal, and Leigh-Mallory, Eisenhower had prevailed. On 17 April he laid out in greater detail the mission of the air forces, which three days earlier had been placed under his authority: the weakening of the German fighter arm and the destruction of the French rail network were now assigned overriding priority. In view of the difficulties encountered in nighttime raids on industrial targets inside Germany, the Bomber Command now solicited the assistance of the USSTAF, in the hope of delivering a crippling blow to the war economy of the Reich.[8]

Eisenhower's gamble was not without risk, however. Even though German military movements in France mobilized a relatively small share of overall transport, U.S. experts estimated that it would be necessary to destroy between 80 and 90 percent of the French rail network in order to weaken the Wehrmacht's capabilities in Normandy significantly. Portal and the War Office could not guarantee interruption of more than 30 percent of rail traffic, however—not enough to block the inflow of German troops. The Allied intelligence services calculated that each German division needed 350 tons of fresh provisions per day: supplying the fifty divisions in the theater therefore required forty trains. With the arrival of additional troops, it was estimated that the number would rise to between seventy-eight and eighty-six trains per day. Even so, shutting down only a part of the rail network could do relatively little to disrupt the supply lines of the German forces; at most, it might help slow the rate of troop reinforcements, but only if the carrying capacity of the two principal through-lines were reduced by more than 20 percent—and here no guarantee was possible.[9] Even in the event that German rolling stock sustained substantial damage, the enemy could always commandeer locomotives from the French railway system, disregarding the needs of the French people.[10] Despite the reservations of his technical advisers, Eisenhower held to his course. Disappointing though the results might prove, everything possible would have been done to improve the chances of OVERLORD's success.[11]

In order to isolate Normandy, the plan therefore called for ninety days of daytime air attacks on thirty-nine objectives located in Germany and thirty-three targets in Belgium and France. In April 1944 the German theater was abandoned in favor of the Franco-Belgian theater, though not without a good deal of indecision:

> Everyone is talking glibly about switching the priorities of the strategic transportation plan nearer D day. . . . There is a great deal of muddled thinking; everything is semi-official; no one is coming out into the open. As a result no decision is being taken by commanders because the problems are not being presented clearly to them. . . . What must be made clear at this stage is the object of a "tactical air plan," the general types of target whose attack would most achieve the object, and the approximate number of such targets for the guidance of the air forces. Then, we can start getting down to particular targets, and fighting over details.[12]

In the event, priority continued to be attached to the principal rail hubs and repair sheds. The Eighth U.S. Air Force was to strike the east of France and Belgium; the British Bomber Command the west and the Paris region; the American Expeditionary Air Forces (AEAF) northern France and Belgium. In March the first attacks were launched against the rail lines; rail centers and locomotive depots were targeted next, beginning in April.[13] Then came the bridges, when P-47 Thunderbolt fighters and B-26 Marauder bombers attacked Vernon, Oissel, Orivel, and Mantes-Gassicourt on 7 May 1944. The success of these operations, as well as their modest cost—only twenty-two tons of bombs were needed to destroy a bridge—led the air staffs, to act on a suggestion made by Air Marshal Sir Arthur Coningham, the New Zealander who com-

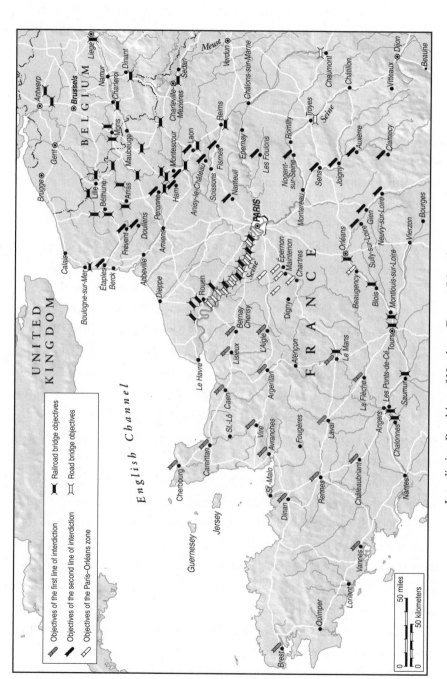

2. Interdiction Bombing of Northern France (May–August 1944)

manded the British Second Tactical Air Force and order a campaign of systematic destruction. Almost at once, however, a report intercepted by the British secret services revealed that the German Third Air Fleet (Luftflotte 3) had deduced from the location of the targets that the landing would take place between Le Havre and Cherbourg.[14] A halt to the bombing was therefore called on 10 May, and though the campaign started up again two weeks later for the Seine, its resumption was pushed back until 6 June for the Loire.[15] Altogether, the Transportation Plan consumed considerable resources. By D-Day, 76,200 tons of bombs had been dropped: 71,000 on rail centers, 4,400 on bridges and other civil engineering structures, and 800 on rail lines.[16]

Other objectives were not wholly neglected. The Bomber Command scaled down its attacks against Germany substantially, directing only 8 percent of its tonnage at targets within the Reich in June 1944, but the Americans carried on with the campaign.[17] The Combined Service Intelligence Committee recommended that the Fifteenth U.S. Air Force, based in Italy, attack the Luftwaffe's aircraft factories and storage facilities in Austria and southern Germany, rather than the rail centers, to pin down the German fighter force and weaken the enemy's military potential.[18] Beginning on 12 May, the USSTAF took aim at synthetic oil plants in Brussels, Böhlen, Merseburg-Leuna, and Zeitz as well, a program that mobilized 11.6 percent of Spaatz's bombers in June, 17 percent in July, and 16.4 percent in August.[19]

The secret weapons being developed by the Germans also obliged the Allies to react. A first raid conducted against the rocket research center at Peenemünde, on the Baltic coast, during the night of 17–18 August 1943 had led the Reich to scatter its launch sites and place its installations underground. In December 1943, noticing an increase in the number of launching pads, the Allies began sending the heavy bombers of the Eighth Air Force on precision bombing missions as part of an operation that Churchill whimsically named CROSSBOW. The threat posed by Hitler's "retaliation weapons" *(Vergeltungswaffen)* was hard to gauge, and though the Allied Supreme Command did not feel that it necessitated rethinking the overall plan, it did shift OVERLORD's forces to the west of Southampton in March 1943, beyond the reach of the pilotless bombers

(V-1s) and rocket-launched ballistic missiles (V-2s). Churchill, meanwhile, was concerned about the danger to the civilian population in southeast England. He invoked the escape clause in the agreement that placed the Bomber Command under Eisenhower's direction: the United Kingdom being directly menaced, the primary mission of the air force in March and April became to destroy the V-1 and V-2 sites (in Holland and Belgium, respectively)—while continuing to aim at targets that threatened to compromise the safety of the landing. Between August 1943 and August 1944 the strategic air forces devoted 13.7 percent of their sorties and 15.5 percent of their bombs to these sites; and between May 1943 and August 1945 the tactical air wings carried out four thousand sorties from bases in the United Kingdom, most of these directed against the launching pads.[20]

The military operations in northwestern Europe in general, and France in particular, posed a political and moral dilemma, in that they exposed civilian populations to the risk of heavy casualties. It was not the Allies' intention to punish whole industries or cities as such: unlike the campaign that Harris carried out against the Reich, the bombing of targets in France—a friendly country—was not in any way conceived as a terrorist operation; in Germany, as indeed in Italy (where the bombing of Rome was aimed at hastening an armistice), the situation was different. Even so, no matter how cautiously the Transportation Plan was put into effect, it was liable to be very costly in human terms, as Supreme Headquarters readily acknowledged.

British fears rested on predictions that were pessimistic, to say the least. At the beginning of April the War Cabinet estimated that Allied raids could claim 80,000–160,000 victims—half of them fatalities. But the British government did not consider the question from the point of view of morality or compassion. It worried instead that the large number of casualties would set the liberated against their liberators, both during the war and afterward. The foreign secretary, Anthony Eden, argued that railway workers—the group likely to be hardest hit—would withhold their support from the Resistance in the first instance, and later from Allied troops. In the longer term a policy that in many respects appeared to be criminal risked irremediably tarnishing the reputation of Great Britain in the eyes of the French people.[21] Both Vichy and Berlin lashed out against the Allied bombing. Churchill, for his part, noting with alarm that the RAF was dropping twelve times as many bombs on France as the USAF was, feared that the prestige of Great Britain would suffer by comparison with that of the United States.[22]

In a message addressed to Eisenhower on 3 April Churchill asked that the Allied high command reject a murderous strategy. Eisenhower replied two days later, saying that although he was trying to do "everything possible to avoid loss of life among our friends," it would be "sheer folly to abstain from doing anything that can increase in any measure our chances for success in Overlord."[23] On 29 April, in the wake of a meeting of the War Cabinet two days earlier, Churchill pressed for assurances that the objectives selected would cause fewer than 100 civilian deaths per site.[24] Eisenhower agreed at once to suspend attacks against twenty-seven targets but then changed his mind several days later, on the grounds that "such a modification would emasculate the entire plan."[25] Total casualties, he pointed out, were lower than anticipated (including three thousand to four thousand deaths, according to the estimates of his staff).[26] With the support of Roosevelt, who urged him to reject "any instruction that might interfere with the commanding in the field," and General Marie-Pierre Koenig, who considered the risks to the civilian population to be acceptable, Eisenhower stood firm.[27] The offensive resumed on 5 May, but on the express condition that every attempt would be made to spare the most heavily populated areas (among them two objectives situated very near Paris). Churchill insisted, yet again, that civilian fatalities must not exceed ten thousand in all.

The Allies therefore officially ruled out a strategy of massive destruction with regard to France. On 2 June Eisenhower reminded the air force chiefs, "Much of the air fighting will take place over the heads of friendly people, who have endured the savagery of the Germans for years. Humanity and the principles for which we fight demand from our pilots scrupulous care to avoid any but military targets."[28] As a practical matter, however, this amounted to a rather empty hope, since neither the aircraft used (four-engine bombers) nor the method employed (carpet bombing by the RAF) allowed for precision. Ultimately, the Allies were unwilling to allow the fate of the civilian population to interfere with a strategy that, rightly or wrongly, was considered vital to the success of OVERLORD. Faced with the difficult choice between forgoing particular targets and pursuing the objectives of the Transportation Plan, they sought to minimize the carnage of the campaign in Normandy by taking all possible steps to prevent the enemy from transferring additional forces to the theater. All things considered, this approach was both circumspect and restrained.

It nonetheless was responsible for a great many casualties. Between June 1940 and May 1945, some 600,000 tons of bombs were dropped on France (or roughly 22 percent of the total dropped by Anglo-American forces in Europe), causing 67,078 deaths. Of this number, 503,000 tons fell during 1944 alone, which, with its 35,317 fatalities—53 percent of the total number—was by far the most murderous year. The raids on the marshaling yards at La Chapelle on 20 April 1944 (670 dead), Cambrai on 27 April (127 dead), Saint-Étienne on 26 May (1,084 dead), and Rouen during the week straddling the end of May and the beginning of June (260 dead) were particularly lethal.[29]

Disabling the transportation network in France, with all its gruesome consequences, was probably the price that had to be paid if NEPTUNE was to go forward with a reasonable chance of success and if a favorable relation of forces vis-à-vis the Reich was to be established in the long term.[30] For this purpose, cooperation with the Soviets was essential as well.

## COOPERATING

Until late fall 1943, interallied relations had been poisoned by mutual mistrust. The guarantees obtained for OVERLORD during the Teheran Conference, together with promising developments on the eastern front, led Moscow to regard the situation with somewhat greater equanimity. "Roosevelt has given his word that large-scale action will be mounted in France in 1944," Stalin confided to Marshal Zhukov. "I believe he will keep his word. But even if he doesn't, we have enough of our own forces to complete the rout of Nazi Germany."[31] The Soviet defeat of the Germans at Stalingrad in February, the failure of the Wehrmacht's Operation

CITADEL at Kursk in July, and finally the success at Teheran in extracting the promise of a landing combined to produce a change of attitude that did not escape the American leaders' notice. "It appeared that the whole propaganda machine was turned on to promote enthusiasm for the 'Historic Decisions' at Teheran which had solidified Allied unity in the common purpose to shorten the war and to secure the peace."[32] Other factors reinforced this optimism.

Until 1943 the aid approved for the Soviets within the framework of lend-lease had been relatively modest. Whereas the United States had given the equivalent of $5.8 billion to Great Britain in 1941–1942, it provided the Soviet Union with only $1.2 billion during the same period. Great Britain's assistance was smaller still, amounting by June 1943 to £188 million, or approximately $750 million.[33] The defensive successes of the Red Army at Moscow and Leningrad, as well as its victory at Stalingrad, therefore owed little to Allied aid. From 1943 onward, however, the Anglo-American financial contribution weighed more heavily, in both quantitative and qualitative terms. Between 1943 and 1945 the USSR received $9.3 billion from the United States and 1.24 billion pounds (about $5 billion) from Great Britain, with 57 percent of lend-lease transfers by value being made during the eighteen months between July 1943 and December 1944.[34] Contrary to what is usually supposed, military matériel—airplanes, guns, and tanks—by no means made up the main part of this assistance; indeed, it fell off in relative terms, declining on the American side from 63.2 percent of the total amount in 1942 to 49.9 percent in 1943, and then dropping further, to 43.8 percent in 1944.[35] The balance consisted of industrial goods, vehicles, foodstuffs, and agricultural products.

The economic impact of lend-lease and other forms of mutual assistance, though hardly negligible, should not be overestimated, for these mechanisms accounted altogether for only 4 percent of the total American and British expenditures during the course of the war. For the years 1943–1944, net imports added roughly 10 percent to the Soviet GNP.[36] Nonetheless, the contribution made by Washington and London proved to be decisive in two respects: first, high-technology products, by increasing the striking power of the Red Army, allowed it to take the offensive against Nazi forces; second, the transfer of merchandise gave the Soviet economy breathing room it desperately needed, enabling Moscow to replenish a stock of fixed capital assets that had been severely depleted by military operations and, no less important, to feed its people. Between October 1941 and May 1945 the Americans sent 4.5 million tons of foodstuffs—canned foods, sugar, salt, and "some terrible-looking greasy white food called fat-back which the Russians loved to spread on black bread."[37]

Of every dollar of lend-lease aid, only twenty-five cents went directly toward Soviet military expenditures, the remainder serving to replace machinery, increase transport capacity (especially trucks), and improve the alarmingly low standard of living of the civilian population.[38] What is more, almost all this aid reached Russia safely. Whereas 12 percent of lend-lease shipping was sunk by U-boats in 1942, 99 percent made it through the German Navy's defenses unscathed in 1943, thanks to better-protected convoys. To further limit the risk of attack, shipping routes were diversified: some seaborne cargo was sent through Vladivostok, thus avoiding the Arctic Ocean; other freight passed overland through the Persian corridor.[39] Whatever its other effects may have been, by alleviating the mistrust that Russia felt toward America and Britain, the assistance given by the West unquestionably helped strengthen Allied unity.

There was no question either, by the end of 1943, that Moscow intended to see the war through to the end. In the meantime, however, Germany and the Soviet Union had initiated diplomatic contacts, in the utmost secrecy. Edgar Klaus, a German military counterespionage agent stationed in Stockholm, enjoyed good relations with the Soviet delegation there and served on several occasions as an intermediary between the two governments. In March 1943 a compromise peace had been suggested by Hitler's private secretary, Martin Bormann. Meetings subsequently took place in the Swedish capital between the Reich's ambassador, Victor Prinz zu Weid, and his Soviet counterpart, Alexandra Kollontai. In June 1943 another meeting occurred, between the Soviet diplomat Mikhail Nikitkin and the press spokesman of the German Ministry of Foreign Affairs, Paul Karl Schmidt.[40] During the summer, Stalin toyed with the idea of a separate peace with Germany, on the condition that the Reich withdrew from the territories it had occupied in the East and guaranteed Russian autonomy over a part of this region, notably Poland. Discussions along these lines resumed in Stockholm in the fall with Goebbels's support.[41] Shrouded in a "fog of contradictions," they ran aground over Hitler's obstinacy; but there were objective reasons for the impasse as well. "For the moment," Goebbels remarked, "concluding a peace with [Stalin] is a utopian idea. What we want, Stalin needs, and what he does not wish to give up, we have: Ukraine, which provides us with food, and the Donets Basin, which provides us with coal and iron, and thus assures our production of steel. We could not relinquish these, for in that case we would lose the war."[42]

Throughout this period, then, Moscow was not averse to entertaining German overtures, communicated at regular intervals by discreet emissaries. In the beginning, Stalin probably had a real interest in a separate peace, which promised to rescue his country from what then appeared to be imminent defeat. Later, having regained the upper hand militarily in the aftermath of the Battle of Kursk, he used these desultory discussions as a means of putting pressure on the Western governments to open a second front. On the German side, envoys from the SS, Wilhelmstrasse, and the intelligence services approached the Soviets through the Swedish channel without Hitler's knowledge. Although they may well have inquired into the possibility of a negotiated settlement, it is more likely that their main purpose was to sow discord among the Allies. In the end, these talks—always initiated by the Reich—were undermined by the mutual hostility of the two dictators: neither Hitler nor Stalin could have renounced their war aims, even supposing they had wanted to. At all events, Russo-German conversations (the importance of which was sometimes exaggerated after the war) came to nothing.

Whatever their motivation may have been, the Soviets decided well before the Moscow and Teheran Conferences to come clean with their Western partners. They officially notified Washington and London of the Stockholm talks and alerted them on 16 September 1943 to Tokyo's offer to act as an intermediary between Berlin and Moscow.[43] After the tensions of the previous months, the USSR now offered proof of its good faith, by forsaking its maneuvering with the Reich. Indeed, it had every interest in cooperating, especially inasmuch as the prospect of OVERLORD had now provided a more concrete basis for Allied collaboration.

The conference of foreign ministers held in Moscow between 18 and 30 October was a step in this direction. From the diplomatic point of view, it produced some movement toward settling postwar issues. The USSR gave its support to the principle of a common authority for the occupied countries, whose future would be decided by a European Advisory Commission—a way to avoid carving up the Continent into spheres of influence. Germany was to hand back the territories it had seized since 1938, give up East Prussia, and pay reparations to its conquerors. A declaration on German atrocities, calling openly for the punishment of war criminals, was also adopted.[44] On the strategic level, the Soviets suggested that Turkey be encouraged to enter the conflict and suggested seeking permission from Stockholm for the use of Swedish bases to intensify the air offensive against the Reich—proposals that met with a cool reception from Great Britain and the United States.[45] The Americans, for their part, demanded sharing of meteorological information, improved military communications, and the right to use Soviet airfields for conducting shuttle bombing missions against targets in Germany and the oil fields in Romania (aircraft taking off from bases in Italy and Great Britain would land in the Soviet Union in order to refuel, thereby shortening flying time and increasing the number of missions that could be flown). "These proposals hit the Soviet representatives as a bolt from the blue," but they agreed to them in principle.[46] With Stalin's promise a month later at Teheran that the Red Army would launch an offensive to coincide with the start of OVERLORD, East-West cooperation had finally gone beyond the mere declaration of good intentions.

Already in October Washington and London had dispatched military missions to Moscow, led respectively by General John R. Deane and General Sir Giffard Le Quesne Martel (and later, beginning in February 1944, by Lieutenant General M. Brocas Burrows) in order to work out the details of the new entente. The results were on the whole disappointing. In December General William J. Donovan, head of the U.S. Office of

Strategic Services (OSS), negotiated an agreement with the Russian secret police and intelligence service, the NKVD, that provided for an exchange of agents. Roosevelt, alarmed at the prospect of Soviet spies operating in the United States in the months leading up to a presidential
election, suspended the arrangement in March 1944. Moscow had nonetheless agreed at the end of January to the establishment of an American
radio station in Moscow that would provide "instant and reliable communication between the United States and the Soviet Union."[47] Exchanges of meteorological data were made possible by the creation of a
network of some one hundred stations covering the United States, the
Atlantic, Western Europe, and Russia (though not the Far East, owing to
a lack of adequate facilities in Siberia). Finally, following long discussions
in February, the Soviets made three bases available to the U.S. Air Force,
beginning in May. On 2 June seventy-three Fortresses took off from Italy
and, after bombing the airport at Debrecen in eastern Hungary, landed
for the first time in Ukraine, at Poltava. On the night of 21–22 June, however, the Luftwaffe managed to reach this base without encountering resistance from Soviet antiaircraft artillery or fighters, destroyed more than
forty American planes, and killed thirty-two soldiers (two Americans and
thirty Soviets). Although neither Allied government publicly blamed the
other for the debacle, dissension, mistrust, and resentment filtered down
through the ranks on both sides, dimming the prospects for future cooperation. From then on Poltava was used mainly as a base from which to
recover aircraft forced to land behind Soviet lines. In all, only eighteen
USAF raids relied on Soviet bases for refueling.[48]

If military·cooperation was confined to a few perfunctory exchanges,
this outcome was not due to any lack of effort on the part of London and
Washington. Apart from the matériel furnished in the form of lend-lease
and other transfers, the Soviets benefited from a constant stream of information about Allied strategy. Beginning in October 1943, the Americans
provided them with a regular statement of operations, without asking for
anything in return. On 29 February 1944, for the first time, the Allies
summarized the progress made in preparing for OVERLORD, thereafter
transmitting a second report on the same subject on 25 March and, on 13

May, a final update.[49] Notified of the date of the landing on 6 April, Deane and Burrows forwarded the information on the tenth to Marshal Aleksandr Vasilevsky, chief of the general staff, Roosevelt and Churchill having notified Stalin by telegram the day before—less as a point of courtesy than for the purpose of giving the Red Army as much time as possible to plan the companion operation promised at Teheran.[50] The Soviets were rather less forthcoming, however. It must be said that their mode of government, founded on institutionalized paranoia, hardly favored openness—not least because the strident anti-Bolshevism current in Britain and America since 1917 had left its mark on a generation of Soviet political and military leaders. Roosevelt and Churchill, "not believ[ing] that a leopard could change its spots overnight," were in any case guarded in their expectations.[51] Moscow felt much the same way, as General Sergei Shtemenko later recalled: "We did not forget, of course, that the nature of the anti-Hitler coalition was contradictory and might produce all kinds of surprises. The agreed date for the opening of the second front was very much in doubt. Even at Teheran it had been hedged about with all kinds of reservations by the Allies. The watchword of both GHQ [general headquarters] and the General Staff was, therefore: rely on the Allies but don't be caught napping ourselves."[52] Similarly, the USSR refused to allow its hands to be tied with regard to postwar arrangements. "As I look back over the pattern of Russia's collaboration with the Western allies," General Deane wrote in 1947,

there emerges constantly evidence of Russia's desire to avoid any entanglements from which she would have difficulty in extricating herself in the postwar world. Russia wanted to fight and end the war with none of the heterogeneous mixture of troops, divided responsibilities, and mutual obligations which the British and Americans were prepared to accept with regard to each other. Russia's position at the end of the war was to be that which she herself had won—a position which Russia would control free of obligations and interference from her allies. True, she was ready to conduct her military operations so as to assist the

Western powers if this would hasten the defeat of Germany, but she would conduct them alone and with the minimum conversation with her British and American friends.[53]

Nonetheless, it is clear that the invasion of France remained a matter of paramount concern for the Soviets. Nothing aroused Moscow's mistrust more than the procrastination of the Western governments, which, having promised a second front so many times, had just as often pushed back the starting date. "The more I contact Russians here the more convinced I am that they will never forgive us if OVERLORD has to be postponed," General Burrows emphasized two months before the invasion, recommending that a policy of the greatest possible transparency be adopted toward Russia.[54]

Two contradictory sentiments troubled the Soviet leadership with regard to the landing in Normandy. On the one hand, the Kremlin feared that the war would end more quickly than expected, thus prompting its partners to cancel OVERLORD. An invasion of France, without being absolutely crucial, nonetheless had the great advantage of lightening the Red Army's burden and limiting its losses. On the other hand, worry that rapid Anglo-American successes would tarnish the glorious achievements of the Red Army led Stalin to launch a preemptive propaganda campaign, lamenting the delay in opening a second front, minimizing the difficulties inherent in the enterprise, and criticizing Eisenhower's strategy (particularly the concern for avoiding casualties). The idea that London and Washington were dragging their feet, waiting for the moment when circumstances would favor minimal losses of troops and equipment, seems to have found a receptive audience.[55] A joke making the rounds in Moscow had it that an "Old Believer" was someone who thought that the second front would really be opened one day.[56]

In the face of such recalcitrance, the Anglo-American military missions were no more likely to bring about an era of radiant confidence than other attempts to promote trust and cooperation. "We never make a request or proposal to the Soviets that is not viewed with suspicion," General Deane noted with exasperation. "They simply cannot understand giving without taking, and as a result even our giving is viewed with suspicion. Gratitude cannot be banked in the Soviet Union. Each transaction is complete in itself without regard to past favors. The party of the second part is either a shrewd trader to be admired or a sucker to be despised. . . . In short, we are in the position of being at the same time the givers and the supplicants. This is neither dignified nor healthy for U.S. prestige."[57]

The British and Americans persevered nonetheless, showing a patience toward the Soviets that bordered on the angelic. This poorly rewarded strategy has sometimes been regarded as further proof of Roosevelt's naïveté. But there was more than a little self-interest in his calculations. Already for almost three years the Soviet Union had borne the greatest share of the war's burdens alone. At the beginning of June 1944, 239 German divisions—some 62 percent of the Wehrmacht's troops— were still fighting in the East.[58] If helping the Red Army fight the Reich was manifestly in the interest of the Western powers before the invasion of Normandy, persisting in this course was all the more necessary after 6 June, to prevent the German high command from taking advantage of a lull on the Russian front to transfer surplus troops to the French theater. However much reluctance London and Washington may have felt about supporting Moscow, it was overcome by a prudent regard for their own safety. "The US and British views were fundamentally similar," noted Field Marshal Sir John Dill, the senior British representative to the CCS, "in that the principal objective was to assist the Russians to kill Germans and later Japanese and not to ask too much in return from the Russians."[59] Russia fought bravely and well, General Deane allowed after the war, "but she did it to save her own skin and for no other purpose. On the other hand, we should be honest with ourselves and admit that our most compelling motive in sending supplies to Russia was to save our [own] skins."[60] The Western powers therefore enjoyed a very small margin of maneuver in negotiation, since by 1944 they had more need of the Soviet Union than the Soviet Union had of them. That the Soviets should have been disinclined to cooperate with their partners beyond the minimum degree necessary merely emphasized the naked realities of the situation—realities of which the Western leaders were at bottom perfectly aware.

## Deceiving

In addition to the Transportation Plan and the Soviet summer offensive, the Western Allies counted on the element of strategic surprise to prevent the Germans from massing their troops in Normandy. In view of the unfavorable relation between the attacking and defending forces at the moment of landing, it was necessary to mislead the Germans not only about the place where the Anglo-American forces would come ashore, but also the day and the hour of the invasion. This meant having to create in the mind of the enemy a false idea of the real objectives of OVERLORD. The Allies enjoyed three considerable advantages: the ability, thanks to Ultra, to decode a large portion of German military communications; the geographical character of Great Britain, whose insularity offered protection against enemy infiltration; and the consummate expertise of Great Britain in matters of espionage.

General Morgan and his staff had envisaged deploying weapons of disinformation from the first, without, however, advancing beyond the planning stage: until strategy had been agreed upon, the spies could not act. There was no point, quite obviously, in diverting the enemy's attention toward the Pas de Calais if in the end the Allies were to decide to land there. Moreover, a disinformation campaign had already been mounted in the first half of 1943 to protect operations in the Mediterranean. Within the framework of the COCKADE plan, scenarios were conceived to suggest to the Germans that the invasion of Europe would take place in Norway (code name TINDALL), Brittany (WADHAM), and the Pas de Calais (STARKEY)—an unfortunate initiative, to say the least, at a moment when the Allied high command was contemplating landing forces in the northwestern part of France.[61] The people at COSSAC had little choice but to recast the terms of the deception. Rather than disavow an intention to invade along the Channel coast, which the Germans in any case suspected, it sought to mislead the enemy with regard to the exact place and date. Once Normandy had been selected as the landing site, the Pas de Calais was to be held in reserve as a lure. On 20 November 1943 a directive was issued tracing the main lines of Operation FORTITUDE. There were three main objectives:

a. To induce the German Command to believe that the main assault and follow up will be in or east of the Pas de Calais area, thereby encouraging the enemy to maintain or increase the strength of his air and ground forces and his fortifications there at the expense of other areas, particularly of the Caen area.

b. To keep the enemy in doubt as to the date and time of the actual assault.

c. During and after the main assault, to contain the largest possible German land and air forces in or east of the Pas de Calais for at least fourteen days.[62]

In spite of the Americans' skepticism, the Teheran Conference explicitly reserved a prominent role for these stratagems, to which Churchill gave the code name BODYGUARD. "In wartime," he memorably observed, "truth is so precious that she should always be attended by a bodyguard of lies."[63] On 24 December, after being amended seven times, BODYGUARD was presented to the Combined Chiefs of Staff, who gave it their blessing. The Germans were to be led to believe that the Allies would intensify the bombing of Germany (Operation POINTBLANK) and strengthen the offensive in Italy. In the spring, with the help of the Soviets, they would strike out into Norway, and in the summer turn south toward Denmark. The brunt of the Anglo-American effort would nonetheless be aimed at the Balkans. To the Canadian and American forces fell the task of establishing control over the Dalmatian coast, while the British were to take sole responsibility for Greece. The Soviets were to take part in this action as well, joining British forces in making a landing on the Black Sea coast of Bulgaria and Romania. The cross-Channel attack would be postponed until late summer or fall, when the fifty divisions supposed to be necessary would finally be in place.[64]

Hitler was not fooled by the feints toward the Mediterranean and Scandinavia. In designating northern France, by the terms of Directive no. 51 of 3 November 1943, as the place "where the enemy must and will attack," and in reinforcing the defenses along the Channel coast, he forced COSSAC to change its tactics.[65] Although the Allies were unaware of the exact provisions of the Führer's directive, renewed German activity along the coast from the Cotentin Peninsula to Belgium, together with messages intercepted by the British intelligence services, indicated that the German high command anticipated an invasion in northwestern Europe.[66] In the circumstances, asking the enemy to believe that three great Allied offensives would take place in 1944—in the Balkans, Scandinavia, and northern France—was unlikely to succeed; indeed, the Joint Staff Planners frankly recognized the possibility that BODYGUARD might collapse under its own weight. But while admitting the "general weakness" of the scheme, they found themselves incapable of proposing an "acceptable alternative concept."[67]

The overall arrangement was nonetheless thoroughly reexamined in February 1944. To protect the cross-Channel operation, another plan, known as FORTITUDE, was developed within the framework of BODYGUARD that comprised two wings. The first, FORTITUDE NORTH was intended to make Berlin believe that on or about 1 May the Allies would invade Norway, landing at Stavanger and proceeding from there toward Oslo. Two weeks later, supported by the Soviets, they would open up a supply route through northern Norway and Sweden. Stockholm's cooperation was to be solicited as well, so that the Allies, moving from Swedish bases in a final phase, could attack Denmark in the summer.[68] To make this threat credible, a phantom British Fourth Army with 350,000 men was created and placed under the notional command of General Sir Andrew Thorne. Radio traffic was fabricated beginning on 22 March;[69] double agents working for the XX Committee of MI5 (the "Double-Cross System") were used to persuade their German controllers of the veracity of the scheme; misleading information was deliberately leaked to the press and radio. British agents in Norway began to make "discreet, but not too discreet, inquiries about the snow levels in the Kjölen Mountains, the great spine of Norway. Would the bridge over the Rauma at Åndalsnes support medium infantry tanks? Was the 142nd Infantry Battalion of the SS Mountain Division Prinz Eugen still at Stjordalshalsen?"[70]

The Soviets gave unusually strong support to this plan. Colonel John H. Bevan, chief of the London Controlling Section (LCS), a secret unit under Churchill's personal authority having special responsibility for deception schemes, went to Moscow for five weeks, from 30 January to 6 March, accompanied by his American subordinate Colonel William H. Baumer, for the purpose of coordinating Russian participation.[71] In order to keep German forces in the Balkans until D-Day, they asked for the Soviet Union's help in simulating large-scale attacks against the Bulgarian and Romanian coasts, and attacks against Norway and Finland, to distract Hitler's twenty-seven Scandinavian divisions. Finally, and most important, Soviet assistance was requested to persuade the Germans that the Red Army would not launch its grand offensive until the beginning of July.[72]

Discussions became bogged down over the Soviet Foreign Ministry's unwillingness to threaten Sofia, with which Moscow still maintained diplomatic ties. Eventually Molotov gave way, signing the draft agreement on 4 March 1944.[73] The Soviets undertook, first, to bomb objectives in Finland and Norway, using maps furnished by the British.[74] They agreed furthermore to mount raids on both these countries, which would lend credence to the idea of an all-out Allied attack against Scandinavia. In order to allay fears in Stockholm and Oslo that the Soviets might be tempted to stay indefinitely, the British Foreign Office directed its ambassador to Moscow, Sir Archibald Clark Kerr, to urge Molotov that he give the Norwegian ambassador assurances of the purity of his government's intentions.[75] In May 1944, true to their word, the Soviets feigned naval attacks in the north of Scandinavia and, marshaling ships, troops, and equipment on the Kola Peninsula, carried out aerial and naval reconnaissance of the Norwegian coast between Vardø and Berlevag. And, again as promised, they put out rumors that their offensive would not be launched before summer, issuing false instructions to the commanders of reserve units to prepare their troops for action in July.[76] After 1 June FORTITUDE NORTH was put to bed, but not before the Germans had been encouraged to believe that the Allied assault on Scandinavia would occur only after the cross-Channel invasion of France, in the spring of 1945. In the event, Hitler not only kept his divisions in Norway, but reinforced them—a very considerable force that might otherwise have been deployed in Normandy.[77]

The main thrust of BODYGUARD nonetheless depended on its second wing, FORTITUDE SOUTH—the attack on the Pas de Calais that Hitler himself had forecast in November 1943. The deception in this case consisted in leading the Germans to believe that the Allies would invade at the end of July, with six divisions launching an initial assault to the east and south from Cape Gris-Nez; in all, some fifty divisions would participate in a grand offensive aimed at taking Antwerp (for its port) and Brussels (for its communications network).[78] In order to give substance to this threat, the Allies devised a stratagem called QUICKSILVER, in hopes of persuading the Germans that the landing in Normandy—impossible to deny once it had begun—represented only a diversion: the real attack would take place later, farther to the north on the Channel coast, spearheaded by the First U.S. Army Group (FUSAG) under the command of General Patton (twenty-two divisions in all, belonging to the First Canadian Army and the Third U.S. Army). By the summer of 1944 FUSAG would enjoy a very real existence under the authority of General Bradley, but for the time being this embryonic group of armies was little more than a figment of FORTITUDE's imagination.

To lend credence to this fable, the Allies left no stone unturned. Patton was under orders from Eisenhower to keep a low profile—a role that scarcely suited his temperament. Immediately following his appointment in late January, the fiery general went to the theater in London and then to a reception at the Savoy Hotel, where journalists at once noticed his presence. In April he went to Knutsford, where he made his unfortunate speech about "manifest destiny." Several things—notably the surprising media coverage of the event—suggest that Patton, well known to be constitutionally incapable of holding his tongue, had been made an unwitting accomplice of a plan meant to reveal to Berlin both his presence and the nature of his command.[79] Other stratagems were employed as well. Beginning on 24 April 1944, radio traffic was generated to suggest the presence of an assembling army and staff. If the Luftwaffe was to draw erroneous conclusions from its aerial reconnaissance, however, "the Quicksilver army group had to be seen as well as heard. There had to be troop concentrations, tank parks, petrol dumps, hospitals, pipelines, sewage farms—all the weft and warp of life created by the existence of a million men. And these military installations began to appear on the British landscape—fabricated, much as Hollywood might create a film set, out of lumber, rubber, wire and cardboard."[80] At the beginning of June, 240 dummy LCTs floated in ports between Yarmouth and Folkestone and a giant oil storage facility was constructed near Dover.[81]

The Allied high command nevertheless placed little hope in these subterfuges, for they mobilized a great many actors for a very small audience. Not only were the few Abwehr agents left in Great Britain by the spring of 1944 all working for MI5, but the Luftwaffe was no longer in a position to conduct sustained reconnaissance of the British archipelago (in the six weeks before D-Day it was able to carry out only 129 overflights).[82] The once legendary capabilities of German radio monitoring had markedly deteriorated too, and as a result the prospects for successful deception were still further reduced.

The Allies were therefore obliged to resort to networks of double agents run by MI5's XX Committee. The most effective of these networks was directed by the mythical "Garbo," a Catalan named Juan Pujol who managed to get himself hired by German military intelligence at the beginning of the war, in hopes of then being sent to Great Britain to serve the Allies. Still today, Pujol's motivations remain obscure.[83] Was he seeking a way to fight for what he considered a just cause, or merely a path to social advancement? Whatever the case, his initial offer to work for the British, made to MI6 in Madrid in January 1941, was rejected, and he turned to the Germans. Working from Lisbon, Pujol sent his Abwehr superiors an endless stream of highly detailed intelligence reports about Allied preparations in Great Britain—the product of his extraordinary imagination, supplemented by miscellaneous information gleaned from guidebooks and reference works. Thanks to Ultra, the British intercepted these messages and, convinced by February 1942 that the Germans had complete faith in Pujol, brought him to England via Gibraltar later the same year, in order to make use of his exceptional skills.

After working for a time on behalf of the COCKADE plan, Garbo was assigned to FORTITUDE SOUTH—a heaven-sent opportunity, as it happened, since on 5 January 1944 his German controller asked him to find out the date and location of the cross-Channel operations planned by the Allies, and to provide details about the enemy's order of battle. Garbo was delighted to comply, communicating to Berlin a wealth of information that he claimed to have gathered from a network of highly placed informers, twenty-seven in all.[84] One operative worked at the War Office; another had succeeded in corrupting a Greek sailor with Communist sympathies, as well as a talkative lieutenant of the Forty-ninth Infantry Division.[85] Other imaginary agents ("Donny," "Dick," and "Derrick") monitored the troop movements at Dover, Brighton, and Harwich. Garbo himself had a privileged vantage point, for he worked part-time at the Ministry of Information.[86] To communicate with the Reich, he made use of a clandestine wireless channel, in addition to messages written in invisible ink and sent to Madrid, and from there duly forwarded by his controller to Berlin. In all, this incomparable agent wrote 315 secret letters and transmitted some 1,200 radio messages, all of them feverishly scrutinized by the Abwehr.[87] On 21 January he reported that "the Anglo-American offensive against the Continent, *should this take place,* would not happen for a long time." On 21 April he emphasized that although he could not altogether rule out the possibility that a second front might become a reality one day, "what I am able to guarantee you once again is that for the moment our strict vigilance has not noted any fact from which we can stress to you the danger of the supposed action. . . . I recommend therefore once again calm and confidence in our work. The Allies have used tricks to date, and it is deplorable that those in Germany should give credence to the majority of them."[88]

Other double agents also helped make FORTITUDE SOUTH—and QUICK-SILVER in particular—a success. Dusko Popov, a young Yugoslav operating under the code name Tricycle, was recruited by the Abwehr in 1940 to spy for Germany in London. After various missions, he returned in February 1944 to Lisbon, armed by MI6 with a counterfeit order of battle for OVERLORD that the German intelligence services, despite some initial hesitation, took at face value.[89] Captain Roman Garby-Czerniawski, a Polish officer associated after the fall of France in June 1940 with Interallié, a Franco-Polish resistance network, had been arrested by the Germans in Paris the following year. Turned by the Abwehr, he was sent as a German agent to Great Britain, but not before having made contact in Madrid with a British escape-line officer who recommended him to the XX

Committee.[90] On the eve of the landing, Garby-Czerniawski performed the very useful function—at least in the eyes of the Germans—of acting as Polish liaison with the staff of FUSAG.[91]

Through the brilliant use of these double agents, the Allies were able to persuade the Germans that the landing would take place in the Pas de Calais. There were, however, a few close calls. On 18 February 1944 Admiral Wilhelm Canaris was dismissed by Hitler as head of the Abwehr, which subsequently came under the authority of Walter Schellenberg, the chief of the Sicherheitsdienst (SD), the security arm of the SS. The poisoned atmosphere that had long reigned between the two services and the witch hunt that was launched threatened Pujol. But the SD, handicapped by its eclectic methods of recruitment, had too great a need for experienced spies to be able to afford the luxury of persecuting Canaris's best men. Very fortunately, then, Pujol slipped through the net.[92] The Artist affair, by contrast, posed a more serious danger. In July 1943, Johann Jebsen, the Abwehr officer who earlier had recruited Popov in Lisbon, approached MI5 and offered reliable information about secret weapons and the Schwarze Kapelle (Black Orchestra), the highly secret anti-Nazi movement founded by Canaris that was plotting to overthrow Hitler. The British enlisted Jebsen's services, giving him the pseudonym Artist. But the SD, suspecting Jebsen of irregular financial dealings in Lisbon (though not of links with Popov), arrested him on 29 April 1944.[93] Drugged and placed in a tin trunk, he was brought from Spain to France before being sent on to Germany. The whole edifice of Allied deception threatened to fall apart if Jebsen broke under torture and revealed the Double-Cross System. Supreme Headquarters staff were filled with the greatest anxiety. In the event, Jebsen—executed by firing squad shortly after D-Day—carried his secrets with him to the grave, preserving the mystery of FORTITUDE.[94]

Additional plans were incorporated into the general framework of the BODYGUARD plan. OAKFIELD, meant to mislead the Germans about Allied operations in the Mediterranean, had to be revised in January 1944 to accommodate Operation SHINGLE (which announced landings at Pisa and Rimini aimed at blocking German exit routes from Italy).[95] A new scenario for the region (ZEPPELIN) was therefore devised that warned of an

Allied attack on the Balkans, Crete, and the Peloponnesus, on the one hand, and against the Istrian Peninsula and Dalmatia on the other, in hopes of inducing the Germans to keep their forces on the Mediterranean perimeter rather than shift them to the French theater. Another fictitious formation—the Twelfth British Army—was given responsibility for the Greek wing of the operation, and the Seventh U.S. Army had responsibility for the Yugoslav wing.[96] Pressure was also to be exerted on the Turkish government, through the dispatch to Ankara of a British military mission charged with involving Turkey in the war. But this scheme ran aground for lack of troops: the transfer of so many Allied divisions from the Middle East to Italy, leaving only three modest formations in place, would deprive an attack on the Balkans of virtually all credibility. In mid-April, General Sir Henry Maitland Wilson proposed moving the Second British Division from India to the Middle East—a ploy that together with various ruses would make it possible to raise the presumptive number of divisions available for the offensive to the more plausible figure of eight.[97] General Brooke declined this suggestion on 17 April. The Foreign Office, for its part, advised against bringing pressure to bear on Ankara on the grounds that the contemplated military mission would run "contrary to our present policy of indifference and aloofness" toward Turkey.[98]

ZEPPELIN was therefore amended to prevent German forces stationed in the South of France from being moved northward, and an attack in the western Mediterranean, aimed at the Sète-Narbonne sector of the French coast (Operation VENDETTA), was substituted for the pretended assault on Greece. Intense activity was simulated at Oran, Bône, and Ferryville on the Algerian littoral, complete with dummy landing craft. A full-scale amphibious exercise took place between 9 and 11 June: thirteen thousand men and two thousand vehicles embarked at Oran and took to the sea for three days. The Allies in the meantime (knowing that word would make its way to Berlin) had asked the Spanish government for permission to evacuate wounded combatants to hospitals in Spain.[99] Another scheme, ROYAL FLUSH, was proposed as a means of giving the appearance of diplomatic contact with Turkey, Bulgaria, and Sweden (all of them neutral countries), causing the Germans to suspect that Allied military intervention in those regions was imminent.[100] Additional measures involved the emission of false sonar signals by Allied submarines and a plan to reduce the bombing of Normandy by a factor of two in relation to other areas in the weeks leading up to D-Day.

This vast disinformation campaign therefore took its place alongside two others—the effort to cripple the French transport network and the launching of a Soviet offensive—aimed at slowing the increase of enemy troops in the Norman theater. By means of these devices, in concert with a logistical plan that the Allies counted on to bring up their own reinforcements precisely on schedule, the planners at Supreme Headquarters sought to obtain both a strategic and a tactical advantage. The chances of success, however, remained uncertain. If the Allies' logistical and military plans were to achieve their objectives, the Germans had to fall into the traps that the Allied intelligence services had set for them. For in the late spring of 1944 the Third Reich remained, despite many reverses, a very formidable power indeed.

# 6

# THE OTHER SIDE OF THE HILL

THE SUCCESS OF THE LANDING DEPENDED first and foremost on the military strength the Allies could muster, which is to say their ability to bring to bear sufficient forces to defeat the Germans. But it also depended on the accuracy of their assessment of the German order of battle and their capacity to weaken the Wehrmacht's strategic position in the months preceding NEPTUNE.

## GERMAN STRATEGY

The resistance of Great Britain in the summer of 1940, no less than the invasion of the Soviet Union in June 1941, had significantly altered the military situation facing the Third Reich. All hope of eliminating its major adversary in the West by means of a decisive campaign, before opening a front in the East, sank in the sands of Dunkirk and vanished in the skies over London, where the Royal Air Force inflicted a stunning defeat on the Luftwaffe during the Battle of Britain. Having lost the opportunity to achieve aerial and naval dominance, Hitler had to abandon the idea of invading Great Britain. As a consequence he was forced to adopt a defensive posture in the Western theater. On 26 April 1942, following the failure of Operation BARBAROSSA before the gates of Moscow the previous December, he ordered an Atlantic "wall" to be erected that would extend from Norway to the Bay of Biscay. By equipping the coastline with a uniform set of defenses on the model of the West Wall (known to the Allies as the Siegfried Line, built in the late 1930s along Germany's western frontiers), and manning these fortifications with a minimal number of troops, the Führer counted on being able to repel an enemy landing, if not actually to discourage any attempt at invasion in the first place. The Channel coast being considered especially vulnerable, a deliberate effort was made to fortify the Pas de Calais beginning in August 1942, even though the weakness of the United Kingdom and the unpreparedness of the United States at that moment hardly seemed to justify heroic measures. The disastrous raid on Dieppe the same month, though it demonstrated to the general staff on both sides that the Allies were in no position to mount a Continental assault in the near future, also suggested that such an operation now occupied a prominent place in their priorities. On 29 September Hitler therefore ordered fifteen thousand fortified positions to be constructed along the Channel coast before the following summer, with a view to achieving a ratio of ten to twenty strongholds per kilometer.

Circumstances changed radically in 1943, once the Anglo-American forces had gained control of North Africa and invaded first Sicily, then Italy, and the Wehrmacht had suffered a crushing rout at Stalingrad, followed by the decisive setback at Kursk. The prospect of a landing in northwestern Europe, dim the year before, suddenly acquired real urgency, obliging the Reich's high command to rethink its strategy. In November 1943 Hitler ordered that construction of the Atlantic Wall be accelerated.

After three years of war, German planners were neither vain nor naive enough to believe that a few batteries strung out along the French littoral would suffice to drive enemy forces back into the sea. Field Marshal Gerd von Rundstedt, who by virtue of his appointment in March 1942 as chief of the armies stationed in the West (OB West) was responsible for the defense of northwestern Europe, expressed grave reservations about the value of the Atlantic Wall. Not only did the system of fortifications lack depth, but the troops at his disposal were insufficient in both quantity and quality. Rundstedt therefore asked to be granted an operational reserve of nine armored and motorized divisions that could be brought up immediately in the event of an Allied landing. From the strategic point of view the stakes could not have been higher, for by repelling a cross-Channel invasion the Reich would avoid having to fight on two major fronts—a situation that had been partly responsible for Germany's defeat in the First World War. Once the threat of an attack in the West had been removed, the High Command of the Armed Forces (OKW) could transfer troops to the Russian theater, as Hitler made clear to his generals on 20 March 1944: "The destruction of the enemy's landing attempt means more than a purely local decision on the Western front. It is the sole decisive factor in the whole conduct of the war and hence in its final result. The 45 divisions which we now have in Europe, excluding the Eastern front, are needed in the East, and will and must be transferred there so as to effect a fundamental change in that situation as soon as the decision in the West has been reached."[1] In committing all its forces to the struggle against the Soviet Union, the Reich could hope to achieve the victory that had eluded it for almost three years. Indeed, success in turning back an Allied landing might even make it possible to conclude a negotiated peace with Great Britain, bled dry by this point and incapable of contemplating a new invasion, with or without American aid.

Hitler's gamble was based on three assumptions: that in spite of Allied bombing the German economy could manage to furnish planners with an adequate flow of supplies; that in conducting the campaign on the Russian steppes, OKW could avoid drawing down reserves in the West too far; and that coastal defenses could be strengthened, if not to the point of preventing a landing altogether, then at least enough to make the attackers' task more arduous.

## An Economy under Siege

Between 1940 and 1944 the German war economy continued to grow: production of airplanes rose from 10,247 to 39,807, of tanks from 2,200 to 27,300, and artillery pieces from 5,000 to 41,000.[2] But these impressive statistics conceal quite uneven performance. Between 1939 and 1941 growth in the aeronautical sector was flat, and the manufacture of tanks and other armored vehicles in 1941 represented only a third of the British output. The Nazi regime had nonetheless invested considerable sums since 1936: 55.9 billion Reichmarks (RM) were devoted to the military budget in 1940–1941 and 99.4 billion RM in 1943–1944, out of total public expenditures of 80 and 130 billion RM, respectively. By 1941, however, the results had proved disappointing and placed the Reich in a quandary, as its leaders fully recognized. They therefore committed themselves to a vigorous program of standardization and rationalization. Led first by Fritz Todt, the engineer responsible for building the West Wall, and then, following his death, by the architect Albert Speer, whom Hitler had promoted to minister of armaments and munitions in early February 1942, this initiative bore its first fruits later that year. Whereas Messerschmitt had been bringing out 180 Me-109 fighters per month from seven factories, it was soon producing 1,000 per month at only three sites.[3] Against an index of 100 in 1939, German armament productivity rose from 75.9 in 1941 to 160 in 1944.

Increases in military production were made possible by an abundant labor supply—this in spite of the heavy demands on the able-bodied male population imposed by the army, which conscripted two million men in 1943 to make up for losses at the fronts. A policy of virtually universal conscription allowed the Reich to maintain impressive troop levels: still in June 1944, 6.5 million men were serving in the German armed forces. The reduction in the work force after so many young men were called up for active duty was partly offset by reliance on young and middle-aged women, who in 1944 made up 51 percent of the labor force (as opposed to 36.2 percent in Great Britain), but to an even greater degree by the peoples in conquered territories who found themselves enlisted for service in the German war machine. In a few cases these were volunteers attracted by the promise of work and the illusion of high wages, but more often they were civilians (male and female alike) and prisoners of war forced to work in the factories of the Reich, to say nothing of the vast contingents of slave labor in concentration and extermination camps. In February 1944, 2.5 million prisoners of war worked in Germany, in addition to 7 million civilians who had, as of June that year, been recruited abroad, either willingly or by force. Roughly a third of the Reich's labor population was composed of foreigners—a figure that does not include employees of industrial firms in the conquered territories that directly or indirectly contributed to the German war economy. All these factors help explain why the level of production of military equipment and supplies was 2.85 times greater in 1944 than in 1940.[4] Far from being on the verge of collapse on the eve of D-Day, German industry was indeed capable of furnishing the Wehrmacht with the matériel it needed—on three conditions.

First, a way had to be found to increase armament production still further. Allied production had been growing steadily; in 1943 it overtook that of the Reich. And if total German production the following year still exceeded that of Great Britain and the Soviet Union, it was nonetheless two and a half times less than American output.[5] By mid-1944 the Reich's armament production was only a fifth that of its enemies. The Soviet Union alone brought out 40,246 airplanes and 28,963 tanks that year, whereas Germany manufactured 39,807 and 27,300, respectively.

Second, a way had to be found to protect plants and factories against Allied bombing. Though the strategic bombing campaigns had succeeded in disrupting the German war machine, they had hardly brought about the collapse of the industrial sector, no matter what fantasies the Allied air chiefs may have entertained in that regard. Anglo-American sorties destroyed no more than 5 percent of the Reich's military production over the course of the war, even though the figure in 1944 exceeded 10 percent—a modest advantage that was dearly purchased. The British Bomber Command and the U.S. Eighth Air Force alone lost some ninety thousand men (forty-six thousand and forty-four thousand, respectively), quite apart from the enormous resources this effort mobilized (between 1940 and 1945, the Allies constructed 130,620 bombers; the Bomber Command, at the height of its raids on Germany, absorbed 12 percent of British military expenditures).[6] To reduce Nazi industrial potential by 10 percent at most, this was a very high price to pay.

Yet this accounting captures only a part of the reality. For the Allies aimed neither exclusively nor even primarily at the enemy's military-industrial complex. More than half the raids were directed at cities and transport links, as contrasted with 12 percent aimed at fuel depots and refineries and 9 percent at aircraft factories.[7] The effect of POINTBLANK was to offset the increase in overall war production in several ways: "The underlying basis for production in the future was slowly but surely eroded by bombing, while bomb attack produced cumulative disruption to the sensitive production and distribution web established to cope with the deficiencies of air production demonstrated in the early part of the war. Bombing inhibited further rationalizations, and produced a situation in which managers and workforce alike were compelled to work within certain organisational and even moral limits that the opposing economies never faced."[8] German adaptation, spectacular though it was, must not be allowed to obscure the massive disruptions caused by Allied raids. There can be no question that RAF and USAF bombing prevented the Reich's system of war production from performing to full capacity, by destroying significant segments of it and otherwise obliging Germany to shut down a great many installations and to mobilize thousands of men to defend its skies—and to clear away the rubble on the ground.

Finally, a way had to be found to restore the Luftwaffe's offensive capability. By directly threatening Germany itself, Allied pilots obliged the Luftwaffe to divert resources to protecting civilians and industrial installations. Forced to increase production of fighter planes, the German air force could no longer replace its bombers at the same rate; it was thus deprived of an essential advantage. In March 1943 it had 1,522 bombers in operation, as compared with 2,028 fighters, a ratio of 0.75; in June 1944 this proportion had fallen by more than a third, to 0.47 (1,089 bombers as against 2,301 fighters).[9] In part the difference was due to the severe setbacks the Luftwaffe had suffered in combat. For the year 1944 it lost 1,311 aircraft in January, 2,121 in February, and 2,115 in March.[10] Although German factories managed to make up the difference in fighter planes, replacing men was more difficult: experienced pilots were now a scarce commodity (2,540 were put out of action in April, and 2,461 in May)[11]—a deficit that aroused anxiety among the Nazi leadership: "The problem has to do not so much with the aircraft as with the crews," Goebbels noted. "It is also apparent that our fighter pilots are gradually becoming tired and demoralized, at least to some extent. We are losing a third of them per month, which means that at the end of three months the air squadrons are completely exhausted. They are not all dead, but some are gravely wounded, others taken prisoner, and still others lost in one way or another. An aerial formation that is subjected to such considerable losses can hold itself together only through extraordinary mental exertions."[12] Moreover, the training of replacements was hampered by a lack of fuel: the Luftwaffe's allocation had been drastically cut, falling from 180,000 tons in April to 50,000 in June.[13] Pilot training was correspondingly curtailed, instruction being reduced from 260 hours in 1942 to 110, or in some cases even as few as 50 hours, in 1944.[14]

Nevertheless, to the extent that the Third Reich was not threatened by economic collapse on the eve of D-Day, the verdict concerning the Allied strategic bombing campaign must be considered mixed at best.

## ALL QUIET ON THE WESTERN FRONT

On 5 June 1944 Germany was still conducting large-scale operations in two theaters, Italy and the Soviet Union, in addition to fighting a low-intensity war in the Balkans. For several months, the virtually certain prospect of a landing in northern France obliged the Reich to consider the implications for the distribution of its troops. An alarming report from Rundstedt in October 1943 led Hitler to reinforce defenses in the West, despite the tense situation on the Russian front. The forces under the authority of OB West between November 1943 and June 1944 grew from forty-six to sixty divisions, now armed with 1,608 tanks and self-propelled guns, not counting equipment salvaged from the enemy. The mission of repelling the Allied assault thus fell to the 950,000 men serving in the army and the Waffen SS[15]—an assault that at dawn on 6 June consisted of only nine divisions (three of them airborne) and 176,000 men.

German soldiers, many of them battle-hardened from service in the East and commanded by commissioned officers of great talent as well as highly competent noncommissioned officers, enjoyed a degree of experience that their adversaries for the most part lacked. Every time elite German units—the Afrika Korps, airborne troop formations, panzer divisions—had faced Anglo-American forces on equal terms, whether in Africa or in Italy, they had won. On average, the German infantryman inflicted losses 50 percent higher than those of his British or American counterparts. Moreover, the proportion of combatants as a share of total troop strength favored the Reich. In June 1944, 54.35 percent of the German army was composed of fighting soldiers, in contrast to 38 percent for the U.S. Army; 44.9 percent of its men (almost one in two) served in combat rather than support units, as opposed to 20.8 percent (or one in five) among the Americans.[16] German armament often outclassed that of the Allies as well, in quality if not in quantity. The Wehrmacht's tanks, light machine guns, 88 mm antiaircraft guns, and mortars were superior to those of its adversaries, with the exception of certain weapons—notably the American M55 12.7 mm antiaircraft gun.

The forces of OB West were far from invincible, however. In the so-called static (or garrison) divisions that manned the pillboxes along the coast, many officers no longer met the standards of modern warfare. The average age of infantry battalion commanders was 42.7 years, and 44.5 in the case of artillery divisions.[17] Moreover, the loyalties of the sixty thousand *Hilfswillige*—auxiliary volunteers rounded up from the Reich's former borderlands, few of them very willing and most only distantly German—were doubtful.[18] Nor were the top field commanders altogether exempt from criticism. Even Rommel, despite his many daring exploits in the battle of France and later in North Africa, was no longer at the height of his powers after El Alamein.[19] And Rundstedt himself, in the account given by Major General Leo Geyr von Schweppenburg after the war, though "a gentleman, both wise and clever, [was] undoubtedly one of the most lazy soldiers I [ever] met in higher quarters. And he didn't like my tendency to disturb quiet waters. In 1944, he was an ageing man. Physical ill-health and psychic resignation certainly had something to do with [his] state of lethargy"[20]—together with a notorious weakness for alcohol.

Moreover, the navy and the air force could no longer claim to play leading roles. In the Channel-Atlantic sector, the Kriegsmarine had only five destroyers, five motor torpedo boats, thirty-six fast patrol boats, thirty-seven submarines, and five hundred low-tonnage ships (minesweepers, submarine chasers, and so on)—hardly an imposing force, in the face of which the Allies could confidently expect to rule the seas. The skies belonged to them as well, for the Luftwaffe had paled into insignificance in the West. On 25 May 1944 the Third Air Fleet counted 915 aircraft, of which only 510 were available. Its 438 fighters and combat aircraft could scarcely hope to compete with the thousands of planes that the RAF and USAF were to deploy on 5–6 June 1944, especially since a good many German bases and radar stations had been destroyed in the weeks leading up to D-Day.[21] The possibility could not be ruled out, of course, that the retaliatory weapons that Germany was building in the utmost secrecy would succeed in reversing the situation. Hitler placed great stock in the V-1 and V-2 rockets, which he counted on to sow chaos in Great Britain; but their effect on the outcome of the looming battle in France was difficult to foresee, for the Führer refused to use them before the Allies invaded—or perhaps, because of the long delays in manufacturing these revolutionary devices, he was simply not in a position to use them earlier.

Deprived of meaningful support from either the Luftwaffe or the Kriegsmarine, German planners had no choice but to put their faith in the ground forces. On the eve of 6 June, sixty-three divisions were stationed in France, Belgium, and the Netherlands. The fifty-five divisions based in France were of uneven quality: six of them, depleted and exhausted from the rigors of service on the eastern front, were regrouping; four were Luftwaffe field divisions, the residue of ground crews no longer needed by a shrunken air force; six divisions, cobbled together from underage and unfit recruits, were in training; five were static units whose usefulness in defending coastal strongholds even OB West considered limited. Rundstedt could reasonably rely only on twenty-seven widely dispersed infantry divisions: six stood watch over the Mediterranean; one guarded the Pyrenees; seven were stationed in Brittany; and one occupied the Channel Islands. Protection of the coast across from England ultimately rested on twelve divisions (not counting eight others stationed in Belgium and Holland), supported if need be by nine armored divisions, along with another two panzer units temporarily detached to the Russian front.[22] In principle, Germany had enough troops to resist an invasion; but they suffered from poor mobility (90 percent of the units depended on horse or rail transport); even the armored units were underequipped, each one on average having only 120 armored tanks.

As a practical matter, the Germans enjoyed only two advantages: in armored divisions and coastal defenses. When the landing came, "the main battle," Rommel believed, would "be on the beach."[23] Named inspector of fortifications in the West on 5 November 1943, then commander of Army Group B on 15 January 1944, he set about reinforcing the defenses at once. "I therefore consider that an attempt must be made, using every possible expedient, to beat off the enemy landing on the coast and to fight the battle in the more or less strongly fortified coastal strip," Rommel concluded in a report of 31 December 1943. "This will require the construction of a fortified and mined zone extending from the coast some five or six miles inland and defended both to[ward] the sea and to[ward] the land."[24] The construction of fortified positions proceeded at a steady pace, and by the following spring six thousand earthworks had been finished in the Fifteenth Army sector (extending from the mouth of the Dives River to the Escaut), fourteen hundred of them in the area occupied by Eighty-fourth Corps (from the Dives to the Couesnon).[25] An inspection of defenses in Denmark in January 1944 gave Rommel the idea of constructing underwater obstacles—"artificial coral reefs" that would not only prevent the enemy from approaching the beaches but also destroy the landing equipment of the Allies and wipe out their troops.[26] By 13 May, 517,000 obstacles of this type had been installed, of which 31,000 carried an explosive charge.[27] Similarly, beginning in March, Rommel sought "to ensure that all territory which might conceivably be used for landing airborne troops is treated in such a manner that enemy aircraft and gliders will break up while landing, and the enemy as a result suffer severe losses in men and material—in addition to those caused by the quick opening of our defensive fire."[28] The fields were therefore dotted with "Rommel's asparagus"—tree trunks more than eleven feet high, rammed into the ground at intervals of about thirty feet and connected with barbed wire—and a campaign of intensive mining of the shoreline was undertaken. By mid-May, 4.2 million mines had been laid along the Channel coast.[29]

Yet Rommel was not satisfied. At an average of 100 pilings per man-day of labor, a team of 850 men had to work for thirty days to cover as many miles—the length of the front assumed to be occupied by an invading division. "Generally, the troops do not do enough work to complete the positions," Rommel observed. "The urgency is underrated. The inclination to form reserves everywhere results in a weakening of the coastal front."[30] Often begun by French civilians dragooned for two or three days a week in the coastal villages, these preparations were typically completed by soldiers, and therefore interfered with their training. The real problem was that they had gotten a late start. "It will be asked why the work was not started earlier, for that would have enabled a far stronger barrier to be built," Rommel noted. "The answer is that form of obstacle was not thought of earlier."[31] As a result, the Atlantic Wall presented worrisome gaps. In all, five million mines were laid—only a quarter of the twenty million planned. The fortification program was only half completed, and relatively few of the gun batteries were reinforced with concrete. Whereas 93 of 132 batteries (or 70 percent) were casemated in the Pas de Calais, the proportion fell to 27 of 47 (57 percent) in Normandy.[32] And as for the fortifications that OKW had planned during the summer of 1943 to construct behind the coastline, this second line of defense was only partly finished, for lack of money and resources. As Rommel's chief of staff, General Hans Speidel, observed, "in its manning and armaments the Atlantic Wall was no more than a thin line, without depth or substantial reserves."[33] This crucial weakness could not fail to improve the Allies' position, especially since the German command was both divided and hesitant.

## QUARRELS AND CONFLICTS

The organizational structure of Allied Supreme Headquarters placed all three services under Eisenhower's direct and exclusive command. The Germans were denied this advantage: despite repeated requests, first from Rundstedt and then from Rommel, that the lines of authority be redrawn, Admiral Theodor Krancke, the head of Naval Group West, continued to take his orders from Grand Admiral Karl Doenitz, while Field Marshal Hugo Sperrle, commander of the Third Air Fleet, remained under Goering's immediate supervision. This situation was to prevent the defenders from mounting a coherent and coordinated response once the

Allied invasion was underway. Rundstedt had responsibility for both Army Group B, led by Rommel, and Army Group G, stationed south of the Loire under the authority of General Johannes von Blaskowitz. Rommel, as chief of Army Group B, commanded the Fifteenth Army, positioned to the northeast between the Dives and the Scheldt (Escaut) rivers, and the Seventh Army, positioned to the southwest between the Dives and the Loire. In theory he was subordinate to Rundstedt, but by virtue of his rank as a field marshal Rommel was able to go around him by appealing directly to the Führer and OKW. Rundstedt also had authority over Panzer Group West, created in November 1943, whose six reserve armored divisions were commanded by General Geyr von Schweppenburg.[34] "This concept of 'divide and rule,'" General Speidel later observed, "broke the unity of the Western Command and delivered it to the forces of confusion."[35] Indeed, a chain of command this cumbersome was likely to prevent decisions from being made rapidly because the generals themselves were in sharp disagreement over strategy.

In Directive no. 40 of 23 March 1942 Hitler had laid down the main principles to which the German forces were expected to adhere. By concentrating all their sea, air, and land resources, they were to destroy the enemy fleet before its troops could come ashore. In the event that the expeditionary force should nonetheless manage to establish a beachhead, immediate counterattacks were to be launched to hurl it back into the sea.[36] Rundstedt, as we have seen, believed that the Allies would succeed in breaching the Atlantic Wall, which led him to demand that armored divisions be placed at his disposal by way of reinforcement. Where they should be stationed and when they should be committed to battle—two points that Hitler had left unspecified—remained to be decided.

The commanders of the forces in northern France, Belgium, and Holland urged that the armored divisions be placed near the coast, so that a vigorous riposte could be delivered at once. Stationing them far from the coast carried a major risk, namely, that the attackers' air force and naval artillery would prohibit any movement. Rommel, convinced of the necessity of winning the battle on the beaches, shared this view. Mindful too of the lessons of North Africa and Italy, he felt sure that neutralizing enemy aircraft and naval fire would prove decisive: "The dispositions of both

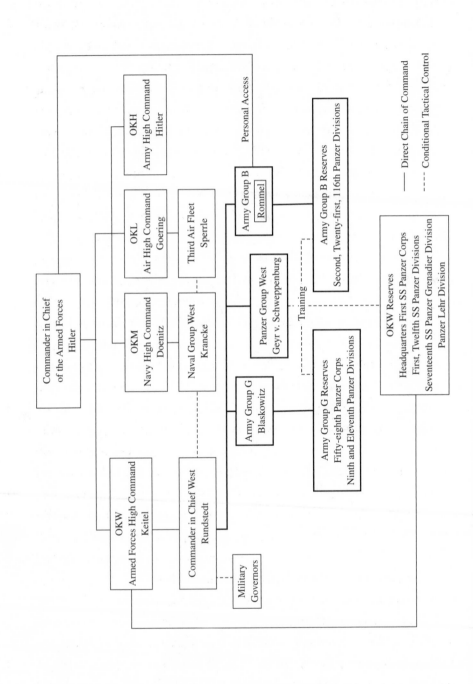

**Commander in Chief of the Armed Forces**
Hitler

**OKW**
Armed Forces High Command
Keitel

**OKM**
Navy High Command
Doenitz

**OKL**
Air High Command
Goering

**OKH**
Army High Command
Hitler

**Commander in Chief West**
Rundstedt

**Naval Group West**
Krancke

**Third Air Fleet**
Sperrle

Military Governors

**Army Group G**
Blaskowitz

**Panzer Group West**
Geyr v. Schweppenburg

**Army Group B**
Rommel

Personal Access

Army Group G Reserves
Fifty-eighth Panzer Corps
Ninth and Eleventh Panzer Divisions

Training

Army Group B Reserves
Second, Twenty-first, 116th Panzer Divisions

**OKW Reserves**
Headquarters First SS Panzer Corps
First, Twelfth SS Panzer Divisions
Seventeenth SS Panzer Grenadier Division
Panzer Lehr Division

—— Direct Chain of Command

---- Conditional Tactical Control

combat and reserve forces should be such," Rommel argued to General Alfred Jodl, chief of the operations staff of OKW, "as to ensure that the minimum possible movement will be required to counter an attack at any of the most likely points."[37] To win his case, Rommel counted not only on Jodl's support but on that of Hitler himself.

General Geyr von Schweppenburg, though, recommended placing five to six armored divisions sufficiently far from the coast, preferably north of Paris, that they would be protected against naval artillery and aerial attacks. The virtue of this strategy, he believed, was that by refusing to commit forces to precise positions in advance, it left open a range of tactical options. In the meantime, the garrison troops and local reserves would absorb the brunt of the assault, while awaiting the arrival of the panzers, which would be moved up to the front by night. In support of this view, the commander of Panzer Group West sought the approval of General Heinz Guderian, a renowned theoretician of armored warfare, and of Rundstedt.

These opposing conceptions reflected the diversity of actual battlefield experience. The "Africans" had faced the Allies in North Africa and Sicily and felt they knew which type of strategy would have to be employed if the German army was to prevail. The "Russians," who had practiced an entirely different style of warfare in the East, brought another perspective to bear. Personal rivalry further complicated the situation: Rommel had a very low opinion of Geyr von Schweppenburg's abilities, and vice versa. "If I am to wait until the enemy landing has actually taken place, before I can demand, through normal channels, the command and dispatch of the mobile forces," Rommel wrote to Jodl on 23 April 1944, "delays will be inevitable. This will mean that they will probably arrive too late to intervene successfully in the battle for the coast and prevent the enemy landing. A second Nettuno, a highly undesirable situation for us, could result."[38]

Hitler moved to resolve the dispute. On 26 April he assigned three armored divisions to Rommel, in addition to the three armored divisions attached to Army Group G. Panzer Group West was allocated three armored divisions, one SS motorized division, and the staff of the First SS Panzer Corps. With this partial victory in hand Rommel tried in May to press his advantage by asking for overall control of the armored forces—only to be turned down by Rundstedt and OKW.[39] Ultimately, Hitler's compromise had resolved nothing: Geyr von Schweppenburg failed to obtain the operational reserve he had sought, and Rommel was denied the forces he was convinced were necessary to win the battle on the beaches.

The difficulty of deciphering Allied intentions did not help matters. In the absence of detailed information about the day and hour of the invasion, Rundstedt had no choice but to spread out his forces over some three thousand miles of coastline. Small wonder, then, that the Germans should have done everything they could to penetrate the secret of D-Day.

## THE URGE TO KNOW

Correctly guessing Allied intentions would have made it possible to improve defensive arrangements by concentrating forces in exactly the area where the expeditionary forces would attack. With regard to intelligence, however, the Reich was at a great disadvantage. The severely weakened Luftwaffe was prevented from conducting aerial reconnaissance, and the few nighttime bomber missions that could be mounted in the spring of 1944 produced little useful photographic evidence of activity in English ports—the joint result of harassment by the RAF and poor weather conditions. Moreover, the interception of Allied radio communications had declined, both in quality and quantity, not least because of the exemplary discipline exhibited by the Allies in this domain.[40] There remained only espionage.

Attempts by the Reich's secret services, the Abwehr primarily, to penetrate the United Kingdom were mostly unsuccessful. Agents were infiltrated among the stream of refugees from Germany before the war, and between 1943 and 1944 four spies were parachuted into the country. Others were sent to Canada and Bermuda. The Abwehr also tried to expand its recruitment, bribing Spanish and Portuguese sailors to serve as couriers and informants on transatlantic traffic.[41] But on the whole the gleanings were meager. Arousing suspicion by their clumsiness, almost all the agents operating in the United Kingdom were arrested; others were turned and used to mislead their former masters. One notable exception, Elyez Bazna (known by the alias Cicero), valet to the British ambassador to Ankara, offered his services to the local station of the Sicherheitsdienst. Beginning in October 1943, he microfilmed documents removed from his employer's safe and managed to obtain information about the major conferences at Moscow, Cairo, and Teheran.[42] Bazna seems even to have transmitted information about OVERLORD that mentioned Normandy as a possible landing site.[43] Both Hitler and Walter Schellenberg, head of the SD, doubted their authenticity, however; surely it seemed odd that the ambassador to Turkey should have been informed of secrets that had nothing to do with him. Nonetheless, in the wake of these reports Hitler was constantly at pains to draw his generals' attention to the perils that threatened Normandy.[44]

For want of experienced spies, the Germans fell back upon proven methods. In July 1942, Wilhelmstrasse instructed its representatives abroad to transmit any information that might throw light on the enemy's intentions. The Foreign Ministry immediately found itself inundated with vague reports that attacks against coastal targets would occur from Norway to the Mediterranean—evidence, as OKW suspected at once, of a vast campaign of disinformation.[45] The press in neutral countries, as well as America and Britain, was thoroughly scrutinized. Revelatory details were few and far between, however, and in most cases planted by the Allied intelligence services. The results obtained from interrogation of captured Anglo-American agents and members of the French Resistance were considered untrustworthy. A 10 April 1944 report from Foreign Armies West (Fremde Heere West, or FHW), a department of the OKH having primary responsibility for the collection and analysis of intelligence about the Western Allies, in citing the testimony of such witnesses, gave a probable date for the landing of late May or early June, while emphasizing that the very agreement among their statements "causes us to conclude that they speak under instruction and hence to doubt their truth."[46] Between January and May the Germans intercepted some twenty messages announcing a landing that did not occur—and so during the first three days of June, when they heard the verses from Verlaine's "Chanson d'automne" announcing the invasion, they paid little attention, prior experience having aroused their skepticism. "I learn from the bureau of investigation," Goebbels noted on 3 June (with reference either to the SD or the Abwehr), "that England has given the order through its secret transmitters to the French underground movements to prepare themselves for an imminent invasion. According to this information, it ought therefore to be launched in the next few days. For one cannot reasonably suppose that the English, in order to fool us, would sacrifice their French partisans to the Germans, who are lying in wait for them. But in the current maelstrom of events, or indeed their absence, one no longer knows what is white and what is black."[47] This fruitless quest for reliable information reflected the ineffectiveness of the German spy services; but to an even greater degree it was a tribute to the extraordinary measures taken by the Allies to protect their secrets.

Since 1940, the Inter-Service Security Board (ISSB) had been charged with maintaining the security of British military operations. At the end of 1943 a special committee was created, with responsibility for guarding the secrecy of OVERLORD, choosing code names, and establishing procedures for the circulation of confidential documents. In February 1944, in order to further reduce the risk of leaks, the committee suggested isolating sensitive areas (especially coastal zones) and denying unauthorized visitors—some six hundred thousand people per month—access to them. It also proposed suspending communications between foreign embassies and their governments; censoring all mail coming from or going to Ireland (whose neutrality gave opportunity for shelter to German spies); delaying outgoing mail from German prisoners of war by three months; and canceling flights to and from Great Britain operated by Aer Lingus and the Swedish carrier AB Aerotransport. Although these measures displeased the Foreign Office, which objected to the breach of customary diplomatic practice, the prime minister readily agreed to them. Civilian passage between Ireland and Great Britain was interrupted on 9 February; a quarantine of the coast from the Wash to Cornwall, as well as around the Firth of Forth, was imposed on 1 April; the termination of diplomatic contacts took effect at midnight on 17 April (exceptions being made for the United States and the Soviet Union). The Allied embassies were authorized to communicate with their governments on the condition that they deposit a copy of their codes with British censors and submit all messages for their review.[48] The same rule was strictly applied to the London headquarters of the French Committee of National Liberation (CFLN)—the Allies suspecting, not unreasonably, that there would be leaks between Algiers and Vichy. De Gaulle, however, infuriated by the Allies' lack of trust, broke off talks then under way in preparation for the landing. Similarly, mail to the United States was delayed by ten days, beginning on 25 May, and British personnel taking part in OVERLORD saw their correspondence systematically censored.

British and American censors closely monitored representatives of the media stationed in England, deftly wielding carrot and stick. They gave one broadcaster permission on 12 March to say that "the time is drawing near for the Allied invasion of Nazi Europe," since the phrase "is drawing near" could refer to any day in the months ahead without in any way indicating to the enemy which one D-Day would be. But they were less conciliatory in the case of a journalist who had submitted the following dispatch for approval: "There has been a good deal of comment as to continuous Allied bombing of the Calais invasion coast obviously an indication of invasion and it has been suggested that this region is best from the point of view of tactical advantages because it is closest to England and with flat country back of the range of hills of the beach. . . . But what we do not think of in worrying about the success of this great invasion . . . is the part which the French civilian population will play." The censors insisted on three changes: the phrase "obviously an indication of invasion" was to be deleted; "this region is best" was to be changed to "this region would be good"; and the phrase "the civilian population of conquered countries" was to be substituted for "the French civilian population."[49] In April 1944 another journalist aroused alarm when he ventured the opinion that "the invasion [would] come off in the next three weeks." He was forced to say instead: "As to the invasion date, a lot of people seem to be guessing but about all I can say is no one seems to know."[50] Censorship posed considerably greater problems for the CFLN, which beginning on 20 May was to provide Resistance forces inside France with fairly precise instructions, without thereby alerting the Germans.

In the end, the mystery surrounding OVERLORD was preserved, despite occasional blunders. In March 1944 a package containing secret documents was sent by accident to a private address in a predominantly German neighborhood of Chicago, by a clerk who was himself of German origin and who had inadvertently substituted his sister's address for that of the War Department in Washington. The error was caught in time, but not before causing Eisenhower intense anxiety.[51] On 18 April at the restaurant in Claridge's Hotel, Major General Henry J. F. Miller, commander of the Ninth Air Force Service Command, drunkenly complained to a nurse that certain articles would not be able to reach Great Britain before 15 June at the earliest, well after the landing. Miller was relieved of his duties at once, demoted to the rank of lieutenant colonel, and sent back to the United States.[52]

In addition to missteps of this sort, there were disturbing coincidences. Captain Basil H. Liddell Hart, a well-known British military expert, somehow acquired information that he ought, in the interests of national security, to have kept to himself. During a mid-March meeting at the Park Lane Hotel in London with Duncan Sandys, minister of Supply, Liddell Hart showed Sandys the draft of an essay that cast serious doubt on the soundness of the plan the Allies intended to follow. He knew the beaches well where the troops were to land, Liddell Hart added, having played on them as a child—a revelation that astonished his interlocutor. "In the light of this knowledge," Sandys reported, "I formed my impression that Captain Liddell Hart was in possession of precise information about future military operations."[53] Sandys resolved to bring the matter to the attention of Churchill's chief of staff, General Sir Hastings Ismay, so that it might be submitted to official inquiry. This was done—and all the more vigorously as Liddell Hart, a sharp critic of the British command, was alleged to have argued in 1942 in favor of "a compromise peace" that had a strong whiff of defeatism about it.[54] His telephone was tapped and he was shadowed by the police, before finally being summoned to an interview with Ismay and Lieutenant Colonel (later Sir) Ian Jacob, military assistant secretary to the War Cabinet, on 20 March.

The suspect limited himself to denying the charges that had been brought against him. "Liddell Hart maintained that no one had ever told him what the OVERLORD plan was. His knowledge of it was arrived at by inferences drawn from his own observation of the preparations which are being made and the like." He nonetheless displayed a certain pique that cast light on both his deep motivations and his personality, observing in particular "that if he had been told the OVERLORD plan, it would have been proper for he is a military expert and in the last war military experts, such as Colonel Repington, were consulted from time to time by Ministers and Generals."[55]

Informed of the incident, Churchill flew into a rage. "Captain Liddell Hart must be prevented from touring around the Armies collecting confidential information and giving the impression that he is in our secrets, and thus obtaining confidences. The time is now coming when this story will have to be told to General Eisenhower." Returning to the matter a few days later, he told General Ismay, "It seems to me that it would make L. H. much more careful if we began a prosecution against him, even if we did not succeed in a conviction."[56] The evidence was inconclusive, however, and on 22 March the attorney general advised, "No effective action is possible in view of Liddell Hart's attitude, and . . . the matter should be allowed to lapse. No further steps are therefore being taken by the War Cabinet office, and Liddell Hart will now return to his home."[57]

Even so, the cause for alarm was real: despite all the precautions that had been taken, a leak was quite possible. This at any rate was the opinion of the investigating officer, who insisted in an appendix to his report on stating his personal view of the matter:

> For the convenience of those who may have to refer to this file at some future time it is well to say that the document in the envelope at 3a contained in its original form the names of places in France. These places were all within the Neptune target area and it was quite clear that Liddell Hart had been told of the actual

area where the landing in Normandy was to take place. . . . We do not know how Liddell Hart obtained the information. . . . It is quite clear that at the end of May, Liddell Hart was discussing the invasion plan with General Pile.[58] Whether it was the latter who gave him the information we do not know. There is no doubt that any one of a number of Liddell Hart's contacts might have done so.[59]

Worse was yet to come. On 3 June, the Associated Press actually announced the landing. A young teletype operator, Joan Ellis, was conscientiously rehearsing the prearranged procedure for D-Day, unaware that she was directly connected to the Telex network. Moscow, Berlin, and CBS all picked up the dispatch before the AP succeeded in denying it twenty-three minutes later.[60] This scare came hard on the heels of a bizarre coincidence, in which the answers to crossword puzzles appearing in the *Daily Telegraph* between 2 May and 1 June included five of the invasion's code names—notably OVERLORD, OMAHA, and UTAH.[61]

Happily, none of these slips did any harm. The Germans nonetheless suspected that a landing would occur in northern France during the spring or summer of 1944, since the Allies would require a period of good weather. "As far as the invasion is concerned," Goebbels noted in mid-April, "the Führer is quite sure that it is imminent. When, naturally he cannot say. Perhaps sometime this month."[62] The Western military commanders, meeting in Paris on 9 May, reckoned that the attack would take place either in May or between the fifth and the seventh of June; OKW forecast a date of 18 May.[63] Moreover, from their experience in North Africa and Italy the Germans had a good idea of the sort of strategy their enemies would adopt. Although they did not expect either one of these campaigns to be reproduced exactly, the high command did anticipate that Allied aerial bombardment would begin on the eve of the invasion, in advance of the landing of commandos and paratroops. Naval artillery would then be brought to bear, to provide cover for the expeditionary force as it came ashore. Tanks would be committed fairly quickly afterward with the purpose of seizing ports and airfields. By the evening of the first day, however, the enemy would be so vulnerable that "an immediate and energetic counterattack conducted by the troops of the defensive system would suffice to repel him."[64] This turned out to be on the whole a fairly accurate analysis.

By contrast, the most complete uncertainty reigned regarding the place where the assault would occur. Almost all the military commanders—Rundstedt foremost among them—thought that the landing would take place in the Pas de Calais, in view of the advantages this region presented: the narrowness of the Channel there facilitated the task of the air force and navy; the launching pads of the V-1 and V-2 rockets offered tempting targets; the Ruhr was not far away; and in the meantime the attackers would be in a position to capture valuable port facilities. Rundstedt did not rule out the possibility of other operations, aiming at Normandy, Brittany, the Bay of Biscay, or the South of France, but he considered them to be secondary maneuvers meant to lead the Wehrmacht astray, by encouraging it to withdraw its forces from the Pas de Calais.

A few discordant voices were raised in opposition to this view. Rommel himself thought the Allies would attack between Cherbourg and Le Havre. Naval Group West planners pointed out that the Allies would be foolish to attack just where the Germans expected them to—an argument supported by the concentration of Allied ships that had been observed near the Isle of Wight.[65] The commander of the Eighty-fourth Army Corps, General Erich Marcks, favored the sector he was assigned to defend, which happened to be Normandy. The crews of the Third Air Fleet interpreted the Allied bombing of bridges on the Seine as part of a plan to isolate Normandy—further evidence that the assault would be attempted between Le Havre and Cherbourg. Indeed, on 6 May Jodl called Rundstedt's chief of staff, General Günther Blumentritt, to emphasize that "the Führer attaches exceptional importance to Normandy and its defence. Measures to be improvised to strengthen Normandy against attack, especially by air landing troops."[66]

The Germans had in fact come close to discovering the truth, but they had no way of knowing this—in large part owing to the many deceptions concocted by the Allies. To be sure, OKW did not fall into all the traps that had been set for it. FORTITUDE NORTH, for example, was only partly successful: although the Reich did end up keeping twelve of its divisions in Norway, it decided not to reinforce its defenses in Denmark, considering that the threat to this area would of necessity be limited.[67] Nor did Allied intervention on a large scale in the Middle East seem likely, once the Turks' evident reluctance to be drawn into the war and the secret information transmitted by the British ambassador's valet were taken into account.[68] Finally, the quite considerable resources mobilized in support of the pretended assault on southern France left the Germans utterly unmoved. An attack between Sète and Narbonne made little sense.

Nevertheless, in the absence of any hard evidence regarding the Allies' intentions, German planners had no choice but to keep a watchful eye on the whole coastline from the English Channel to the Baltic. As a result, the divisions stationed in Scandinavia remained there; and the number of units committed to the Mediterranean remained stable from February to June: no formation left this theater of operations for northern France before D-Day.[69] Nor was Normandy exempted from this policy. Between 7 and 14 May more than twenty thousand German soldiers took up positions in the department of La Manche[70]—a sign that in spite of FORTITUDE SOUTH, Normandy was very much present in their commanders' minds.

On balance, however, the success of the scheme exceeded the Allies' wildest expectations. Well into July 1944 the German high command was to interpret NEPTUNE as a feint masking the decisive assault yet to come in the Pas de Calais. The success of this deception is partly explained by the careful preparations of the British intelligence services and the value of their double agents. Moreover, owing to their ability to intercept and decipher the enemy's communications, the Allies were able to adapt their plans to changing circumstances, eliminating the less plausible stratagems, while placing greater emphasis on elements that the Reich had shown itself ready to believe. There were two further advantages as well. First, FORTITUDE SOUTH flattered the enemy's expectations: persuaded that the Allies would strike at the Pas de Calais, the Germans fell into a form of wishful thinking that led them to credit information that reinforced their preconceptions and ignore evidence to the contrary. Second, they vastly overestimated the strength of the assembling Allied forces. In January 1944 the Reich's intelligence services reckoned that the Allied high command would deploy fifty-five divisions in Great Britain, as opposed to the eighteen actually in place; by the end of May, the estimate had jumped to seventy-nine divisions, whereas in fact only fifty-two were stationed across the Channel.[71] On 29 February the Japanese ambassador to Berlin advised Tokyo that according to Ribbentrop seventy-five to eighty-five divisions were preparing to cross the Channel to storm Europe.[72]

It may be that a sense of quiet desperation had begun to set in. Relentlessly harried by Allied bombing at home, turned back in North Africa and Russia, battered in Italy, Germany might well have supposed that the coalition had virtually unlimited resources. Here again, however, the possibility of deception cannot be ruled out—only in this case deception of quite a different kind. The information that Colonel Alexis von Roenne, head of Foreign Armies West, supplied to OKW was filtered through the Sicherheitsdienst, which insisted on satisfying itself about the accuracy and coherence of FHW's analysis. To please Hitler, though, and to prove to him that it had the situation well in hand, the SD was in the habit of reducing by half the figures concerning enemy troop strength. In early 1944 this gave rise to a very serious unintended consequence. Reassured by news of his adversary's weakness, Hitler agreed in March to transfer formations from the Atlantic Wall to the eastern front. Roenne was mortified. Knowing that the SD would halve subsequent estimates of the Allied order of battle, Lieutenant Colonel Roger Michel, head of FHW's Group England, suggested doubling them so that OKW would end up with approximately realistic figures. Roenne agreed, and in May sent a report indicating that between eighty-five and ninety divisions were gathered in England, not counting seven airborne divisions. Contrary to all expectation, the SD accepted this deliberately inflated estimate without batting an eyelash. Could it be that Michel was working for British or American intelligence services? Or did he perhaps make a simple mental error? The question remains unresolved.[73] Nor is it clear how much importance should be attached to this incident, for the error made by German intelligence occurred, as the Japanese ambassador's telegram confirms, well before Roenne delivered his report to the SD. Whatever the case may be, an overestimate on this scale could only strengthen the credibility of FORTITUDE SOUTH, by suggesting that Eisenhower had enough troops to launch both a diversionary operation in Normandy and a large-scale attack on the Pas de Calais. The Allies, for their part, had scarcely dared to hope for such a success. Indeed, in July 1943 Colonel Bevan, fearing that his agents risked being discredited if they tried to persuade the German high command that the Allies had twice the forces actually available to them, suggested that exaggerating the true order of battle by 20 to 30 percent would be a more reasonable ambition.[74]

In addition to their uncertainty over the place of the landing, the Germans were led on account of poor weather conditions to dismiss the chance of an invasion in early June. Although the Wehrmacht's meteorologists did indicate that the weather was likely to improve at dawn on 6 June, they were unable to provide sufficient assurances.[75] Whereas the Allies enjoyed the advantage of having weather stations in Iceland, on the island of Spitsbergen in the Arctic Ocean, and in Greenland, as well as information from ships at anchor in the Atlantic, the Germans were forced to rely on a few submarines cruising the same waters, together with a handful of aircraft flying over western Ireland. Even if their forecasting had been better, though, it would not have altered OB West's response, for Rundstedt believed that the Allies would not go forward unless they could count on several days of good weather in a row, which would be exceedingly improbable in early June.[76] On 4 June, Naval Group West therefore advised that the expeditionary force would not attempt a landing in the near future. "Fears of an invasion during this period were rendered all the less [acute]," Rommel recalled afterward, "by the fact that tides were very unfavourable for the days following, and the fact that no amount of air reconnaissance had given the slightest indication that a landing was imminent."[77]

In their ability to anticipate the situation they would face on D-Day, the dissymmetry between the two sides was total. Whereas the Germans failed to divine the intentions of their adversary, their own disposition of forces was hardly a secret to the Allied high command, which could call on impressive resources: aerial photography had made it possible to survey 80 percent of the coastal defenses, the American Expeditionary Air

Forces (AEAF) alone having carried out more than three thousand reconnaissance missions, and the other air commands having conducted another fifteen hundred or so;[78] on the ground, British agents and members of the French Resistance transmitted plans and details of the order of battle of OB West, roughly 70 percent being provided by the Gaullist Bureau Central de Renseignements et d'Action (BCRA) and the other 30 percent by networks run by British military intelligence. The interrogation of prisoners of war, supplemented by the deciphering of enemy communications, furnished additional information. Thus, for example, in November 1943 the Japanese military attaché to Berlin cabled to his superiors in Tokyo a thirty-two page summary of his recent tour of the French coast, which the Allies intercepted and promptly analyzed.[79] Moreover, despite the risks involved, ground reconnaissance teams were dispatched to Normandy. A number of raids by Combined Operations Pilotage Parties (COPP) were carried out on the coast for the purpose of gathering sand and clay samples, calculating the slope of the beaches, disabling mines, and inspecting German defenses.[80] Already in 1942 these expeditions had succeeded in taking prisoners and bringing them back to Great Britain for interrogation. In February 1944 the Allied high command suspended the COPP missions, particularly in view of the dangers they posed to operations in the NEPTUNE area.[81] Nevertheless, another four raids (Operation TARBRUSH) were launched in May on the Pas de Calais, in order to investigate the types of mines attached to obstacles in the outer beach area.[82]

Last but not least, the British enjoyed one extraordinary advantage. In 1939 they were able, with the help of the Poles, to obtain an exact copy of the German coding machine known as Enigma, analysis of which allowed them to decipher the internal communications of the Wehrmacht. The Secret Intelligence Service (SIS), located north of London at Bletchley Park, was therefore in a position to penetrate the enemy's innermost secrets, with only a few exceptions (telephone conversations escaped SIS surveillance, and the codes used by the Kriegsmarine were not broken until 1942).[83]

By January 1944, Allied Supreme Headquarters had a fairly clear pic-

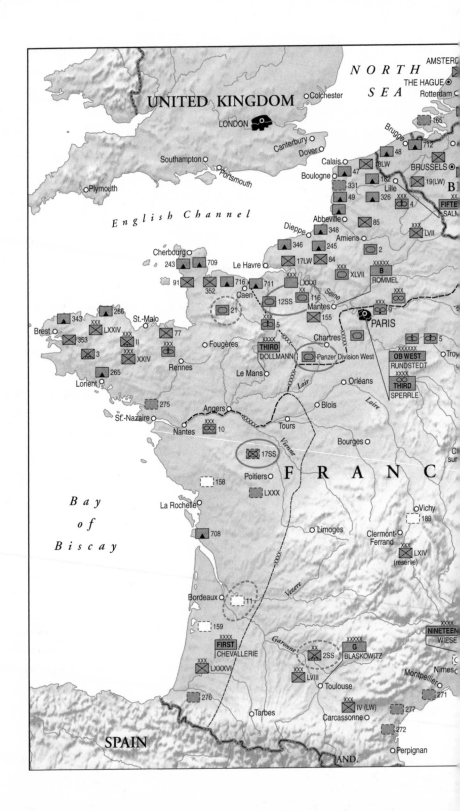

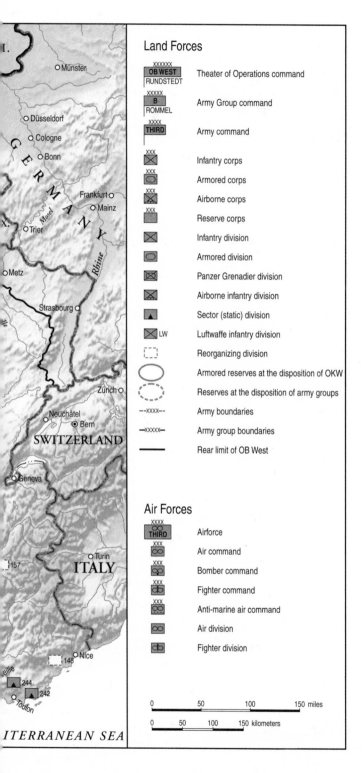

## Land Forces

| | |
|---|---|
| XXXXXX<br>**OB WEST**<br>RUNDSTEDT | Theater of Operations command |
| XXXXX<br>**B**<br>ROMMEL | Army Group command |
| XXXX<br>**THIRD** | Army command |
| XXX<br>⊠ | Infantry corps |
| XXX<br>◯ | Armored corps |
| XXX<br>⊠ | Airborne corps |
| XXX<br>☐ | Reserve corps |
| ⊠ | Infantry division |
| ◯ | Armored division |
| ⊠ | Panzer Grenadier division |
| ⊠ | Airborne infantry division |
| ▲ | Sector (static) division |
| ⊠ LW | Luftwaffe infantry division |
| ☐ | Reorganizing division |
| ◯ | Armored reserves at the disposition of OKW |
| ◯ | Reserves at the disposition of army groups |
| --XXXX-- | Army boundaries |
| -XXXXX- | Army group boundaries |
| ▬▬▬ | Rear limit of OB West |

## Air Forces

| | |
|---|---|
| XXXX<br>**THIRD** | Airforce |
| XXX<br>⊙⊙ | Air command |
| XXX<br>⊙⊙ | Bomber command |
| XXX<br>⊕⊙ | Fighter command |
| XXX<br>⊙⊙ | Anti-marine air command |
| ⊙⊙ | Air division |
| ⊕⊙ | Fighter division |

Scale: 0 — 50 — 100 — 150 miles

0 — 50 — 100 — 150 kilometers

3. Deployment of
German Forces on
6 June 1944

ture of the Wehrmacht's order of battle in Normandy. The Germans, by its reckoning, had at their disposal forty-four divisions—the actual figure was forty-eight.[84] On 4 June the intelligence services of Twenty-first Army Group anticipated that fifty-nine divisions would be stationed in the West on D-Day, with two unconfirmed units possibly being held in reserve—almost exactly the figure of sixty divisions that German records indicate were deployed in France, Belgium, and the Netherlands.[85] Moreover, thanks to the roughly one million aerial photos taken of the defenses established along the Norman coast, fairly accurate maps could be distributed to Allied troops as they set off across the Channel.

The possibility that the Germans would use gas in combat had been discounted early on. A G-3 staff memorandum from mid-January 1944 noted:

We have never captured a German chemical warfare shell. It would have been very difficult for the Germans to destroy or evacuate all chemical warfare shells from Tunisia (had they had stocks). We have never got from the Russians any confirmation of their occasional reports that they have captured chemical equipment. It is obvious that the Germans might be tempted to use chemical warfare if they were convinced it would defeat the invasion and provided chemical warfare would not lead to their ultimate defeat. There is no evidence of any particular German preparation to use chemical warfare against the invasion in the West.[86]

Churchill concurred in a note to General Ismay:

I do not myself believe that the Germans will use gas on the beaches although this is the most potent way in which gas could be used. The reason is that we could retaliate tenfold or more through the greater power of our air forces to deliver upon all their cities. The only reason they are not using gas is that it would not pay them to do so. However, the temptation to use it on the beaches might conceivably be strong enough to override prudence. General Montgomery tells me he is leaving all his anti-gas equipment on this side and his men are not even to carry gas masks. I agree with this.[87]

It should be noted in passing, however, that the prime minister did consider resorting to gas a few months later, in July, primarily in retaliation against Hitler's V-weapons, but also for the purpose of gaining ground in Normandy, where the offensive had stalled. It was "absurd," Churchill felt, "to consider morality on this topic when everybody used it in the last war without a word of complaint from the moralists or the Church."[88] His chiefs of staff did not follow him on this point, arguing in a memorandum of 28 July that the use of gas would have no effect on the outcome of the war. The Allied planners' conviction that the Germans would not use this formidable weapon had the effect in any case of removing a potentially serious constraint, for the need to wear masks would have slowed and interfered with the movement of the disembarking troops, and the likelihood that the masks would get wet as the soldiers came ashore created the additional risk that they would not function properly.[89]

The Allies therefore enjoyed the advantage of strategic and tactical surprise, since the Germans knew neither the place nor the time of the assault. And yet pessimism dominated in the Anglo-American camp, whereas optimism reigned in the German ranks. The experience of Dieppe, Salerno, and Anzio tended to support the view that the attacker is seldom the victor in an amphibious operation, which partly explains the confidence displayed by the Reich's leadership. "The Führer is absolutely sure that the invasion will fail," Goebbels noted in mid-April, "and even that it will be decisively repelled."[90] Earlier, on 19 January, Rommel had written to his wife, "In the West: I believe we'll be able to beat off the assault."[91] General Walter Warlimont, then deputy chief of the operations staff at OKW, later recalled that "Supreme Headquarters and the higher headquarters in the West remained convinced that, in spite of all this, they would be successful in repelling the attack. Looking back it seems that the only grounds for this optimism must have been undiminished

confidence in the superiority of the individual German soldier."⁹² The
Allied command, by contrast, was filled with the greatest anxiety. "I knew
all too well the weak points in the plan of operations," Field Marshal
Brooke later wrote in his diary. "First of all the weather, on which we
were entirely dependent: a sudden storm might wreck it all. Then the
complexity of an amphibious operation of this kind, when confusion may
degenerate into chaos in such a short time. The difficulty of controlling
the operation once launched, lack of elasticity in the handling of reserves,
danger of leakage of information with consequent loss of that essential secrecy."⁹³ Air Chief Marshal Leigh-Mallory was worried mainly about the
fate of American airborne troops: "It seemed to me that to flight in so
large a force at 500 feet over almost the whole of the Cherbourg peninsula (for they were to come from the West and the DZ [dropping zones]
were in the east) was extremely hazardous," he wrote on the day of the
landing.⁹⁴ "I am under no delusions," Admiral Ramsay noted on the eve
of the big day, "as to the risks involved in this most difficult of all operations and the critical period around H Hour when, if initial flights are
held up, success will be in the balance. We must trust in our invincible
assets to tip the balance in our favour."⁹⁵

Eisenhower's aide-de-camp, Captain Harry Butcher, participating in a
briefing with Rear Admiral Bernhard H. Bieri, confessed to being less
optimistic than he had been: "Von Rundstedt is the top commander. He
has under him two army groups, the one [in the] northwest headed by
Rommel, the one in southern France by Blaskowitz. Rommel is expected
to attack quickly in an effort to drive us back into the sea."⁹⁶ On balance,
then, the landing was less a matter of concern in and of itself than the aftermath of the initial operation. "We're going to face three critical periods
in this invasion," General Bradley predicted. "The first will come in getting ashore. It'll be difficult—but we're not especially worried about that
part of it. The second may come on the sixth or seventh day when the
other fellow gets together enough reinforcements for a counteroffensive.
This counterattack will probably give us our greatest trouble. Then once
we hurdle the counterattack, our third critical period will come when we
go to break out of the beachhead."⁹⁷ Bedell Smith had "no misgivings
about our troops getting ashore"; but, he gave an "alarming prediction,"

Butcher reported: "Our chances of holding the beachhead, particularly after the Germans get their building up, [are] only fifty-fifty. But . . . the chance is worth taking."[98]

Looking back, one can hardly fail to be struck by the ambivalence of the top leaders: everyone felt sure that the operation would succeed; everyone feared that it would fail.[99]

# 7

# D-Day, H-Hour

WHILE THE GERMANS BECAME lost in conjecture, the Allies were busy refining their plans. On 8 May 1944 Eisenhower pushed back the date of the assault, set for 1 June, four days, to 5 June. The preparations for the landing now entered their final phase.

## EMBARKATION

By early June, thirty-nine divisions were stationed in the United Kingdom.[1] Although only a fraction of this force would take part in the first two days of the operation, the number of troops needing to be ferried across the Channel was nonetheless considerable. The systematic loading of equipment and supplies had begun the first week of May. Ports were assigned specific tasks: Fowey handled munitions, Talbot gasoline. By the evening of 10 May, 128 coasters and other ships had already been loaded. More important, matériel had reached its various destinations in Great Britain on time and in good condition.[2] The movement of troops began concurrently in three phases: assembly, buildup, and embarkation. The men were directed first toward marshaling areas. In the southwest of England, Torquay received 29,200 men and 4,325 vehicles, and Brixham 11,450 and 1,718.[3] Many of the people in the towns along the assembly route turned out to wish the soldiers well. "The convoys of fresh troops rattled down the streets of the outer suburbs of London, and when they stopped at appointed places, women and girls rushed up with jugs, even pails of tea, thrust packets of cigarettes into the boys' hands, joked a while, and cheered as they drew away; a Dunkirk in reverse."[4] Others were less demonstrative: "Once the invasion troops had departed for Normandy, there was consternation among the prostitutes. The pubs where they used to meet clients were suddenly empty. The George, a pub near the BBC which American officers had made their own, ever after was referred to as The Whore's Lament."[5]

Once the soldiers had arrived in the marshaling area, their equipment was checked and double-checked, particular care being taken to ensure that everything was waterproof. The men were then issued a forty-eight hours' supply of rations, two hundred francs, ten seasickness pills, and water purification tablets. The ever-farsighted quartermasters, resigned to human frailty, did not omit to equip the men with condoms, despite having been solemnly instructed to make "unremitting efforts to control prostitution."[6] Evidently venereal disease was more dreaded than epidemic infections arising from combat injury.

To boost morale, the troops' regular diet was supplemented with white bread, fresh meat, fruit cocktail, even ice cream in some cases. Discipline was relaxed, and certain units were granted the privilege of skipping breakfast in order to get more sleep. Psychiatrists were assigned to each marshaling area in case men broke under the strain of waiting; few did, however, and the underemployed specialists had time to instruct their fellow physicians in the rudiments of their art.[7] Sensibly enough, the soldiers were confined to quarters, but some went over the wall to see loved ones one last time—among them Corporal "Topper" Brown of the Fifth Royal Tank Regiment, who escaped his camp near Felixstowe to visit family in Tonbridge, Kent, 120 miles away.[8]

After a few days of this preferential treatment, the troops were distributed among the various assault formations, organized according to assigned points of departure. They then converged on nineteen boarding stations, where they were herded into the more comfortable LSTs first, then onto the other ships (in a second phase, two or three hours before going ashore, they were to be transferred to smaller landing boats). Once the men were aboard, officers briefed them about their mission, without revealing the secret of either the day or the place of the attack. For the

British, this first phase began on 26 May.[9] The Americans followed, on 30 May for Force "U" (Utah), 31 May for Force "O" (Omaha), and 1 June for Force "B" (reinforcements for Omaha). By 3 June the boarding process was complete.

The troops then began to ponder what lay ahead. Although the food was still good, physical conditions were difficult, owing to overcrowding on the ships' decks and the pestilential odor of diesel fuel mixed with the stench of vomit, many of the men having gotten a head start on seasickness. Most of all, the level of tension had been ratcheted up several notches. "We were very, very cold," recalled the American officer Ralph Ingersoll, waiting to set off for Utah, "and I could not tell whether the cold came from within or without. We had been on the landing craft for three days and two nights and fear came in so many different forms we were very bored with it and not even curious about the symptoms now."[10] Some drew strength from religious faith—prayer services were particularly well attended.[11] Others found escape in reading or playing cards, sometimes for money. Officers turned a blind eye.

In the case of the airborne divisions, the three stages of assembly, buildup, and embarkation were collapsed into one. Units stationed in barracks stayed put, cut off from the world after 30 May; troops that had been lodged in private local homes were recalled to temporary camps set up on the airfields from which they would be leaving.[12] Some officers sought to calm their nerves by screening old films; others, like Lieutenant Colonel Wolverton of the U.S. 506th Parachute Infantry Regiment and Colonel Howard Johnson of the 501st, preferred to urge their men on with impassioned speeches. Many of the paratroopers shaved their heads in the manner of Iroquois warriors and covered themselves with red and white war paint.[13] For everyone, it was a trying time of seemingly endless waiting.

The weather conditions worsened, leading the commanders on 4 June to consider delaying the operation scheduled for the next day. "Admiral Ramsay thought that the mechanics of landing could be handled, but agreed with the estimate of the difficulty in adjusting gunfire. His position was mainly neutral. General Montgomery, properly concerned with the great disadvantages of delay, believed that we should go. Tedder disagreed."[14] After having weighed the pros and cons, Eisenhower decided, at 4:15 on the morning of the fourth, to call off the landing. Supreme Headquarters hastily summoned home the convoys heading for Utah and dispatched two destroyers and a Walrus seaplane to call back 139 ships— most of them transporting tanks—that had not responded to the order.

Later that day, the chief meteorologist, Group Captain James Martin Stagg, announced that a lull of thirty-six hours was probable. Should they take a chance and go ahead? The tide table was such that if they canceled the operation, they would have to wait until 19 June—a delay that would in turn require them either to keep the men on board their ships for another two weeks or to go through boarding procedures all over again. Eisenhower was inclined to risk everything rather than wait any longer. The burden on his shoulders can scarcely be imagined. After receiving confirmation of Stagg's forecast on the morning of 5 June and considering the matter in silence for several minutes, he finally made up his mind at 4:30 A.M.: "O.K., let's go."[15] "No one present disagreed," Eisenhower later recalled, "and there was a definite brightening of faces as, without a further word, each went off to his respective post of duty to flash out to his command the messages that would set the whole host in motion."[16] Before the great departure, the Allied supreme commander visited British troops near his advance headquarters at Portsmouth and then after dinner went to Welford to bid farewell to the men of the 101st Airborne Division before they took off for the Cotentin. He remained at the base until the last plane took off, then went back to headquarters well after midnight to get a few hours' rest.

## OPERATIONS

Two great forces composed the fleet of NEPTUNE. The Eastern Naval Task Force, commanded by Admiral Sir Philip Vian, carried troops of the British Second Army destined to land on Sword, Gold, and Juno: three infantry divisions (less two brigades), one armored division and three armored brigades, and two brigades of commandos, in addition to a support division and nondivisional units. The Western Naval Task Force, directed by Admiral Alan G. Kirk, brought over the U.S. First Army to the transfer area for Utah and Omaha: three infantry divisions, five tank battalions, and two commando battalions, in addition to nondivisional units. In all, more than 130,000 men and 20,000 vehicles were launched during the first three waves. Close by, fifteen hospital ships were poised to intervene, manned by 8,000 doctors and equipped with 450,000 liters of plasma and 600,000 doses of penicillin.

A gigantic armada of 1,200 warships and 5,700 transport ships (including 4,266 landing ships and landing craft)[17] carried the first wave. Regardless of their port of departure, all these vessels (apart from the landing craft, which were stowed on the larger ships) converged on Area Z, unofficially known as Piccadilly Circus, about twenty miles southeast of the Isle of Wight. Preceded by twenty-five flotillas of minesweepers, the convoys made their way through ten approach channels (two per beach, one used as a "fast" lane and the other as a "slow" lane) that had been cleared of charges and marked by illuminated buoys. Two buoy-laying submarines (*X20* and *X23*) marked the area around Juno and Sword beaches for the British and Canadian forces. Allowances having been made for the differences in the tide tables of the five beaches, the assault was set to begin at 6:30 A.M. in the American sector, 7:25 at Sword and Gold, and 7:35 at Juno. To protect the fleet, RAF fighters patrolled the skies all night, and the Eighth and Ninth U.S. Air Force took over at dawn. Four P-38 Lightning squadrons guarded the approach channels; six Spitfire squadrons provided low-altitude cover; three Thunderbolt squadrons carried out surveillance at higher altitudes. In all, fifty-two squadrons were mobilized, in addition to thirty reserve formations.[18]

Subterfuges were employed to confuse the enemy. Two Bomber Command squadrons jammed German radar. Dummies were parachuted in to Maltot (southwest of Caen), Marigny (west of Saint-Lô), and Yvetot (northwest of Rouen). Strips of metal-coated paper were dropped, to suggest the advance of a fleet toward the Pas de Calais. Operations TAXABLE and GLIMMER simulated landings on Cape Antifer and the Pas de Calais, the credibility of which were enhanced by false radio traffic, sonar emissions, and smoke screens.[19] Signals were sent out to mislead the few radar stations still operating along the Channel coast—a wise precaution, despite the Germans' sluggishness that spring.[20] As the Allied intelligence services noted with satisfaction three days before the landing, the enemy did not seem to suspect the imminence of OVERLORD.[21] That lack of awareness was due in part to the degraded state of the Reich's information-gathering capabilities. Not only had bad weather wreaked havoc, leading to the suspension of naval and aerial reconnaissance, but the Allies had devoted 1,650 sorties to bombing German radar stations since 11 May.[22] Many installations had been destroyed: only eighteen radio transmitters (out of ninety-two) and nine radar installations were functioning during the night of 5–6 June, all of them subject to Allied interference, with the result that the approach of the fleet was detected only between 2:00 and 3:00 in the morning—just as the attacking forces, a few miles from the coast, were preparing to board their landing craft.[23]

At the same moment, parachute and airborne troops were about to go into action. On the American side, two divisions—the Eighty-second ("All American") and the 101st ("Screaming Eagles")—were to land in the Cotentin. Beginning at 10:15 in the evening of the fifth, 13,000 men took off in 832 aircraft. Between 1:30 and 2:30 A.M., the paratroops readied themselves for the decisive jump, which would last forty seconds. The men of the Eighty-second Airborne were initially scheduled to be dropped near Saint-Sauveur-le-Vicomte, but the unanticipated arrival of the German Ninety-first Infantry Division, noticed just in time by Allied intelligence, caused plans to be modified on 28 May.[24] The Eighty-second was therefore redeployed to Sainte-Mère-Église, where it was hoped that by taking control of national highway 13 and destroying two bridges on the Douve, the Allies could prevent counterattacking German forces from advancing north toward Cherbourg. The 101st was given the mission of controlling the four roads leading out from Utah, seizing the lock at La Barquette, neutralizing a few coastal batteries, and destroying the rail line to Carentan. In this way the Americans counted on being able to secure the territory behind Utah—a measure that was all the more vital because the naturally marshy character of the terrain, which had been deliberately flooded by the Germans, threatened to block the troops' progress after the landing.

The objectives were achieved for the most part, although the bridges on the Merderet remained intact. Moreover, the arrival of airborne forces obliged the Germans to engage in combat, thus diverting their attention from the beaches. The paratroops were too widely scattered to be very effective, however. Major General Maxwell D. Taylor's 6,600 Screaming Eagles found themselves spread out over a twenty-five-by-fifteen-mile area, and only 1,100 men made it to their rendezvous points.[25] Banks of clouds, together with German antiaircraft fire, worked to break up the formations of C-47s. The pilots took every possible precaution: only twenty or so planes were shot down; but some troops landed as much as twenty miles from their dropping zone. The forces needed to achieve the mission's objectives were therefore much reduced. The Third Battalion of the All-American 501st Regiment, led by Lieutenant Colonel Julian Ewell, had only forty of its full contingent of six hundred men—a handicap that did not prevent it from taking the village of Poupeville, adjacent to exit 1 from Utah.[26] The Allies nonetheless paid dearly for the flawed execution of the landing plan. John Steele, a paratrooper with the Eighty-second who passed a long night caught on the church spire of Sainte-Mère-Église with an injured foot, was luckier than most. The 101st alone lost 1,500 men and 60 percent of its supplies and equipment.[27]

On the British side, Major General Richard N. Gale's Sixth Airborne Division was dropped a little after midnight. The 9,000 British troops landing by parachute or glider were assigned the task of destroying the bridges on the Dives, seizing the bridges spanning the Orne, and neutralizing the battery at Merville. Once again these objectives were achieved—the last owing to the daring of the team led by Lieutenant Colonel Terence Otway, which had rehearsed the maneuver at Newbury nine times, using a replica of the battery. Yet unforeseeable contingencies arose. Airborne troops were to have swooped down on German positions just as Otway's men were about to launch their assault. But only one glider came, landing near the village, a half a mile from its target. At the appointed hour, then, Otway could count on only 110 men and a few explosives. Even so, they managed to destroy the battery at 4:45 A.M., though not without a certain sense of disappointment (the guns were 100 mm, not 150 mm as expected) and at the cost of heavy casualties (seventy men killed or wounded).[28] The troops landed by glider around Bénouville seized the bridges over the Orne and the Caen Canal and succeeded in holding them on their own for thirty hours in the face of a fierce German counterattack.[29] They further distinguished themselves by capturing Ranville—the first village in France to be liberated. General Gale's men nonetheless paid a high price for this honor: 100 out of 355 glider pilots were wounded or killed; casualties for the Sixth Airborne Division as a whole amounted to 40 percent. Nonetheless, in striking contradiction to Leigh-Mallory's gloomy prognosis of a few weeks earlier, they rendered invaluable assistance to the seaborne forces that were poised to attack.

Aerial bombardment was less successful. Between 3:15 and 5:00 A.M., 1,135 heavy bombers of the RAF striking at ten selected batteries (notably Saint-Martin-de-Varreville, Ouistreham, and Maisy) dropped a total of 5,853 tons of bombs. Later that morning, 1,365 USAF "heavies" followed. Then the medium bombers took over. In all, the Allied air forces threw into the battle 3,467 heavy bombers and 1,645 medium bombers, mainly for the purpose of pulverizing the coastal defenses. The results were disappointing. Fearing that they would accidentally hit the troops who were coming ashore, the bombardiers waited too long to open their holds. "Not until later," General Bradley acknowledged, "did we learn that most of the 13,000 bombs dropped by these heavies had cascaded harmlessly into the hedgerows three miles behind the coast. In bombing through the overcast, air had deliberately delayed its drop to lessen the danger of spill-over on craft approaching the shore. This margin for safety had undermined the effectiveness of the heavy air mission. To the seasick infantry, bailing their craft as they wallowed through the surf, this failure in air bombing was to mean many more casualties upon Omaha Beach."[30] Conversely, the medium bombers released their payloads prematurely—a third falling into the water in the vicinity of Utah.[31] Moreover, because many of the bombs failed to penetrate the concrete cladding of the German pillboxes, the Atlantic Wall remained largely intact at dawn.[32] The task of smashing it therefore fell to the navy's artillery.

At 5:45 A.M. the cruisers and battleships opened fire, followed at 6:19 by the destroyers. The barrage reached its height between 5:55 and 6:45. Gun-equipped landing craft came after the large ships, before the troops set foot on the beaches. Here again, the results fell short of expectations:

the siting of German small- and medium-caliber guns in such a way as to enfilade the beach, rather than the sea, may have accounted for their delay in opening fire, but they were protected by "a solid front of concrete to seaward of [the] pillboxes against which naval gunfire had no destructive effect."[33] Moreover, smoke and flame interfered with the accuracy of the artillery on board the LCGs. In the British sector, naval gunfire succeeded in eliminating no more than 8 percent of the mortars, 19 to 23 percent of the machine guns, and 32 percent of the German antiaircraft guns of 37 mm to 88 mm—and even this last figure may be too high. It did, on the other hand, have a certain psychological effect on the defenders: groggy and demoralized, many of them were unable to regain their combat posts; 23.5 percent of their guns were later found undamaged by the Allies.[34] In all, it is estimated that only 10 to 20 percent of the defenses in the British area were destroyed, and that another 10 to 20 percent of the guns were not manned.[35] Because of the air attacks carried out in the weeks preceding D-Day, the Germans had not been able to fortify all their emplacements.

Everything considered, then, Allied aerial and naval bombardment failed to compromise the integrity of the German defenses in any serious way. Terrible ordeals therefore awaited the men who were preparing to attack.

## THE LANDINGS

The invasion plan called for the Anglo-American forces to land at dawn on five adjacent beaches. Nature intervened to complicate their task, however. A stiff wind blowing toward the coast caused the tides to rise half an hour sooner than forecast, and, by covering many of the mines and obstacles, to handicap the engineers in their work. The men, having crossed the Channel in pitiful conditions—many of them tense and exhausted from having thrown up the large breakfast they had been served—were hardly in peak form. The lull that Stagg had promised did not portend good weather: the wind blew at fifteen knots, swelling the waves to a height of three to six feet and making the approach to shore a grueling test of endurance.

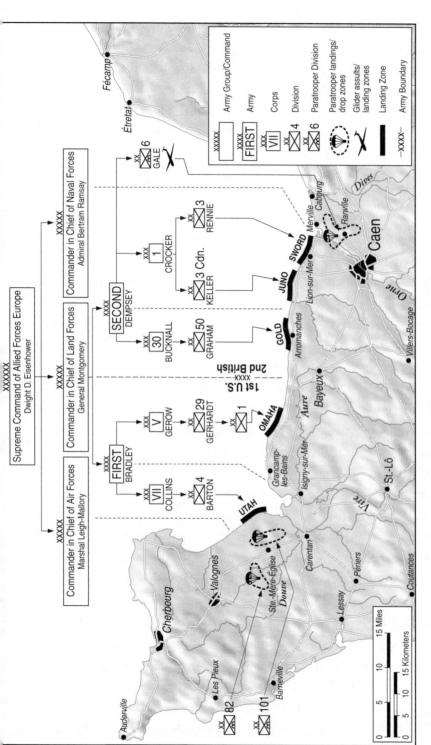

4. Landing of Allied Forces on 6 June 1944

On Omaha the American army came within a hair's breadth of catastrophe. The terrain strongly favored the enemy, it is true. Although almost four miles of sand stood exposed at low tide, the beach rose in its upper part to a pebbled embankment bordered by a low stone wall. Above this loomed dunes, hills, and cliffs on which the Germans had laid out their defensive positions. Anticipating a landing at high tide, they had placed their obstacles near the upper reaches of the shoreline—hence the Allies' decision to disembark at low tide, in order to have time to destroy them.[36] The change in tidal onset thwarted this plan. Complicating matters was the fact that the men of the Twenty-ninth Infantry Division, commanded by Major General Charles H. Gerhardt, were inexperienced and their officers undistinguished. This weakness had led Supreme Headquarters to assign to Omaha an elite unit, the First Infantry Division ("Big Red One") led by Lieutenant General Clarence R. Huebner, which was to arrive in the first wave. But the overall success of the assault nonetheless rested in part on novice troops that would land later in the day. Moreover, both soldiers and vehicles were overloaded. In theory, an infantryman carried about forty-five pounds of equipment, in addition to his personal effects; in practice, he often hauled as much as sixty-eight pounds, various other essential articles (grenades, life vest, raincoat, and so on) having gradually been added to the basic kit. Weighed down by so much gear, many soldiers sank straight to the bottom on jumping out of their landing craft, and all the more quickly since the gear weighed still more when wet. Moreover, the difficulty of moving through choppy seas and along the soft, undulating surface of the beach hindered their progress.

On coming ashore at Omaha, the Americans expected to encounter the German 716th Infantry Division, a second-rate garrison unit composed partly of Russians. Instead, the troops that landed found themselves facing the 352nd, a mobile and much more substantial formation. And whereas SHAEF planners had reckoned the number of opposing battalions at four, in fact there were eight. The 352nd had been in the area since March but somehow had escaped detection—an almost inexplicable failure, considering the high standards of Allied intelligence.[37] Be that as it may, the attackers got off to a rocky start.

They were dogged, too, by bad luck. The aerial bombardment, as we have seen, had failed; and because the landing began almost an hour earlier on the American beaches than it did in the British sector, the naval bombardment was briefer in the first as well. As a result, the German defenses were almost wholly intact when the first soldiers disembarked. The landing craft, carried off course by the current, rarely came ashore at their target locations. In the ensuing disorder, the men tended to converge on the middle section of the beach, where they huddled together for protection—an ideal target for German gunners. In principle, infantry assault formations were to have landed first and knocked out enemy defenses, thereby allowing demolition teams to set to work clearing the shore of obstacles. But since the current had carried the advance units too far to the east, the engineers arrived before them, only to find that they had to work without protection against enemy fire and without much of the equipment they needed.

A few figures will summarize the scale of the disaster. Out of sixteen demolition teams, only five reached their designated area; they had at their disposal only six of the sixteen armored bulldozers assigned to them; 40 percent of the engineers were killed or wounded. As a consequence, not only were they unable to clear the beach of obstacles, but the exit routes along which men and stores were to be evacuated remained closed. The rising tide worsened the chaos. Of the sixteen teams of beachmasters that were supposed to run up flags to guide the landings, twelve became lost and the other four arrived at the wrong place. Attempts to bring amphibious vehicles ashore led to tragedy. In the case of the Sherman dual-drive (DD) tanks, equipped with impermeable canvas skirts to keep them afloat, "thirty-two were launched, their skirts deployed, but in high seas and (doubtless because of fear) too far from land. Twenty-seven sank with their complete crews, a tribute to stubborn hope, for tank after tank was launched *seriatim,* each sinking like a stone, observed by everyone on the launching ship."[38] The soldiers, for their part, were unable in many cases to establish contact with their commanders, more than three-quarters of the radios having been lost during the first wave.

Scenes of panic multiplied. The pilots of a Rhino barge loaded with tanks and trucks simply abandoned it, almost a half mile out, leaving their drivers no choice but to wait until the tide brought them ashore. Junior officers, many of them inexperienced, often failed to lead by example.[39] The situation soon became so alarming that at 8:30 A.M. all movement of matériel was suspended on Omaha. Headquarters feared that with 25,000 men and 4,400 vehicles scheduled to land in the second wave, the beach would become impossibly congested. The rising tide was beginning to cover the obstacles, vehicles were piling up on the shore, hundreds of barges were going around in circles, radio communications were interrupted. General Bradley began to prepare for the worst: "When V Corps reported at noon that the situation was 'still critical' on all four beach exits, I reluctantly contemplated the diversion of Omaha follow-up forces to Utah and the British beaches."[40] This solution would have been disastrous: in human terms, it would have meant sacrificing the combatants at Omaha by depriving them of reinforcements; as a strategic matter, it would have opened up a gap between Utah and Gold of some thirty-five miles that enemy forces could not fail, sooner or later, to occupy and exploit.

Gradually the situation improved. Two landing craft, finding no place for the men on board to disembark, headed at full speed toward the beach and, throwing caution to the winds, opened fire. The men jumped ashore and managed to silence several German positions. Other boats and barges followed their example. Despite the fear of harming their own troops, eleven destroyers—among them the *Shubrick, McCook,* and *Satterlee*—approached the coast and supported the attackers with covering fire. Scarcely less important was the exemplary courage of a few officers—notably Brigadier General Norman Cota, second-in-command of the Twenty-ninth Infantry Division—who galvanized their men into action. As a result, the engineers were at last able to get down to work freeing jammed ramps on landing craft and pushing aside destroyed vehicles on the beach, without regard for the original plan. At 1:09 P.M. General Gerow sent his first positive report—so positive, in fact, that Bradley gave up the idea of abandoning Omaha.[41] Only a few minutes earlier a first exit had been opened up. An hour later the first tanks rolled out from the beach. But the clearing of the landing area did not begin in any meaningful way until late afternoon. By evening three exits were operational, further relieving the pressure.[42] Even so, although the trucks, jeeps, and tanks were now able to move inland, the artillery remained in place. Because of the chaos, little matériel had gotten through. By D + 5, only 46.6 percent of the scheduled tonnage had been unloaded at Omaha, a deficit that immediately posed the problem of resupplying the troops that had landed.

The fighting at Pointe du Hoc, just west of Omaha, was still bloodier. The elite Second Ranger Battalion, led by Lieutenant Colonel James E. Rudder, had responsibility for taking this high ground, thought to shelter a formidable battery of six 155 mm guns. One part of Rudder's force was to fight on the beach at Omaha; the other would scale the adjacent cliffs. The Rangers fought in horrifying conditions: of the sixty-eight men in Company C, only thirty-one made it ashore; equipment went missing—only one of the twenty-five-meter extension ladders supplied by the London Fire Department could be erected, and the attackers, in order to climb to the top, were forced to resort to grappling irons and ropes shot out by rocket guns. There they were astonished to discover that the 155 mm cannon had been removed from their casements and replaced with telephone poles; later the guns were found half a mile inland, in a make-shift and well-camouflaged battery, and immediately disabled. This success nonetheless exacted a heavy toll: by the end of D-Day, only ninety of two hundred Rangers were still in a position to fight.[43] In total, Fifth Corps lost 8.8 percent of its men: of some thirty-four thousand men who landed, three thousand were killed, wounded, or missing in action.[44] This figure, though high, was yet far below the projected losses of 12.5 percent. When darkness fell, 65 percent of the obstacles installed by the enemy were still in place.

The situation appeared in a quite different light on Utah, where the terrain was less hostile: the beach rose toward the shore along a gentle slope, and the absence of bluffs deprived the defenders of the advantage they enjoyed at Omaha, although flooded areas inland threatened to slow the advance of troops. The American assault followed the same plan as at Omaha, except that in this case the demolition teams landed right on schedule. Since the obstacles were not yet submerged by the rising tide, the engineers were able to work quickly—all the more so since the obstructions were relatively few in number. From the first wave on, then, the beach was able to be cleared. Other problems that handicapped the American forces to the east did not arise at Utah. The aerial bombardment was effective on the whole. The current, though it carried the troops away from their landing points, brought with it luck as well. The men of the Fourth Division, for example, instead of being deposited in front of the heavily guarded dunes at Varreville, landed at Sainte-Marie-du-Mont, a less strongly defended position. Crucially for the support of the infantrymen, twenty-eight of thirty-two DD amphibious tanks arrived safely on shore. While the troops set to work neutralizing German resistance, the engineers managed to open up an approach route permitting reinforcements and additional equipment to be distributed along a relatively broad front; four breaches having been opened in the seawall, it became possible to evacuate the troops and stores and so to avoid treacherous overcrowding on the beaches.

Successful though it was, the assault on Utah was not free of complications. Losses of landing craft were relatively high; indeed, the commander of Force U, Rear Admiral Don P. Moon, considered suspending landing operations at night.[45] There were instances of panic in the Fourth Infantry Division, a unit composed largely of untested soldiers. One officer, trying to establish contact with elements of the Eighty-second Airborne Division, experienced the greatest difficulties in assembling some sixty men, but managed finally to rally, he said, "some stragglers from God knows where and all the glider pilots I could catch. The last six or seven I had literally to catch, making motions at them with a pistol—for they had become very, very enthusiastic about carrying out their orders to get back to England."[46] Movement of troops and stores encountered delays in the face of continuing enemy resistance: ships were forced to anchor farther from the coast than planned; communications broke down; in some cases landing craft discharged cargo at sea, in order to avoid enemy fire, with the result that many vehicles stalled or sank on clearing the ramps. Only 6,614 tons of matériel were unloaded in the first three days, or 26.6 percent of the planned tonnage. The problem of resupplying the troops, difficult from the first, became more acute over time. And yet by the evening of 6 June there was reason for optimism on Utah. The beach had been rid of mines and other obstacles; exits were open; food and supply depots had been established; 21,300 men had been safely landed. The total cost in lives was astonishingly low: 300, or 1.4 percent—a happy contrast with "bloody Omaha."[47]

The British sector displayed great differences with its American counterpart. Extending over some twenty-five miles, the former was divided up for operational purposes into three beaches forming a discontinuous front of about five miles.[48] More built-up than the American sector, this area obliged the attackers to engage in intense fighting in the villages that lined the shore. Moreover, the sector was guarded by a series of German batteries distributed between Riva-Bella (six 155 mm guns), Houlgate (six 155 mm guns), Merville (four 100 mm guns), Longues (four 155 mm guns), Ver-sur-Mer (one battery of four 100 mm guns and another of four 122 mm guns), and Ouistreham (four 155 mm guns). And although the region's well-developed road network promised to assist the Allies' progress inland, the narrow streets in the coastal villages threatened to create bottlenecks at the outset.

On Gold Beach, the Fiftieth (Northumbrian) Infantry Division landed without encountering strong resistance in its zone, adjacent to the villages of Asnelles and Ver-sur-Mer. The fortified German positions at Le Hamel and La Rivière held out for several hours, but already by 11 A.M. Major General D. A. H. Graham's men had managed to open up seven corridors to the interior for evacuating troops and armored forces. Shortly thereafter, the division's four brigades launched an assault on the hills overlooking Arromanches, which they seized by the end of the afternoon, as well as the heights dominating Port-en-Bessin the following day. Of some 25,000 men who came ashore, only 413—or 1.7 percent—were lost.[49]

On Juno, operations began at 7:45 A.M., having been pushed back ten minutes because of choppy seas. In the meantime, the rising tide had covered some of the obstacles on the inner beach, with the result that 20 of the first 24 landing craft to go forth were lost or damaged—the fate of 90 of the 306 vessels deployed at Juno that day.[50] The Third Canadian Division, led by Major General Rod Keller, encountered particularly lively resistance: aerial and naval bombardment had succeeded in knocking out only 14 percent of the coastal defenses, leaving intact most emplacements of 88 and 75 mm guns. To make matters worse, the bombardment was interrupted at 7:30 A.M., five minutes before the originally scheduled hour of landing; but since the Canadians arrived later than planned, the Germans had time to regroup. General Keller's men nonetheless enjoyed considerable advantages, particularly with regard to the relation of forces, since only 400 Germans faced 2,400 Canadians. In view of the weather conditions, the Canadians decided to offload their Sherman DD tanks as close to shore as possible (only six hundred yards out in some cases), while trying to bring them in all the way if they could. Fourteen of the first nineteen tanks made it ashore safely. The first wave of oncoming troops sustained heavy losses, in a scene reminiscent of the tragedy at Omaha; but they were able to find shelter fairly quickly: they took cover behind the tanks or concealed themselves behind the seawall at the upper end of the beach—opportunities denied to the First and the Twenty-ninth Divisions on Omaha. As a result, the first wave at Juno rapidly succeeded in seizing Courseulles and Bernières but managed to take Saint-Aubin only eighteen hours later, after fierce street fighting. By the evening of 6 June some 24,000 men had come ashore, at the cost of 805 casualties (3.35 percent of the total), including 300 dead.[51]

Finally, Major General T. G. Rennie's Third Infantry Division, reinforced by a special commando brigade under the command of Brigadier General Simon Lovat, was to land on Sword. Here the German batteries played only a minimal role. Otway's men of the Sixth Airborne had destroyed Merville; the guns of Ouistreham had been silenced; and the German battery at Le Havre, confused by the smoke and disabled by fire from the British battleship *Warspite,* did not have the range to reach the shore. The enemy's 88 mm guns and submerged obstacles and mines nonetheless caused severe damage at Sword. At 7:25 A.M. a vanguard of LCTs and LCAs began discharging DD tanks, troops, and twenty-one pieces of specialized armor: Crocodiles (Churchill tanks fitted with flamethrowers), Crabs (Sherman tanks equipped with rotating cylinders of weighted chains, or "flails," that exploded buried mines), and AVRE tanks (also known as Petards, for their petard demolition mortars) used to remove underwater obstacles and clear immobilized vehicles.[52] Thanks to these devices, a beachhead was rapidly established, and the troops of the Third Infantry immediately set about liberating Ouistreham with the help of Commando Kieffer, an elite naval unit of 177 men led by Philippe Kieffer—the only Free French ground force to take part in operations in Normandy on D-Day.[53] The engineers had cleared away all the wreckage on Sword by early afternoon, in addition to opening up three exits; 28,800 men had been brought ashore, with light losses, everything considered: 630 dead and wounded, or 2.2 percent of the total.[54]

The special misfortune of the forces landed on Omaha was not a consequence of more concentrated enemy defenses. Neither obstacle belts nor artillery pieces were more numerous there than on the other beaches. Other elements were of greater importance: the topography favored the defenders; aerial bombing had spared the coastal batteries; naval bombardment was considerably less intense. The ratio of pounds of shells discharged per yard by the navy ranged between 0.22 and 0.26 on Utah and 0.09 on Gold, but only between 0.04 and 0.08 on Omaha because of the shorter time allowed for naval bombardment there. To destroy German positions on Omaha, Americans had nothing to rely on but their own courage. Tellingly, they had no DD tanks available to them— whereas the British and Canadians could look to the support of ninety-six on Gold, eighty-eight on Juno, and forty-seven on Sword.[55] In electing to transfer men and tanks from transport ships to barges and small landing craft at a great distance—eleven or twelve miles—from the Norman coast, the Americans had chosen unwisely. Their amphibious tanks were swamped, and the troops that made it ashore endured a difficult crossing that lasted three hours—a trial that the British had avoided by opting for a shorter trajectory, roughly seven miles.[56] To be sure, the Commonwealth forces arrived in a pitiful state, their quartermasters having forced them to consume a solid breakfast washed down by rum that was soon thrown up.[57] But they were supported by specialized armor and equipment of the Seventy-ninth Armored Division—Churchill Crocodiles, Sherman Crabs, AVREs—that the Americans lacked.

On the evening of 6 June, then, the Allies could look back with satisfaction on the events of the day. Some 156,000 men had gained a foothold on the Norman shore: 23,000 men parachuted onto the Cotentin and in the vicinity of Caen; 55,000 had landed on Utah and Omaha, 78,000 on the three beaches of the British sector. Contrary to persistent legend, casualties were relatively light. Whereas Supreme Headquarters had anticipated 25,000 victims, the actual number of dead, wounded, or missing was only 10,000. Omaha accounted for a quarter of the total, with the Eighty-second and the 101st Airborne Divisions jointly making up another quarter.[58] British casualties (excluding airborne troops) represented only 2.6 percent of the Second Army's ground forces; and although the first wave on Gold, Sword, and Juno suffered substantial losses, the following waves emerged relatively unscathed, the German defenses having been largely destroyed in the interval.[59]

Everything considered, the operation had been a stunning success. But the Allied high command could not be satisfied simply with landing a significant force on the Continent. It needed to profit from this result at once, by taking the offensive and seizing strategic positions.

# 8

# To Win a Battle

FOR THE FIRST PHASE OF the campaign, the Allied high command had set its troops three major objectives: to gain a foothold on the beaches; to consolidate a bridgehead by placing the five landing areas under unified control; and to capture Caen, Bayeux, and Cherbourg. These objectives were the product of both strategic and logistical considerations: establishing a continuous front would reduce the vulnerability of the Anglo-American forces, by depriving the Germans of breaches they could exploit to advantage; enlarging the lodgment area would provide the necessary space not only for assembling additional troops and storing matériel, but also for preliminary maneuver; taking Caen—the major objective—would yield control of a communications center and give access to a vast plain suitable for the establishment of air bases and the deployment of armored formations.

In the event, the attempt to unify and extend the positions achieved on 6 June was not without its share of disappointments. To the west, the men of the U.S. Fourth Infantry Division succeeded in joining up with elements of the 101st Airborne Division on the day of the landing; and moving out from Omaha, the bridgehead was rapidly expanded in the direction of Isigny, Port-en-Bessin, and Caumont-l'Éventé. On Juno, the Third Canadian Division managed to link up with the British forces that landed there later the same morning. The British Sixth Airborne Division, supported in the afternoon by the arrival of Lord Lovat's First Commando Brigade from Sword and in the evening by the division's second unit (brought in by 248 gliders), had the area of Bénouville well in hand. But while the Allied front stretched over some fifty-five miles, there were disquieting gaps between Gold and Omaha (seven miles), between Sword and Juno (three miles), and between Utah and Omaha (eleven miles). Over the next six days the Allies managed to close these gaps. On 7 June elements of the British Fiftieth Infantry Division and Seventh Armored Division entered Bayeux—the first town to be liberated in France, and one all the more envied by its neighbors for having fallen into the hands of its liberators intact. Toward the west, the Americans joined hands with the British, and from 8 June onward Omaha and the British beachheads formed a continuous whole. Finally, Bradley's troops took Isigny on the ninth and Carentan three days later, though not without fierce fighting (and, in the case of Carentan, hand-to-hand combat).[1] By means of this operation, Utah and Omaha were united, with the result that by the evening of 12 June the Allies had succeeded in creating a continuous front fifty miles long and six to eighteen miles deep, depending on the location. In the Cotentin, progress followed a slow but steady course. In the Anglo-Canadian sector, by contrast, Caen energetically resisted: the Germans had no intention of giving up control of a city of such great strategic importance.

## QUIET NO LONGER IN THE WEST

Poor weather conditions and a vast disinformation campaign combined, as we have seen, to mislead the adversary utterly. The Germans' surprise was compounded by the disorganization of the field command: Rommel had left his headquarters at La Roche-Guyon on the morning of 5 June to celebrate his wife's birthday at their home in Herrlingen, near Ulm and, more important, to plead with Hitler that two panzer divisions be placed on either side of the Bay of Veys, between Utah and Omaha; General Friedrich Dollmann, commander of the Seventh Army, had gone to Rennes to take part in war games; Lieutenant General Erich Marcks, chief of Eighty-fourth Corps, was celebrating his fifty-third birthday with members of his staff; General Joseph ("Sepp") Dietrich, of the First SS Panzer Corps, was in Brussels; Major General Edgar Feuchtinger, of

Twenty-first Panzer, is thought to have been seeking solace from the troubles of war in the arms of a female acquaintance. Absence from the front did not in all cases prevent them from regaining their posts quickly; indeed, General Marcks had activated his troops as soon as he heard of paratroop landings, just after 1:00 A.M. Just the same, the Western command was by no means immediately operational—especially since it was to sustain a series of severe blows in the days that followed: on 6 June Major General Wilhelm Falley, who had turned around on reaching Rennes to resume his command of the Ninety-first Division, was cut down by a burst of light machine-gun fire; on the tenth, bombs struck the headquarters of Panzer Group West, killing seventeen senior officers; on the twelfth, General Marcks was killed by a bomber-fighter attack (the fate also, six days later, of Major General Rudolf Stegmann of the Seventy-seventh Division); on the seventeenth, Major General Heinz Hellmich, commander of the 243rd Division, was killed; on the twenty-eighth, General Dollmann died of a heart attack. This string of misfortunes disrupted decision making and deprived the German command, already handicapped by internal rivalries and the fragmentation of authority Hitler had long encouraged, of the cohesion needed to mount an effective response.

Warnings had nonetheless been issued at the earliest opportunity. The Allies were to give advance notice of the attack to the French Resistance by means of a series of radio messages. The last three lines of the first stanza of Verlaine's "Chanson d'automne" had inadvertently been sent in the first days of June to Ventriloquist, a network controlled by an agent of the Special Operations Executive (SOE) of the British Secret Services who had fallen into the hands of the German intelligence. The Germans therefore knew the meaning of the transmission but, as we have seen, discounted it. Even so, when the staff of the Fifteenth Army intercepted the lines signaling an imminent invasion ("Blessent mon coeur / D'une longueur / Monotone") again on the evening of the fifth, at 9:15 P.M., OB West duly issued a preventive alert at 9:45. Three hours later, at 12:50 A.M., the 711th Infantry Division announced drops of parachutists in its sector, north of Caen—a report subsequently confirmed by Fifteenth Army headquarters for the area east of Caen. At 2:30, OKW gave permission for the Twelfth SS Panzer Division to conduct a reconnaissance along the coast but declined to grant Rundstedt the right to make further use of either this unit or the elite Panzer Lehr, both part of its armored reserve.

Those who argue that Rommel, had he been able to use these panzer divisions as he wished, would have been able to push the Allies back into the sea are inclined to make too much of this refusal. Excusing the Western command for its mistakes, these authors attribute sole responsibility for what they consider a crucial blunder to the blindness of OKW, and especially to the cowardice of Jodl, its chief of operations, who, by refusing to awaken Hitler, lost precious time. "Assuming that the four divisions concerned [First and Twelfth SS Panzer Divisions, Seventeenth SS Panzer Grenadier Division, and Panzer Lehr] were the Supreme Headquarters' reserve in the full sense of the word," Jodl's deputy Walter Warlimont later observed, "no one could have considered releasing them at a time when even the forward headquarters still had no clear picture of the situation and before the first enemy landing craft had touched the beach. It was not for instance until 10:30 A.M. that Headquarters Army Group B considered the situation sufficiently definite to inform their Commander-in-Chief, Field Marshal Rommel, who had been in southern Germany since 4 June. The Chief of Staff of Army Group B in his book published later states flatly that it was 'out of the question' and adds that one 'had to have the nerve to wait.'"[2]

Everything considered, warning of the assault had been given reasonably quickly. At 6:30 A.M., German radio announced the news—confirmed only three hours later on the Allied airwaves. Field headquarters were promptly placed on battle alert. Rommel raced back from Herrlingen, arriving at La Roche-Guyon by evening. Hitler, awakened at 10:00 A.M., greeted the news calmly: "Also, Anganga is" ("So, we're off")—evidence that the leadership did not succumb to panic.[3] Plainly the German reaction did not depend on decisions made on the morning of 6 June. It was determined above all by two things: on the one hand, OKW's prior assessment of the situation and, on the other hand, the resources that the field commanders were able to mobilize. Whereas Naval Group West and Seventh Army headquarters did not believe on 6 June that the landings in Normandy constituted a diversionary maneuver, Rundstedt was more hesitant. But however he may have regarded the situation, he was for the moment capable of deploying only modest forces against the Allied attack. Although Twenty-first Panzer was in position, Twelfth SS Panzer did not arrive on the scene until late during the night of 6–7 June, joined on the eighth by Panzer Lehr. Neither of these divisions was fully operational until the next day, 9 June—a bit late, as it turned out. Supreme Headquarters had approved the request for their movement at around three o'clock in the afternoon on D-Day.[4]

Unable to destroy the Allied bridgeheads, the Germans had to settle for local counterattacks. On the first two days, Twenty-first Panzer and Twelfth SS Panzer succeeded in blocking the Caen road against the British advance; and on the seventh, the Third British Division failed in its attempt to break through the enemy defenses at Cambes and in the woods of Lebisey. Twelfth SS Panzer also parried the thrust of the Canadian Third Division, which sought to seize the airfield at Carpiquet, and turned the division back near the village of Authie—committing terrible war crimes while doing so.

Stalled outside Tilly-sur-Seulles, the British tried in the days that followed to outflank the German formations, aiming to close in on Caen by a pincer movement. To do so, they had to capture Villers-Bocage to the west and Sainte-Honorine, Cuverville, and Demouville to the east. Twenty-first Panzer blocked the eastern thrust, however; and SS First Lieutenant Michael Wittman succeeded, in a famously daring raid on 13 June, in repulsing the leading elements of the British Seventh Armored Division at Villers-Bocage, single-handedly destroying some twenty tanks and nearly thirty armored vehicles. These and other local successes closed off the road to Caen, where the Twenty-first and Twelfth SS Panzer Divisions were later joined by a third unit, Panzer Lehr, equipped with 250 tanks and 150 88 mm antitank guns. The Germans were nonetheless unable to mount a broad counterattack. General Geyr von Schweppenburg had hoped to cut off the British forces between Caen and Bayeux, but he was forced to abort the operation on 10 June when the mobile headquarters of Panzer Group West was destroyed by RAF bombers. The three panzer divisions, now striking out northward from

Caen, met with stiff resistance from British forces supported by artillery fire and air bombardment; an offensive launched eastward from the Orne by Twenty-first Panzer and an accompanying infantry division failed just as completely. By a curious paradox, then, the schemes of strategists on both sides were frustrated: if the British were powerless to gain their primary objective, Caen, the Germans proved no more capable of taking advantage of their adversary's missteps.

The Wehrmacht's impotence was clear from the beginning. The vaunted Atlantic Wall had held exactly one day on Omaha, and only one hour on the other four beaches—to the astonishment of the Allied intelligence services: "The defence failed. No other conclusion is possible when it is realised that within an hour of H-Hour, the leading troops were passing through the beaches and that by 9:30, at least two of the coastal batteries had been reported out of action."[5] Rundstedt, as we have seen, did not believe his defensive line was strong enough to repel an invasion; but he did think it would succeed at least in retarding the Allies' advance long enough to be able to deliver a devastating counterattack. Even in this more modest expectation he was to be cruelly disappointed—in part because the land-based obstacles meant to neutralize airborne troops failed in their purpose as well. "The antiglider stakes which Rommel had had installed were ineffectual in preventing the landing," Major General Fritz Bayerlein noted, "as they had neither been wired together nor fitted with mines."[6] Along the shore, under relentless fire from tank gunners, the Germans had difficulty reacting, for they did not imagine that the Allies could transport armored vehicles and heavy equipment together with the first wave of infantry. In claiming that an assault from the sea could not succeed, the Reich's propaganda had the inadvertent effect of undermining the motivation of its own troops, whose eagerness to fight was further reduced by the presence of foreign soldiers in their ranks, recruited from the conquered territories.[7]

Nor was the Kriegsmarine in a position to threaten the Allied armada. The submarines and motor torpedo boats dispatched to the Norman coast played only a limited role; and an Allied bombing raid on Le Havre during the night of 14–15 June destroyed a dozen fast patrol boats. "As a result of the enemy attack on Le Havre," Rommel noted, "the navy lost a large part of the craft suitable for use against the landing fleet."[8] By mid-June, German losses had risen to two destroyers, three motor torpedo boats, sixteen fast patrol boats, nine patrol boats, and three minesweepers.[9] Assisted by the air force, the navy could do little more than lay a few mines and launch small numbers of diver-guided torpedoes. During the first week of 6–13 June, it sank only 64 Allied military and merchant ships, and damaged 106.[10] Although these numbers are not unimpressive, considering the poverty of the Kriegsmarine's resources, they hardly threatened the success of NEPTUNE. Indeed, three-quarters of Allied naval losses on D-Day itself were due to the bad weather, and not to the action of the German forces.[11]

The Luftwaffe was similarly conspicuous by its absence. Not that Goering had shown any reluctance to send reinforcements: on 10 June, 688 fighters were on active duty on the Norman front, as contrasted with 438 on 25 May. But the Reichsmarschall's efforts counted for little. Of 57 planes dispatched from Wiesbaden, only 3 made it safely to Évreux, 7 were reported missing, and 47 were partially damaged on landing. Of the 22 transferred from Cologne, only 2 arrived at Villacoublay.[12] On average, Third Air Fleet lost 38 fighters a day—or a total of 1,040 by the beginning of July. Lacking fuel and proper ground facilities, many planes were based in the airfields of the Paris region and northeastern France, too far from the theater of operations to intervene effectively. These planes were also weighed down with additional fuel tanks, which reduced their maneuverability and made them more vulnerable to Allied fighters and anti-aircraft guns. The Luftwaffe was therefore obliged to scale back its ambitions. It managed only 319 sorties on 6 June, 849 on 8 June, and 376 on 18 June,[13] whereas the Allied air forces carried out some 14,000 missions on D-Day alone, losing a relatively small number of aircraft (roughly 300 in the first three days of fighting).[14] No matter that the Germans had succeeded in inflicting losses on the Allies—their own losses were proportionately greater, a state of affairs that sapped the morale of their soldiers, who mordantly observed that a gray plane was American, a black one British, and an invisible one German. In addition, it exposed the ground forces to attack, by preventing them from moving at will. The Second Panzer Division, stationed some 160 miles distant on the Somme, did not reach the front until 13 June and became operational only a week later. The story was the same for other formations. The Third Parachute Division "required six days for its approach march from Brittany to its battle area north-east of St. Lô (135 miles as the crow flies)," Rommel reported, "during which time it was under constant threat from the air. By the time it arrived, the attack it was due to launch on Bayeux was no longer possible, as strong enemy forces had already taken possession of the Forest of Cerisy. . . . All the reserves that came up arrived far too late to smash the enemy landing by counter-attacks. By the time they arrived the enemy had disembarked considerably stronger forces and himself gone over to the attack under cover of a powerful air and artillery support."[15] Panzer Lehr, on leaving the Chartres district at 5:00 P.M. on 6 June, immediately found itself under attack by Allied planes. By nightfall the unit had lost 20 or 30 vehicles. It was bombed again the next morning, with the result that 80 of its 700 half-tracks and self-propelled guns, 130 of its 1,000 trucks, and 5 of its 140 tanks were destroyed.[16]

Weather conditions nonetheless restricted Allied air supremacy, forcing cancellation of half the scheduled missions in June. "I sometimes think that the Powers above may have fascist tendencies," Leigh-Mallory confessed, "so bad has been the weather."[17] Even so, robbed of the power of free movement, the Germans had no choice but to keep their armored divisions in place, in hopes of containing the thrust of Canadian and British forces toward Caen. Doing so obliged OKW to violate the principles of orthodox strategy, since it meant assigning to tanks a mission traditionally reserved for foot soldiers. In more equal circumstances the place of armor would have been taken by infantry, allowing the panzer divisions to regroup and mount a counterattack. But the Allies' almost total mastery of the skies ruled out any such solution. The Germans therefore threw reinforcements into battle unit by unit, without being able to substitute infantry for armored formations before the beginning of July.

Rommel and Rundstedt, keenly aware of the implications of this strategic impasse, tried to persuade Hitler to modify his plans. The Führer consented to meet with them on 17 June at Margival, the site of his underground Western headquarters near Soissons. Rommel explained that he no longer believed a second landing to be likely and requested complete freedom of maneuver, in addition to armored reinforcements. He furthermore proposed pulling back his forces behind the Orne in order to protect them against naval artillery and, if necessary, launching a counteroffensive on Montgomery's flank. Hitler flatly refused.[18] Heartened by the results of the first V-1 attack on London four days earlier (the V-2 did not become available until September), he proclaimed his faith in these revolutionary instruments of destruction, soon to be supplemented by new submarines and jet fighters.

The Führer's reprisal weapons were indeed a lethal threat: the flying bombs killed a total of 6,184 people, the missiles 2,754—and spread fear among the civilian population. But they did not shake its resolve. "The pilotless plane continues to rival the invasion of Normandy as a topic of conversation," noted a government report. "Much anxiety is expressed, but this seems chiefly on account of those living in danger areas, particularly friends and relations. The use of the flying bomb is thought to indicate Germany's weakness and her need to bolster up home morale at all costs, and it is variously described as 'Jerry's last kick' and 'the product of despair.' The general feeling is that flying bombs cannot affect the outcome of the war."[19] In the meantime, the accidental boomerang of a V-1, falling on the Margival compound just after the departure of his generals, led Hitler to cancel a promised visit to Seventh Army headquarters the following morning and return to Germany—leaving Rommel and Rundstedt to deal with an increasingly dire situation by themselves.[20]

The reasons for the stalling of the Anglo-Canadian assault on Caen and Carpiquet, which were to have fallen the first day, have been the subject of much debate, both during the war and after. The Commonwealth forces suffered in the first place from the confused situation on the beaches. The Twenty-seventh Armored Brigade, which had been instructed to strike out toward Caen without delay, found two-thirds of its tanks stuck in the sand or else pinned down by fighting along the coast. The entire weight of the thrust toward the city therefore rested on the 185th Infantry Brigade, led by Brigadier K. Pearce Smith. And yet its supporting tanks, the Shermans of the Staffordshire Yeomanry, were themselves delayed by the massive congestion on Sword.[21] For the British to take Caen, the Staffordshires would have had to reach the Norman capital before Twenty-first Panzer—a result that could be achieved only in the event of a total collapse of the German coastal and inland defenses. This and other conditions proved impossible to fulfill.[22] On Juno the Ninth Canadian Infantry Brigade landed between Bernières and Saint-Aubin, but it too suffered from the disorder that raged all around. By itself, however, the fact that bottlenecks on the beaches in the British sector prevented the armored units from dashing toward their objectives inland does not explain the failure at Caen.

It should be noted, first, that the Commonwealth field commanders displayed great caution. General Dempsey, fearing a German counteroffensive, ordered his three divisions to halt their advance early in the evening of 6 June to take stock of the situation, although both Caen and Carpiquet were within sight. His exhausted men showed little will to push on. Some set to digging trenches—a sign that memories of 1914–1918 had not been entirely erased. It was in any case difficult to ask these soldiers, who had crossed the Channel before dawn and then broken through the Atlantic Wall, to give any more of themselves that day. And because the military and psychological preparations had placed greater emphasis on the landing than on the fighting that was to follow, by the evening of D-Day the Allies could be forgiven for supposing that the hardest part was over. Among troops in the British sector the tendency was "to stop to brew up a tea and congratulate themselves on having accomplished their objective—getting ashore."[23] Some units, of course, had been fighting for three years; they were filled with weariness, compounded by the desire to stay alive now that victory seemed within reach. The Desert Rats of the Seventh Armored Division, having fought their way from El Alamein to the shores of Normandy, no longer showed the same determination; they felt that they had done their part and so earned the right to limit the risks to which they were exposed.[24] Many of the officers, by contrast, exhibited a kind of pointless audacity, marching at the head of their formations, where the talc coverings of their map boards, glinting in the sun, drew the attention of German snipers.[25]

But perhaps the greatest impediment was inadequate coordination between infantry and armor. The commander of Seventh Armored, Major

General G. W. J. Erskine, told Brigadier James Hargest, attached as an observer to Thirtieth Corps, that he would rather advance alone because the foot soldiers could not keep up with the pace set by his tanks. But in that case, of course, infantry would no longer be in a position to move in and hold ground once it was conquered. Hargest concluded:

> Our tanks are badly led and fought. . . . They bunch up—they are the reverse of aggressive—they are not possessed of the will to attack the enemy. . . . My opinion is that a great deal of their failure is due to the retention of the absurd Regimental system. Because there is no work for cavalry the Cavalry Reg[imen]ts were given tanks. The officers are trained in armour not because they like armour but because they are cavalry men. . . . An airman is a good airman because he loves being in a plane. Not so with armour. . . . At the moment we suffer because of the incompatibility and the lack of the "will to fight" in the Armoured Corps.[26]

In fact, it was Montgomery's very awareness of these weaknesses that led him to keep the Sixth Airborne Division at the front, a decision that occasioned some grumbling in the ranks. "In spite of the fact that the Div[ision] realised the valuable part it was playing in holding the left, this role, an unexpected one for Airborne tr[oo]ps was bound to lead to a sense of disappointment and frustration."[27]

The troops' lack of drive, by allowing the enemy to bring up reinforcements and organize its defenses, doomed offensive initiatives aimed at taking Caen quickly and made stalemate inevitable.

## FRUSTRATION AT CAEN

The Allies, as we have seen, counted on taking Caen the first day. Although German resistance had initially thwarted their designs, Montgomery's determination to capture the city remained undiminished. Toward the end of the first week of operations, he contemplated launching an airborne operation, which on 13 June the airmen refused to carry out—to his great anger.[28] He nevertheless persisted. "The immediate task of this Army will be to capture Caen," he told Eisenhower. "I shall hope to see both Caen and Cherbourg by June 24."[29] This ambition led to the planning of the first major offensive of the campaign, code-named EPSOM.

In the wake of the debacle at Villers-Bocage, Montgomery proposed to attack on a narrow front toward the Odon River, west of Caen, in order then to surround the city from the south. Thirtieth Corps was to launch an assault on Rauray, which, by forcing Panzer Lehr to fight instead of assisting Twelfth SS Panzer, would protect the right flank of the spearhead, Eighth Corps, commanded by Lieutenant General Sir Richard N. O'Connor.[30] Sixty thousand men would be engaged, supported by 550 tanks and 300 antitank guns. The great storm that hit Normandy between 19–22 June delayed the operation, which finally began on the twenty-fifth with the thrust toward Rauray. Despite German resistance, the British gained ground: forward elements penetrated as far as the left bank of the Odon by 27 June, permitting the Eleventh Armoured Division to push onward to Hill 112, near Esquay-Notre-Dame. The next day O'Connor's forces took the bridge at Gavrus as well, thus forming a narrow salient roughly five miles long by two miles wide, called the Scottish corridor after the Fifteenth Scottish Division, which carried the main attack toward Caen. The Germans hastened to turn away this challenge, launching a counterattack on 29 June led by the Ninth and Tenth SS Panzer Divisions, just arrived from Galicia, in Poland. Although Allied air forces succeeded in halting the enemy advance the next day, Montgomery was forced to abandon the operation. In less than a week, the Eighth Corps had lost more than five thousand men and seen its infantry reduced by half.[31]

Was EPSOM a victory or a defeat for the British? The answer depends on the strategy that Montgomery meant to follow. Caen, so far from falling the first day, managed to hold out against Twenty-first Army Group until 9 July. Yet Montgomery later claimed that the city was only a secondary objective, a red herring designed to give the Americans room for maneuver in the Cotentin by distracting the bulk of the German forces. "I was convinced that strong and persistent offensive action in the Caen sector would achieve our object of drawing the enemy reserves on to our eastern flank: this was my basic conception. From the beginning it formed the basis of all our planning."[32] Eisenhower, in his own memoirs, obligingly confirmed this version of events:

> Our frustration in the attainment of our immediate tactical goals in the eastern sector involved no change in the broad purposes of the operational plan. It was merely another example of the age-old truth that every battle plan comprises merely an orderly commitment of troops to battle under the commander's calculation of desirable objectives and necessary resources, but always with the certainty that enemy reaction will require constant tactical adjustment to the requirements of the moment. As quickly as it became certain that the enemy intended at all costs to hang on to Caen as the hinge of his operations it instantly became to our advantage to keep him so preoccupied in that region that all other Allied operations would be facilitated.[33]

This view seems nonetheless to be at variance with the historical record. Montgomery's insistence on the paramount importance of seizing the capital city of Calvados was well known to his subordinate commanders. "It is clear," he wrote to Generals Bradley and Dempsey on 18 June, "that we must now capture Caen and Cherbourg as the first step in the full development of our plans. Caen is really the key to Cherbourg; its capture will release forces which are now locked up in ensuring that our left flank holds secure. . . . The immediate task of the army will be to capture Caen and provide a strong eastern flank for the Army Group."[34] Indeed, Montgomery's fellow service chiefs at Supreme Headquarters, equally familiar with his views of the matter and less well disposed to him personally than Eisenhower, were quick to level criticism. "I confess to being very much disappointed by the Army," Leigh-Mallory noted in his diary. "I don't say that another Anzio is probable but it is certainly possible. They cannot expect the Air to do everything for them, and on dead days like this when the weather is bad it is up to them to push for-

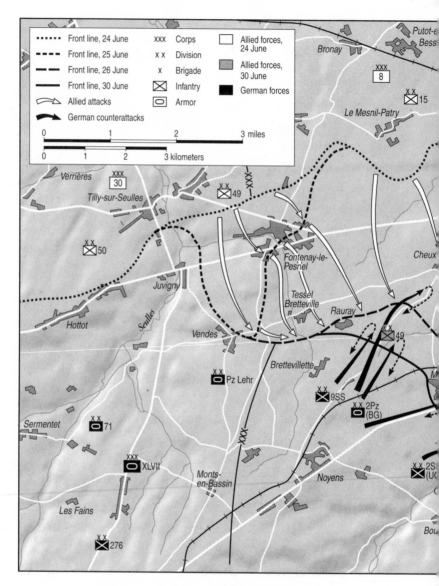

5. Operation EPSOM (24–30 June 1944)

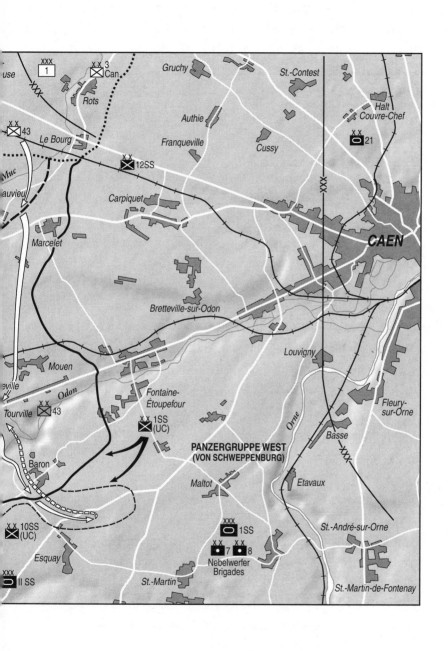

XXX
1

XX 3
Can

Rots

Gruchy

St.-Contest

Halt
Couvre-Chef

XX
43

Le Bourg

auvieu

Muc

XX 12SS

Authie

Franqueville

Cussy

XX
21

Carpiquet

CAEN

Marcelet

Bretteville-sur-Odon

Louvigny

Mouen

Fleury-
sur-Orne

eville

Odon

Tourville

XX 43

Fontaine-
Étoupefour

XX 1SS
(UC)

PANZERGRUPPE WEST
(VON SCHWEPPENBURG)

Orne

Basse

Baron

Maltot

Etavaux

XX 10SS
(UC)

XXX
1SS

St.-André-sur-Orne

Esquay

XX 7  XX 8
Nebelwerfer
Brigades

XXX
II SS

St.-Martin

St.-Martin-de-Fontenay

ward."[35] Nor have Montgomery's retrospective justifications convinced many historians. "It was 'Monty's way,'" Liddell Hart observed, "to talk as if any operation that he had conducted had always proceeded exactly as he intended, with the certainty and precision of a machine—or of divine providence. That characteristic has often obscured his adaptability to circumstances, and thus, ironically, deprived him of the credit due to him for his combination of flexibility with determination in generalship."[36]

The fact remains that the British forces wore down the German armored divisions in a battle of attrition, to the advantage of the American forces to the west—as Montgomery's commanders in the Caen sector, assessing the situation at the end of June, frankly recognized. Going forward, Dempsey noted, the Second Army's task was "to attract to itself (and to defeat) all the German armour and, when opportunity offer[ed], to take Caen."[37] Its sixteen divisions were holding at bay two infantry divisions and more than seven panzer divisions—two-thirds of the enemy tanks—along a front more than thirty miles long. In the Cotentin, by contrast, thirteen American divisions were confronted by only seven German divisions.[38] A Solomonic judgment seems therefore to be in order:

> Epsom had not been a victory. It had certainly not achieved its objectives, which lay not across the Odon but the Orne, five miles to the south. Yet it had achieved, in a roundabout way, an important purpose. Hitler's strategy, conceived long before the invasion and implemented as soon as it began, was to use his armour to drive a wedge between the Allies and drive them both eventually into the sea. The necessity of stopping 15th Scottish Division's march down the "Corridor" had diverted his armoured reserve from that mission and so damaged its units that days would be needed to restore them to an offensive state.[39]

The controversy was not over, however. A fresh offensive, launched by Montgomery a few weeks later, was to give it new life. In the meantime, taking advantage of their relative freedom from German pressure, the Americans were slowly but surely marching on Cherbourg.

## THE CAPTURE OF CHERBOURG

Having joined up the forces that came ashore at Utah and Omaha, the U.S. First Army sought to cut off the Cotentin in order then to take Cherbourg, which the logisticians at Supreme Headquarters considered vital for securing lines of supply. On 9 June General Bradley ordered Collins's Seventh Corps, blocked after its landing at Utah by German resistance at Sainte-Mère-Église, to march toward the Atlantic to cut off the peninsula. A week later, on 16 June, the Germans withdrew from Saint-Sauveur-le-Vicomte, and Barneville fell during the night of 17–18 June. Bradley then directed the Eighty-second and 101st Airborne Divisions and the Ninetieth Infantry Division to move southward without assigning them specific offensive missions, because of a lack of munitions and the priority attached to Cherbourg. On 19 June, the Fourth Infantry Division finally succeeded in breaking through the German defenses that had barred the road to Cherbourg, entering Montebourg before going on to seize Valognes the next day. Elements of Seventh Corps prepared then to advance northward along three corridors: the Fourth Infantry Division, departing from Montebourg, was to pass to the right, while the Seventy-ninth and the Ninth, moving from a line that cut halfway across the Cotentin, from Barneville to Saint-Sauveur-le-Vicomte, would initiate thrusts to the center and the left, respectively. After two days devoted to marshaling the artillery, the grand offensive began.

Operations in the Cotentin were severely hampered by its distinctive terrain, the most outstanding feature of which—farmland partitioned into small irregular fields by thick hedgerows, the infamous *bocage*—had almost inexplicably been neglected by Allied planners. Indeed, an inquiry after the campaign revealed that, of one hundred junior officers, none had received either information or training for conducting combat in such an environment.[40]

> In reality the hedgerows are sturdy embankments, half earth, half hedge. At their base they resemble dirt parapets and vary in thickness from one to four feet with heights that range from three to fifteen feet. Growing out of this earthen wall is a hedge that

consists of small trees and tangles of vines and brush. This vegetation has a thickness of between one to three feet and varies in height from three to fifteen feet. Originally intended to serve as fences to mark boundaries, to keep in livestock, and to prevent the erosion of the land by sea winds, the hedgerows surround each field, breaking the terrain into numerous walled enclosures. . . .

The military features of the bocage are obvious. The hedgerows divide the country into tiny compartments, provide excellent cover and concealment for defenders, and present a formidable obstacle to attackers. Numerous adjoining fields can be organized to form a natural defensive position echeloned in depth. The thick vegetation provides excellent camouflage and limits the deployment of units. The hedgerows also restrict observation, making the effective use of heavy caliber direct fire weapons almost impossible and hampering the adjustment of artillery fire. Anyone occupying a high place that afforded a clear view of the surrounding countryside would have a distinct advantage.[41]

If the German forces had neither the mobility nor the cohesiveness to mount counteroffensives in the Cotentin, prior experience nonetheless enabled them to exploit to the fullest the advantages offered by the terrain and in this way destroy the enemy's momentum. Small forward detachments were assigned the task of defending a series of fields, connected with one another by sunken roads. A set of gun and artillery positions spread out at intervals behind them constituted the principal line of combat. Light machine guns, whose grazing fire picked off enemy soldiers scrambling for cover, were the predominant weapon. Heavy machine guns, 88 mm antiaircraft guns (adapted in this situation for ground defense), and the Panzerfaust (a hand-held antitank weapon equipped with a single-shot, shaped-charge projectile) completed the roster of infantry weapons, which were reinforced by mortars. German mortar fire alone may have caused as many as three-quarters of the Allied casualties for the entire Normandy campaign.[42]

In the *bocage* of Normandy in general, and of the Cotentin in particu-

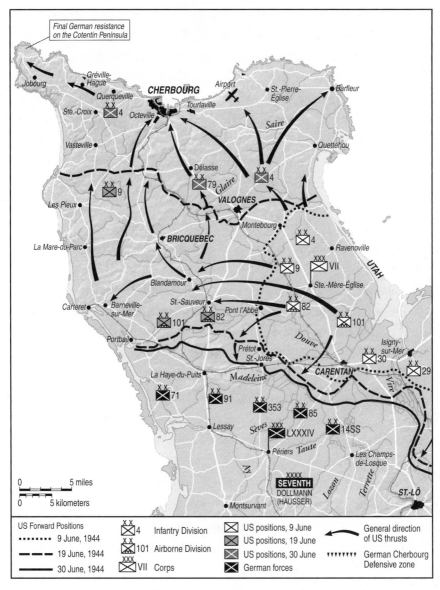

Final German resistance on the Cotentin Peninsula

6. The Capture of Cherbourg (3–30 June 1944)

lar, both the density of the vegetation and the proximity of the German defenders made the movement of heavy artillery problematic. Its use was complicated by the fact that fighting often took place at a range of less than three hundred yards. As a consequence, soldiers were liable to be hit by their own supporting fire; and because the embankments were raised up above the bordering roads and paths, the force of exploding artillery shells was apt to be absorbed by their earthen bases. The *bocage* also reduced the effectiveness of the Allies' tanks: by limiting maneuver and visibility, on the one hand, it obliged them to keep to the main thoroughfares, where they presented an easy target for German artillery; if, on the other hand, they tried to climb up the embankments, their exposed and unarmored undercarriages made them even more vulnerable to lethal attack. As a result, tank forces were unable to capitalize on either their mobility or their firepower. The option of blowing up the hedgerows was considered and quickly dismissed. A company of tanks covering a mile and a half would have to clear thirty-four separate rows in a typical assault, using seventeen tons of explosives in the process.[43] Quite apart from insuperable problems of cost and supply, this stratagem was evidently self-defeating to the extent that it could not fail to arouse the Germans' attention. In the Cotentin, therefore, the Americans had no choice but to adopt "a form of jungle or Indian fighting in which the individual soldier plays a dominant part"[44]—an unexpected return to a premodern form of combat.

And yet Allied strategists had in fact emphasized the dangers of the hedgerows before the invasion. A report of 7 May by Brigadier (later General Sir) Charles Richardson lucidly summarized the situation:

> An outstanding characteristic of this entire area is the "bocage"— close terrain consisting of small hedge-lined fields, often embanked, interspersed with thickets, woods, orchards and pastures. The bocage contains numerous narrow, often sunken, unsurfaced roads. Military observation is considerably restricted. Generally speaking the area will not be an easy one for forces to advance through rapidly in the face of determined resistance, but it will likewise be most difficult for the enemy to prevent a slow and steady advance by infiltration. . . .
>
> "Bocage" country may not be suitable for the employment of armour in mass, although tanks can penetrate most of the hedgerows and could no doubt work in small groups with infantry to good advantage. Anti-tank guns will not have adequate fields

of fire. It is difficult to judge whether such terrain favours defending or attacking infantry. It provides excellent cover for coming to grips with the enemy but its closeness and the shortened local observation mean that forward movement would probably be slow. . . . Generally speaking it may be supposed that attacking forces could move steadily but slowly forward through such terrain, that considerable difficulty would be experienced in maintaining contact between small units and control over them. The tactics to be employed in fighting through bocage country should be given considerable study by formations to be employed therein.[45]

This wise counsel appears to have been quite simply neglected, by both the British and the Americans. Their only thought was to make their way out of the bridgehead and gain access to favorable terrain as rapidly as possible.

*Bocage* warfare, which had therefore to be improvised on the spot, delayed the capture of Cherbourg: planned for D + 8, it was pushed back by almost two weeks, to 26 June. General Collins had requested additional support from Admiral Kirk, who dispatched two naval groups charged with silencing enemy batteries in the city and outlying areas. The bombardment began on 25 June and lasted for three hours. Although the siege did not succeed in destroying all gun emplacements, it profoundly affected German morale and led the commander of the Cherbourg garrison forces, Major General Karl Wilhelm von Schlieben, to disregard Hitler's orders by surrendering the next day.[46] "As if to content himself in captivity with the memory of better days," Bradley recalled, "he carried with him the menu of a dinner at which he had been the guest of honor in Cherbourg less than a month before: Lobster and hollandaise, *pâté de foie gras,* baked bluefish, roast leg of lamb, peaches and cream, château wines, vintage champagne, and Napoleon brandy." The American soldiers, for their part, wished to celebrate their victory in more tangible ways. For them, Cherbourg's "strategic worth was soon overshadowed by the wealth of its booty and it was there that the term 'liberate' came into popular use in the army."[47] The crucial fact remains, however, that once the Allies had taken Cherbourg, they finally held a large deepwater port capable of handling the cargo they desperately needed.

## Delays and Shortages

Victory, as we have seen, depended just as much on logistics as on strategy and tactics. The Allies had to transport not only reinforcements and additional stocks of equipment to support the later stages of the campaign, but also stores and munitions for the troops already fighting on the Continent—a titanic task, since initially they could rely on neither ports nor artificial harbors. Before the invasion, the Quartermaster Corps had anticipated being able by D + 17 to convey thirty-eight thousand tons of matériel per day—half of this in the form of fuel and munitions.[48] To meet this target, ad hoc measures turned out to be necessary. On D + 2, despite fears about damaging the hulls of the largest transport ships, the navy agreed to beach LSTs, so that they could unload at low tide directly onto the beaches, where they would subsequently be refloated by the rising waters. During the two first weeks, this method was adopted on Omaha for two hundred LSTs. In the meantime, the capture of secondary ports had yielded some happy surprises: the Germans had inflicted relatively little damage, and handling capacity was greater than expected. Even so, the Mulberries had to be brought into service by D + 21, to pick up the slack until the large ports—Cherbourg, Le Havre, Antwerp, and Marseille—were available.

The defects of these improvised arrangements were fairly quickly exposed. The large ships, unable to dock, were forced to anchor at sea, where they were unloaded by Rhino barges and DUKWs capable of transporting two and a half tons of matériel each. Many LST captains, acting on their own initiative, sought to position themselves far enough from the shore to avoid enemy fire. This tactic only increased the demands on the ferries, by lengthening shuttle times and reducing the number of trips per day. To complicate matters further, almost to the point of chaos, the ships had to be unloaded in accordance with preprepared cargo lists. On 10 June the U.S. First Army abandoned this system and instead began discharging ships in the order of arrival. Two days later, headquarters lifted the blackout that had been in effect until then. Freight could now be unloaded throughout the night, and the rate of resupply accelerated. Rough seas nonetheless slowed the transport of troops and stores, creating a backlog that was not eliminated until 15 June, or D + 9. By that point, freight was being handled more efficiently on the beaches, and depots were beginning to be established inland.

By mid-June, despite the lack of port facilities, things were looking up. Each day 150–200 ships were disgorging seven thousand vehicles, fifteen thousand tons of provisions, and forty thousand men. On 18 June the Allied forces counted twenty-one divisions, compared with eighteen for the Germans. Nonetheless, the delays of the first days had not been made up: on D + 12 only 72.8 percent of the projected tonnage had been unloaded—and that only by resorting to minor ports such as Courseulles and Port-en-Bessin, which had been opened six days earlier.

Then, between 19 and 22 June, a storm suddenly arose whose severity cannot be underestimated, even if the deluge of biblical proportions reported by many witnesses was an exaggeration. Winds approaching gale force (twenty-one to thirty-eight miles per hour) roiled the seas, whipping up waves almost ten feet high and causing considerable damage. Twenty-four of the large buoys protecting the Mulberries broke loose from their moorings. Waves rushed in, knocking down piers and destroying the treadways they supported. Some of the concrete caissons were set adrift, and boats roamed like mad dogs within the anchorages: only eight of thirty-two Phoenixes remained in place on the third day; eight hundred ferries sank or were damaged. Overall, however, the British installation at Arromanches (Mulberry B) held up fairly well. But the same was not true on the American side at Saint-Laurent (Mulberry A), where the breakwaters had been anchored in waters that were too deep and the blockships had been staggered to facilitate unloading.[49] The waves, crashing through the breaches, wreaked havoc.

The storm is estimated to have been responsible for the loss of 20,000 vehicles and 140,000 tons of various stores, aggravating the shortfalls due to earlier delays. The logistics experts therefore had to revise their plans. Mulberry A was abandoned, and its surviving facilities dismantled and cannibalized for use at Mulberry B. By increasing the flow of matériel to

Arromanches, redirecting traffic to small ports, and bringing as many ships ashore as possible, the Allies still managed to compensate for the loss of Saint-Laurent. Whereas on 22 June unloading was reduced to 57.4 percent of its scheduled daily level, only four days later operations had returned to normal. By contrast, the deficits recorded in the first days had not been made up: by 30 June, the delay in delivering vehicles had risen on the American side to thirteen days. Moreover, 22 percent of the soldiers were late in reaching their assigned positions, only 452,460 men having been landed out of a planned total of 578,971. The results on the British side were scarcely better: twelve and two-thirds divisions had been brought over by 30 June, or roughly 475,000 men, a full two divisions fewer than the fourteen and two-thirds that had been counted upon.[50] There was a deficit of 19,866 vehicles as of 25 June and of 276,346 men as of 5 July.[51] The Quartermaster Corps had nonetheless made every possible effort: it mobilized 570 Liberty ships, 788 freighters, and 2,899 ships of other types during the month of June in an unflagging attempt to resupply the Twenty-first Army Group.[52]

Unavoidably, however, these shortfalls adversely affected the conduct of military operations in the Cotentin. On 15 June General Bradley imposed restrictions on munitions, in view of unexpectedly intense fighting and the illicit establishment of ancillary depots by divisional commanders keen to have immediate access to their own reserves. The rationing order was lifted on 2 July, but in the meantime it prevented General Collins's Seventh Corps from advancing more rapidly toward Cherbourg and limited the freedom of maneuver of General Middleton's Eighth Corps at the base of the peninsula. "For two weeks Middleton waited for ammunition supply on that front while the enemy stiffened his defenses on the lower side of the bogs," Bradley recalled in his memoirs. "When eventually we slugged through that neck in preparation for the breakout, we discovered how profitably the Germans had utilized that time." From then on, until the American armies reached the Ruhr, "we never had enough ammunition to shoot all we needed."[53]

All of this casts doubt on the actual value of the artificial harbors. In three days, the storm had swallowed up two-thirds of the facilities. It is true that between 35.5 percent and 48.5 percent of total British cargo tonnage, depending on the estimate, passed through Arromanches between 6 June and 31 August.[54] In the first weeks, however, the share was considerably smaller: 12 percent on 12 June, and 19.6 percent on 3 July. The contribution of the Mulberries was therefore limited from the beginning.[55] Indeed, the Americans, deprived of Saint-Laurent in the wake of the storm, nonetheless managed to unload more matériel (ten thousand tons a day) than the British (six thousand tons per day). If we take into account the American performance, the Mulberries' share of total tonnage was modest at best, probably less than 25 percent. Considering, too, that construction of the Mulberries had mortgaged the labor of twenty thousand men and cost twenty million pounds sterling (about $80 million), it is legitimate to ask whether the Allies would have been better off employing those colossal sums for other purposes. "As events turned out," wrote Sir Walter Monckton, assigned in late December 1944 the task of drawing up a report on the scheme, "it is probable that we could have achieved a successful invasion without the Mulberries and this conclusion is to some extent confirmed by the American experience at Mulberry A."[56]

This opinion nonetheless overlooks one crucial element. The raid on Dieppe had persuaded the Germans that the Allies could launch a ground campaign in Europe only by seizing a major port at the outset. The Mulberries, by relieving the Anglo-American forces of this necessity, offered them the advantage of strategic surprise—especially since aerial photography had led the Germans to conclude that the prefabricated elements were meant to replace the damaged wharves of existing facilities, not to create new harbors from scratch.[57] In retrospect, then, the Mulberries' justification depends not on their logistical value, but on their contribution to the overall strategy of OVERLORD.

At the end of June the situation therefore appeared in a mixed light. The Allies had succeeded in landing an expeditionary force and in breaking through the Atlantic Wall, at the price of losses they were prepared to accept. Furthermore, having taken Cherbourg, they now controlled a port of prime importance, which together with smaller coastal installations appeared to augur a satisfactory solution to the logistical problems of the first three weeks—even though enemy sabotage kept Cherbourg from be-coming operational until 16 July. Finally, the Allies had firmly in hand a continuous lodgment area. Though the Germans had so far managed to contain it, they had not, despite determined efforts, succeeded in reduc-ing it.

A few shadows darkened the picture, however. In the east, Caen con-tinued to resist, denying the Allies access to the open country beyond, and with it the necessary space to maneuver and establish air bases. The lodgment area itself covered not even a thousand square miles—far less than the almost ten thousand square miles that Supreme Headquarters had been counting on. With a million men on both sides fighting along a front a hundred miles long, the constant influx of reinforcements and supplies threatened to worsen the congestion still further. Moreover, the narrowness of the bridgehead limited the armored forces' freedom of ac-tion, and bad weather obliged the air force to cancel half its missions in June, a development that prompted Allied high command to urge that bases be established on the Continent as quickly as possible, to avoid costly shuttling to and from Great Britain.[58] But in this regard there was little the armored divisions could do to help: to the east, the Allies' Shermans were outclassed by the German Tigers and Panthers; to the west, the *bocage* forced commanders to rely on infantry warfare; on both fronts, the enemy's 88 mm guns and Panzerfausts had wreaked great dev-astation. On the British side, by 30 June, casualties had risen to 20,475 (including 3,184 dead and 7,314 missing); combined with Canadian losses of 2,978, they amounted to 6.46 percent of a total force of 362,584.[59] On the American side, for the same period, they amounted to 36,229 (in-cluding 5,025 dead and 5,521 missing).[60] Between 6 June and 10 July the ranks of the 101st Airborne Division alone were reduced by 3,559 (31.5 percent of the overall number), including 642 dead and 810 missing.[61]

In gaining a foothold onshore in the dawn of 6 June, the Anglo-American forces had won a battle. Yet almost a month later, they were still a long way from winning the war in the West.

# 9

## STALEMATE

IN SPITE OF THE CAPTURE of Cherbourg and the war of attrition being effectively waged outside Caen, the Allies had made no real headway in Normandy. Powerless to break through the German lines, for want of a lodgment area large enough to receive reinforcements of troops and matériel, they were unable to engage in mobile warfare through the massive deployment of armored forces. This impasse forced the high command to recast its strategy at a moment of great tension between the Americans and the British.

### BOGGED DOWN

At the beginning of July, then, the Allies found themselves bogged down in the Norman countryside. To the west, the Germans retained their hold on the lower Cotentin, preventing the Americans from escaping the peninsula in search of open expanses more suitable to a rapid campaign. To the east, the Anglo-Canadian assault on Caen was stalled. Eisenhower directed his commanders to redouble their efforts.

On 4 July the Canadians attacked the airfield at Carpiquet. On the eighth the British renewed their attack on the Norman capital, this time with the aid of large-scale naval and air bombardment. From 7–9 July, 1,598 aircraft of the RAF dropped 2,570 tons of bombs—to no great effect, as it turned out, for the Germans had placed their defenses outside

the city. Looking back on the operation, the planners at Supreme Headquarters noted that the targets chosen by the Twenty-first Army Group
appeared to be "most unsuitable."[1] The results were all the more unsatis-
factory because although Carpiquet had finally been conquered, as of the
ninth the British and the Canadians held only the left bank of the Orne:
bomb craters and the rubble of the ruined city had slowed their progress,
and they could go no farther.[2] The Americans did their best to put this
fresh setback in a favorable light. "It was found necessary to rationalize
[the] inability to advance by pointing out to [war] correspondents that
while British troops were not advancing freely, they were holding down
German armor that may have been used to better advantage facing American troops on the right."[3]

Montgomery therefore found himself obliged to draw up a new plan of
attack. The result, GOODWOOD (named, like EPSOM, after a famous race-
course in England), was destined to arouse heated debate among historians. Montgomery's supporters readily accept that he wanted neither to
capture Caen nor to achieve a breakthrough, but primarily to draw off
German forces just as Bradley's First Army was preparing to launch Operation COBRA in the south of the Cotentin.[4] In seeking to eliminate enemy armor in the area between Caen and Falaise, to the southeast, the
Second Army's mission was to be carried out in close conjunction with
the American offensive. But once COBRA was postponed, GOODWOOD became an independent enterprise, which it had assuredly not been to begin with.[5] A note drafted by Montgomery on 15 July confirms this view of
the matter. Ordering a secure bridgehead to be established to the east of
the Orne and the positions on the eastern flank to be strengthened, he
called for the destruction of "German equipment and personnel, as a
preliminary to a possible wide exploitation of success. . . . The eastern
flank is a bastion on which the whole future of the campaign in NW Europe depends; it must remain a firm bastion; if it became unstable the operations on the western flank would cease. Therefore, while taking advantage of every opportunity to destroy the enemy, we must be very
careful to maintain our own balance and ensure a firm base."[6] Later on, in
his memoirs, he elaborated on this idea:

It is important to understand that, once we had secured a good footing in Normandy, my plan was to *threaten* to break out on the eastern flank, that is in the Caen sector. By pursuing this threat relentlessly I intended to draw the main enemy reserves, particularly his armoured divisions, into that sector and to keep them there—using the British and Canadian forces under Dempsey for this purpose. Having got the main enemy strength committed on the *eastern* flank, my plan was to make the break-out on the western flank—using for this task the American forces under General Bradley. This break-out attack was to be launched southwards, and then to proceed eastwards in a wide sweep up to the Seine about Paris. I hoped that this gigantic wheel would pivot on Falaise. It aimed to cut off all enemy forces south of the Seine, the bridges over that river below Paris having been destroyed by our air forces.[7]

But time was short. The German command had begun to replace its armored divisions with infantry units, in order to be able to send its tanks to the American front. To block this maneuver, the British had to make credible the threat of a breakthrough that would force the enemy to keep its panzers on the eastern flank. Goebbels conceded afterward that they succeeded. "The enemy mystified us at Caen," he wrote in his diary in early August. "We were expecting a great offensive in this sector and had massed troops there; in fact, the enemy attacked along the American flank."[8] Just the same, the immediate purpose of distracting German forces did not exclude the possibility of a breakthrough in the east as well. Leigh-Mallory and Tedder both saw GOODWOOD as a major operation, and they expected a great deal from it. The scale of the resources allocated, notably to the air forces, and the fact that General Dempsey as early as 13 July had mentioned Falaise as the objective, gave grounds for optimism. Nor did Montgomery attempt to conceal his confidence. "Plan if successful promises to be decisive," he cabled Tedder the following day, 14 July.[9]

Operation GOODWOOD opened at dawn on 18 July with a gigantic bom-

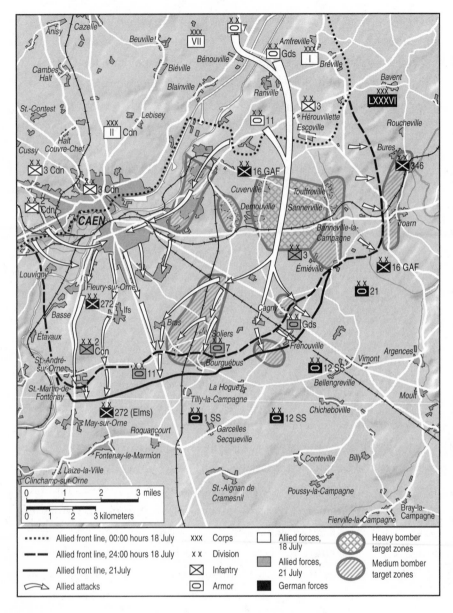

7. Operation GOODWOOD (18–21 July 1944)

bardment by two thousand aircraft dropping almost seven thousand tons of bombs. Strong artillery preparation followed. Three corps then launched the ground offensive. To the east, Lieutenant General J. T. Crocker's First Corps enlarged the modest bridgehead that British paratroops had established on 6 June by pressing on to Troarn and Bavent.

Second Canadian Corps, led by Lieutenant General Guy G. Simonds, crossed the Orne between Blainville and Louvigny and proceeded to liberate the right bank of the river southwest of Caen. Finally, and most important, General O'Connor's Eighth Corps, fortified by three armored divisions, wheeled to the south, gaining the plain below the Bourguébus Ridge and from there driving on toward Falaise. The success of the operation depended on two key assumptions: that the aerial bombardment would neutralize the German forces by playing the role usually assigned to artillery, which for lack of room had to wait for the armored forces to depart before it could enter into action; and that the tanks' firepower would allow them to penetrate the German defenses (hence their massive presence—750 Shermans, Churchills, and other armor took part in the offensive). In the event, the element of surprise worked in the Allies' favor.

And yet it turned out to be of only marginal importance. At 5:45 in the morning of the eighteenth, two waves of bombers began pounding the German defenses. The psychological effect was intense, giving encouragement to the Allies while stunning the Germans both literally and figuratively (70 percent of the prisoners taken remained deaf for twenty-four hours). Nonetheless, the delay between the bombing and the ground attack was too long, leaving the enemy time to reorganize, particularly in the area around Bourguébus. Moreover, the attacks on Troarn were not sufficiently vigorous, nor were the hundred-pound bombs of the Eighth U.S. Air Force powerful enough to destroy enemy artillery, for they spared German tank and antitank guns in the area of Cagny, Émiéville, and Bourguébus.[10] On the ground, bringing the eight thousand vehicles of Eighth Corps's three armored divisions quickly and in secrecy from their start line to Bourguébus Ridge, more than seven miles away, presented a difficult problem. The Germans' position in the towers of Colombelles gave them an excellent vantage point.[11] To complicate matters further, the mines that the Allies themselves had laid to protect their supply lines slowed the tanks' advance; and the need for so many vehicles to cross six bridges over the Orne in single file caused a massive bottleneck that prevented the divisions from going into battle together. As it turned out, the assault was carried out by just one armored division. But things went badly from the first: the aerial bombardment inflicted only minimal damage on the enemy defenses, and troop movements were quickly detected. Already by 11:00 A.M. the British offensive had lost its momentum.

For the adversary's response was not slow in coming. Under the direction of Lieutenant General Heinrich Eberbach, commander of the Fifth Panzer Army, the Germans had conceived a layered defense in four belts, each nearly ten miles deep, with a fifth held in reserve, and mobilized significant resources—300 antitank guns, 300 mortars, 230 tanks.[12] Although the Germans had been staggered by the aerial and naval bombardment, the Allies' delay in advancing gave them time to regroup and reorganize their lines of defense. German resistance was unrelenting. On the first day, Montgomery lost 270 tanks and 1,500 men, and the next day another 131 tanks and 1,100 men.[13] On 21 July he gave up the fight. The Canadians, for their part, had suffered similar disappointments. General Simonds dispatched his Second Infantry Division to the south, to secure the western flank once the armored divisions had seized the heights around Bretteville-sur-Laize. Simonds was bent on taking the Verrières Ridge, but he underestimated the strength of the Germans, who had deployed some one hundred armored vehicles, in addition to artillery. His mistake was to send his troops into battle before the tanks had accomplished their mission. Spurred on by glorious memories of the First World War, the Canadian commander intended to be worthy of his predecessors: "Verrières was to be Simonds's Vimy."[14] Instead he was forced to abandon his attack on 22 July, before the high ground could be taken, meanwhile sustaining very heavy casualties.

Operation GOODWOOD, and with it the Allied high command's hopes of achieving a decisive result, lay in ruins. The Germans had contained the advance of the Anglo-Canadian forces and given them a thrashing in the process. Between 18 and 21 July Dempsey lost 6,168 men (in addition to the 3,000 casualties sustained earlier by Twelfth Corps, which had undertaken a clearing operation to the west of the Orne between 15 and 17 July) and 36 percent of the British tanks, all for a gain of some twenty square miles.[15] To be sure, the Germans did not emerge from the confrontation unscathed. One hundred nine tanks from Twenty-first Panzer and First SS Panzer Divisions were destroyed, and the counterattack, launched on 21 July from the east bank of the Orne below the city, failed.[16] The transfer of armored forces to the American front was delayed as well. Still, in view of the great expectations aroused by GOOD-WOOD, the operation was judged to be a failure—notwithstanding the justifications offered by Montgomery and his eulogists, both at the time and afterward. As the official American historian of the battle noted, "He had held the eastern flank firmly and had continued to keep a great part of the German strength on the British front. But if this had been General Montgomery's basic intention, his apparent determination to take Caen had obscured it."[17]

The fiasco was the result, as one might imagine, of several miscalculations. No doubt it was unrealistic to suppose that the armored forces could by themselves have achieved a breakout, with the infantry reduced to merely holding the ground conquered by the tanks. Everything considered, however, as a British postmortem of the operation concluded,

> the timing of the attack was the key of its failure. The air support program was based on the estimated speed of movement of the armour. This estimated speed was never achieved due to delays in the corridor, by minefields, by the railway embankment and the surprise of sudden tank casualties [in] the area of BOURGUEBUS reported by scout cars to be clear of the opposition. As a result, the air bombardment effects wore off before the attack reached the bomb areas and the enemy defence in the bombed areas has resumed a large part of its efficiency.[18]

Montgomery erred also through excessive caution, moving to protect the flanks of his armor, though they were not exposed. A well-coordinated tank-infantry attack in the area of Bourguébus would surely have been more effective.

Yet it is not clear that Montgomery had any real choice in the matter. Severely depleted infantry reserves forced him to count heavily on the armored divisions for much of his strength. Not only were the ranks of the Twenty-first Army Group severely reduced going into the campaign, but they had been taxed to a far greater extent than anticipated. The War Office reckoned that in periods of intense combat 48 percent of the casualties would be sustained by infantry, 15 percent by the armored corps, and 14 percent by artillery. But in the Canadian ranks alone, the proportion of infantry losses rose to 76 percent, while the others fell to 7 percent and 8 percent, respectively.[19] Montgomery, whether he liked it or not, could not help taking these figures into account in devising his plans. The lack of foot soldiers obliged him to give up any idea of launching an integrated offensive—particularly since American unwillingness to assign infantry divisions to the British sector made unbalanced reliance on tank forces unavoidable. Given, too, that the bulk of the German panzer forces were dedicated to the defense of Caen, Montgomery's setback is perhaps not surprising. In any case, the consequences were momentous. The GOODWOOD debacle forced the Allies to revise their strategy thoroughly and entrust the breakthrough, and then the breakout, to the American forces instead. This in turn brought about a crisis within the Allied high command.

Until the last days of June, reports from the front were confident and Montgomery's authority remained unquestioned, despite the failure of EPSOM. Eisenhower contented himself with exhorting the commander of ground forces in Normandy to increase the pressure on Caen—and indeed had instructed him on 7 July to avoid a deadlock by all possible means. But deep down, Eisenhower was seething with anger and frustration. His aide-de-camp, Harry Butcher, claimed that the effort made by the British before Caen "was a holding operation to contain the German Army while the Americans took Cherbourg and resumed their push southward. Ike has been smoldering and today burst out with a letter to Monty which, in effect, urges him to avoid having our forces sealed into the beachhead, take the offensive, and Ike would support him in every way, as if it were necessary to say this."[20]

Montgomery's repeated reverses made it necessary to reconsider the situation, however. Signs of unease were already apparent by the end of June. "The situation is full of difficulties," General Brooke wrote in his diary on the thirtieth; "the Americans now begin to own the major strength on land, in the air and on the sea. They therefore consider that they are entitled to decide how their forces are to be employed." The American challenge to Montgomery's leadership of the ground forces was all the more ominous in view of the fact that displeasure with his performance was now growing on the British side as well, with Churchill rebuking him on 6 July "because operations were not going faster."[21]

Operation GOODWOOD was the last straw. On the evening of 19 July, Butcher recounted, "Tedder called Ike and said Monty had, in effect, stopped his armor from going farther. Ike was mad. . . . With 7,000 tons of bombs dropped in the most elaborate bombing of enemy front-line positions ever accomplished, only seven miles were gained—can we afford a thousand tons of bombs per mile? The air people are completely disgusted with the lack of progress."[22] Partisan accounts in the press— "Second Army Breaks Through / Armoured Forces Reach Open Country / General Montgomery Well Satisfied" read the London *Times* headline on 19 July—aggravated tensions within the coalition leadership and inflamed public opinion on both sides of the Atlantic.[23] A German report that had recently fallen into the Allies' hands further sharpened the sense of dismay at Supreme Headquarters. Pointing out the weaknesses of British infantrymen, it concluded with the recommendation, "It is best to attack the English, who are very sensitive to close combat and flank attack. . . . They rely largely on the artillery and air force support. In the case of well-directed artillery fire by us they often abandon their position in fight. The enemy is extraordinarily nervous of close combat. Whenever the enemy infantry is energetically engaged, they mostly retreat or surrender."[24] Invidious comparisons of overall British performance with American performance stirred up resentment as well. Montgomery's chief planner, Brigadier Richardson, reported on 7 July that eight divisions held a front of 77,500 yards in the British sector, whereas in the American sector nine divisions controlled 108,000—almost 20 percent more terrain as a proportion of the total Allied front.[25] Increasingly, the war effort became a contest of national pride, with each side cheering on its champion. The British complained about the lack of understanding shown by the Americans, who in turn suspected Great Britain of deliberately sacrificing thousands of GIs to ensure the survival of its Tommies. The absence of direct contacts between top American and British generals did nothing to smooth over these differences. Eisenhower and Montgomery, to cite but one example, met only nine times during the Normandy campaign.[26] The growing tendency of each army to take care of its own operations without regard for the other's requirements created frictions that ultimately made it necessary to restructure the high command. In the meantime, the crisis led to a resolution of the strategic impasse—only in the Manche, rather than Calvados.

## Breaking Through

After capturing Cherbourg, General Bradley planned to launch an offensive to the south, in order both to prevent the Germans from blocking the exit routes from the Cotentin and to profit from terrain more favorable to the maneuver of his armored units. Looking to the longer term, as Montgomery reminded him on 21 July, the Allies would still need to "gain possession of the whole of the Cherbourg and Brittany peninsulas. The whole weight of the Army Group will therefore be directed to this task, we require the Brittany ports so that we can develop the full resources of the Allies in western Europe, and we must get them soon."[27] A week later Montgomery emphasized once again to his field commanders, "We must secure the Brittany ports before the winter is on us."[28] Postponed many times for lack of adequate supplies, the offensive finally began in early July, with the overall aim of reaching a line running from Coutances through Saint-Lô and Caumont—thus giving the American armies a solid base from which to launch a further attack, which promised in turn to free them at last from the constraints of fighting among the hedgerows and marshes. The success of this operation was by no means assured. Apart from the fact that the Germans held the lower part of the Cotentin, Bradley had to send the right wing of his army through land to the west of Carentan that had been flooded to block or otherwise slow the passage of Allied vehicles.

Bradley decided to commit his forces in stages. On 3 July General Middleton's Eighth Corps set out from Saint-Sauveur to take Lessay and Coutances but ran up against the German 353rd Infantry Division near La Haye-du-Puits. After fierce fighting that lasted almost a week, the

Americans finally prevailed on 9 July, having gained a mere six miles at the appalling cost of ten thousand men.[29] General Collins's Seventh Corps moved out on 4 July toward Carentan, intending to join up with Eighth Corps; but the front between the Gorges marshland and the Taute River was so narrow, and the ground so sodden after the previous month's rains, that the Eighty-third Infantry Division had difficulty advancing.[30] There were other complications as well.

> Poor reports from subordinate units, incorrect map locations, and weak communications made accurate artillery support almost impossible and effective aid from the few tactical planes in the air on the second day difficult. Lax command control and discipline resulted in an inordinately large number of stragglers. Regimental and battalion commanders did not seem able to coordinate their attached units, institute reconnaissance in time, or press their attacks with vigor. Tank-infantry coordination was especially bad, and mutual complaint and recrimination resulted. . . . The inexperience of the division was apparent on all echelons.[31]

To Nineteenth Corps, led by Major General Charles H. Corlett, fell the formidable task of taking Saint-Lô, the administrative seat of the Manche and a vital crossroads. As a major logistical node for enemy forces in the Cotentin, it had to be captured at any cost. Launching an attack on 7 July, the Thirtieth Infantry Division succeeded in crossing the Vire by surprise and opening a bridgehead around Saint-Jean-de-Daye. Its advance nonetheless ground to a halt outside Pont-Hébert, forcing Bradley to redirect the thrust of the assault along the main road connecting Saint-Lô and Périers rather than the Coutances–Saint-Lô road. On 11 July Collins's Seventh Corps renewed the offensive and after a week of hard fighting managed to take the city, which, having been evacuated by the Germans during the night of 17–18 July, now lay in ruins.

By 19 July, however, the First Army—twelve divisions strong—had advanced little more than seven miles to the west of the Vire and not quite four miles to the east. And though the Lessay-Périers line had been reached, these two small towns nevertheless remained in enemy hands. Saint-Lô had indeed been captured, but only with great difficulty: Collins's men were hampered not only by rain and a stubborn German defense but also, as we have just noted, by their own lack of coordination between armor and infantry. Even so, the Americans had learned a great deal about *bocage* combat in the past six weeks and had improved their method of attack considerably. In a reversal of orthodox tactics, an infantry company's armored support now laid down suppressive fire across the front hedge of a field; the infantry closed in on the enemy beyond it, meanwhile, advancing as far as the rear hedgerow, as engineers placed explosive charges in the center of the front row. Once the field was taken, some of the tanks moved forward into the field, the rest holding back in case more enemy elements were flushed out.[32] This assault technique made it possible to gain ground, but still slowly and at a heavy cost in men: First Army recorded some 40,000 casualties, 90 percent of them among the infantry.[33]

By mid-July, then, the Allied position was a source of genuine concern. The British and Canadian forces had still not managed to conquer Caen and the high ground surrounding the city. And yet the Americans' success at Saint-Lô suggested that a breakthrough might be possible in the western sector. At this point, however, disagreements over strategy intervened, threatening to undermine the unity of the Allied high command. Logistical difficulties darkened the outlook still further.

Insufficient reinforcements and unexpectedly high casualties had combined to produce a shortage of manpower. On the American side, 452,460 men had been landed by 1 July (78 percent of the projected number of 578,971), supplemented by another 415,202 men in the next three and a half weeks (96 percent of the goal for the period), which brought the overall number of U.S. troops in Normandy to 867,662 (86 percent of the projected total) on 25 July.[34] The Quartermaster Corps had therefore done what had been asked of it, at least in July. And yet the deficits in supply resulting from the great storm of 19–22 June had not been wholly erased. On the American side, the relatively low level of reinforcements was a consequence not of insufficient reserves, but of a lack of equipment and transport ships, which slowed the arrival of fresh troops.

On the British side, however, the problem was a lack of manpower, pure and simple. Whereas on 29 June Montgomery could count on immediate infantry reinforcements of 7,335 men, this figure—quite low to begin with—fell to 2,837 after GOODWOOD.[35] By the end of July, noting the toll of the fighting on existing units, the general staff officer responsible for monitoring troop levels advised that it would soon be "imperative to implement the next stage of infantry cannibalization."[36] On 19 August General de Guingand, Montgomery's chief of staff, took the requisite measures, ordering the dissolution of twenty-one infantry battalions and assigning the maximum number of conscripts to the infantry, even if it meant depriving other branches of the army (reconnaissance regiments, for example) of recruits.[37] By the end of the month, the worsening situation caused the Fifty-ninth Infantry Division to be disbanded and its remnants divided up among the other units. Even so, including the 640,000 soldiers serving in the British armies, Allied forces on the eve of Operation COBRA in late July numbered 1,452,000 men, distributed among thirty-six divisions—a respectable figure.[38]

Yet the new recruits who arrived in Normandy did not always meet the requirements of the commanders in the field, whether in the short or the medium term. For immediate purposes additional foot soldiers were needed, and these were in short supply. On the American side, planners had estimated that casualties in June would amount to 70.3 percent; in the event, for infantry alone, they came to 85 percent.[39] To make up the shortfall, 95 percent of the infantry reinforcements needed to be trained in the use of rifles and artillery, a considerably higher proportion than the War Department's estimate of 76 percent; but in fact only 39.7 percent of the reserves sent to Normandy by mid-July had received such training. From that point on, the shortage of fighting soldiers became critical, with disturbing implications for American strategy. To reinforce the offensive capability of the units landed on D-Day, the proportion of support troops assigned to noncombat missions (supply, vehicular maintenance, and so on) had been reduced at the divisional level to the strict minimum—16–

18 percent of the total contingent. In theory, this quota was to increase gradually, rising to 21 percent on D + 15 and finally reaching 30 percent on D + 40.[40] But on 26 June support troops still represented only 16 percent of the forces landed on the Continent[41]—a proportion that would be unmanageably low once the Allies managed to establish a capacity for mobile warfare, which could be expected to place additional demands on the Quartermaster and Transportation Corps, for lines would push forward at an increasingly rapid rate. Drivers, depot personnel, nurses, postal workers, and the like, were therefore of crucial importance in assuring the success of the offensive. In mid-July, the prospect of a breakthrough seemed distant, if not unrealistic; but it might nonetheless suddenly become a matter of urgent priority. This possibility posed a dilemma for Supreme Headquarters. Should the proportion of support staff be increased, at the risk of compromising COBRA for lack of fighting troops? Or was it necessary instead to increase the share of infantry, at the risk of crippling a breakthrough attempt for want of service corps personnel? The logisticians did their best to anticipate the dispatch of new combat units to the front, so that support troops could be moved into position at just the right moment, but they found themselves hampered by weak port capacities and poor communications.[42]

Finding enough soldiers was only part of the problem. The Allies also needed matériel. Small-arms ammunition, essential for hedgerow combat, was in particularly short supply. Here again the difficulty had to do not with insufficient production, but with delays in delivery: whereas the First Army required 7,500 tons of munitions a day, the Quartermaster Corps in mid-July was able to distribute only 3,000.[43] It was not possible to make up entirely for tank losses. Bradley's forces lost 187 tanks in June (26.6 percent of the total number at hand), and 280 in July (24.4 percent)—more than three times the 7 percent forecast by the War Department. "It became immediately apparent that the planned percentage of replacements in tanks was not sufficient to maintain the losses to be expected in modern combat."[44] And yet Washington turned a deaf ear to requests from the field commanders, with the result that logistical problems were aggravated by underestimation of actual force requirements and compounded by the skepticism of the War Department.

In Italy the Americans had succeeded in restoring normal operations at the port of Naples in a few days. That success made them believe that Cherbourg could quickly be put back on track as well—a futile expectation, as it turned out. By 25 July Cherbourg was supposed to have unloaded 150,000 tons; but in fact the 18,000-ton threshold had only just been reached, and the first troop convoy waited until 7 September to dock. It was therefore necessary to redistribute the burden to the small Norman ports (30,000 tons) and the beaches. Of the 447,000 tons transported between 1 and 25 July, 88 percent were deposited directly on the shore.[45] This system, as we have seen, limited turnaround and restricted both strategic and tactical flexibility. As of 9 August, eighty preloaded ships were permanently anchored off the French coast waiting to be unloaded, not counting the ones moored in British waters, waiting to set sail for the Continent.[46] In July 66 out of 102 vessels sat idle at the wharves for more than a week; some took as long as forty-six days to go from the United States to Great Britain and from there to France and back to the United States.[47] The delays caused scarce shipping resources to be wasted. They also forced Supreme Headquarters to incorporate logistical factors into strategic planning—hence the repeated insistence on taking the Breton ports, and Eisenhower's support for the idea of a landing in Provence to capture Marseille. On balance, the lack of port facilities was a severe constraint on the conduct of operations, inasmuch as the shortage of equipment and supplies retarded a number of offensives, particularly in the Cherbourg peninsula.

Nevertheless, the point should not be overstated. The logistical situation facing the Allies, though far from ideal, did not amount to a crisis and in any case bore no comparison to the drastic shortages that handicapped the Germans (Panzer Group West, to name but one example, was supplied with only 400–900 tons of provisions per day in July). Moreover, happy surprises occasionally awaited Bradley's forces. In addition to the stocks of gasoline discovered at Cherbourg, they found they were able to dock 1,300-ton tankers at Port-en-Bessin (rather than the 300-ton vessels originally budgeted for). It turned out, too, that the First Army had a smaller appetite for fuel than expected: the 55 tons consumed per day in June and 75 tons in July were far lower than the daily consumption rate of 121 tons anticipated by the logisticians.[48] Part of the reason for the Allies' ample supplies of gasoline, of course, was that the front had remained more or less stationary. But the situation was to change dramatically in August, when the Allied armies, breaking through the enemy defenses at last, began their headlong rush toward the borders of the Reich. In mid-July, however, the Germans' firmness in holding their positions made such a prospect appear quite remote.

## German Resistance

The resistance displayed by the Germans in Normandy until the American offensive of 25 July may seem surprising in view of the prevailing balance of forces. But it should be kept in mind that the Wehrmacht still had considerable resources at its disposal. In the West, it could rely on an average of 125 tanks per unit (as against only about 50 in the East). By 1 May more than half its armored vehicles were stationed in the Atlantic sector, to which a third of the total had previously been allocated, the other two-thirds being assigned to the Russian front.[49] As we have seen, the effects of the Transportation Plan must not be overestimated. Beginning in April, the Germans accelerated delivery of supplies and equipment to armored formations in France. On 5 June, the day before the invasion, more than 200 trains transported matériel to the divisions of OB West.[50] Thereafter, despite the attacks of the Anglo-American air forces, the enemy was still able to dispatch as many as 250 trains per day.[51] Furthermore, German military needs absorbed only a third of French railway capacity—not, as Allied experts believed, two-thirds.[52] At least at the outset, then, the Transportation Plan penalized French civilians more than their occupiers. The Twelfth SS Panzer and Panzer Lehr divisions were delayed in reaching the front by only twenty-four hours in all.

German armed forces were bolstered further by the recall of Second SS Panzer Corps from Galicia in June—a disturbing sign that the likelihood of a Soviet offensive was not enough to arrest the transfer of units to Normandy.[53] Even the Kriegsmarine and the Luftwaffe, despite their much reduced state, posed problems for Allied logistics. From D-Day until the end of July, the German air force laid between three thousand

and four thousand mines, in addition to the ones emplaced by the navy, which caused considerable damage.[54] In July and early August four Allied ships were sunk or damaged each week because of mines; altogether, during those two months forty-seven ships were sunk and another sixty-seven partially destroyed as a result of mines, torpedoes, and other devices.[55] Admiral Vian complained of these losses, and all the more insistently since the mines were of a new type that his experts were unable to disarm.[56] Moreover, the navy found it difficult to defend against the bombers that laid them: radar interference prevented its ships from responding with precisely targeted fire; and the nighttime identification of enemy aircraft was no straightforward matter, either, for Allied planes, likewise, operated at night.[57] On the ground, the terrain favored the German defenders, who made masterful use of antitank guns and mortars—the cause of 70 percent of British and Canadian casualties in July.[58] Poor weather conditions worked against the Allies as well: half the scheduled aerial support could not be employed on account of rain, despite the nine hundred missions carried out by the U.S. Ninth Tactical Air Command (TAC) between 26 June and 24 July.[59]

Yet these challenges must not be overestimated. Already in June the Wehrmacht's capabilities had been significantly impaired. Even before the landing, the mobility of many divisions was compromised by a lack of motorized transport. Only two-thirds of the elite Second SS Panzer ("Das Reich") Division, for example, were prepared to go into battle on D-Day; and the lack of available vehicles made it necessary for its elements to be brought from Toulouse to the Norman front in five stages, between 8 June and 20 July.[60] Defending against the Allied invasion made a difficult situation worse. Over time the Germans suffered substantial losses in matériel that were all the more calamitous because OKW proved to be incapable of remedying them: between 6 June and 9 July the Germans lost 150 Mark IVs, 85 Panthers, 15 Tigers, 167 75 mm antitank guns, and 30 88 mm guns (equal to the equipment of two SS Panzer divisions)[61] that were not replaced, both because of shortages and owing to the decision to allocate 90 percent of the equipment arriving from Germany to newly formed units.

In a report sent to Hitler on 17 July Rommel gave a grimly realistic assessment of the German position. "The situation on the Normandy front is growing worse every day and is now approaching a grave crisis. . . . As against 97,000 casualties (including 2,360 officers)—in other words, an average of 2,500 to 3,000 a day—replacements to date number 10,000, of whom about 6,000 have actually arrived at the front. Material losses are also huge and have so far been replaced on a very small scale; in tanks, for example, only 17 replacements have arrived to date as compared with 225 losses."[62] The following week brought further confirmation of this bleak estimate: by 23 July the Germans had lost 116,863 men; as of 25 July they could oppose to thirty-four Allied divisions at most twenty-six of their own, eight of them armored.[63]

Yet additional resources were available to OKW, particularly in the Pas de Calais. The Reich's chief strategists persisted, however, in crediting rumors of a second landing. "According to investigations made by the Supreme Command on the basis of prisoners' statements and captured documents," the Japanese ambassador in Berlin cabled the Foreign Ministry in Tokyo on 22 June, "there were in England, in addition to the army group under Montgomery, twenty-three divisions under the command of General Patton ready to carry out an invasion. This was another reason why the Germans had [refrained] from pouring their armies into Normandy. . . . The Germans still considered that there was a great likelihood of Patton's army group landing between Dieppe and Boulogne and were prepared for this."[64] Operation FORTITUDE evidently continued to cast its spell: wounded soldiers, repatriated to England from Normandy, generated false radio traffic; two infantry battalions composed of low-grade recruits maintained fourteen flotillas of dummy LCTs; two hundred men lit fires in the woods, hung out laundry, and drove around in vehicles to simulate the life of phantom units. In all, 1,500 men managed to hold the twenty or so divisions of the German Fifteenth Army at bay for almost two months, to the great amusement of the officers in charge of the deception.[65] It was not until the end of July that Kluge came to his senses and these idle forces were mobilized to defend against the enveloping Allied armies.[66]

The shortages of matériel intensified the effects of reduced troop strength. Forces at the front required 1,100 tons of munitions, 1,000 tons of fuel, and 250 tons of supplies per day[67]—needs that were satisfied for a time by depots established before D-Day. On 6 June the German armies had a sixty-day supply of rations, and the panzer divisions enough fuel to travel 300 miles. From July onward, by contrast, the depletion of these stocks was compounded by the now devastating effects of the Transportation Plan. Supplying the troops with adequate provisions required thirty-six trains a day; but only nine were able to reach the Seine-Loire triangle daily between 10 June and 11 August. In the northeast area of the triangle, through which 98 percent of the military traffic passed, the volume of entering trains dropped in May by 50 percent by comparison with January–February, rose again to 80 percent of this level in the three last weeks of June, but then fell precipitously to 39 percent in July. In the Seine area, rail traffic fell from 213 trains during the first week of April to 50 for the last week of May, but then almost vanished—averaging only a single train per week in the months that followed.[68] The shortfall of gasoline at the front was to have especially dramatic consequences. At the end of June the commanders of the Seventh Army complained that their panzers were unable to counterattack southwest of Caen, for lack of fuel.[69] Supplies of airplane fuel to the Luftwaffe declined sharply as well, from 180,000 tons in April to 50,000 in June, before finally plummeting to 10,000 in August.[70] As a result, it played a negligible role during the battle of Normandy, with the consequence that the Allies were able to gain aerial supremacy. But the lack of matériel became truly critical only in August, when stocks—which had been at their highest levels between May and July[71]—were finally exhausted. The Transportation Plan therefore did not seriously disrupt enemy logistics until the beginning of July, after which German movements became increasingly disorganized. Locomotives were more and more urgently needed; damaged engines, hastily repaired for the most part, were by then more likely to be immobilized by mechanical failure, impeding rail traffic still further.[72]

Allied air attacks had two additional consequences. First, they obliged ground units to take alternate routes, which increased the time needed to reach their destinations. Second, by forcing these units to travel at night, the air campaign slowed their rate of advance, because motorized vehicles could not use their lights. Moreover, the fatigue of the drivers, aggravated by conditions of poor visibility, increased the number of accidents; and the short summer nights reduced the time available for movement. "Every attempt to advance in daylight has proved to be useless," noted General Guderian in a report of 20 June 1944. "The many charred vehicles along the roads are the consequences of such attempts at daytime movement."[73] Without having been completely interrupted, the transfer of troops to the Norman sector therefore suffered from serious delays. The Ninth and Tenth SS Panzer Divisions had to travel more than a thousand miles from Poland; setting out on 12 June, they reached Lorraine by train on the sixteenth but arrived at Alençon only on the twenty-fifth.[74] Similarly, First SS Panzer left Belgium on 17 June, but it was not until 9 July that the entire division had reached the battlefield.

Finally, the Allied bombing, though sometimes ineffective from the tactical point of view, placed enormous strain on the nerves of the combatants. "The psychological effect of such a mass of bombs coming down with all the power of elemental nature upon the fighting troops, especially the infantry," General von Kluge advised Hitler, "is a factor which has to be given serious consideration. It is immaterial whether such a bomb carpet catches good troops or bad, they are [all] more or less annihilated"[75]—along with their equipment and supplies. If attacks of this kind recur, Kluge warned, the soldiers' ability to stand their ground is put to the most severe test—a circumstance that had ominous implications for German strategy, which was predicated in large part on the troops' courage in withstanding the Allied onslaught.

Indeed, the courage of German soldiers in general, and of the SS in particular, made life difficult for their adversaries. The German army fought well on the whole. Its obstinate resistance was possible in part because morale did not collapse as it had toward the end of the First World War; nonetheless, the will to resist was undermined by the growing sense that Germany had lost the war, and the presence of middle-aged men and foreign elements in many units in Normandy further weakened the determination to fight to the last cartridge, as Hitler demanded. The presence of a hard core of fanatics, whose blind obedience and unquestioning loyalty to the Führer limited the loss of faith within the ranks, offset this effect to some degree. So too did the residual influence of military training and naked coercion, as interrogation of prisoners taken after the surrender of Saint-Malo and Boulogne revealed: "German officers and soldiers will fight on desperately even though their morale is low. They do so partly because they are well disciplined soldiers and continue to obey orders, and partly because some of them fear being shot by the officers or fear reprisals against their families. Others fight on (and most are ardent Nazis) because they are convinced that continued resistance might, by some miracle, bring victory for themselves and their country."[76] Of 853 prisoners captured between 6 June and 17 July, 50 percent took defeat for granted, whereas 20 percent believed that victory would be theirs.[77] While recognizing that it served no useful purpose to speculate about the possibility of a general psychological collapse in the German army,[78] the Allies nevertheless broadened their propaganda effort to encourage deserters, guaranteeing them six points: "Immediate removal from the danger zone. Decent treatment as befits soldiers. The same food as American soldiers ('the best fed army in the world'). Hospital care. Postal privileges. Return home after the war 'as soon as possible.'"[79] Only a handful of enemy soldiers gave in to these alluring promises: by the end of June, thirty to forty men had surrendered, presenting the leaflets that had reached them.[80] These soldiers turned out to be foreign troops for the most part, primarily Polish and Alsatian.[81] The failure of the Allied campaign was a corollary of the fact that German soldiers had been inundated by Nazi propaganda about atrocities committed by the Americans against prisoners of war and were terrified of going over to the other side, lest they be tortured and killed.[82] To thwart such rumors, a million leaflets had therefore been dropped on the garrison towns of the Cotentin, mostly in vain.[83]

Although German soldiers themselves blithely trampled on the laws of war in dealing with French civilians and members of the Resistance, they did respect them in combat, taking care for the most part to spare medical personnel wearing a Red Cross badge on the left arm. When the Allies realized that doctors and nurses were typically wounded in the right arm, which was unprotected by this sign, they required that the red cross be displayed on both arms and on the helmet.[84] Barbaric acts were nonetheless commonplace. Snipers—detested by soldiers on both sides—were typically killed without any form of trial.[85] A battalion commander of the Seventeenth SS Panzer Grenadier Division forbade the taking of African-American prisoners. Two American military doctors were killed "because one looked so Jewish and the other was ugly too."[86] On or about 8 June twenty-six men (the vast majority of them Canadian) were assassinated at Château d'Audrieu, where elements of the Twelfth SS Panzer Division (composed of soldiers trained in the Hitler Youth) had established a command post. The same band executed seven Canadian soldiers at Le Mesnil-Patry between 7 and 11 June, and committed a further atrocity near Authie. Taking back a village on 7 June that had briefly been captured by the North Nova Scotia Highlanders of the Canadian Ninth Brigade, the Germans deliberately shot twenty-eight soldiers, robbed them, and mutilated their corpses, rolling a tank over one of the bodies and allowing funerals to be held for the dead only on 13 June. On 17 June around six o'clock in the evening, seven Canadian soldiers were marched under escort by three men to the mayor's residence in Mouen, occupied by the Twelfth Engineering Battalion of the same SS division. After interrogation, the prisoners came out at ten o'clock. A detachment led them into a field, lined them up, and shot them.[87] The Twelfth SS Panzer stood out among the German units in Normandy for its sadistic brutality. It was responsible for the majority of the crimes committed in the first months, including the assassination of 178 prisoners and dozens of French civilians in all.[88]

Germans had no monopoly on atrocities, however. The commander of the 101st Airborne Division instructed his troops not to take prisoners; one of his men killed a wounded German soldier who had tried to surrender.[89] Allied pilots machine-gunned vehicles marked with the Red Cross during operations on Falaise. Members of the First Polish Armored Division left SS prisoners to die rather than be burdened with them, or indeed with any soldiers who had fought against their country in 1939.[90] Some Canadian soldiers of native Indian origin scalped their captives. And some German prisoners were killed by their American captors on trying to escape. A board of inquiry found that some of the "attempts to escape" seem to have been nipped in the bud, to say the least, but in no case could it be said that there was no reasonable ground for shooting. It is probable that the rumors of shooting of PWs were grossly exaggerated, part of the folklore of the war—isolated incidents having been enormously magnified and multiplied in the retailing. More solid bases of fact are to be attributed to the widespread reports that prisoners of war were systematically deprived of their personal property—money, watches, decorations and insignia etc. . . . . A number of the reports make it clear that, insofar as treatment of prisoners of war was concerned, stealing of personal property from prisoners of war at the time of the first search was the most frequent offense committed by United States soldiers.[91]

On the whole, however, the violence visited by the Germans on their adversaries in Normandy cannot be compared with the brutality of the fighting they faced on the eastern front. The Americans and British enjoyed a better reputation among German soldiers than did the Russians, which helped to curb a growing tendency to dehumanize the enemy. Despite an underlying suspicion of Anglo-American motives in the ranks, German commanders insisted that the principle of what Rommel called "war without hatred" be upheld. "The enemy [in North Africa] was reputed to say: 'Kill the Germans wherever you encounter them,'" he told officers during an inspection tour in the South of France prior to the invasion. "Such behavior is alien to us. We fought as respectable soldiers—though as tough as the others. The crushing defeat of the enemy attack at the coast of France [will] be our contribution to vengeance."[92] The directives of Nazi military commissars were more troubling. "Who is attempting now to invade Europe?" asked an order from Berlin, read out by Major General Viktor von Drabich-Wächter to the officers and men of the 326th Infantry Division shortly after the Allied landing.

They are Poles, French, Americans, Canadians and Englishmen, people of the most varied races and nations who, in spite of their differences, are united on one point—their boundless hatred against everything that is German. These are the same people who machine-gun from their planes our women and children working at home in the fields, who attack our children in their play grounds; who in fact wish to fulfill what the Jew Kaufman as spokesman for America demands:

1. The German army will be divided into groups which will be assembled in strongly barricaded areas and the men will be immediately sterilized.

2. The civil population, men, women and children, will be placed in special areas and sterilized.

3. Germany will be divided up and its territories given to others.

4. The German population will be compelled to learn the language of the state to which it is assigned.

What does that mean to us? This struggle gives us the possibility to avenge ourselves for the suffering visited upon our women and children and for the loss of our possessions. It gives us the possibility to repel and to annihilate those who wish to deprive us of every right to live. We must now recognize no bounds in our hatred against our mortal foe.[93]

The effects of this kind of rabid exhortation are hard to judge. In the event, the 326th fought well and hard, and on the whole without the blind rage that party officials demanded.

Nonetheless, not all soldiers cherished the hope of dying for the Reich and their Führer. In early August, General Eberbach deplored "an increased number of cases of looting, cattle stealing and so called 'purchase' accompanied by a show of weapons." Even as the prospect of crushing defeat loomed, divisional vehicles were used to ride around or "to cultivate some female acquaintance—in spite of the shortage of fuel."[94] Forceful arguments were sometimes employed to induce men to fight. Between January and September 1944, the Wehrmacht executed some 4,000 men—1,605 of them for desertion.[95] One regimental commander of the Seventeenth SS Panzer Grenadier Division positioned himself behind the front lines in order to shoot down soldiers who shrank from the assault of American armor.[96] Nor did SS divisions always display greater enthusiasm for combat than regular army formations. Even though it is true that fewer prisoners were taken from the ranks of the SS than from those of the Wehrmacht—prima facie evidence of their superior will to fight—closer scrutiny of actual battlefield performance tells a different story. Thus, for example, the Hitler Youth Division destroyed twenty-three Allied tanks in close combat during the first three weeks of the Normandy campaign, whereas the rather less impressive 352nd Infantry Division took out thirty. Before the fall of Caen, SS infantrymen refused to support the panzers in their counterattacks. The SS command, for its part, took care to prevent its troops from being recklessly sacrificed, at every stage of the campaign withholding a portion of its total forces. After 18 July Twelfth SS Panzer was withdrawn from the front, apart from a few elements that were selectively deployed. Indeed, no SS division fought in a continuous and organized way for the entire ten weeks of the Normandy campaign.[97] The familiar view of an army determined to fight to the end in order to stave off disaster must therefore be qualified to some degree.

In the meantime, both the sheer number of the casualties sustained during the month of June and the inability to promptly bring up reinforcements to the front obliged OKW to reconsider its options. The Führer's field marshals pleaded for a strategic retreat that would slow the Allied advance and make it possible to mount a counteroffensive, by shortening supply lines and exploiting the defensive advantages of natural obstacles (notably the Somme and the Seine). But Hitler, as we have seen, refused to yield an inch of ground: "Present positions are to be held," he instructed his commanders on 1 July. "Any further enemy breakthrough is to be hindered by determined resistance or by local counterattack."[98]

This iron resolve has usually been attributed to the unreasoning obstinacy of a mad dictator. But Hitler's position was not wholly without justification. Retreat would deprive Germany of two major assets: the V-1 and V-2 rockets launched from the Channel coast and the submarines stationed in French bases on the Atlantic. Also, by giving the Allies room to establish airfields, it would further strengthen their command of the skies. Finally, and perhaps most important, it would allow the Anglo-American armies to wage a war of rapid movement that the Wehrmacht was poorly equipped to defend against. In attempting, through a battle of attrition that made the most of the defensive advantages of the Norman terrain, to contain the expansion of the Allied bridgehead, while at the same time retaining control of the Atlantic ports, Hitler's strategy was not absurd on the face of it.[99] As a practical matter, however, the mounting casualties and lack of supplies to which Rommel had called attention made the approach untenable. Not only did Hitler remain unmoved by the desperate appeals of his commanders, but he dismissed those who dared to contradict him. Rundstedt made the mistake of trying to explain the hopelessness of the German position to General Keitel, chief of OKW, in a telephone conversation during the night of 1 July. "'What should we do?' cried the despairing Keitel. 'What should we do?' 'Make peace, you fools,' said von Rundstedt. 'What else can you do?'"[100] Relieved of his duties the following day, Rundstedt was replaced as head of OB West by General von Kluge. Blinded by the Führer's grand illusions during a two-week stay at Berchtesgaden in preparation for assuming his new duties, Kluge began by insisting on the total obedience of his subordinates ("Even you," he told Rommel, "must obey unconditionally from now on. This is good advice that I am giving you").[101] Once directly confronted with the realities of the situation, however, he rapidly changed his views, recognizing that what OKW saw as alarmist reports from the field were only a sober assessment of the actual state of affairs. "Despite all our efforts," he wrote Hitler on 21 July, "the moment is fast approaching when our hard-pressed defenses will crack. When the enemy has erupted into open terrain, the inadequate mobility of our forces will make orderly and effective conduct of the battle hardly possible."[102] Gloomy reports of this sort could not fail to displease the Führer, and indeed Kluge was eventually to be dismissed in his turn. In the meantime, Rommel was obliged to surrender his command following a strafing attack by a British fighter on 17 July that left him with four skull fractures. By a singular coincidence, he was thrown from his staff car near a village bearing the ancestral name of his British adversary, Sainte-Foy-de-Montgommery. Brought at once to a field hospital in Bernay, Rommel was transferred after a few days to Le

Vésinet, outside Paris, before finally being invalided to his family home in Upper Swabia on 8 August. In mid-July, then, Kluge was assigned responsibility for both OB West and Army Group B—a moment of deep crisis for the German high command that curiously seems to have escaped the notice of the Allied intelligence services.

Unlike Hitler, the German generals were in no doubt that collapse in the West was inevitable in only a matter of weeks. It is against the background of the deteriorating situation in Normandy that the assassination attempt against the Führer on 20 July is to be understood. The German historian Klaus-Jürgen Müller has argued that the purpose of this attempt was wholly symbolic, OVERLORD having undermined "the very basis on which the conspirators' plans rested until then: the landing had taken place before Hitler could be overthrown. . . . Until then, political and military considerations had the same weight as ethical considerations; henceforth the latter came to the fore."[103] According to this view, the sole motivation of the conspirators, knowing that the cause was lost, was to show the world that another and better Germany had managed to survive the tyranny of the Third Reich. But it must not be forgotten that the moment finally chosen coincided with a situation in the West that held out the chance, no matter how slight, that the leaders of a reformed German nation might yet be able to persuade the Allies of the desirability of concluding a separate peace—one that would enable the United States and Great Britain to claim victory while sparing themselves many months of further costly fighting. July therefore presented a favorable opportunity, for in June the Germans had still counted on being able to hurl the Allies back into the sea, and by August the chance of suing for peace would have passed. "For all negotiations a firm Western front was a prerequisite," General Speidel, Rommel's chief of staff and himself one of the plotters, later recalled. "The stability of the Western front was, therefore, our constant concern."[104] On 2 July, emphasizing the importance of cooperating with the Western powers, Rommel cautioned: "It is high time . . . for the politicians to act as long as we hold any kind of trump."[105] The strategic retreat he and other generals advocated to Hitler offered precisely the hiatus required for negotiating a political solution, the necessary condition of which was, of course, the removal of the

Führer himself. Ethical considerations may have played a role, but they did not exclude geopolitical calculation.

The German generals nevertheless mistook their wishes for realities. The Allies, as we have seen, had no intention either of negotiating with the Reich or of exempting its elites—generals included—from criminal responsibility. Faithful to their declaration at Casablanca, the Americans and British refused to renounce the principle of unconditional surrender or otherwise to risk the rupture of their coalition with the Soviets. On the German side, the conspirators could count on the support neither of a majority of the people nor of the various organs of the Nazi state apparatus. Hitler, having miraculously survived, moved at once to reassert his control and to punish all those who, directly or indirectly, had taken part in the conspiracy. Rommel, to cite only the best-known example, was invited to choose between a public trial and suicide. On 14 October he decided to take his own life.

The failed attempt of 20 July 1944 was therefore only an epiphenomenon, albeit one that unmistakably portended the dark days that lay ahead for the German armies. They were not alone, however, in having suffered repeated setbacks and massive casualties. The British and American armies underwent a severe crisis as well, whose repercussions for the morale of their troops were to be both profound and long-lasting.

# 10

# PSYCHONEUROSES

THE VOLUME OF CASUALTIES SUSTAINED by Allied soldiers in hedgerow combat, the inadequacy of their training, the unsuitability of their equipment on terrain that left them utterly exposed to enemy fire, the labyrinth of sunken roads, which deepened the fear, bewilderment, and loneliness they felt—all these things unavoidably affected morale. "For the ground forces," an official report observed, "the 'old fashioned' trench warfare which readily permitted relief and rest of units was no longer used. The soldier was more of an individual or a specific part of a small team and therefore more dependent for survival on his own resourcefulness and initiative. . . . These and many other factors make it evident that stresses and strains were greater and tested fully the capacity of the individual to adjust to 'total war.'"[1] The campaign in Normandy obliged troops to adapt to a new way of fighting, the like of which they had never encountered before—in many cases because it was their first experience of battle. After the bloody but exhilarating frenzy of the landing on D-Day came dreary, seemingly endless weeks bogged down in the marshes of the Cotentin and stalled in profitless encounters before the gates of Caen, weeks that fed the sense of despair and dehumanization. "Over a stretch of such days, you become so dulled by fatigue that the names of the killed and wounded they checked off each night, the names of men who had been your best friends, might have come out of a telephone book for all you knew. All the old values were gone, and if there was a world beyond this tangle of hedgerow . . . , where one barrage could lay out half a company like a giant's club, you never expected to live to see it."[2]

The rain, falling in amounts not seen since 1900, both demoralized and exhausted the men—and all the more since they were not to receive a change of uniform until mid-September.[3] For many weeks, cold rations constituted their only nourishment. Fatigue weighed especially heavily upon them, for the length of the summer days (almost nineteen hours, from 4:45 A.M. to 11:15 P.M.) prolonged the fighting.[4] Many units were slow to be relieved. The U.S. Second Infantry Division, which landed at Omaha on 8 June, spent 303 days at the front.[5] The British Third Infantry Division, although it had sustained some six thousand casualties, fought for seven weeks without a break.[6] As of 18 July no leave policy had yet been announced on the American side.

Commanders, though they were not always in a position to improve matters, sometimes made them worse through unfortunate remarks. "We can't fight the Boche without incurring casualties and every soldier must know this," General Simonds cynically told his officers on 16 July. "For example, if the operation is worthwhile and I call it off with 50 per cent casualties incurred then I have achieved nothing but a waste of lives; if I continue, and incur a further 20 per cent casualties and bring the operation to a successful conclusion then the operation is worthwhile."[7]

The U.S. Quartermaster Corps did its best to alleviate the physical and psychological suffering of the troops. Films were screened beginning on 25 June. Almost two weeks later, on 6 July the first mail reached the front—well behind the target dates of D + 3 for postal service and D + 10 for package delivery.[8] A brothel was set up at Rennes for the Twenty-ninth Infantry Division.[9] Clergymen also ministered to the soldiers' needs, though in a rather different way. Members of the Chaplain Corps landed on 23 June and set about comforting the troops of Nineteenth Corps at once. Two priests and a rabbi began conducting funeral services on the twenty-eighth. The other chaplains, stayed with the men on the front, to help relieve the anguish of seeing so many cadavers removed from the field of battle.[10]

The quality of the soldiers' food improved as well. Between the offensives of early July and COBRA on the twenty-fifth, the First Army was granted a week of hot meals (B rations) instead of K and C rations; even so, preferential treatment of this sort was dispensed in the rear and seldom reached the forward lines.[11] None of these measures could conceal the harsh realities of the war. With little immediate hope of victory, straining to move forward over unforgiving terrain and surrounded on all sides by a terrible slaughter, men cracked.

## Breakdowns

Some soldiers tried to avoid being sent into battle, either by deserting or by disabling themselves for combat. During the battle of Normandy, the Canadians recorded 95 cases of suspect wounds and 20 or so desertions per month. On the British side, the Second Army counted 52 cases of self-inflicted injury for the first three weeks of June, and 179 cases for the thirteen-week period ending on 30 September.[12] Courts-martial punished 216 desertions in July and 522 in August—as against 27 in June; moreover, cases of unauthorized absence rose sharply, jumping from 312 in July to almost 500 in August (as against 129 in May).[13] On the American side, whereas tribunals having jurisdiction over the Twelfth Army Group punished only 3 cases of self-inflicted injury between June and November 1944, they handed down sentences in 231 cases of AWOL, 169 of alleged misconduct toward the enemy, and 141 of refusal of dangerous duty. For the month of August alone, the First Army recorded 120 AWOLs, a figure probably lower than the actual number, since not all cases came before the courts.[14]

But many more Allied soldiers in Normandy were victims of a range of psychiatric disorders. Simple fear was responsible for widespread incontinence: about 20 percent admitted to losing control of their bowels; 10 percent to urinating on themselves.[15] At the other extreme, suicides were not officially recognized, instead being hidden within the category "Killed in Action" (KIA).[16] In most cases, however, soldiers were simply incapable of continuing to fight: "Not always counted in the casualty reports, they nonetheless totalled an additional 25 to 33 percent of the number of men physically wounded."[17]

Casualties associated with psychological disturbances of various kinds were therefore a matter of great concern. In the U.S. Army, 590 cases were reported between 9 and 16 June (or 13.9 percent of injuries); 1,399 between 7 and 14 July (33.2 percent); and 755 between 28 July and 14 August—a far lower figure than the single-week figure for July but one that nonetheless accounted for 46.1 percent of the total number of battlefield injuries for this period.[18] In all, the First Army acknowledged 5,669 psychiatric cases and the Third Army 1,831, or 36 percent and 18 percent of nonfatal casualties, respectively.[19]

The experience of the British and Canadians was comparable. At the end of July, 17 officers and 506 soldiers of the Third Infantry Division were diagnosed to be suffering from this pathology, or roughly 20 percent of illnesses and injuries.[20] The Second Army as a whole reported 8,930 cases in the middle four months of 1944, accounting for 10.3 percent of nonbattlefield casualties (including traffic accidents and other injuries) and 20.2 percent of battlefield casualties (directly caused by fighting alone). Psychiatric disorders affected 2.5 out of 1,000 men at the beginning of July, a figure that more than doubled, to 5.63, on 22 July, before declining during the month of August.[21]

The incidence of these disorders followed a clear trajectory reflecting the course of the campaign. At the outset, the success of the landing and the consolidation of the beachheads encouraged optimism, and few troops were affected by psychological trauma. On 12 July psychiatric cases on the American side represented only 8.5 percent of the sick and wounded.[22] But with the setbacks in the fighting around Caen and the difficulties of combat in the hedgerow country of the Cotentin, patients flooded the field hospitals and medical aid stations.[23] In all, between a quarter and a third of the victims were treated not as a result of physical injuries, but because they were suffering from what the veterans of the Great War had called shell shock—a syndrome known to those who came after them as psychoneurosis or combat exhaustion. Deliberately vague terms were intended to characterize a group of personality disorders that, though they struck novice soldiers disproportionately, particularly reinforcements who had been rushed into battle without proper training, also affected veterans, typically after four months of combat.[24]

Psychiatric ailments and desertions in the broad sense represented two aspects of a single phenomenon: 56 percent of AWOLs complained of psychosomatic problems (as contrasted with 33 percent for all troops) and, conversely, combat exhaustion was cited in justification for 20–30 percent of desertions and unauthorized absences. Army psychiatrists, skilled in the art of understatement, noted that in both cases the men were "attempting to escape from what they consider[ed] an unpleasant environment."[25] The connection between the symptoms was not thought to suggest the need for a single form of treatment, however. As one medical historian of the campaign put it, "The physical escape of the deserter and the psychological escape of the hysteric were expressions of the same mechanism but the former was severely punished and the latter treated with sympathy in hospital."[26]

No matter that the phenomenon of combat exhaustion was not new, the Allied command found itself confronted in Normandy with a loss of troop strength on a scale it had scarcely anticipated. The earlier campaigns in North Africa and especially Italy had impressed on them the unsuspected fact that even well-adjusted men could crack. "Ordinarily neuropsychiatric disorders are thought to occur only in weaklings or individuals with personality defects," noted an official American report in October 1943. "This is not true. Information at hand indicates that a significant proportion of the neuropsychiatric casualties are occurring in individuals who give no history suggesting predisposition. Under the extremes of stress and fatigue of modern combat, the most stable individual may reach his breaking point. Thus, the presence of neuropsychiatric disorder must be looked for in normal as well as predisposed individuals."[27] All this seems obvious enough to us today: under the exceptional strain of battle, any man, however sane he may be, has a threshold beyond which he can no longer fight. But at the time it was a new idea. Once it came to be accepted, "exhaustion went from being a pathology to 'a normal reaction to an abnormal situation.'"[28] As one military doctor put it, "Psychoneurosis is a condition, not a disease, which results from an individual surrendering to an adverse situation."[29] The experience of soldiers in World War II, particularly during the Italian campaign, also gave rise to what was subsequently called Old Sergeant Syndrome, affecting noncommissioned officers who had been on the front lines for an extended period. Otherwise stable and highly reliable, these men began to fall apart on realizing that their chances of survival were diminishing. Having had in many cases to assume unforeseen responsibilities owing to the death of their superior officers, they doubted their capacity to discharge them and, on being evacuated from the front, were ashamed at having lost their nerve and let down their men.[30]

## Diagnosis

The Allied field commanders were not slow to react to a problem that, in quantitative terms, threatened to reach alarming proportions as the war went on. On the British side, it was decided in July 1943 to assign a psychiatrist to the medical command of each military region. Emergency medical service neurosis centers were established in recognition of the need to treat psychiatric patients separately from soldiers suffering from physical injuries. In September two psychiatrists were also dispatched to tend to the troops landed at Salerno. On the American side, on 26 April of the same year General Bradley insisted that the term "exhaustion" be used, in order to forestall any tendency to pass moral or other pejorative judgment on those exhibiting symptoms. He was particularly opposed to systematic evacuation of patients to the rear, instead mandating a week of observation and care closer to the lines, to facilitate their return to combat units.

The Italian experience, apart from showing that men of sound mind were susceptible to combat exhaustion, demonstrated that the incidence of psychiatric casualties depended more on specific triggering events and the morale of individual units than on personal weaknesses. Military psychiatrists observed that homesickness, the absence of female companionship, the feeling of not being respected by superiors, and a lack of confidence in the abilities of their commanding officers all played a determining role. Other factors included the difficulty of the fighting itself, fatigue, danger, exposure to cold and heat, hunger, isolation, and confusion; also the fear of appearing cowardly or of losing one's self-control, and the sense of being responsible for the life of others. Doubts about the cause one was called upon to serve sometimes led to breakdown as well.[31]

But if his commanders in the field grasped the implications of these facts at once, Eisenhower appeared to be both surprised and disconcerted by the scope of the phenomenon a year later. "Late Monday afternoon," Captain Butcher noted on 15 August 1944, "Ike took General De Witt on a visit to the 5th General Hospital near Carentan. When he returned, he said he was depressed and he looked it. There were about 1100 SIWs—meaning those with self-inflicted wounds—and numerous cases of psychoneurosis or battle anxiety. He said it was always difficult to prove that a soldier had shot himself. This is usually done through the left hand or foot. The soldier always will say that it was an accident."[32] A British battalion commander, reporting on three days' fighting in the Caen sector in late June, counted five cases of self-inflicted injury and noted, "75 percent of the men react adversely to enemy shelling and are 'jumpy.' Each time men are killed or wounded a number of men become casualties through shell shock or hysteria."[33]

In truth, the risk—and the dread—of psychiatric trauma hung over even the most battle-hardened soldiers. Two examples gleaned from the vast medical history of the campaign in northwestern Europe will give some idea of the physical and moral duress to which the combatants were subjected:

A private first class of a machine gun crew was admitted after 14 days of combat. He went to the rear for rations, and when he returned to his foxhole was tired. His buddy and fellow member of the crew said he would stand his guard. While the patient was sleeping a mortar shell landed near[by] and killed his buddy. The patient became upset, very tense and apprehensive, and was evacuated. He felt responsible for his friend's death and could not banish the thought. He was told that his friend, not he, suggested the change in guard duty and that such incidents were bound to occur in combat. It was obvious that his anxiety was due in part to identification with his buddy and this was explained to him. Also he was reassured that he was not to blame and that no one would do so. He was sedated and reassured once or twice daily and made a rapid recovery.

A rifleman in heavy weapons was brought. . . . Complete aphonia was present. . . . He was given a pencil and paper and he wrote "I killed a man," and wept even more bitterly. . . . He saw a German wandering around and shot him with his rifle. He approached the German and saw that he was not dead, and afraid of trickery, hit him in the head with his rifle butt, tearing away the right side of his face and head. The German screamed in agony. The patient said the German was a nice kid with loved ones at home like himself. He was a murderer and could not kill anymore. He spoke of his girl friend and said he wanted to marry her but now would have to tell her he was a murderer. He had always abhorred violence.[34]

Incidents such as these did more than undermine the morale of the men and their officers. Multiplied by the thousands, they threatened to reduce troop strength dangerously at a moment when casualties from other causes were growing at an alarming rate. Unable to withstand this additional loss of manpower, ground commanders cast about for ways to limit psychiatric injuries. Yet incomplete medical understanding of the underlying pathology made it difficult to arrive at agreement about the best way to manage its effects. Victims of battle exhaustion had typically been regarded either as cowards, if not actually malingerers, and referred to courts-martial; or they were considered to be sick and treated as such. After considerable debate, the second view prevailed—evidence of a degree of compassion foreign to both the Red Army and the Wehrmacht.

Accepting that combat exhaustion was a matter to be dealt with by hospitals, rather than military tribunals, was nevertheless only a partial solution. So long as the causes of the condition remained unknown, no remedy could be proposed. If psychoneurosis struck only unstable personalities, the right sort of tests would settle the question by eliminating emotionally fragile recruits at the outset. But if it affected men of sound mind and temperament, as all the available evidence suggested, then preventive measures were not enough. Combat exhaustion would have to be cured.

## TREATMENT

Before the Italian campaign, as we have seen, prevention was the preferred method for reducing the incidence of psychoneuroses. On entering the war, the United States relied on psychologists and psychiatrists to select conscripts—an approach that initially enjoyed little favor in Great Britain. "It is very wrong," Churchill averred in December 1942, "to disturb large numbers of healthy, normal men and women by asking the kind of odd questions in which the psychiatrists specialize."[35] But official thinking gradually changed. Psychiatric selection was instituted in October 1940 for troops, and early 1941 for officers.[36] Conscripts later found to be suffering from psychiatric illnesses were not returned to civilian life: they remained in the military, receiving treatment in hospitals and subsequently being reassigned to more appropriate duties in other branches of the armed services.[37] Military physicians in Canada, feeling that they were fully capable of detecting doubtful cases, were reluctant to cede a portion of their authority to psychiatrists. As a result, psychological testing did not really come into force there until 1941.[38] In all, 22,000 Canadians and 1.5 million Americans were rejected as unfit for service on psychological grounds during the course of the war.[39]

This regime presented certain oddities of its own, however. In early 1943 the Canadians recognized the disadvantages of turning down young men who were guilty of nothing more than immaturity or a lack of motivation, but who were otherwise capable of being trained to fight.[40] Nonetheless, there was resistance to investigating alternative approaches to the problem in both Canada and the United States, where military physicians such as Major F. H. Van Nostrand argued against a policy of hospitalization and intensive psychotherapy that they considered unlikely to do much good.[41] But it was really the campaigns of 1942–1943 that exposed the inadequacy of the screening process: in North Africa army staffs found themselves confronted with a sharp increase in psychiatric maladies, which affected fifteen out of every thousand men in 1943; in Italy 16 percent of sick and wounded Americans exhibited psychological problems—a proportion that rose to 35 percent during periods of intense fighting.[42] Whether tests were administered before their induction into the armed forces or afterward, a disturbing number of soldiers were later found to be psychologically traumatized.

There was disagreement over what should be done. The Canadians and Americans argued for battlefield treatment, whereas the British favored evacuation. By the time OVERLORD began, no unified policy had been established. At the outset of the campaign the British referred all cases of combat exhaustion in the first instance to a regimental aid post, where emergency treatment was administered. Patients were then sent to a corps exhaustion center for specialized care, or else they joined the masses of sick and wounded awaiting evacuation. The Americans, by contrast, recommended treatment close to the front lines so that soldiers would be in a position to rejoin their combat units as soon as possible. But no one foresaw the explosion of cases that would occur as the campaign wore on. On D + 13, British physicians had been pleased to discover that psychiatric casualties were lower than forecast.[43] But they were to be rapidly disillusioned in the wake of the twin failures of EPSOM and GOODWOOD. In the Fifty-first (Highland) Division, to take but one example from the offensive launched on 24 June, such cases represented 30 percent of the sick and wounded.[44]

U.S. Army units in the Cotentin faced a similar situation. Unlike the British or even the Canadians, however, the Americans were able to come to grips with it, in part because they had less difficulty admitting the reality of a condition that their allies preferred to cloak in euphemism. To be sure, the consensus within the army medical corps was not absolute.

Unfortunately, however, there is a certain proportion of soldiers who are more afraid of the enemy and what the enemy can do to them, than they are of being cowardly. Nevertheless, a still more potent fear can be generated in such soldiers; and this is the fear of certain punishment which is as bad as the worst the enemy can inflict. If every soldier *knew* that he would be executed for cowardice, for malingering, or for a self-inflicted wound, the vast majority of weaklings would choose the more favorable odds offered in facing the enemy. . . . The plain fact is that—aided, abetted

and confused by too much psychiatry theory—our war department and our commanders have not faced this problem in a realistic manner. But there is one fact that no psychiatrist can explain: *psychoneurosis is not a problem in the Russian Army.* The
Russians punish cowardice with death.[45]

In spite of dissenting voices such as this one, the American command
declined to attribute the phenomenon to lax discipline or shameful pusil-
lanimity, and instead treated it as a genuine illness—an opinion that had
long been shared by those with direct experience of the problem: 79 percent of the officers serving in the Mediterranean and 68 percent of the officers serving in the Pacific felt that the majority of cases ought to be regarded as instances of a distinct pathology; only very small minorities (6
percent and 3 percent, respectively) demanded that such men be considered cowards and punished accordingly.[46] Notwithstanding that the vast
majority of generals and psychiatrists supported the principle of medical
treatment, they also urged that the ailing soldiers rejoin the struggle at
the earliest opportunity. As the Manual of Therapy of the European Theater of Operations succinctly put it: "The treatment objective is twofold:
to return to duty as many men as possible and to minimize the consequence of disability."[47] A paradoxical alignment of interests therefore
emerged between military physicians, who were concerned above all with
restoring the health of their patients, and the generals in the field, who
were under pressure to restore flagging troop levels.

As a result of this providential consensus, psychiatrists were encouraged to speak frankly to soldiers about their fears, for example by ex-
plaining that self-inflicted injuries are a sign of a neuropsychological
problem: "Do not tell the patient that it is 'all in his mind,' 'stop imagin-
ing things,' or 'forget it.' The physiological manifestations of emotions are
not imaginary and there is no conscious control over conversion hysteria
symptoms. . . . However, courage and fear are not opposites. It may be
helpful to the soldier to know that courage consists of doing one's duty
though one is terrified. Doing a duty without fear is not courageous or
brave, just as it is not virtuous to refrain from sin which one has no desire
to commit."[48] Both commanding and attending officers were instructed to

anticipate the occurrence of breakdowns. In one American corps fighting in Normandy, each company was assigned a medical attaché whose job was to monitor the behavior of the men on the front lines. If a soldier seemed disturbed—anxious, jumpy, on the point of cracking—his name was given to the sergeant in charge, who promptly pulled him out of action and placed him in the custody of the Quartermaster Corps. In most cases the men quickly asked to return to the front.[49]

In the event that more serious symptoms presented themselves, soldiers received attention for twenty-four hours near the lines, in battalion or regimental collecting stations, where they could rest, have a hot meal, and bathe. Those who recovered quickly were sent to the replacement depot, and from there to the medical battalion of the corps or division that was responsible for returning them to their original unit. But those whose state of mind remained precarious after a day's rest were sent to division clearing stations, where psychiatrists prescribed a cure of seventy-two hours (extended in some cases by another twenty-four or forty-eight hours). There, in addition to hot meals, the patient received sedatives and an explanation of the difficulties he was experiencing. Only the most serious cases were referred to surgical hospitals and exhaustion centers, where patients underwent psychotherapy and pharmaceutical treatment; if necessary, they were then transferred to evacuation hospitals.[50] In most cases, however, the first stage of treatment sufficed to restore ailing soldiers, if not quite to health, at least to battle readiness. The U.S. First Army treated 9,101 neuropsychiatric cases in July; in 77.8 percent of these the soldiers were able to return to combat.[51] For the Normandy campaign as a whole, the casualty collecting and clearing stations sent 62 percent of their 11,150 psychiatric patients back to the front; and 13 percent were reassigned to noncombat duties, with the balance—25 percent—being evacuated to Great Britain.[52] For the First Army, the number of men returned to service represented 58 percent of the exhaustion cases recorded between 6 June and 24 October 1944[53]—evidence of the progress that had been made since the previous year, when only 44 percent of the patients treated returned to fully active service in combat units.[54]

Skeptical at first, the British were gradually persuaded of the usefulness of American methods. From July 1944 on, they discouraged systematic evacuation to Great Britain, in large part because of the harm of this practice to the morale of the troops still on the front lines. By sending victims of combat exhaustion to aid stations for a brief course of treatment, psychiatrists were able to keep many of the men in the theater of operations, thus stemming at least to some extent the chronic manpower shortage. "Rightly or wrongly," a Second Army report noted, "the impression grew that the incidence of psychiatric disabilities was exorbitant, and that evacuations across the channel constituted an easy means of escape for those of poor morale. . . . From the beginning the Corps Psychiatrists were aware of their responsibilities in preventing the merely frightened or unwilling man from taking this route of escape. . . . At the end of the month, conditions allowed the policy of evacuation of psychiatric casualties to be reversed, so that now the wheels are turning in the opposite direction and the emphasis is on conservation."[55]

The new policy of treating battle exhaustion in the field was itself handicapped by a lack of trained psychiatrists. Field ambulances and dressing stations administered simple treatments. Soldiers exhibiting mild or moderately severe states of anxiety were given a bath and a good night's sleep (in pajamas), with the aid of sedatives, followed by two days' rest to allow the effects of the barbiturates to wear off, during which time military discipline was nonetheless gradually reimposed.[56] More serious cases were referred to one of several corps exhaustion centers, operational beginning in mid-June, and then, depending on the number of available beds, to a division exhaustion center for a week's rest and treatment. The most severe cases were transferred to the Second Army's rest center at Vaux, open from 4 July on, where a brief period of convalescence was followed by reassignment to noncombat duties.

## Prognosis

This reversal of policy produced satisfactory results on the whole. The rates of return to combat units grew, rising in the case of the British Thirtieth Corps from less than 15 percent in June to 45 percent in July—although what became of these men and whether they were able to maintain their psychological equilibrium once returned to the front is not known.[57] Between periods of intense fighting the return rate rose to 65 percent; 50 percent of the men treated reassumed their old posts and 15 percent took new ones.[58] Nevertheless, the situation was hardly an easy one for these patients. Many doctors and nurses regarded them as being responsible, because of their lack of courage, for the repeated failures in the British sector. Then, one day in July during the assault on Caen, the medical staff witnessed the arrival of "these filthy, exhausted, tremulous, stuttering men, huddled under their blankets"—a day of violent bombardment that provoked a panic, shared by staff and patients. "This event was followed by a sudden swing of opinion. It was decided that the patients were still sick men, that they needed peace and quiet, that everywhere in Normandy was too noisy and that they must all be sent to England immediately."[59] We do not know whether the British high command made an exception to its new rule in this instance.

The Canadian military leadership, it should be noted in passing, long resisted the psychiatric diagnosis of combat exhaustion. In the view of Generals Crerar and Simonds, stricter discipline would suffice to arrest the rising casualty rate and discourage shirking and malingering. In this they were opposed by junior officers and psychiatrists, who took it upon themselves to send psychologically traumatized men to reserve or noncombatant units.

The vexed question of how best to cope with psychiatric injury was ultimately resolved by the successes that the Allied armies began to achieve in late July. By mid-August, the morale of the men in the evacuation hospitals was improving, and the incidence of self-inflicted injuries, in particular, had sharply declined. "Soldiers like to play on a winning team," noted General Patton.[60] On the British side, cases of psychoneurosis in the Second Army fell to 1,736 for the last four months of 1944 (or 4.8 percent of all casualties and 14.3 percent of battle casualties).[61] Whereas 5.63 men out of every thousand suffered from combat exhaustion on 22 July, in September it affected only between 0.37 and 1.02 of every 1,000 soldiers.[62] Desertions and unauthorized absences also fell, dropping respectively from some 500 in August to 288 in September and from 500 to 187.[63] The decline was less pronounced on the American side. In the First Army, symptoms affected 2,609 men (or 21.3 percent of the sick and wounded); in the Third Army, 5,143 (or 27.4 percent of the sick and wounded).[64] These figures were nonetheless substantially lower than those recorded in August, which, as we saw earlier, often exceeded 30 percent.

The crisis of the summer of 1944 was therefore dramatic not only in human terms. It also revealed a structural defect in the composition of the Anglo-American forces. Poorly selected in the first place, assigned to the infantry by default, less well educated than sailors or airmen, the men who fought on the ground took little pride in the units in which they served. And yet, though they were the weakest element in the Allied forces, the burden of the fighting fell disproportionately on their shoulders, as the grim balance sheet of the Normandy campaign attests: infantry alone sustained 76 percent of the combat casualties and accounted for 74 percent of the psychiatric cases. Confronted by a gruesome spectacle of slaughter, advancing slowly over difficult terrain against a fiercely determined enemy, the foot soldiers were likeliest to fall apart as the arms of death closed in upon them. But beyond the extraordinary violence these men endured, the figures also indicate a lack of motivation. Infantrymen were all the more susceptible to psychological collapse in that they doubted the cause they had been summoned to serve—an observation that is confirmed by considering the opposite case. Thus, for example, the French troops of Major General Philippe Leclerc's Second Armored Division, placed under American command, were almost untouched by the scourge of psychoneurosis, which in August struck only one man (or 0.3 percent of the sick and wounded). It might be objected that this unit, which did not arrive in Normandy until 1 August, was seriously engaged in combat only a week later, on 7 August, at Avranches. Possibly so. But it needs to be kept in mind that 7.9 percent of the casualties sustained by the U.S. Seventh Armored Division, which first saw action only on 14 August, were due to battle exhaustion. Similarly, the U.S. Eightieth Infantry Division posted a rate of 4.55 percent, although it began fighting in Normandy on 8 August. Considering the American Third Army as a whole, the proportion of psychiatric casualties for Leclerc's division was by far the lowest; others ranged from 5.2 percent (Fifth Armored and

Fifth Infantry) to 13.7 percent (Fourth Armored), even 14.4 percent (Second Infantry).[65] Surely it is not implausible to conclude that the discrepancy between these figures can be accounted for by the fact that the French Second Armored Division was made up primarily of volunteers who enlisted in the firm belief that the survival of their nation was at stake.

Postwar accounts by American and British authors have propagated a triumphalist image of brave men who unhesitatingly sacrificed their lives to liberate France and crush Nazism. Certainly their courage and valor cannot be denied; but too often the myth has obscured their frailties and suffering, which found expression in the form of psychiatric disorders, self-inflicted wounds, and flight from battle. In the face of unbearable violence, minds and bodies rebelled—not out of cowardice, but because a yet poorly understood psychophysical limit of endurance had been exceeded. Some GIs and Tommies sought to escape the hell of battle and to make it home alive; others sank temporarily or permanently into a state of combat exhaustion. But even if the majority fought without displaying outward signs of mental injury, few were unaffected by the experience afterward. A study done in late 1944 of 5,127 soldiers who returned to the United States revealed that 69 percent of the infantrymen, 66 percent of the engineers, and 73 percent of the men serving in the Quartermaster Corps were suffering from psychiatric problems.[66]

The profound trauma indiscriminately inflicted on soldiers by the unprecedented brutality of modern warfare, first revealed to the Allies during the campaigns in North Africa and Italy, reached the height of its intensity among the hedgerows of the Cotentin and in the stalled columns laying siege to Caen. The hope that was reborn with the prospect of breaking through the German defenses in late July, though it by no means amounted to a cure, did nevertheless succeed in easing the mental anguish produced by weeks of deadlock.

# 11

# From Avranches to Paris

E VEN BEFORE THE REPEATED reverses suffered by Montgomery, German resistance had delivered a powerful blow to the morale of the Allied armies. Where could a breakthrough be expected to occur, then, if the British had shown themselves incapable of piercing the enemy defenses outside Caen?

## Going on the Offensive

On 10 July, General Bradley sketched a plan based on a relatively simple idea: "First, we must pick a soft spot in the enemy's line; next, concentrate our forces against it. Then after smashing through with a blow that would crush his front-line defenses, we would spill our mechanized columns through that gap before the enemy could recover his senses."[1] This scheme depended in the first instance on large-scale aerial bombardment, with 2,200 aircraft releasing some 4,700 tons of explosives in four successive waves. Next, ground forces would attack along the road connecting Saint-Lô with Périers and Lessay, with three infantry divisions (Fourth, Ninth, and Thirtieth) opening a breach that could be exploited by armor for the purpose of encircling the German Eighty-fourth Corps, positioned between Coutances and Lessay. By destroying the bulk of the adversary's forces in the lower Cotentin Peninsula, it would become possible to go on to capture its ports in Brittany.

In proposing to operate on a narrow (rather than a broad) front, with a view to enveloping the enemy (rather than mounting a frontal attack), Bradley dared to break with the classic orientation of American military strategy. His plan also entailed a considerable degree of risk. The tanks had to traverse forty miles of arduous terrain before entering an expanse of flat land in Brittany. "Bradley had no evidence whatever that the Bocage country could be forced without casualties he couldn't afford," one observer remarked, "and an armored blitz through the terrain that lay ahead looked almost like madness, especially after Caen."[2] Not only were the flanks of the armored units unprotected, but supply lines would be restricted to a single road running along the west coast of the Cotentin, where traffic jams threatened to slow the transport of equipment and supplies. An additional set of problems would arise if the Germans, as the Americans feared, had organized their defenses along the road from Périers to Saint-Lô. And then there was the worry, of course, that the enemy might employ V-1 and V-2 rockets, or indeed other even more lethal secret weapons.[3]

The U.S. First Army possessed certain advantages of its own, however. First, the weight of forces was in Bradley's favor, for his fifteen divisions were opposed by only seven German divisions (three of them armored); and Lieutenant General Paul Hausser's Seventh Army had only 110 panzers to defend against his 750 tanks. The element of surprise worked in favor of the Americans, as well, since OB West scarcely imagined that they would launch an offensive on such unfavorable terrain. Perhaps most important of all, the Americans had refined their tactics. A sergeant named Curtis G. Culin in the Second Armored Division's 102nd Cavalry Reconnaissance Squadron had the idea of equipping tanks with a row of tusklike blades, made out of iron salvaged from German beach obstacles, that would enable the Shermans to advance by shearing off the hedgerows at the base. Bradley approved the device on 14 July, and the Quartermaster Corp put a team of twenty-eight welders to work at once; by the time COBRA began on the twenty-fifth, they had produced more than five hundred sets of hedgerow cutters. By the end of July, three-fifths of the First Army's Shermans had been converted into "rhino tanks" (so called on account of their iron horns). Owing to this expedient, it became possible to coordinate the simultaneous assault of artillery, tanks, and infantry, which until then had been obliged to operate separately.[4]

Air-ground coordination was improved as well, though not without difficulty. Major General Elwood R. ("Pete") Quesada of U.S. Ninth Tactical Air Command initially was of the view that the air force should not concern itself with targets that could be destroyed by artillery. With the deadlock of the early summer, however, his thinking changed and he became the staunchest advocate of providing ground troops with close air support. Equipping tanks with very high frequency (VHF) radios allowed the Shermans and Quesada's Thunderbolts and Mustangs to communicate with one another, the ground forces indicating objectives to the airmen and vice versa. From then on, Ninth TAC was unstinting in its efforts. On a typical day, 40 percent of its missions were devoted to close support of the American First Army, 30 percent to close support of the British Second Army, 10 percent to knocking out rail lines and communications fifty to seventy miles behind enemy lines, and the rest, some 20 percent, to carrying out fighter raids and providing ground assault cover.[5] Altogether, the three tactical air wings (Nine, Nineteen, and Twenty-nine) flew 69,326 close-support missions, accounting for more than 32 percent of the overall tactical effort undertaken on behalf of the Twelfth Army Group.[6] Each sortie lasted about fifteen minutes, each pilot carrying out an average of five missions a day.

In view of the preeminent role assigned to the air force, it was left to Air Marshal Leigh-Mallory to fix the date of the operation. Bad weather forced it to be pushed back from the original date of 21 July to the twenty-fourth, then finally the twenty-fifth. It was named COBRA for a curious reason: "There was a story current that a planning officer on the First Army Staff, thinking that the sneaking columns would turn and wrap themselves about the German army, had wanted to name the plan for a snake which crushed its victims—but the only snake whose name he could remember was the cobra."[7] The inauspicious weather gave way to tragic miscalculation in the first stages of the operation, however. Before being postponed a second time, some 1,500 heavy bombers of the Eighth Air Force and almost 400 aircraft of the AEAF had taken off on the twenty-fourth, and not all of them could be called back.[8] The third wave of 300 planes mistakenly dropped seven hundred tons of bombs when a malfunctioning bomb door caused its leader to release his load outside the target area; the bombers following did the same, with the result that twenty-five Allied soldiers were killed.

The air campaign the next day was still more disastrous. Bradley had directed that it be carried out parallel to the road from Périers to Saint-Lô, to avoid hitting his own forces.[9] The crews of the more than 1,500 heavy bombers of the Eighth Air Force were unaware of this order, however, which would have required them to fly for two and a half hours over a narrow strip guarded by German antiaircraft defenses.[10] The bombing was instead carried out at right angles to the road and once again struck American troops, killing 111 (among them General McNair) and wounding 490.[11] Supreme Headquarters staff, believing it advisable to cover up this blunder, reported that McNair had been killed by the enemy. "A loud wail of protest went up from all Correspondents who knew the facts and charges were made in the press that Public Relations officers were seeking to cover up. Later, the true story was told but the mistake had already been made."[12]

To make matters worse, the bombing initially seemed to have been ineffective. As the official history of the operation noted, "Many American troops had expected the bombardment to eliminate resistance in the target area," but this was not the case.[13] Preliminary reports suggested that only 10 percent of enemy troops had been put out of action, a relatively low figure, considering the resources deployed. In reality, however, the attacks had a devastating impact on German operations, disrupting communications and sowing chaos.[14] "The shock effect on the troops was indescribable," reported General Bayerlein. "Several of the men [went] mad and rushed dementedly round in the open until they were cut down by splinters."[15] This account was confirmed by the Seventh Army chief of staff, Colonel Rudolf Christof Freiherr von Gersdorff, who told General von Kluge, "Yesterday's heavy fighting was successful for the enemy only because he paralyzed all our movements by employing fighter-bombers on an unprecedented scale."[16]

The Americans did not immediately appreciate their good fortune,

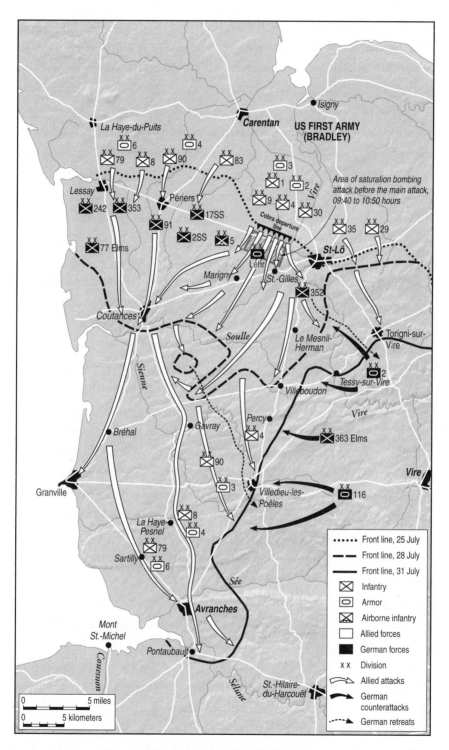

8. Operation COBRA (25–31 July 1944)

however, because at first they encountered stubborn resistance. Moreover, the casualties resulting from the mistakes of 24–25 July had undermined morale, and the men of Seventh Corps were unable to do more than cross the Saint-Lô road on the first day, a gain of only a mile or so. And yet appearances were deceiving: unbeknownst to both General Collins and his troops, the enemy defenses were utterly destroyed and resistance would soon begin to crumble. Collins therefore decided to bring up two of his armored columns, notwithstanding the chance that they might get stuck in a gigantic bottleneck—a risky gamble, but one that in the event was crowned by success. With forward support from the tanks, themselves protected by four fighter-bombers flying half-hour sorties in succession, the scope of the advance broadened from 27 July on.[17] Nineteenth Corps moved toward Tessy, and Eighth Corps toward Coutances, which it took on the twenty-eighth, then reaching Avranches, the gateway to Brittany, two days later. In the meantime, air support was unremitting: between 25 and 31 July, Ninth Tactical Air Force carried out 655 reconnaissance missions and 9,185 sorties, dropping 2,281 tons of bombs.[18]

In the view of Ralph Ingersoll, an officer attached to General Bradley's staff, "Bradley's greatness emerged now in his dual appreciation, first, of the fact that the relatively untried American armies were strong enough, with the superiority we had in the air, to bet everything on a decisive battle and win and, second, of the truth that this battle had to be fought immediately, could not wait until we had more troops ashore or pause for more supplies, but must be fought now."[19]

It fell to General Patton to make the most of this sudden advantage. Before assuming command of the Third Army on 1 August, he had supervised the advance of Middleton's Eighth Corps with his customary energy. On 28 July he directed the armored divisions to press on ahead of the infantry formations—a daring stroke that soon proved its worth, for with the fall of Avranches the spearheads of his Third Army were in a position to rush into the breach that had been opened. Within seventy-two hours, seven divisions and some 10,000 vehicles had crossed over the Sélune at Pontaubault without meeting any effectual resistance. Kluge, concerned by the risk to his unprotected left flank, had asked Hitler for permission to transfer armor from the British front to the American sector, but the speed of Bradley's advance foreclosed this option, with the result that German counterattacks on the twenty-eighth and the thirtieth failed for lack of panzer support. At the same time, the failure of Eighth Corps to penetrate beyond the road from Lessay to Périers permitted much of the enemy force to escape. "Aided by the terrain, the weather, the darkness, the absence of Allied night fighter planes, and the extreme caution of American troops, who had come to respect the ability of the Germans to fight in the hedgerows, the German troops facing the VIII Corps had neatly slipped out of the trap set by COBRA."[20]

### BREAKING THROUGH

In the east, the British and the Canadians made less clear-cut progress, although from mid-July onward they had expanded operations in support of the upcoming American thrust in the Cotentin. In Eisenhower's view, continuing the Anglo-Canadian offensive begun on 18 July was essential. Three days later, notwithstanding the disappointment of GOOD-WOOD, he wrote to Montgomery:

> The recent advances near Caen have partially eliminated the necessity for a defensive attitude, so I feel that you should insist that Dempsey keep up the strength of his attack. . . . As Bradley's attack starts Dempsey's should be intensified, certainly until [Bradley] gains the space and airfields we need on that flank. In First Army, the whole front comes quickly into action to pin down local reserves and to support the main attack. Dempsey should do the same. The enemy has no immediately available major reserves. We do not need to fear, at this moment, a great counter offensive. . . .
>
> I realize the seriousness of the reinforcement problem for Dempsey. That is another reason, in my mind, for getting the business straightened out quickly. Eventually the American ground strength will necessarily be much greater than the British. But while we have equality in size we should go forward shoulder to shoulder, with honors and sacrifices equally shared.[21]

Tedder considered this letter too accommodating, because it contained no order. And indeed Montgomery held to the guiding principle of his scheme, which aimed to draw off the main part of the German forces, while the American First Army attempted to break through to the south. Dempsey noted on 25 July, "[The Allied plan] will have no geographical objective but will be the continuation of the policy which held good the whole time—that 2nd Army shall deal with the main enemy force whilst 1st Army swings forward with its right."[22]

The British command nonetheless hoped to make up for a perceived loss of prestige. On 16 July Churchill had directed General Ismay to see to it that the record of "British casualties, dating from the outset of operations, . . . be issued . . . at regular monthly intervals covering the same period as the fortnightly Allied casualties. I am particularly anxious that the Canadian casualties although stated separately should be included in the British publication of casualties, otherwise they will be very readily assumed to be part of the American casualties. The point is of Imperial consequence."[23] In the circumstances, the prime minister naturally expressed eagerness for Montgomery to bring back an important victory before long. "I am very glad that the Americans had a good success today," Churchill wrote him on 27 July. "It would be fine if this were matched by a similar British victory. I realise that you have the main weight of the enemy against you and I am sure you will overcome them. This is the moment to strike hard."[24]

Two days earlier, the Canadian Second Corps had launched an attack on Falaise (Operation SPRING) in support of COBRA. Noticing that no German panzer division opposed the British troops to the west of Noyers, General Dempsey also ordered a fresh assault (Operation BLUECOAT) on 30 July that was to move rapidly from Caumont to La Forêt-l'Évêque and Bény-Bocage, and then on to Vire. This maneuver, if successful, would suddenly land the British behind the Germans' forward positions in the lower Cotentin, within ten miles of the U.S. Fifth Corps, while preventing the Germans from taking advantage of Mont Pinçon, near Vire, to cover their retreat.[25]

The results of these two operations were bound to disappoint the prime minister: SPRING turned out to be a fiasco, and BLUECOAT was on balance a failure. Bad weather once again prevented the Allied air forces from intervening effectively. And because the Allied intelligence services had not been able to indicate with any precision the areas where enemy forces were concentrated, the Germans were free to use the surrounding hills and hedgerows to the fullest advantage.[26] Eisenhower grew impatient. Emphasizing that Bradley had enough troops to make a dash forward, he instructed Montgomery to order the Canadians to redouble their efforts and block the Germans' exit routes from Caen, so that Dempsey's attack to the west, coupled with Bradley's in the Cotentin, could succeed in clearing the entire area to the west of the Orne of German resistance.[27] Montgomery therefore ordered Dempsey to "throw caution overboard and take any risks he like[d] and to accept any casualties and to step on the gas to Vire," while at the same time dismissing General Erskine from his post as commander of the Seventh Armored Division, along with Lieutenant General Bucknall of Thirtieth Corps, for their lack of vigor in prosecuting the attack.[28] But to no effect: despite the entry of the British Second Armoured Division into Bény-Bocage on 1 August, Mont Pinçon remained in German hands—at the very moment when the American forces were sweeping into the Breton peninsula.

The British and Canadians enjoyed numerical superiority in both July and August, however, when they fielded four times as many tanks as the Germans; but this advantage was eroded by the poor quality of English equipment, together with the effectiveness of German artillery. It took two British tanks to destroy one German tank, and five to destroy two when panzers could count on support from antitank and self-propelled guns. Despite the disproportionate aid given by the Royal Air Force and an apparently favorable ratio of armored forces, the difficulty of the terrain and the concentration of German firepower combined to deny the Anglo-Canadian armies a decisive victory. Between 6 June and 12 August the British lost 1,267 tanks, the Canadians 300, and the Germans 1,250.[29] The human toll was heavy as well: as of 31 July the Second Army had recorded losses of 55,221 men (including 7,803 dead and 8,572 missing in action).[30] Not even the chaplains were spared, twelve having died as of 7 August in the exercise of their ministry.[31]

On the American side, the unexpected success of the breakthrough led Bradley to revise his plans. He decided to limit the forces assigned to the liberation of Brittany to Middleton's Eighth Corps, which carried out its mission brilliantly: Rennes fell on 4 August, Vannes on the fifth, and Nantes on the tenth; the only shadow, but that a considerable one, was cast by the inability of Gerow's Sixth Armored Division to obtain the surrender of the German garrison at Brest, which did not fall until 19 September. By mid-August, the Reich no longer had enough soldiers to defend the peninsula. Lieutenant General Wilhelm Fahrmbacher's Twenty-fifth Corps numbered fewer than thirty thousand men, less than a third of its strength at the beginning of July, in part owing to the transfer of two divisions of paratroops, three infantry divisions, and two combat groups to Normandy. The German command therefore resigned itself to an enemy victory, while doing everything it could to hold three essential positions, the ports of Brest, Lorient, and Saint-Nazaire (the last two resisted until 8 May 1945). This situation in no way worked against the Americans, who by substantially reducing their presence in the west were correspondingly able to reinforce the columns sweeping eastward. In the first days of August, Fifteenth Corps of Patton's Third Army rushed headlong toward the Seine, liberating Mayenne on the fifth and entering Le Mans on the eighth. Between 5 and 9 August this unit covered more than ninety miles.

In the aftermath of the breakthrough at Avranches, the Germans sought to halt the Allied advance by mounting a counterattack. Conceived by Hitler himself, this riposte was intended by the planning staff of OB West to buy time—six to ten weeks—to reorganize their lines of defense along the Marne and the Somme. But the Führer had grander ambitions. By driving westward to the sea at the base of the Cotentin, he aimed to destroy the main part of the American armored forces and to drive a fatal wedge between the First and Third Armies. Operation LÜTTICH called for three panzer columns to head toward Avranches along as many corridors, protected by air cover, in order to split the American forces. To take the fullest advantage of the opportunity for tactical surprise, the Germans dispensed with artillery preparation. One of Hitler's orders to General von Kluge underscored the magnitude of what was at stake: "The enemy must not, under any circumstances, have free access [to the interior of the country] for operations. . . . The outcome of the campaign in France depends on this attack."[32] The very name he chose for the operation was meant to inspire his generals, in recalling the glorious offensive that Ludendorff had launched exactly thirty years before at Liège, in Belgium.

In the event, LÜTTICH went badly wrong. On 2 August the Ultra system had intercepted an order from the Führer demanding that the American breakthrough be ignored in favor of his counteroffensive. This instruction seemed so implausible that Tedder personally checked with the intelligence services, which confirmed the message. As a result, the Americans had four days to prepare. In order to confound the Germans' plans, Bradley had the idea of allowing Kluge's divisions to penetrate his lines before launching his own counterattack.[33] The trap worked perfectly—even a bit more flawlessly than he could have hoped. The German assault began on 6 August and forced the Americans in the south to yield Mortain and hole up at Hill 317; to the north, progress was equally encouraging, but the German 116th Panzer Division, surprised by its unexpected success, hesitated and practically came to a halt. The U.S. First Army, now under the command of General Courtney H. Hodges, took advantage of this respite to regroup while his air force destroyed the enemy's armor. In a little less than a week, the battle was over. Operation LÜTTICH had sounded the death knell for Hitler's illusions, at least in the Cotentin, which was irretrievably lost. It now remained for the Allies to capitalize on their breakthrough.

## The Battle for Falaise

The German collapse at the beginning of August presented the Allies with an opportunity to achieve a decisive victory in the West. By pulling the American forces back around along a tight eastward arc toward the Seine and urging the Canadians onward to Falaise, Eisenhower hoped to encircle and destroy the bulk of the German Seventh Army and Panzer Group West—a plan that seemed all the more likely to succeed because the belated transfer of German units to the American sector had weakened the Reich's defenses in the British sector.

On 7 August Simonds's Canadian Second Corps launched Operation

TOTALIZE. At the same time, part of Patton's Third Army, Fifteenth Corps under Major General Wade Haislip, began its drive to the east. Haislip's orders were to pivot at Le Mans and continue northward, with a view to meeting up with the Canadians at Argentan, thus trapping the remainder of the German forces in a "short hook." The American advance proceeded at a satisfactory pace. Alençon fell on 12 August, offering a first success to the newly landed French Second Armored Division, and by the evening of the thirteenth Haislip's forces were approaching Argentan. The Canadians had made little headway, however, despite the tactical innovation of bringing infantry forward on armored vehicles, guided by green and red tracer shells, to attack at night—the skies being illuminated by antiaircraft searchlights, whose reflection against the clouds created a sort of artificial moonlight.[34] Care was taken, too, to synchronize bombing and ground assault, in order to prevent the Germans from reforming their lines. But when the lead bomber in one wave on 7 August was hit by flak, the rest dropped their loads at once, killing more than seventy soldiers and wounding some three hundred, principally in the Canadian ranks.[35] Of some 390 bombers sent out that day, at most 150 reached their objectives.[36] As a result, Simonds suspended air operations.[37] In the meantime, the troops carrying out the ground assault had managed to advance three miles. But during the night of 7–8 August a German smoke screen disoriented Canadian armored units.[38] The Twelfth SS Panzer Division was able to pull back to the Laison River and blocked the enemy's pursuit. On the evening of the tenth, the Canadians found themselves still six miles from Falaise.

At this point the question arose whether to abandon the "short hook" toward Argentan in favor of following a wider arc of encirclement along the Seine (the "long envelopment"), as Montgomery suggested. The Allied command reaffirmed its commitment to the original plan, but with fifteen miles still separating Simonds's Second Corps and Haislip's Fifteenth Corps on 16 August, Bradley ordered a halt to their advance out of fear that one or both might inadvertently cross the boundary established by Montgomery five days earlier to avoid any collateral damage. Bradley readily acknowledged the danger: "To have driven pell-mell into Montgomery's line of advance could easily have resulted in a disastrous error

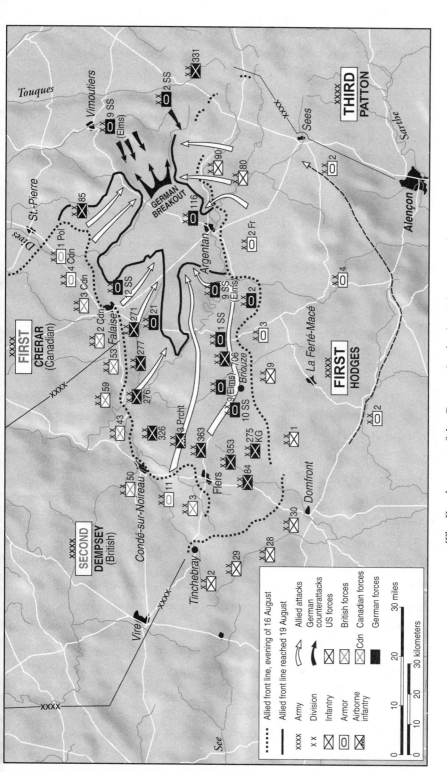

9. The Envelopment of the German Armies (1–16 August 1944)

in recognition." Moreover, with the better part of Patton's Third Army rushing on toward Orléans and Paris, the forces left to Bradley were hardly adequate to block the retreat of nineteen panic-stricken German divisions determined at all costs to find a way out of the closing Allied noose. He may also have suspected that the Germans were likely to succeed in escaping the net to one extent or another, by holding the flanks of the pocket until the order was given to withdraw and then slipping through the Argentan-Falaise gap. However it was, Bradley was content to err on the side of caution ("I much preferred a solid shoulder at Argentan to the possibility of a broken neck at Falaise").[39] Leaving only four divisions in place, he ordered Haislip's Fifteenth Corps to head out on 14 August for Dreux, west of Paris, and Major General Walton H. Walker's Twentieth Corps to proceed as swiftly as possible to Orléans.

The task of closing the Falaise pocket therefore fell to the British and Canadians. Montgomery approved this operation but refused to reinforce the Canadian troops, either because he thought it was too late or because he thought they were capable of carrying out their part of the mission on their own. Or perhaps it was because he counted on being able to sweep up the remnants of the German Seventh Army farther to the east, as Bradley believed: "Rather than close the trap by capping the leak at Falaise, Monty proceeded to squeeze the enemy out toward the Seine. If Monty's tactics mystified me, they dismayed Eisenhower even more."[40]

Operation TRACTABLE was launched on 14 August. Despite considerable enemy resistance, Falaise fell two days later. Recognizing at last that defeat in Normandy was imminent, Hitler ordered his forces on the western flank of the pocket to pull back to the east bank of the Orne. A race against the clock now began. Three days later, on the nineteenth, the Falaise pocket was closed. Even in the face of harassment by Allied air forces, a good many German elements still managed to escape during the night through the gully lying between Trun and Chambois. On 21 August the curtain finally fell in the Norman theater.

On balance, then, the campaign in Normandy had been a success— though hardly a brilliant triumph, and still less a decisive one. Having made little headway for some six weeks, the Allies managed at last to break through the enemy lines and destroy a part of the German army.

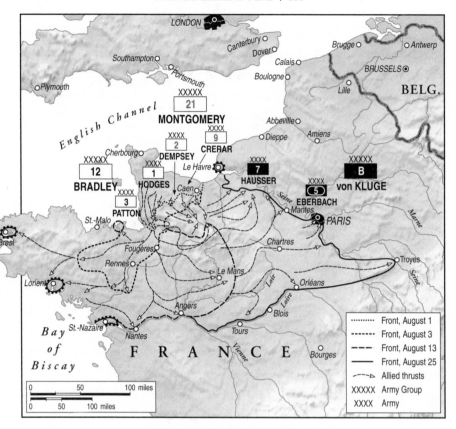

10. The American Breakout (August 1944)

From Avranches the Americans swept to the east on a forced march: Fifteenth Corps reached Mantes-Gassicourt on 18 August, Twelfth Corps having liberated Orléans the day before, and forward patrols of Twentieth Corps reached the outskirts of Fontainebleau on the twentieth. Acceding to de Gaulle's wishes, Eisenhower agreed to detach from Patton's command the French Second Armored Division under General Leclerc, who was to have the signal honor of accepting Major General Dietrich von Choltitz's surrender on 25 August at the Gare Montparnasse in Paris. The British and Canadians, for their part, having closed the gap at Falaise, now turned northward. Rouen fell on 30 August, followed the next day by Amiens and, on 4 September, by Lille, Antwerp, and Brussels. The agony of static warfare, recalling the worst horrors of 1914–1918, had finally given way to the war of rapid movement that the Allies had sought to establish from the beginning, and at which they excelled, owing to their aerial supremacy and their lightly armored but rapid and highly maneuverable tanks. The increased reliance on mechanized forces compensated to some degree for the massive troop losses sustained in the Norman theater, which in the case of the British had made the chronic manpower shortage still more acute.

## THE AFTERMATH

The victory in the northwest of France was reinforced by successes in the south. On 2 July the Combined Chiefs of Staff had ordered that operation ANVIL, long advocated by Eisenhower, be scheduled "at the earliest possible date."[41] A landing in Provence, the Allied supreme commander argued, would provide cover for OVERLORD's southern flank, while at the same time giving the Allies control over Marseille, a vital port for resupplying troops in anticipation of the breakout from Normandy. Churchill and his chiefs of staff were firmly opposed to this plan. On 12 July in a cable to Washington the BCOS pressed its view that ANVIL did not constitute "the correct strategy" for the Allies.[42] A week later Churchill intervened with Roosevelt through his adviser, Harry Hopkins, urging that the operation be called off, in view of the dangers of Soviet penetration in Eastern Europe.[43] On 4 August Churchill came back to Roosevelt with a proposal for an alternate attack in Brittany, north of Saint-Nazaire, and restated his position in conference with Eisenhower. "Ike argued so long and patiently that he was practically limp when the PM departed and observed that although he had said no in every language, the Prime Minister, undoubtedly, would return to the subject in two or three days and simply regarded the issue as unsettled."[44] Eisenhower's prediction came true on 9 August at 10 Downing Street. Nonetheless, the BCOS capitulated the following day, leaving Churchill with only a very modest moral victory: ANVIL was renamed DRAGOON, in recognition of the prime minister's displeasure at having to give in to the Americans against his wishes.[45]

In the event, the forces that landed in Provence—two-thirds of them French—brilliantly attained their objectives, in forcing Hitler on 16 August to order the retreat of Army Group G. The South of France was

rapidly liberated, rather to the surprise of the planners at Supreme Headquarters, whose original forecast anticipated substantial delays. In a memorandum of 17 August they cautioned against excessive optimism: "Whatever scale of resistance is met by the Dragoon forces, owing to the great
distances to be covered, it appears impossible that these forces will reach
the Dijon area before November."[46] As it turned out, they were wrong by
almost two months: OVERLORD and DRAGOON forces joined up on 12 September near the Burgundian capital. Two weeks earlier, on 23 August,
Marseille had been captured, with General Jean de Lattre de Tassigny's
French Army B playing an important role. By 28 September, 905,512
men had entered southern France via Toulon, Port-de-Bouc, and Marseille. Of a total of 4,459,168 tons of matériel transported to the western
front between November and January, 1,434,930 had been unloaded in
Mediterranean ports; the tonnage passing through Marseille and its satellite ports was to be exceeded by Antwerp only in the first month of
1945.[47] The fact remains that Eisenhower, in steadfastly preferring ANVIL
to Churchill's scheme for a Balkan operation aimed at sending General
Alexander's forces through the Ljubljana Gap into the plains of the Dan-
ube, gave the Soviets a free hand in Eastern Europe, for which Churchill
harshly reproached him after the war: "This is not to deny that the operation as carried out eventually brought important assistance to General
Eisenhower by the arrival of another army to his right flank, and the
opening of another line of communications thither. For this a heavy price
was paid. The army of Italy was deprived of its opportunity to strike a
most formidable blow at the Germans, and very possibly to reach Vienna
before the Russians, with all that might have followed there-from."[48]

This view of the matter failed to take into account several crucial
points. In the first place, northwestern France had long been considered
the decisive theater of operations. It was therefore necessary to concentrate Allied efforts there—particularly given that an impasse in Normandy
was liable to be perceived as a defeat, from which the world—and especially the Soviet Union—would draw their own conclusions.[49] In June
1944 with the promised Russian offensive about to begin, Washington
had no intention of creating a *casus belli* with Moscow, and in any case it
had already committed itself at Teheran to mounting an operation in the

South of France. The conquest of the Ruhr, moreover, represented a more substantial prize than did that of Italy or Austria. But as a logistical matter, achieving this goal depended on the prior conquest of a major port, and nothing guaranteed the Anglo-American forces a rapid victory in either Italy, where delays in landing six divisions were unavoidable (owing to the surviving German defenses) or Istria (which had no port facilities to speak of). Furthermore, while de Gaulle readily agreed to deploying French forces in Provence, his consent would have been more difficult to obtain for an offensive in Yugoslavia.[50] Going ahead with the landing in Provence was therefore a sensible decision, hastening the Allied advance and the liberation of France, while giving Eisenhower the port he needed.

In the meantime, the Soviets launched their summer offensive—Operation BAGRATION, also promised at Teheran—on 22 June with 1,254,000 men and 4,070 tanks.[51] The rapid advance of the Red Army, which by 1 August had brought it to the outskirts of Warsaw, was not entirely to the liking of the Western powers, however, for the Soviets' mission was to keep the bulk of the German forces pinned down on the eastern front; already by late June, it will be recalled, two divisions (Ninth and Tenth Panzer) had been transferred from Poland to Normandy. Moreover, the surprising speed of Moscow's victories aroused alarm in London and Washington over the possibility that Eastern Europe might come under Soviet control. At the outset of the campaign, however, Stalin had not yet decided on a course of action. On 8 July he convened a meeting of his generals, to draw up a strategy for Poland and the Balkans—a sign that he had not, until then at least, been following a preestablished plan.[52]

Indeed, a week before the launching of BAGRATION Stalin made a public show of welcoming the first successes of his partners in Normandy. The statement he gave to *Pravda* on 14 June was subsequently broadcast throughout the country: "In summing up the result of the battles that have been waged for a week now by the liberating Allied troops in northern France, one may declare without hesitation that the vast crossing of the Channel and the massive landing of the Allied troops in northern France have totally succeeded. There can be no doubt that our allies have achieved a brilliant success. It must be acknowledged that in the history of war there has not been a comparable undertaking, in respect of the scope of its purpose, its spectacular scale, and the mastery of its execution."[53] The Russian people did not seem to share their leader's enthusiasm, however. On D-Day itself, the chief of the American military mission, General Deane, was surprised as he proudly made his way through the streets of Moscow at the general indifference toward news of the invasion: "When I started out I thought the appearance of an American officer on the streets would be received with such acclaim that I would have difficulty avoiding the cheers of the men and the embraces of the women. Actually I covered the entire distance without being noticed by anyone. The news had been broadcast over the public radio and it received due notice in the press. There was a general feeling of relief that the British and Americans were on the Continent, but there was no demonstrative outburst of enthusiasm."[54] His British counterpart, General Burrows, was taken aback by the questions asked at a press conference in Moscow the same day, which, as he remarked in a cable to the Chiefs of Staff, "showed [an] extremely low standard of knowledge of what launching Overlord entails."[55] Having survived a long, grueling, and barbaric war in their own land, the Russian people may understandably have found it difficult to join Stalin in praising their allies' exploits in the West.

For want of popular support, this *entente cordiale* was therefore confined to the higher echelons. The Western powers invited the members of the Soviet mission in Great Britain to witness their triumphs across the Channel. On 13 June Admiral N. M. Kharlamov embarked on the HMS *Mauritius,* with Lieutenant General A. F. Vasiliev and Lieutenant General A. R. Sharapov sailing aboard the *Warspite.*[56] Two weeks later, on the twenty-eighth, Stalin suggested to the American ambassador in Moscow, Averell Harriman, that the Allied war effort on both fronts be coordinated by a combined general staff that included representatives of all three powers. The Joint Chiefs of Staff in Washington declined the offer, however, arguing that such an arrangement would only hamper the day-to-day conduct of operations and that it would be more sensible to steer a middle course between the bilateral deliberations of the Anglo-American Combined Committee and informal consultation with Moscow.[57]

The month of August was a bleak one for the Reich. Driven back on the Russian front, besieged in Italy, forced to retreat in France, the German army found itself perilously close to disaster on all sides. That it was nevertheless able to resist defeat for almost a year only confirms the unfinished character of the victory won by the Allies in Normandy.

The battle of Falaise ended in the escape of a large part of the German Seventh Army from the net that the Allies had drawn around it. To be sure, preliminary estimates suggested that General Hausser's forces had left behind somewhere between five thousand and six thousand dead, some thirty thousand to forty thousand prisoners, and a considerable amount of equipment; the British and Canadians claimed to have destroyed 571 antiaircraft guns, 358 tanks, and 4,715 other vehicles.[58] These figures are now thought to be on the low side.[59] The German command in the West was also badly shaken. General von Kluge, having narrowly escaped an attack by Allied fighter-bombers on 15 August that left him temporarily unable to communicate with OKW, became suspect in Hitler's eyes and was replaced by Field Marshal Walther Modell. After writing a letter to the Führer emphasizing his personal loyalty, Kluge committed suicide on 19 August, on his way back to Germany. In the space of ten weeks, then, between 6 June and 17 August, the leadership of OB West had changed hands twice—in stark contrast to the stability of the Allied command. What is more, the savagery of the fighting, the air attacks, the firing of artillery almost within sight all combined to plunge the battlefield into chaos. A British officer attached as an observer to the Twelfth Army Group who had personal experience of the battlefields of World War I and of the bombing of London in 1940 noted:

> The grass and trees were vividly green as in all Normandy and a surprising number of houses [were] . . . untouched. That rather peaceful setting framed a picture of destruction so great that it cannot be described. It was as if an avenging angel had swept the area bent on destroying all things German. . . .
>
> I stepped over hundreds of rifles in the mud and saw hundreds more stacked along sheds. . . .

I saw no foxholes or any other type of shelter or field fortifications. The Germans were trying to run and had no place to run. They were probably too exhausted to dig. . . . They were probably too tired even to surrender.

I left this area rather regretting I'd seen it. . . .

Under such conditions there are no supermen—all men become rabbits looking for a hole.[60]

And yet between twenty thousand and forty thousand Germans, perhaps even as many as one hundred thousand, succeeded in fleeing this hell in the two or three days before the pocket was closed, and the Allies captured only a fifth of the corps commanders and division generals.[61] In all, as many as two-thirds of the troops threatened with encirclement may have escaped the trap set for them. The Canadian troops, took thirteen days to cover barely thirty miles.[62] Taking advantage of their slow advance toward Chambois and of the torrential rains, the Germans also profited from SHAEF's undue reliance on airpower to destroy their armies. Forgoing heavy bombers, the air command ordered harrying nighttime raids and targeted daytime attacks that together caused probably a third of the total enemy casualties.[63] Even so, Allied fighters were unable to prevent the Germans from crossing the Seine. In addition to the prefabricated bridge installed at Pont-de-l'Arche, the retreating troops used twenty-three ferries between Les Andelys and Quillebeuf. In the course of five nights, between twenty thousand and twenty-five thousand vehicles and some three hundred thousand men crossed the river.[64] Carrying four trucks per crossing and making four round trips per hour, the ferry at Les Damps alone, operating for three days and five nights, transported some fifteen hundred vehicles.[65]

The Reich therefore managed to avoid a second Stalingrad in Normandy, having succeeded in rescuing a substantial proportion of its troops. The Allies were to pay a high price for failing to block the German retreat. In the judgment of the author of the official American history of the campaign, Martin Blumenson, "What was, in fact, a great Allied victory in Normandy was, in long-range terms, inconclusive. Substantial remnants of the Germans defeated at Argentan and Falaise and harassed at the Seine River would reappear and again face the Allied armies."[66] These remnants were reinforced by the troops pulled back from the South of France: General Blaskowitz's success in reaching Dijon with 130,000 of his original force of 209,000 men was a substantial achievement, notwithstanding their inability to bring more than a small part of their equipment with them.[67] Even so, their presence helped stiffen the resistance that the Allies were to encounter on the western front during the fall and winter of 1944–45. The Germans also managed to retain control of the Breton ports, which in the eyes of Supreme Headquarters represented a major strategic objective, as Eisenhower had reminded Marshall on 7 August—even though Churchill had been overruled regarding ANVIL.[68] Still, Allied troop losses for the Normandy campaign were slightly more than half those of the Germans. For if the British, Canadians, and Poles suffered 83,825 casualties (including 21,138 dead) between 6 June and 1 September, and the Americans 125,847 casualties (including 20,838 dead), German casualties were still greater during the same period: 393,689 wounded or missing in action, of whom 54,754 had been killed.

## TENSIONS AT THE SUMMIT

The delay in breaking out from Normandy aggravated tensions at the upper levels of command between the Americans (and indeed the Canadians) and the British, as we saw earlier. The growing power of the U.S. Army, underscored by the activation of General Patton's Third Army, had led Bradley on 19 July to request the formation of an American Twelfth Army Group under his command. Montgomery agreed to this on 25 July, setting an effective date of 1 August. The Canadians obtained control of their own forces as well, and the headquarters of the Canadian First Army, placed under the authority of General Crerar, became operational on 23 July. The reasons for this concession were more political than strategic, Crerar having been given command of a cosmopolitan force that included the First Belgian (or Piron) Brigade, the Polish First Armored Division, and the Czech Brigade, in addition to his own divi-

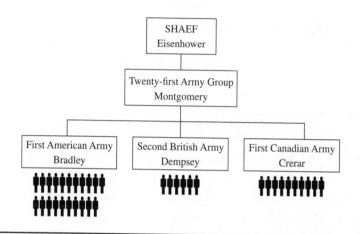

Allied Ground Forces Command
31 July 1944

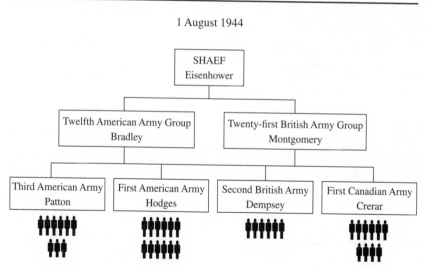

1 August 1944

3. Allied Ground Forces Command (31 July/1 August 1944)

sions. Just the same, Canada was henceforth a full partner in the undertaking, with responsibility for the sector that had formerly been entrusted to the British. As of the beginning of August, Montgomery nonetheless remained in command of the ground forces.

In the meantime, however, the failure of GOODWOOD forced Eisenhower to act. On 21 July he moved to take over direction of the armies himself, effective 1 September, thereby substantially limiting the scope of Montgomery's command. To be sure, this development had long been planned.[69] But it came at a very bad time. In mid-August, owing to a censor's mistake, the press reported that Bradley's promotion as the head of the Twelfth Army Group made him Montgomery's equal—something that was technically incorrect at the time. When British newspapers rose up in arms, SHAEF's public relations department was in the awkward position of having to set the record straight by confirming Montgomery's preeminence. It was then the turn of the American press to erupt in anger, claiming that the British dominated the alliance and that Eisenhower was no more than a figurehead. As a result of the contretemps, Marshall urged Eisenhower to take over command of the ground forces at the earliest possible moment.[70]

To Montgomery's mind, the announcement could only be interpreted as a disavowal. To salve this latest wound to his easily injured pride, King George VI elevated him to the rank of field marshal on 1 September. Yet the promotion could not conceal a loss of prestige whose roots were hardly new by this point. "Because of their shortage in manpower," Bradley later observed, "the British bid for face in the European campaign depended largely upon Montgomery's retention of his role as Allied ground commander. While Monty commanded all Allied ground troops, even those of the United States could be properly labelled 'Montgomery's forces' for whatever the reference might be worth to the British in prestige."[71] Eisenhower's assumption of his new duties shattered this illusion, further increasing the tensions between the Allies, as Montgomery was later to note in his memoirs: "But just when final victory was in sight, whispers went round the British forces that the Supreme Commander had complained that we were not doing our fair share of the fighting. I do not think that great and good man, now one of my greatest friends, had any idea of the trouble he was starting. From that time on-wards there were always 'feelings' between the British and American forces till the war ended."[72] British public opinion did not attach great significance to this affair: only 4 percent of those polled in early Septem-ber said that Montgomery's nominal fall in stature mattered, though 59 percent were closely following the Allied advance into northern France and Belgium. But among the small number who cared about his demo-tion, the sense of injustice was keen: "He has been badly treated, and lowered in the eyes of the world"; "Eisenhower has been jealous of him"; "the Yanks want all the glory."[73] Eisenhower himself acknowledged that "British newspapers greeted the story with great resentment, alleging that Montgomery had been demoted because of his success. The American press, on the other hand, hailed the story with considerable satisfaction because it indicated that the American troops, in their own channel of in-vasion, were now operating on a truly independent basis."[74] Whatever the case, Montgomery was bitterly chagrined.

In one sense his dispossession signaled nothing more than a reversal of the balance of forces within the Allied coalition, which the dramatic American midsummer successes had plainly achieved. Between 21 July and 20 August the now exclusively Anglo-Canadian Twenty-first Army Group had conquered some 3,800 square miles; but the newly created American Twelfth Army Group, emancipated at last from British tute-lage, had seized more than 21,500 square miles during the same period.[75] The plain fact of the matter is that the Americans were no longer willing to be ordered around. Tired of being treated as novices in the arts of war, they were determined to direct the campaign in the West as they saw fit.

While controversy over the perceived affront to Montgomery's dignity filled the columns of newspapers on both sides of the Atlantic, a strategic debate of a wholly different order was playing itself out behind closed doors. On 18 August, Montgomery laid out for the Imperial General Staff his plans for advancing toward the borders of Germany:

> After crossing the Seine 12 and 21 Army Groups should keep to-gether as a solid mass of some 40 divisions which would be so strong that it need fear nothing. The force should move north-

wards. 21st Army Group should be on western flank and should clear the channel coast and the Pas de Calais and West Flanders and secure Antwerp. The American Armies should move right flank in Ardennes directed on Brussels, Aachen and Cologne; the movement of American armies would cut the communications of enemy forces on channel coast and thus facilitate the task of British Army Group. The initial objects of movement would be to destroy German forces on coast and to establish a powerful air force in Belgium. A further object would be to get enemy out of V1 or V2 range of England. Bradley agrees entirely with above conception. Would be glad [to] know if you agree generally. When I have got your reply will discuss matter with Ike.[76]

In the aim of concentrating the Allied forces in a single northward thrust, this plan was by no means indefensible. But it confined Patton's Third Army to a subordinate role, guarding the southern flank of a force whose overall command Montgomery was bent on claiming for himself. Political considerations, sharpened by the prospect of Roosevelt's presidential campaign that fall, made this mission unacceptable to the Americans. Eisenhower was left with a difficult choice. On the one hand, favoring the Third Army would enable Patton to reach the banks of the Rhine more rapidly, but it was less clear whether his forces would be sufficiently strong to launch the conquest of Germany by themselves. Assigning priority to the Twenty-first Army Group, on the other hand, though it promised to establish a secure and extensive base of operations in Belgium, would make poor use of Patton's undoubted talents and give the Germans more time to fortify their border defenses. Eisenhower elected to split the difference. Precedence was to be granted initially to the British armies, with a view to achieving all the objectives outlined by Montgomery in his message of 18 August, and so to preparing the way for an invasion of the Ruhr.[77] Once Antwerp had been liberated, the Allied forces would revert to the basic plan, which called for a two-pronged advance toward the Rhine across a broad front, striking at the Ruhr to the north, and the Saar to the south of the Ardennes.[78] First proposed on 23

August, this rough-and-ready compromise was ratified on 4 September. But it succeeded only in arousing bitterness and contempt among Eisenhower's generals, American and British alike. "Eisenhower's plan of two thrusts, one to the Ruhr and one to the Saar," Montgomery was to remark later in his memoirs, "meant that everything had to be split—forces, air, maintenance, transport, rolling stock, etc. We were throwing overboard the principle of concentration of effort."[79] Thirteen years after the war, he was "still firmly convinced that had we adopted a proper operational plan in the middle of August, and given it a sound administrative and logistic backing, we should have secured bridgeheads over the Rhine and seized the Ruhr before the winter set in. The whole affair if properly handled would not only have shortened the war; it would also have held possibilities of bringing it to an end in Europe with a political balance very much more favourable to an early and stable peace than that which . . . actually emerged."[80] Eisenhower remained firm: "General Montgomery was acquainted only with the situation in his own sector," he wrote in his own memoirs. The British commander "understood that to support his proposal would have meant stopping dead for weeks all units except the Twenty-first Army Group. But he did not understand the impossible situation that would have developed along the rest of our great front when he, having outrun the possibility of maintenance, was forced to stop or withdraw."[81] Patton, for his part, was furious. He accused Eisenhower of siding with the British and enlisted Bradley's support in trying to win the Allied supreme commander's approval for his plan to advance directly through Lorraine to the Saar. Once again, however, differences over strategy gave way to logistical necessity.

In early August, the supply situation appeared in a favorable light. The American forces still had available to them a nine-day supply of munitions and a sixteen-day supply of fuel. The British had twenty-seven days of food rations, sixteen days of fuel, and between fourteen and twenty-one days of munitions.[82] But circumstances changed rapidly. By D + 98 (12 September) the Allies had reached a line that they had been forecast to reach only the following spring, on D + 350. In effect, 260 days of campaigning had been compressed into 19. This frenzied advance massively increased consumption by armored and infantry units. By 24 August, Hodges's First Army had used up 782,000 gallons of gasoline, and by the end of the month reserves were exhausted, with less than a third of a day's supply remaining (0.31); the Third Army had almost no gas left at all (0.007).[83] In addition, a deficit in medium tanks threatened operations (it amounted on the American side to 432 vehicles, or 25.3 percent of the total number actually allocated). The problem, however, had to do neither with supply shortages nor with extravagant demand, but with severely overstretched supply lines. On 31 August on the British side they covered 45 miles; on the American side, 120 miles—and 350 miles in September.[84] Virtually all provisions (90–95 percent) at this time were still being stored in base depots near the beaches because of the difficulty of establishing advance depots between the front and the Norman coast, some 300 miles away.[85] An advance depot had indeed been established on 13 August at Laval for the Third Army, but by this point Chartres and Dreux, outside Paris, were preparing to welcome their liberators. For the Quartermaster Corps, the constraining factor was no longer so much access to ports as the speed with which inland depots could handle deliveries.[86]

The logisticians hoped to be able to solve the problem by means of a special delivery system, the Red Ball Express, using trucks that traveled along two parallel highways between Saint-Lô and Chartres, one reserved for outbound traffic and the other for trucks returning to the base depot.[87] But the first convoys did not roll until 25 August. Nor did pipelines carrying petroleum, oil, and lubricants (laid by 7,200 support troops with the assistance of 1,500 prisoners of war) meet the case: hasty and inexpert construction resulted in defects, which in turn caused frequent interruptions in supply; moreover, the armies were operating 250 miles from the head of the pipeline in Cherbourg, which by the end of August barely reached Alençon.[88] Air transport proved incapable of remedying these deficiencies. The Allies had hoped to send three thousand tons of stores and equipment per day by plane; but between 19 August and mid-September a mere twenty thousand tons were actually delivered.[89] On balance, the insufficiency and irregularity of supply not only slowed the march of the Allied armies toward the Reich, but also limited their room for maneuver by further complicating the contentious business of drawing up plans for the fall campaign. Far from being the humble servant of strategy, logistics from now on dictated its own terms.

A couple months of slogging through the hedgerow country of Normandy, rewarded by a lightning but inconclusive breakthrough into the plains of northern France, therefore did not amount to victory. Conquering a vast territory and destroying an adversary are not the same thing, as Clausewitz observed long ago. Having failed to destroy their adversary in Normandy, the Allies were obliged to fight on for the better part of a year. All the same, thanks to their successes, France was, at least in large part, now liberated.

# 12

# THE BATTLE OF FRANCE—
# AND FRANCE'S BATTLE

T HE ALLIES WERE CONCERNED about the effects of the Normandy invasion on France itself for two reasons. The first had to do with uncertainty regarding the attitude of the French people: Would they take an active part in expelling the occupiers or would they, like Sleeping Beauty, passively await the arrival of their liberators? The second had to do with uncertainty regarding the political consequences of the invasion: Who would govern France until elections could be held? For the French in general, and members of the Resistance in particular, the answer to the second question was clear: General de Gaulle, alone among French citizens, was entitled to form a provisional government. But the Allies were of a different mind. Right up until the eve of the landing they tried their best to marginalize de Gaulle, refusing to acknowledge his claim to broad authority as head of the Provisional Government of the French Republic (GPRF in its French initials), created on 3 June 1944 as the successor to the CFLN.

## IN SEARCH OF RECOGNITION

Relations among Churchill, Roosevelt, and de Gaulle were both complicated and antagonistic. In June 1940 Churchill had shown great generosity in welcoming de Gaulle to London—a gesture that de Gaulle never forgot. But the cordial atmosphere of those early days quickly dissipated in quarrels over Syria, and then Madagascar. As their interests came into conflict, Churchill found it increasingly difficult to endure de Gaulle's haughty manner and inflexible attitude, all the more so because accommodating his wishes risked putting Britain at cross-purposes with the United States.

Until late 1942 Roosevelt had been content to deal with Vichy, believing that when push came to shove, Marshal Pétain would resist German demands. But in greeting the arrival of American forces in North Africa with gunfire and accepting the German invasion of the unoccupied zone of France without a word of complaint, Pétain disappointed that expectation. Taking de Gaulle for an apprentice dictator, Roosevelt set out in search of a third man, whom for a time he believed he had found in the courageous General Giraud. Giraud, who had been taken prisoner by the Germans in 1940, subsequently made a daring escape from the German fortress of Königstein. From the patriotic point of view his credentials were impeccable; moreover, his Vichyist sympathies reassured reactionary circles in France that endorsed Pétain's domestic policies, while rejecting collaboration with Nazi Germany. The Americans therefore arranged for Giraud to come by submarine from occupied France to Algeria, where as Darlan's deputy and head of French forces in North Africa he became their devoted supporter. His willingness to confine his attention to military questions, without involving himself in politics, further increased Roosevelt's confidence in him.

Nevertheless, by his determination to retain Pétainist legislation—anti-Semitic measures included—and his refusal to release hundreds of political prisoners, Giraud quickly alienated democratic-minded progressives both in France and abroad, where he came under sharp attack from the press in Britain and America. Moreover, by refusing to talk to de Gaulle, he incurred the wrath of the various elements of the internal Resistance, now allied under the auspices of a national council, the Conseil National de la Résistance (CNR), founded by Jean Moulin; in May 1943, declining to endorse a man who was committed to carrying out the policies of

Vichy in France's overseas colonies, the CNR announced its support for de Gaulle instead. Despite the wise counsel of Jean Monnet, charged by Roosevelt with converting Giraud to the virtues of democracy, the president's protégé was slow to react; and when at last he did, his clumsiness undermined any claim to credibility. Having infuriated his own supporters by his readiness to serve the interests of the United States, Giraud was finally obliged to negotiate with de Gaulle, whom he received in Algiers on 30 May 1943. After two rounds of talks they agreed to share power in a provisional government, the Comité Français de la Libération Nationale (CFLN), which was to "exercise French sovereignty" and "direct the French war effort in all forms and all places."[1]

The Allies had a rather different conception of the CFLN's mandate. In a joint statement issued on 23 August the United States regarded it merely "as the body governing the overseas French territories that recognize its authority,"[2] a view similar to the one expressed by Great Britain. The Soviet Union, more generously, looked upon the committee as "the representative of the governmental interests of the French Republic and as the leader of all patriotic French people fighting against the Hitlerian tyranny" and agreed to "exchange plenipotentiary representatives with it." Whereas Washington was careful to emphasize that its declaration in no way amounted to recognition of "a government of France or of the French empire," Moscow did not rule out this possibility.[3] But whatever formulas may have been employed, they offered little guidance for the future. The challenge facing the Allies was to develop a set of principles that would apply not to a body having jurisdiction over France's colonial dependencies, but to the government of metropolitan France once Operation OVERLORD had succeeded in liberating the country.

London and Washington dragged their feet, although the CFLN (presided over by de Gaulle alone from 9 November 1943 on) had asked them to open negotiations almost at once. In early September de Gaulle sent to Harold Macmillan and Robert Murphy, respectively, the British and American representatives in Algeria, a "draft agreement" specifying "the terms of cooperation to be established from the day when the Allied forces [would] land in France, between these forces on the one hand and the authorities and the people on the other." The plan distinguished between three spheres of competence. In the combat zone, authority would be vested in the Allied high command; in the militarized zone, all necessary facilities (including ports and so on) would be made available to the Allied forces, but power would be exercised by civilian French authorities; and in the nonmilitarized zone farther inland, "all decisions [would] be taken by the appropriate French authority."[4] Anticipating that the Allied landing in France would occur in the near future, the CFLN moved to assert its political prerogatives and police power at the earliest possible opportunity—mindful too that two months earlier, on 17 July, military control had been imposed in Italy by the Allied Military Government of Occupied Territory (AMGOT) in denial of Italian sovereignty. From the perspective of Algiers, this created a dangerous precedent that had to be overturned at all costs.

To counter the perceived threat to French sovereignty, the CFLN made use of every diplomatic channel at its disposal. Its representative to His Majesty's government, Pierre Viénot, formerly undersecretary of state for foreign affairs in Léon Blum's cabinet before the war, was instructed to initiate talks with the British authorities. Jean Monnet, who shortly after arriving in Algiers had thrown his lot in with de Gaulle, was dispatched to Washington, where it was hoped that his personal acquaintance with Roosevelt and other high officials would enable him to bring about a change in American policy. In this he was aided by René Massigli, the committee's commissioner for foreign affairs, and Henri Hoppenot, head of the French mission in Washington—but to no avail. Hints of progress could occasionally be detected. "The American government, one is told, has today formally recognized that the CFLN is qualified to administer the reconquered territories," Viénot reported in late November 1943. "It admits the principle of the 'delegate of the Committee' that is the basis of our proposed agreement. . . . Our distinction between zones of combat, a civilian zone, and purely civil administration is accepted."[5] And in early February 1944, Massigli notified Viénot that "M. Monnet informs me that the decision to recognize the Committee as the sole authority in France at the moment of the landing has just been taken in Washington."[6] Yet these turned out to be false hopes. Although there had been a measure of success in allaying hostility toward de Gaulle in some quarters of London and Washington, and although the CFLN could now count on the support of friendly officials in both the Foreign Office and the State Department, Roosevelt nonetheless refused to deal with the committee. "It must therefore be admitted that the responsibility for delay lies entirely with the President," reported Hervé Alphand, the committee's director of economic affairs.

> He seems to feel a certain embarrassment, not to say a certain aversion to acting in a way that could be interpreted as going against his past policy. . . . The Vichyist policy whose abandonment is being considered nonetheless leaves behind traces and memories. It is altogether as though Roosevelt were waiting for some miraculous event or other that would prevent him, at the last moment, from carrying out his decision. This state of mind may evidently lead him to modify the text of the formula that has been submitted to him; it is impossible to guess at the reactions that may arise from such a psychological state. As for the English attitude, it is explained by the extreme weakness of the diplomacy of the British cabinet, by the subjection in which it is held by Washington; in this domain, of such grave importance for the European future, the British decision is being taken at the White House and Churchill has relinquished his powers, which are now in Roosevelt's hands.[7]

Indeed, the prime minister acknowledged as much himself: "We ought not to quarrel with the President for fear of offending de Gaulle. De Gaulle, for all his magnitude, is the sole obstacle to harmonious relations between Great Britain and America on the one hand, and the skeleton and ghost of France on the other. . . . He will be the bitterest foe we and the United States have ever had in France."[8] In spite of the Francophile sympathies of his foreign secretary, Anthony Eden, Churchill therefore refused to put pressure on Roosevelt to accept de Gaulle's claim to represent the French people.

## THE SOVIET OPTION

This impasse led the CFLN during the winter of 1943-44 to explore contacts with the Soviets, which until then it had neglected. The committee informed Moscow of the talks that were then under way with the United States and Great Britain—something it had not always done in the past[9]—and sought to involve it in settling their differences, in the hope that the entry of the Soviet Union into discussions about the future of Europe would force its Western allies to give way in the matter of France. The instructions sent by Massigli to Roger Garreau, the committee's representative to the Kremlin, made this line of argument explicit. "[If the Soviet Union] has indeed reserved to itself a right of intervention in the arrangements to be concluded between the Anglo-Saxon powers and the occupied States of Western Europe," he wrote, "and if its own feeling about the position of France in the war is in fact the one recently expressed by your interlocutors, it is its responsibility to intervene with London and Washington so that an end may be put to a situation that is eminently contrary to the cohesion of the interallied war effort."[10] Once again, however, the CFLN's expectations were to be disappointed, as Moscow limited itself to amiable expressions of solidarity.

The Soviets' unwillingness to intervene with the Western powers on behalf of the Gaullist cause did not mean that good relations with France were of no consequence to the Kremlin. Stalin, in his ongoing campaign to obtain firm assurances that a second front would be opened, had long considered de Gaulle an ally;[11] moreover, looking beyond the war, he anticipated that de Gaulle's support would prove to be invaluable in preventing a rapid German recovery. As Maurice Dejean (Massigli's predecessor as commissioner for foreign affairs and at that time ambassador to the Allied governments in London) observed, "The Soviets will trust us only to the extent that they have [the] impression that the new France has nothing in common with Vichy and that its European policy is essentially oriented, like that of the Kremlin, toward elimination of the German peril." Indeed, de Gaulle's support was all the more to be desired, Dejean argued, given that British and American intentions aroused suspicion in Moscow: "They have many reasons to wonder whether the Anglo-

Saxons are resolved to be done with the German danger and whether they accept the idea of seeing Germany disappear as an important factor in world politics."[12] The Soviet interest in having a say in questions of postwar European reconstruction that London and Washington had reserved for themselves to decide, particularly with regard to France led the Russians to lobby for a central role to be given to the European Advisory Commission (created in the wake of the Teheran Conference) and to argue that any agreements negotiated by the Western powers should be subject to formal review by that body. Similarly, the threat of British and American overreaching in France in the wake of the landings in Normandy inspired the Soviet press to inveigh against AMGOT, which it called "an exceptional institution deprived of the indispensable assistance of the democratic forces now represented in a legitimate government."[13]

The CFLN was not slow to appreciate the usefulness of encouraging Soviet intervention, with a view to winning the unanimous support of the Big Three for a single draft agreement regarding French sovereignty. "This last way of proceeding would present the advantage of not appearing to play off one ally against another," the committee's economic affairs department noted in an internal memo of early April 1944. "It would nonetheless make it possible to introduce Russia into the negotiations and perhaps to open the way to a fundamental conversation on the question between Moscow and Algiers. It would avoid moreover giving the Russians the impression—an impression they are perhaps inclined to share—that we are turning to them after having exhausted our chances with the Anglo-Saxons."[14] This gambit did at least succeed in arousing anxiety in the West. "I saw in one of the papers that Russia was about to recognize the provisional Government of France," Churchill noted with alarm on 23 May. "Russia has no right to take this step without consultation with her two allies who are doing all the fighting in the West."[15] In the event, the risk remained conjectural. "To the extent that the governments of Great Britain and the United States are of the opinion that it is not appropriate at the present moment to recognize the CFLN as the provisional government of France," Fedor Gusev, the Soviet ambassador to London, declared the same day, "the Soviet government declares itself ready to support the position of its allies and to act in this matter in common with the governments of Great Britain and the United States." Everything considered, the suggestion that it was prepared to recognize the Provisional Government of the French Republic before the British and Americans did was more a diplomatic ploy on the part of the Soviets aimed at putting pressure on their allies than a commitment to aid France.[16]

Indeed, Molotov expressly declined, in the wake of the events of 6 June, to act on Gaullist overtures,[17] for reasons given by Vladimir Dekanosov, the deputy foreign affairs commissar: "We fully sympathize with the committee and General de Gaulle, we approve their attitude, and we are convinced that they will win their case. But you will also understand that the necessities of war oblige us to take into account the views of our allies, so as not to upset them."[18] Dekanosov went on to say, "The government of the USSR for the moment desires not to offend the American government through the hasty recognition of a de facto state of which it approves and which it knows must one day be established by force of circumstance. . . . It would be awkward to seek to rush a decision that as a practical matter has already been taken and that will be made official at the appropriate time."[19] At a militarily decisive moment, then, the Soviets clearly sought to avoid exacerbating tensions. It seems likely that they also hoped, at least initially, to create a place for themselves in the collective management of European affairs on a consensual rather than a conflictual basis. Moscow's reluctance to act more forcefully on behalf of the CFLN prevented it from being formally recognized by the coalition as a whole. This refusal had a number of harmful consequences, chief among them the failure of Supreme Headquarters to integrate French forces into military preparations for OVERLORD. The Allies were therefore unable to count on the support they had anticipated receiving from members of the Resistance.

## THE PRICE OF INDECISION

In the early stages of planning the invasion, little thought was given to coordinating the activities of underground elements in France. In July 1943

General Morgan had deliberately downplayed the assistance that the *armée des ombres* might be expected to give the British and American forces:

> These groups are concentrated in centers of population and thus could not operate in effective numbers in the coastal defended areas. Moreover, leaders of groups on the Continent could not be warned in advance of the date and time of the operation. Consequently, no assistance from resistance groups can be expected during the initial assault.
>
> After the assault has taken place, however, pre-arranged plans could be put into effect for the demolition of railway communications in certain specific areas and for guerilla activities on the German lines of communication. . . .
>
> At a later stage in the invasion local uprisings in the rear of the enemy lines could be organised with a view to immobilising enemy troops in the protection of rearward installations. General uprisings should be limited to the areas to be occupied by our forces, as otherwise the functioning of organized groups will be disrupted. . . .
>
> The assistance of the groups should therefore be treated as a bonus rather than an essential part of the plan.[20]

Less than a year before the landing, then, the Resistance scarcely figured in Allied plans—particularly because British parachute drops had provided it with very few arms. Beginning in September 1943, however, the development of organized guerrilla elements led COSSAC to reconsider its assumptions. As a result, the French underground was assigned responsibility for dismantling the rail system, disrupting enemy communications, interfering with the movement of German reinforcements, and carrying out other acts of sabotage behind enemy lines. By the spring of 1944 official thinking had changed: "The support which Resistance Groups can be expected to give to the land fighting in France while not having a direct bearing on the immediate tactical situation should appreciably affect the strategic development of military operations."[21]

In the meantime, the Gaullist secret service, the Bureau Central de Renseignements et d'Action, moved quickly to make the necessary preparations. Although it had been deliberately kept in the dark about the date and place of the landing, the BCRA devised a series of plans in support of the operation: VERT, aimed at paralyzing rail transport for a period of two weeks; BLEU, at sabotaging the electrical grid; TORTUE at hindering, by means of guerrilla activity, concentration of enemy forces; VIOLET, at cutting long-distance telephone and telegraph lines, in order to force the Germans to communicate by radio messages, which could then be intercepted and deciphered. The CFLN, for its part, had been tireless in its efforts to support the Resistance militarily, by dispatching regional delegates, and politically, by establishing a clandestine network of mayors, prefects, and regional commissioners who would be ready to seize power once the day of liberation was at hand.

The Allies nonetheless did everything in their power to prevent the Resistance from taking measures before 6 June, for fear that premature action would cause additional German divisions to be moved into France and lead to bloody reprisals—an apprehension shared by de Gaulle himself. Accordingly, the expression "national insurrection" was banned from the airwaves of the BBC between September 1943 and May 1944. The section of the British secret services responsible for subversion in the occupied countries, the Special Operations Executive, likewise tried to discourage "a spontaneous and open resistance as far as possible in order to conserve resources until D-Day," while recognizing that a delaying strategy could not be wholly successful, "because of the Communist Party's plan to wage the 'ceaseless offensive.'"[22] Supreme Headquarters, though it did not rely on the French underground to assure the success of its plan, no longer regarded its contribution as merely a "bonus." From February 1944 on, the British began to arm the Resistance more systematically, and the BBC extended friendlier treatment to the head of the Gaullist secret service, the pseudonymous Colonel Passy, though he continued to be harshly criticized by other elements of the British press. Yet as the winter wore on without a decision to recognize an authority competent to coordinate internal paramilitary activities with Eisenhower's staff, the CFLN grew concerned. "Is there not a risk, in the absence of specific agreements, in the absence of a declaration known to the public before the landing, of seeing a period of troubles, of uncertainty and anarchy emerge in our country?" Alphand cabled Algiers on 21 March. "Is there not a risk of seeing certain groups take advantage of the American and British hesitation to attempt, on our territory, to set up governments, of Pétain seeking directly or indirectly an agreement with the Allies, the Communists to create a central authority in Paris, and so on?"[23]

In the economic sphere, an important technical question remained to be decided regarding the currency that was to be put into circulation in France once it was liberated. In November 1943 the CFLN suggested that the Allies purchase some thirty billion francs. "The issuance would be handled by the Committee of Liberation, which would make the necessary sums available to the Allied armies according to a formula that has already been accepted by the Belgian, Dutch, and Norwegian governments."[24] The Americans rejected this offer the following month, however. The War Department's view, Hoppenot reported, was that the question was purely military in nature and that in any case "the decision to provide the invasion troops with a currency issued by the interallied command had just been confirmed by Mr. Stimson and was irrevocable."[25] At bottom, the French ambassador believed, it was the committee's insistence on the use of a French currency—which would imply recognition of its authority over the liberated territories—that caused the American government to turn down de Gaulle's proposal.

This rebuff was accompanied by humiliating security precautions. The British and Americans refused to keep the French informed about their plans, fearing some indiscretion. "Operational information concerning 'OVERLORD' will not be passed to the French until such time as the Supreme Commander of the Allied Expeditionary Force may direct," General Bedell Smith instructed subordinate commanders in late March 1944. "This measure is necessary because any information which the French may obtain is liable to be passed into France, and thence to the enemy. It must be borne in mind that liaison with the French in respect of 'OVERLORD' is not permitted at present."[26] The CFLN not only had no overall view of Allied strategy; it was further hobbled by the censorship imposed after 17 April on virtually all foreigners present in Great Britain, which had the effect of shutting down communications between London and Algiers. "This precaution," de Gaulle recalled in his war memoirs, "taken unilaterally by the Anglo-American powers in regard to the French, whose forces, like their own, were to play an essential role in the operations, affected us as an outrage and an insult."[27] Talks with the Allies were therefore suspended, for "so long as it will not be possible for the provisional Government to communicate in French code with its diplomatic and military representatives in London."[28]

Ultimately, however, the Allied policy was untenable, for the simple reason that Eisenhower could not proceed with OVERLORD unless he had a firm understanding about the extent of his authority over the country he was about to invade.

## MILITARY OR CIVIL GOVERNMENT

Roosevelt, having dithered for so long, now had to make up his mind. On 15 March he issued instructions to Eisenhower in his capacity as Allied supreme commander:

> You will have ultimate determination of where, when and how civil administration in France shall be exercised by French citizens remembering always that the military situation must govern. . . . In order to serve the setting up of any such civilian administration in any part of France you may consult with French Committee of National Liberation and may authorize them in your discretion to select and install the personnel necessary for such administration. You are, however, not limited to dealing exclusively with said Committee for such purpose in case at any time in your best judgment you determine that some other course is preferable. . . . You will have no talks or relations with [the] Vichy regime except for the purpose of terminating its administration in toto.[29]

It may appear that the discretion granted to Eisenhower amounted to a concession to the CFLN, which now became the Allies' favored partner. But it could just as well be interpreted as a way of encouraging rivals to challenge the Gaullist authorities. "As a practical matter," Pierre Viénot asked Anthony Eden, "what will happen? In one town, the Supreme Commander will appoint, for example, an official who is allied with the CFLN. In another district it will be a Vichy sympathizer, and in still another a Communist. Who except the French Committee will be able to coordinate these various authorities? Even so, it would be a terrible burden for [Eisenhower], and in the end he would be obliged to run France [himself]."[30] It is possible, of course, that Roosevelt wished to do precisely this—strengthen Eisenhower's hand by giving him the authority to adjudicate the competing claims of the various French factions. Be that as it may, the directive in no way amounted to acceptance of de Gaulle's claim to represent the French people, as Roosevelt reminded Eisenhower on 13 May: "I know you will understand that any matters relating to the future government of France are a political and not a military matter. . . . We must be certain that the words 'free determination' which date back to the Atlantic charter shall be preserved in substance and in spirit. Therefore no existing group outside of France can be given the kind of domination over the French people in France which would dominate the free expression of a choice."[31] In the end, however, the president's instructions were too vague to satisfy the Allied supreme commander. On 19 April, he directed General Bedell Smith to seek permission from the Combined Chiefs of Staff to open negotiations immediately with General Koenig, commander of the French Forces of the Interior, in order to settle outstanding questions on a purely military basis.[32] The request was turned down.

It has long been supposed, mistakenly, that Roosevelt contemplated placing France under the rule of AMGOT. This arrangement was reserved for enemy countries that were to be occupied by the Allies, whereas France, as a friendly nation, was to enjoy the status of a liberated territory. The government would therefore be run by the French themselves, not, as in the case of Germany, for example, by foreigners. In October 1943 Major General John H. Hilldring, director of civil affairs in the War Department, had argued that civil affairs should come under the authority of a French citizen, with the French moreover being given a voice in the matter: "Any arrangement which does not give leadership to [the] French would unnecessarily initiate and perhaps provoke French [citizens] to troublesome counter-activity before and after the landing period. . . . To consider any [such] arrangement . . . would be completely unacceptable to any group of Frenchmen and would probably precipitate a crisis between the French and Anglo-American Allies and complicate the situation before the landing period."[33] On 9 April of the following year, the secretary of state, Cordell Hull, made it clear that the United States had neither the intention nor the desire to govern France or to administer its affairs, except insofar as it might be necessary for the purpose of conducting military operations against the enemy. "It is of the highest importance," he emphasized, "that civil authority in France be exercised by a Frenchman."[34] The invasion plan therefore made no provision for AMGOT, as the staff of the Third United States Army was at pains to emphasize yet again several days after the landing: "It is not intended that Military Government be established in liberated France. Local civil administration will, as the rule, be conducted and controlled by the French themselves. Only when the French Civil Authorities fail to carry out a required action of the military commander, and the success of the military operation is jeopardized and/or allied security is threatened as a result, may direct controls be initiated."[35]

The matter in dispute, in other words, did not have to do with the status reserved to France. It had to do instead with the power to name the administrators of liberated France—a right that the CFLN claimed for itself, whereas the Allies insisted that it be vested in the supreme commander. Many observers expected that military operations would drag on long enough that this issue would eventually resolve itself—as the Russians continued to predict in late June—especially since the relationship of trust that de Gaulle had established with Eisenhower in North Africa suggested that a spirit of benevolent pragmatism would govern Allied policy. But those observers failed to anticipate that the American proposal to lodge authority with the Allied supreme commander would infuriate de Gaulle, who not surprisingly saw it as an intolerable insult to French sovereignty.

## The Force of a Symbol

In the military sphere, it had been agreed that a French force would take part in the operations in Normandy. In December 1943 de Gaulle requested that "a French division . . . be transported to Great Britain in time to participate in Operation Overlord and to liberate Paris."[36] Eisenhower, immediately on assuming his new duties at the end of the month, magnanimously gave his approval. His assistant chief of staff (G-3) at Supreme Headquarters, Lieutenant General Harold R. ("Pinky") Bull, viewed the situation with cool detachment: "The advantages of having a French formation in the Neptune build-up are purely political viz. to ensure French collaboration with us in other theaters such as in Italy and North Africa and in the Anvil threat. On the other hand, this political factor is of overriding importance and every effort must be made to meet it."[37] And so it was agreed that a formation marching under the French flag would liberate Paris; which one remained to be decided. Because transporting an armored unit would entail logistical problems, the Allied command preferred the less costly option of bringing an infantry division from North Africa. In the end, however, General Leclerc's Free French Second Armored Division was selected. These men were renowned for their valor in capturing the oasis of Kufra in Libya in March 1941. (Some of them had also served with General Koenig's First Free French Brigade the following year in the heroic battle of Bir Hakeim.) The British and the Americans, although they had no particular interest in honoring them, perceived that Leclerc's formation presented two considerable advantages: on the one hand, it could be moved at once from its base in Morocco; and, on the other, it was composed mainly of white soldiers. For it was inconceivable that Paris should be liberated by soldiers of color: "Anything other than the French Metropolitan troops in the U.K. would be accepted with reluctance," General Bull noted in a memorandum of 15 January 1944.[38] General Bedell Smith concurred two weeks later: "It is most desirable that the division . . . consist of white personnel and this would indicate the 2nd Armored Division which, with only one fourth native personnel, is the only French division operationally available that could be made 100 percent white. If the demands of shipping make it impossible to transport an armored division, then we may find it necessary to make up a mixed force of all arms, consisting of white troops and given a division designation."[39] The British did not demur. "I am concerned that it is of paramount importance that amongst the first troops to enter Paris shall be Frenchmen," General Morgan had already noted on 14 January. "The more important the dimensions of this French contingent the better."[40] Morgan added that both he and General Ismay had impressed on de Gaulle's military chief of staff, Colonel Pierre de Chevigné, the difficulties of receiving nonwhite troops in Great Britain. "He has taken the point well. It is unfortunate that the only French formation that is one hundred per cent white is an armored division in Morocco, round about Casablanca and Rabat. Every other French division is only 40 percent white. I have told Colonel de Chevigné that his chance of getting what he wants will be vastly improved if he can produce a white Infantry division. In doing this he sees no insuperable difficulty and is forthwith investigating the matter."[41] De Gaulle himself was sensitive to this aspect of the matter: "Our infantry divisions comprise many natives, and the English would be opposed to their presence," he had written to Eisenhower on 30 December 1943. "Our armored divisions, by contrast, are composed essentially of French elements."[42] Ultimately, the Second Armored Division was chosen for four reasons: no infantry unit was available; the formation was very well trained;[43] it was composed mainly of French soldiers; and it was commanded by a man who had been a personal ally from the very beginning—a point that mattered greatly to de Gaulle. Leclerc's unit was nevertheless improvised and heterogeneous.[44] In mid-April it was transferred from North Africa to England, where it underwent a further round of rigorous training, and on 1 August 1944 it disembarked in Normandy.

In fixing Eisenhower's prerogatives and integrating the Second Armored Division into the plan for OVERLORD, the British and Americans had acted out of expediency rather than principle. As D-Day drew nearer, however, pressure mounted to work out a more satisfactory agreement with de Gaulle's provisional government—more satisfactory to all parties concerned.

## A Test of Wills

The practical implications of the invasion itself made it imperative that a compromise be reached as soon as possible with the GPRF, which on 3 June had been proclaimed as the successor to the CFLN. Eisenhower wanted de Gaulle first to go on the BBC, to speak to the French people; after that, the various questions relating to administration of a liberated France could be dealt with. The British began to debate the question among themselves in May. At a meeting of the War Cabinet on the nineteenth, Churchill proposed inviting de Gaulle to come to London from Algiers after the launching of OVERLORD "to discuss arrangements for collaboration in the civil administration of French territory. In the meantime, General Koenig and M. Viénot would be allowed to send a certain number of cipher messages, provided that they gave an indication of the contents of the messages and an assurance that no attempt would be made to include any information about military affairs other than those affecting French troops."[45] It was not until 31 May, however, that the Allies decided to issue the invitation. "Come please now with your colleagues at the earliest possible moment and in the deepest secrecy," Churchill cabled de Gaulle on 2 June. "I give you my personal assurance that it is in the interests of France. I am sending my own York [aircraft] and another York for you."[46]

After some initial hesitation, de Gaulle accepted and landed outside London early on the morning of 4 June. From there he went on to Portsmouth, where he boarded a special train sent by the prime minister, with whom he was to meet before being briefed by Eisenhower later in the day about the invasion plan. The morning session went off without incident. But a storm was gathering. At lunch Churchill urged de Gaulle to go to the United States to broach the idea of holding preliminary conversations in Great Britain. The Foreign Office, Eden said, would very much regret it if this proposal were to be rejected; and Ernest Bevin, the minister of labor and leader of the Labour Party, added that his followers would be offended as well. At this de Gaulle exploded:

What! On more than one occasion I have tried to initiate discussions. I have been making proposals since last September. You have never replied. It is therefore pointless to say that the British Labour Party would be offended. The battle is about to begin, and I will speak on the radio. Fine. But as regards discussing the question of administration, it is clear that the President has never wanted to see me, and yet now suddenly I am being told I must go and talk to the President. . . . Why do you seem to think that I need to submit my candidacy for [exercising] authority in France to Roosevelt? The French government exists. I have nothing to ask of the United States in this respect, nor of Great Britain. This being said, it is important for all the Allies that the relations between the French administration and the military command should be organized. Nine months ago we proposed as much. Since the armies are about to land in France, I understand your haste to see the question settled. We ourselves are ready to do so. But where is the American representative? Without him, as you well know, nothing can be decided. Furthermore, I note that the Washington and London governments have made arrangements to do without an agreement with us. I have just learned, for example, that despite our warnings the troops and services about to land are provided with so-called French currency, issued by foreign powers, which the government of the republic absolutely refuses to recognize and which, according to the orders of the inter-Allied command, will have compulsory circulation on French territory. I expect that tomorrow General Eisenhower, acting on the instructions of the President of the United States and in agreement with you, will proclaim that he is placing France under his authority. How do you expect us to come to terms on this basis? *Allez, faites la guerre, avec votre fausse monnaie.*[47]

After this outburst, de Gaulle was driven to Eisenhower's headquarters, where the broad outlines of OVERLORD were explained to him. At the end of his presentation, the supreme commander handed de Gaulle a copy of the speech that he planned to read on the BBC on behalf of the Allies on the day of the landing. Its language and tone displeased de Gaulle mightily. Eisenhower directed the French people to "carry out his orders," announcing, "In the administration, everyone will continue to fulfill his functions unless contrary instructions are received" and assuring his listeners that once France was liberated, "the French themselves would choose their representatives and their government."[48] In short, as de Gaulle later observed, Eisenhower "appeared to be taking control of our country even though he was merely an Allied general entitled to command troops but not in the least qualified to intervene in the country's government."[49] Since leaflets containing the proclamation had already been printed up, in anticipation of their being dropped in massive numbers on D-Day, the changes that de Gaulle had expected to be able to make could not be incorporated into the text.

In assuming that the provisional government would approve their plans without further question, the British and the Americans showed astonishing naïveté, for de Gaulle had long made it clear that he would oppose any attempt to deny the provisional government what he regarded as its rightful authority. At that point, filled with righteous anger, he was not content simply to reject the Allies' scheme; instead, he set about trying to thwart it.

In the first place, de Gaulle refused to address the French people over the airwaves once Eisenhower had finished. "By speaking immediately after Eisenhower," he observed, "I should appear to sanction what he said—of which I disapproved—and assume a place in the succession unsuitable to the dignity of France."[50] It was only at a time of his own choosing, late in the afternoon of 6 June, that he delivered a memorable address. "The final battle is now joined. After so much fighting, fury, and suffering, the decisive clash is now upon us, the clash that has so long been hoped for. This is, of course, the battle of France—it is also France's battle! . . . In the nation, in the empire, and in the armies there is but a single will, a single hope. From behind the heavy clouds of our blood and our tears now reappears the sun of our grandeur."[51] His speech was all the more remarkable, Churchill venomously remarked, in view of the fact that France did not yet have any soldiers in the battle that had just begun.[52] De Gaulle departed from Eisenhower's text on one crucial point, in stressing that "the orders given by the French Government and by the French leaders that it has designated for this purpose must be followed exactly."[53] Moreover, he canceled the departure to Normandy of the Military Mission of Administrative Liaison, which, under the direction of Pierre Laroque, had trained 160 officers and fifty female volunteers responsible for administering the liberated territories in accordance with terms that remained to be specified. Finally, and perhaps most important, the head of the provisional government announced that it did not recognize the francs with which the Allies were preparing to flood the liberated territories.

De Gaulle's speech marked a decisive reversal in the balance of power between the two sides. Until the spring of 1944 the CFLN had been in the position of having to seek diplomatic recognition and material assistance from the Allies, without obtaining any satisfaction. After the landing in Normandy, the attackers needed the assistance of the French—as much in order to make their way through a country they did not know as to administer the territories they looked forward to freeing from German tyranny. In short, the provisional government no longer had to beg for Anglo-American aid or acknowledgment. From that point on everything depended on de Gaulle and the French people, or more precisely on his ability to win the acceptance of the people. Indeed, almost two months before D-Day, de Gaulle was clear about where matters stood. Recalling a conversation on 17 April with the British ambassador to the CFLN, Alfred Duff Cooper, he later noted: "Formal recognition no longer interested the French government; what mattered to that government was to be recognized by the French nation. And that fact was now established. The Allies might have helped us to gain countenance when such accessions were useful; they had not done so. At present, the matter was of no importance."[54]

On the eve of the landing, de Gaulle's obstructionism threatened political and economic disaster. If the general were to refuse to address the French people, they might reject liberators he had not endorsed. If he forbade his military liaison officers to accompany the Allied troops, administrative authority in the liberated areas would be cast into doubt.

And if he condemned the "invasion francs" as counterfeit, the already huge cost of the war stood to rise still further for the Allies. By claiming the right to issue its own money—the very symbol of a nation's autonomy—the Anglo-American coalition had struck a terrible blow against French sovereignty, while at the same time depriving the GPRF of control over the country's money supply, with all the dangers that implied. The Allies could print as many notes as they liked without having to guarantee them. Who would pay in the end? Were France to shoulder this burden, it would commit itself to financing OVERLORD without having any say in the conduct of operations; but in the event that it refused to back the Allied currency, the provisional government would force London and Washington to bear the cost of the war in France by themselves. In crossing swords on this issue with them, de Gaulle was not only fighting for a principle; he was also—and no less—intent on placing the country's postwar finances on a sound footing.

Faced with an extremely embarrassing predicament, Churchill and Roosevelt sought to reassure themselves. For a time the prime minister refused to believe that de Gaulle would dare publicly to disown the Allies' francs as counterfeit: "I should myself think, if I were a French shopkeeper, that a note printed in the United States tendered to me by a British or American soldier and declared legal by General Eisenhower was well worth having whether de Gaulle endorsed it or not."[55] The United States, he reminded the Exchequer and the Foreign Office, held a part of France's gold reserves (amounting to some five hundred million pounds sterling), which would offer "some means of arguing later on."[56] Roosevelt, for his part, reckoned that de Gaulle's obstinacy would lead to the collapse of the franc against the dollar—a grotesque luxury that France could hardly permit itself.[57]

At the same time, the two men could not conceal their doubts. "I have now seen the specimens of the notes in question," Churchill wrote Roosevelt on 10 June. "They do not strike us as very reassuring. They look very easy to forge. Nothing is said on whose responsibility they are issued and who is responsible for redeeming them. Surely there must be some authority behind them. . . . Please my dear friend, look at them yourself and say what we ought to do. Should we let de Gaulle obtain new status as his price for backing these notes or should we take the burden on ourselves for the time being and improve the issue later on and settle up at the Peace Table where there will be many accounts to be presented?"[58] The chancellor of the Exchequer, Sir John Anderson, was asked to weigh the risks. In the absence of an agreement, he advised, "the whole of the burden of financing the conduct of operations inside France might fall on us and not on the French authorities . . . in which [case] we should find ourselves responsible for the serious reactions of this special currency on the internal economy of these areas."[59] On 21 June Churchill yielded. "The notes give no indication of the authority by whom they are issued. Unless we reach an understanding with the French Committee, we shall be morally responsible for seeing that they are honoured. Under the mutual aid arrangements which we are making with the other European Allies, they will bear the cost of civil administration and of supplies and services to our troops in their countries. But if we should become responsible for the whole of the military notes issued in France, the French would contribute no mutual aid to the American and British Armies of Liberation."[60] By confronting London and Washington with the unnerving prospect of having to assume the entire cost of military operations themselves, de Gaulle had found the argument he needed to make them come to terms.

It was all the more persuasive because the great majority of the British press, and a good many of the newspapers in America, had now rallied to his cause. Eden and the British Foreign Office had long argued in favor of recognition; in the meantime, the views of the State Department had changed. And on the ground in Normandy, Eisenhower and his commanders were very favorably impressed by the work of the Resistance. All these considerations finally led London and Washington to agree to open negotiations. The British took it upon themselves to host the initial round of talks alone, partly to avoid giving offense to the Americans, but also in the hope that a way could be found to overcome Roosevelt's objections. On 7 June Eden suggested entering into preliminary discussions with Pierre Viénot.[61] Roosevelt gave his approval to this plan six days later, and on 19 June a Franco-British committee met to work out the basis of an agreement that would subsequently be presented to the United States.[62]

This sudden turn of events was of course the direct result of de Gaulle's intransigence. But it was also due in part to the pressure of public opinion, especially in Great Britain, where both the House of Commons and the press expressed outrage over his treatment at the hands of the Allies. Geopolitical calculations played a role as well: fearing Soviet hegemony over Eastern Europe and doubting the steadfastness of America's commitment once the war was over, Eden sought to ensure that Great Britain would have a solid ally across the Channel. The shift in policy by London and Washington was further hastened by three other factors: the warm welcome the French people gave to their liberators; the success of the Gaullist authorities in maintaining order at the local level; and the surprising military effectiveness of the Resistance.

# 13

## LIBERATORS AND LIBERATED

How the French people would welcome their liberators was the great unknown. There was no guarantee that the population, traumatized by four years of occupation, shaken to the core by the bombing that accompanied OVERLORD, unavoidably caught up in the fighting on all sides, would greet the arrival of British and American troops with enthusiasm. On and after D-Day, the Allies dropped thousands of leaflets encouraging civilians to flee threatened areas—without great success, however, for the winds carried the warnings far from their targets; people stood on their doorsteps, transfixed from a distance by the sight of the leaflets fluttering to the ground.[1] Few took the warnings seriously. Some fourteen thousand civilians perished in the region of Lower Normandy during the summer of 1944, perhaps half of them as a result of the aerial bombardment carried out between 6 and 15 June.[2]

The Allied command also feared widespread insurrection. "Aside from organized resistance," wrote C. D. Jackson, deputy chief of the Psychological Warfare Division at Supreme Headquarters, "I have become convinced that it will be impossible to prevent a general uprising in France on D-Day. This uprising will probably not be a national levee en masse, because it will be conditioned both by the regional character of the inhabitants and by the degree to which German occupation and Vichy rule have been oppressive—so that the overall French pattern will be spotty, with one region all out, another region indulging in isolated vendetta work. But something will be going on all over, with no way of keeping it down."[3]

The first reports from civil affairs officers dispatched to the British beachhead in June, however, suggested that there was little reason for anxiety. "Taking into account the naturally reserved disposition of the Norman," noted Lieutenant Colonel D. R. Ellias, "we have received an enthusiastic welcome. The first troops into Bayeux on D + 1 . . . were cheered and embraced, flowers were showered on them, and a demonstration celebrating the Liberation was held on D + 3 at which the British CAO was tumultuously cheered."[4] Ellias's fellow officers attached to the Twenty-first Army Group filed a similar report in mid-August, once again allowing for "the naturally undemonstrative bent" of the local people: "Our forces have everywhere been received with sincere cordiality. It has been repeatedly observed that persons who had lost relatives or property as a result of battle accepted their loss with philosophic resignation and as a personal contribution to the long [awaited] liberation of their country."[5]

Indeed, the troops were received with open arms more often than not. At Cherbourg, for example, concerts given by the Americans met with applause, and local girls gladly danced with the GIs. But jubilation was sometimes mixed with tragedy. At Carentan, acknowledging the homage of the townspeople near the war memorial, General Taylor saw "coming toward him a little girl, Danielle Lasnay, who held in her arms a large bouquet of roses. But the child did not have time to present her flowers. Shots rang out, fired by a German soldier lying in ambush behind a rooftop chimney. Instinctively the general dived to the ground to avoid the bursts of gunfire. But he was too far from the little girl to pull her down with him. A bullet hit Danielle, passing right through her heart. She was three years old."[6] Similarly spontaneous manifestations of joy elsewhere, even if they did not suddenly give way to grief, were dampened by fears of a German resurgence.[7]

The intensity of the Allied air attacks was a source of perplexity to many Normans. A British reconnaissance report quoted the Gaullist prefect of Calvados, Pierre Daure:

Because I have always been a friend of your country, I feel I can speak frankly. The need for large-scale air bombardment was not understood by the inhabitants, as so few Germans were directly in the town. There could be no comparison between the losses of the civilian population and those of the enemy, the latter being very few. The Germans hide in the woods and not in the towns. As for the argument [that] the bombardment was necessary to block the roads, my answer is that in this part of France there are so many alternative routes and tracks that it made little difference. The power and destructiveness of the bombardment made some people compare it to the well-known methods of the enemy. However, the extensive looting by the SS that followed helped to redress the balance and there is not the slightest doubt that the people are delighted to be liberated.[8]

The spirit of self-sacrifice among the civilians made a deep impression on the Allies. "The population, despite the destruction of their homes, was definitely glad at the liberation of their town," one American intelligence officer in Cherbourg reported. "An optician told me 'If my house had not received some destruction, I would not have felt I had had my part in the liberation.'"[9] Brigadier Hargest, attached as an observer to the British Thirtieth Corps, corroborated such accounts:

Since we arrived here the people have been distinctly friendly. They offer us a welcome, they have acted as guides, they are our best informants. Certainly they are not effusive, but after their gruelling experiences we should not expect effusiveness from them. They have seen us arrive under fire, which destroyed their cattle and crops. Their furniture and effects are in many cases a complete "write off." They must be stunned by the misfortune that singled out their villages for destruction and scattered their life savings. But they are still friendly and glad to be free. They are sabotaging the enemy's L of C [lines of communication] and helping us with ours. Thousands are in the Maquis, thousands have been killed for sabotage and guerrilla fighting.[10]

Hargest then went on to express surprise at the attitude of his troops toward the French, which he was not alone in noticing and deploring: "Yet for some reason there is among the British army, a distrust, a lack of sympathy amounting to marked dislike that puzzles me."[11]

A certain element of the English press deliberately fed this hostility. Thus, for example, a correspondent for one of the London tabloids named Rex North struggled to make sense of what he claimed to have seen in the first days after the landings:

> Soberly and factually I must set it down. Six out of ten of the people over here distrust and detest us, and I have carefully checked the figure. Further, more than half seem to be allies of the Germans so that it is impossible to tell who, if any of them, are our friends. . . . For, like so many others, I expected everyone to fete our victorious forces as they came in. Instead, I have spent a week wondering where the next French bullet was coming from.
>
> I expected to find a starved, oppressed country that would cry out for arms and for the right to stand up and fight with our armies of liberation.
>
> Instead, over half the French I met in Normandy had no wish to be liberated. Men on street corners—wearing German field-grey trousers, let me add—turned their backs on me. Others just happened to spit at that moment. . . .
>
> Why do the French snipe at us—wave excitedly to our troops as they enter a place—[and then] lead them exactly to the position where the snipers want them? . . .
>
> Personally, I find it easier to believe that the Germans, strictly under orders, have behaved so well in Normandy that the French have got used to them. That a whole generation has been growing up with these Nazis, and because their own young men are in German prison camps the inevitable has happened.
>
> They see the Allies now as people who have brought only bombed and shattered houses. Their ignorance of our cause, of the vital importance of our victory to Europe, is appalling. . . .

Decisions of the highest importance must be made. Already there are far too many British soldiers buried beneath wooden crosses in France after meeting with French bullets.[12]

Nonetheless this type of article—which had no basis in fact, as Allied officials hastened to make clear[13]—was very much the exception in the Anglo-American press. Most journalists, though they cared little on the whole about the fate of civilians, took a more nuanced view: "There are French who hate us; French who are indifferent; French who resent the destruction of their belongings; and perhaps a few dozens of French girls who are in love with German soldiers, and are sheltering them and packing a pistol for them," Alan Moorehead wrote in the *Sunday Express* on 25 June. "But as for the great mass of the people whom we have seen, they are overwhelmingly on our side."[14] Still, the attacks of Rex North and his ilk not only created a certain nervousness in the field (especially in the Canadian sector, where the command moved quickly to nip "these mischievous rumors" in the bud);[15] they also skewed the impression that Allied soldiers formed of the French people. In reviving the old Francophobia of the popular London papers, such rumors reflected the contempt in which France had been held since the stunning rout of 1940 and the collaborationist policy of Vichy, which to some extent tempered the genuine sympathy for the Free French that was widely felt on the other side of the Channel.

## FRIENDS OR CONQUERORS

An underlying current of anti-French prejudice may also have encouraged certain kinds of behavior found in armies everywhere, though they were no less odious for that. "There is the usual looting and stealing by British troops, particularly on the coast, which is causing unfavourable comparisons between the behaviour of our troops and the Germans," the senior civil affairs officer for the Second Army, Brigadier R. M. H. Lewis, noted on 14 June.[16] Refusing to pay for their purchases, some soldiers resorted to simple theft, others to actual hold-ups.[17] Following the capture of Saint-Lô, soldiers made off with safe deposit boxes they found sticking out from the rubble in the wake of the bombing of a branch of the Société Générale. Acts of vandalism were also committed: on 15 October the municipal council of Ozeville, in the Manche, protested the pillaging of the town church, where American soldiers had demolished the pews, stalls, and liturgical objects.[18]

Rapes occurred as well. On 4 August 1944 three American soldiers raped a Frenchwoman identified only as Germaine O.; and one member of the trio then committed a second offense against Catherine M. Two days later, the band broke into the home of René F. with the intention of committing theft and rape.[19] On 26 August, in Cherbourg, a florist was raped by four black soldiers.[20] "The liberators have turned into looters, rapists, and killers," lamented the prefect of the Manche.[21] The occurrence of such episodes of brutality is not in doubt, but it is unclear how frequent they were. Military authorities kept records only of individuals who were tried by the courts. Not all cases ended up coming before a tribunal, whether because the authorities sought to hush them up or because victims refused to press charges. In view of the fact that some archives are still closed to public inspection, it seems probable that the number of crimes and misdemeanors, already very considerable, will need to be revised upward.

On the American side, for the months of August and September alone, the First and Third Armies counted forty-seven cases of looting and theft, sixty-seven rapes and attempted rapes, twenty-one murders, and eighteen cases of assault.[22] On 1 July 1945, for the whole of the campaign, U.S. military authorities tallied 169 rapes, 403 murders and cases of voluntary manslaughter, and 305 cases of criminally negligent homicide. Thefts, though not recorded, were also numerous, "rang[ing] from simple acquisition of a mattress for added comfort to armed and violent robberies. Frequently, looting or pillaging was accompanied or preceded by other offenses."[23] An independent estimate by the office of the judge advocate general found that a total of 181 women—French and foreign—were raped by U.S. soldiers in France between June 1944 and June 1945.[24] Discrepancies among official statistics are partly the result of divergent methods of counting: thus a rape committed against a woman by four soldiers could be treated as a single case involving one individual or as four separate cases; some summaries counted only rapes committed in France against Frenchwomen, others all rapes committed against women in France, foreigners included. Here again, however, it seems likely that none of the available estimates give a true idea of the scale of the phenomenon. One recent study has concluded that in the department of the Manche alone American troops were responsible for 208 rapes and about thirty murders during the campaign.[25]

On the British side, courts-martial punished 2,897 thefts, 275 instances of "indecency," and 1,033 offenses of various other kinds against civilians in the theaters of operation outside the United Kingdom—an area comprising Italy and the Middle East in addition to France—for the year 1944–1945. It should be noted that these figures do not include officers and do not specify the number of rapes and murders.[26]

The motivations for these acts, insofar as they sprang from rational impulses, appear to have been many. As armed soldiers, some of the men considered themselves to be in charge of a conquered country and therefore free to take from the inhabitants whatever they liked. "Fighting for others rather than defending his own borders, the GI felt that he was owed a great deal. He therefore took what was offered to him (women particularly) and helped himself to the rest by any means possible."[27] Criminals who had been drafted into military service continued to profit from illegal activities during the war, all the more readily since France—a suddenly impoverished land with a rich artistic and architectural patrimony—presented inviting opportunities for trafficking of all kinds. As for rapes, sexual frustration played an obvious role. These acts were typically committed by support troops (78 percent of the soldiers brought to trial belonged to noncombat units), the majority of whom were black. The question arises whether black soldiers were more inclined to resort to violence in order to satisfy their desires than white soldiers. Probably so, though they appear to have been victims to some degree of the nostalgic reminiscences of African-American World War I veterans and the institutionalized racism of the U.S. military. On the one hand, "Black GIs found themselves in a foreign country whose inhabitants were reputed to be free of racial prejudice and sexually liberated. Moreover, tales they had heard from those among their elders who had seen action in France during the First World War suggested that Frenchwomen had no reservations about sleeping with black men."[28] On the other hand, there are grounds for believing that racist prejudice led military courts to charge African-Americans with crimes more often than other Americans. Whatever the reasons for the disproportionate incidence of cases involving blacks may have been, there is no doubt that alcohol encouraged sexual violence. "Normans were always ready to provide the troops with Calvados but unable, because of language difficulties, to explain the necessity of moderation."[29] Fifty percent of the soldiers convicted of rape were drunk at the time of the offense.[30]

Neither during the operations then unfolding in France nor later in Germany did the Allies use such crimes as a means of achieving victory, unlike certain armies that employed—and still employ today—sexual violence to subdue local populations. Rapists enjoyed no institutional support within the army, nor did their actions form part of American strategy.[31] Few, if any, offenders benefited from the indulgence of their superiors: Allied commanders did nothing to conceal these atrocities, which harmed civilians, damaged relations between liberated and liberator, threatened military discipline, and tarnished the image of a heroic army chivalrously delivering peoples from the Hitlerian yoke. By and large, the guilty were punished.

The American authorities dealt harshly with such crimes. Of 169 men convicted of rape, 29 (4 whites and 25 blacks) were hanged, and 15 others executed for rape and murder. Prison sentences were also commonly issued as well. The three soldiers mentioned earlier, who terrorized a town in the Cotentin in early August, were sentenced the following month to eight years hard labor apiece.[32] With regard to murders, American tribunals in France handed down thirty-five death sentences and forty-eight life sentences in addition to a great many prison terms having an average length of eight years.[33] All told, from 0.5 percent to 1 percent of the American troops engaged in Europe, or between 20,000 and 40,000 soldiers, were brought before courts on charges of misconduct, ranging from petty theft or sale of stolen property to murder.[34] These figures are relatively low as a share of the hundreds of thousands of troops engaged in the European theater of operations, or by comparison with figures from subsequent conflicts. Nonetheless, they present a striking contrast between the traditionally accepted image of the Allies as exemplary liberators and a less flattering reality, whose consequences were felt by the civilian population in a deep and lasting way.

In the event, only with difficulty was criminal behavior curbed—despite the manifest desire to punish it, which derived as much from the need to maintain discipline as from an interest in reassuring the local people. "For the benefit of more amicable relations—the French call it propaganda—all cases of rape, plunder and looting by our forces should be thoroughly investigated and the culprits, if discovered, should be punished," a U.S. Army bulletin advised commanders on 11 July. "Their punishments should be made known thereafter to the civil population. In the case of civilian looting, the culprits should also be apprehended if possible and punished in civilian courts."[35] But this was something more easily said than done. On the one hand, the inquiries usually took place after the troops had passed through; as a result, the search for the guilty parties was often hampered.[36] On the other hand, the effectiveness of punishment in preventing crime was doubtful, as the judicial authorities recognized. "Although courts-martial may serve as a deterrent, such must not be relied upon as a preventative. Solution of this problem is a command responsibility, requiring constant vigilance and the exercise of leadership. . . . Action will be taken to withhold fire arms, knives, and other weapons for personnel whose duties do not require their possession. When deemed necessary, access to and consumption of intoxicating liquors will be controlled or limited."[37]

In the aftermath of extensive bombardment, fighting, and acts of criminal violence, the liberation of the Manche came as a relief rather than a cause for celebration, especially since dislocated civilians experienced the forced exodus from their homes as a tragedy.[38] This reaction seems to have been true of Normandy as a whole. And yet the region remained calm, in part perhaps owing to the dignified reserve for which its people are known; but surely it had at least as much to do with the Gaullist authorities' efforts at conciliation.

## A Permanent Coup d'État

De Gaulle's provisional government had made preparations for the devolution of power by naming its own mayors and prefects in the greatest secrecy. It was nonetheless essential that a way be found to establish its authority in the confused military situation that prevailed in the days immediately following the invasion. The Allies, as we have seen, had long refused to recognize the GPRF. But the obstructionist strategy pursued by de Gaulle, together with the noisy campaigns on his behalf in the English and American press, obliged them finally to make concessions. On 13 June Roosevelt proposed that the general be permitted to go to France.[39] Churchill grudgingly complied and gave orders to General Montgomery:

> I must inflict on you a visit from General de Gaulle tomorrow. This is, on no account, to be a burden to you in any duties you have to discharge. . . . Our relations with him are formal, but we are nonetheless his host. I do not think that you should receive him at the beach. It will be much better he shall make any discourse he wishes after he returns to England. It would surely be undesirable to gather large crowds in Bayeux and have anything in the nature of a political demonstration. If however the people are anxious to welcome him on his way through, it is not for us to deny him.[40]

The prime minister therefore authorized no more than the minimum in the way of notice or courtesy—to the great dismay of the civil affairs officers, who were furious at not having been informed in advance about a visitor of such consequence.

Setting out on 14 June on the French destroyer *La Combattante,* de Gaulle arrived at Montgomery's headquarters at Creully before proceeding to Bayeux, where he gave a brief speech. After going on to Isigny and then Grandcamp, he reembarked for England the same night at Courseulles. Without amounting by any means to a popular referendum, the reception granted to him by the Normans bore the unmistakable stamp of cordiality, contrary to what Montgomery claimed in his report the following day. "His reception in Bayeux and other small towns was definitely lukewarm and there was no real enthusiasm."[41] The civil affairs officers gave a shrewder appreciation:

> The Norman is not a demonstrative person and as this part of Normandy has suffered very little, physically or morally, no white-hot enthusiasm could be expected. However, the people were undoubtedly pleased at seeing French officers who were not under the German boot and there was a natural curiosity to see de Gaulle, the symbol of the Resistance. His visit did give the effect to the inhabitants that they had their sovereignty back. His reception was much more fervent in the devastated areas such as Isigny and other places. In some there were scenes of emotion.[42]

Beyond the telling symbolism of the public moment, de Gaulle had practical plans that he was privately determined to put into effect. Accompanying him on *La Combattante* were François Coulet, a loyal deputy who was to serve as commissioner of the Republic for Normandy, as well as Colonel de Chevigné, poised to assume command of the French armed forces in the liberated areas of the country. During his meeting with Montgomery, de Gaulle had carelessly mentioned that Coulet would concern himself with administrative questions, but the implications of this remark did not register with his host ("He has left behind in Bayeux one civilian administrative officer and three colonels but I have no idea what is their function").[43] These trusted associates proceeded to act at once, without bothering to seek the Allies' blessing. The following day, 15 June, the Vichy subprefect Pierre Rochat was removed from office and replaced by Raymond Triboulet, a local notable and *résistant* who had been in contact with the Committee of Liberation.

Unlike their military superiors, the civil affairs deputies instantly understood what had taken place. "De Gaulle has staged a very clever coup d'état," one senior officer wrote, "with or without the connivance of London. I feel very sore that I got no notice whatever of the visit beforehand, as I would of course have stuck to the man like a leech. I also feel that I should have received some guidance beforehand as to the line I was to take in case of any attempt such as has been made. . . . I have of course kept my commander informed. His attitude is that he will have absolutely nothing to do with politics in any shape or form and has no intention of issuing me any instructions, or making any comment whatever. That of course leaves me to use my 'common sense'; a phrase I am getting rather acclimatized to."[44] The military authorities therefore refused to take a position on the underlying question of principle. "Lacking instructions from London, the SCAO [senior civil affairs officer] decided that his best policy was to accept Gen. de Gaulle's representatives as the de facto civil authority for the region of Rouen, since they appeared to be acceptable to the French themselves, and had already dismissed M. Rochat from the Sous-prefecture of Bayeux."[45] The view from the civil affairs headquarters of Twenty-first Army Group was summarized by General Lewis: "The next days will show whether Coulet and Triboulet can establish themselves and win the people's confidence as the de facto government. Meanwhile we are treating them as such; the high question of 'recognition' has now left the stratosphere of diplomatic exchange and is being decided on the ground."[46]

The refusal to recognize the GPRF officially had therefore led to a curious paradox. In the absence of clear directives, the Allied commanders saw little reason not to leave decisions to the Gaullist delegates. This devolution of authority proceeded smoothly on the whole, and the civil affairs officers were pleased that a satisfactory working relationship had been established with the representatives of the provisional government:

> It is quite apparent that the French administrative authorities appointed by De Gaulle are doing everything in their power to advance the status of the General. This, of course, is understandable, and need not constitute grounds for too great worry so long as they at the same time continue to afford cooperation as has been the case to date. . . . To summarize it would appear that if we accept the administration now functioning in France, and furnish them a reasonable degree of assistance, both administrative

and in a material sense, there is no need to particularly worry about ability or desire of the people to do a good job.[47]

Another report on the state of civil affairs in mid-July expressed much the same view:

> Generally the people appear disinterested in politics but the leadership of de Gaulle through his appointees and liaison officers is unchallenged. His representatives in the higher echelons lose no opportunity to press the political advantage given them by the position we have permitted them to assume. They wear the cross of Lorraine, appear prominently with resistance leaders and encourage display of the resistance armband which is being worn by those claiming membership in the resistance. In these circumstances the public cannot help but feel that we are supporting de Gaulle, whatever we may say in White House press conferences.
>
> De Gaulle's instructions seem to be for his agents to cooperate completely in everything that concerns the military necessity, reserving to themselves the right to control those matters not of military concern. . . . [They] are proving invaluable. . . . Though [the French liaison officers] are patently de Gaullist and clearly pushing the cause of the Provisional Government, there has been no case brought to my attention in which they have failed to comply with any request of the military authorities.[48]

Despite the scale of the difficulties facing them, de Gaulle's agents discharged their duties honorably. Thousands of Normans, having fled their towns in the face of Allied bombing, found themselves without homes. In the area around Coutainville alone, for example, some fifteen thousand refugees had to be housed and fed.[49] In the Manche, eighty-seven thousand houses had been destroyed, and in the towns of Coutances, Mortain, Montebourg, and Valognes more than 70 percent of the buildings suffered damage.[50] From the standpoint of providing these and other towns with fresh supplies, though, the situation appeared less bleak, in part because the population was in good health.[51]

Moreover, Normandy as a whole remained calm, and the people refrained from punishing avowed or presumed collaborators. A small number of newcomers to the ranks of the Resistance caused problems, however. One U.S. Army intelligence bulletin identified them as "young hoodlums" who had grown up during the war years.

> Now unemployed, they find in the Resistance (with the danger passed) a vent for the spirit which in our country go[es] into college fraternity initiations and football rallies. If there is to be trouble in France it will arise as leadership in the Resistance is assumed by these small fry who respect no rights. In one community they have armed themselves, ignored orders of the mayor, appropriated his car, and without authority placed under house arrest persons they suspect of collaboration. . . . In another they have cut off the hair of young girls suspected of affairs with Germans. These incidents are not widespread, but promise trouble if not suppressed.[52]

Such problems as there were turned out to be relatively minor, and the brutal purge predicted by some observers failed to materialize. After its liberation, the Manche recorded only a single summary execution, Calvados 12, and the Orne 43—as against 375 in the Dordogne alone, far to the south.[53] It should be added that the new French administrative authorities did their best to assist the Allies with regard to the sensitive subject of illicit sexual behavior by closing down the brothels in Caen and Bayeux. This measure did not solve the problem, for many women continued to engage in prostitution outside those venues. Packets of condoms were therefore distributed to prevent the spread of venereal disease, and signs exhorting the men to use them were posted prominently, to the great dismay of some inhabitants. By way of compromise, it was agreed that the location of condom dispensers could be indicated more discreetly after dark by a green light.[54]

By early July the new authorities had given proof of their competence both in dealing with the most trifling administrative details and in implementing the most vital measures; and the American information services began encouraging journalists to praise the Gaullists' ability to govern and their incontestable success in maintaining order and rationing food and other supplies. In urging the media to popularize the slogan "Liberated France—run by Frenchmen," the Political Warfare Division broke with the official position of the White House—or perhaps only anticipated its new policy, announced shortly thereafter.[55]

Profiting from the Allies' procrastination and the circumspect benevolence shown by Eisenhower, who after his experience in Algiers had no intention whatsoever of assuming the administrative and political responsibilities of a liberated country, the Gaullist provisional government had therefore succeeded in imposing its authority despite the inevitable frictions between the French people and their liberators. In doing so, the government strengthened its claim to official recognition, and all the more so because the French Resistance had rendered even greater assistance to the armies in Normandy than Allied strategists had anticipated.

## A Call to Arms

The French Resistance consisted of a number of disparate and often rival organizations, which fell into three main groups. The first, made up of movements such as Combat, Libération, and Défense de la France, sought to influence public opinion and to mobilize civilians, whom it recruited and in some cases provided with military training. The second, consisting of networks such as Alliance Réseau, specialized in intelligence, sabotage, and the repatriation of Allied prisoners to Great Britain. Finally, the maquis, operating in force from fall 1943 on, mainly in the Ain (Rhône-Alpes) and in the South of France, was led by young civilians who had resisted Vichy's attempt to draft them for work in Germany under the Service du Travail Obligatoire and who sought to play an active paramilitary role with a group emphasizing guerrilla tactics. These organizations were further divided by sharp political differences: in addition to Gaullist networks under the control of the BCRA and British networks run by the SOE, there were Communist movements, such as the

Front National and the Francs-Tireurs et Partisans Français (FTP), and right-wing movements, such as the Organisation Civile et Militaire. The maquis itself embraced a wide range of political tendencies.

The Allies, as we have seen, had assigned four tasks to the French underground as a whole: disrupting rail traffic, interrupting communications, delaying the arrival of German reinforcements to Normandy, and waging guerrilla warfare. But what place did the various branches of the Resistance inside France—the French Forces of the Interior (FFI)—occupy within the Allied chain of command? On this point the greatest uncertainty reigned. Although all military and paramilitary formations had in February 1944 been nominally assigned to the FFI under the orders of General Koenig in London, his authority was not universally accepted. On the French side, the Conseil National de la Résistance, infiltrated by Communists through its Commission d'Action Militaire (COMAC), disputed the Gaullists' claim to command all clandestine groups within metropolitan France and insisted on the right to issue its own directives. On the American side, though the Special Forces Headquarters (SFHQ) had been set up on 1 May to coordinate the work of British SOE and American OSS agents, Koenig's role was not specified. This omission was remedied only four weeks later. On 31 May the Allies recognized Koenig's full authority over the FFI and stated that he would receive his orders from Eisenhower via SFHQ. A further step was taken two weeks later, on 17 June, when Koenig had been formally inducted into the Allied chain of command. "His status will be similar to that of any Allied Commander serving directly under SHAEF. It will be General Koenig's duty to advise the Supreme Commander if the orders given to him conflict with the political directives or policies of the French Committee of National Liberation, just as senior British or U.S. Commanders are required to do in the event of serious conflict of orders with the policy of their own Governments."[56] By virtue of this order, Koenig obtained the veto power that de Gaulle had long demanded. The Resistance had at last been integrated into Allied strategy—too late to guarantee optimal preparation for the operations entrusted to it, but soon enough to ensure at least some degree of coordination.

The Allies had planned, moreover, on parachuting special troops into

France just before the landing was to take place. Some twenty Jedburgh teams, consisting of three or four men of different nationalities—British, American, and French—were to act as liaison with the Allied command and furnish the Resistance with technical assistance, particularly in connection with sabotage. Elite troops of the British Special Air Service, along with American Operational Group parachutists, some fifteen hundred men in all, were also sent to carry out localized missions. Then, in the wake of the messages broadcast by the BBC on the evening of 5 June (and on Eisenhower's express orders, overriding French objections), the Resistance set in motion all the operations to be carried out on French territory, with a view both to stimulating a massive popular response and to misleading the Germans about the actual site of the landings.[57] The results were uneven. The call for a general uprising had the consequence that many towns were occupied prematurely, triggering exactly the bloody reprisals that the Allies had sought to avoid. But French underground forces also distinguished themselves in combat, exceeding the most optimistic forecasts.

> The achievements of resistance groups during the first ten days of the battle have been greater than could reasonably have been expected. Full reports have not yet come in, but evidence so far received shows that the railway system of France has been so dislocated as to make the movement of both troops and supplies by rail, if not impossible at any rate subject to delays of unpredictable length.
>
> This railway sabotage was particularly successful in southeastern France and in the area of the Rhone valley, where, apart from one or two local trains, movements were at standstill for some days. . . .
>
> The combined result of rail and telecommunications sabotage has been to make it increasingly difficult for the Germans to coordinate or in some cases to effect in any reasonable time the moves of their reserve formations.
>
> 21 Army Group have stated that, in their opinion, the over-all action of French Resistance has resulted in an average delay of 48

hours being imposed on movement of German formations to the bridgehead area. . . .

[Actions carried out by the maquis have created] chaotic conditions in large parts of France, generally hampering the German military machine. In limited areas, Resistance is in complete control.[58]

It was in Brittany that real cooperation between the Allies and the French underground was first achieved. Only in early July did Supreme Headquarters decide to coordinate the action of American troops and Resistance elements. After the breakthrough via Avranches on 3 August it issued an appeal for generalized guerrilla warfare and the next day, in support of local clandestine forces, parachuted in a staff headed by Colonel Albert Eon and Colonel Passy. With the aid of volunteers the FFI succeeded in liberating Saint-Brieuc on 6 August and establishing control over the rail lines connecting Brest with Saint-Brieuc and Rennes, while ensuring that the strategically crucial Morlaix viaduct escaped collateral damage. Additionally, Resistance forces liberated a number of towns and cities—Josselin, Malestroit, and Quimper in particular—before American troops arrived in those places. The FFI was responsible for guiding individual units and performing thankless tasks that nonetheless required large numbers of men, such as guarding German prisoners and protecting lines of communication. But it sometimes played a more active role, in eliminating small pockets of German resistance (at the request of the Third U.S. Army), attacking enemy columns, and laying siege to smaller enemy concentrations entrenched along the Atlantic coast.[59] Some 35,000 men strong by early August, the FFI in the role of forward infantry also supported American armor. "Everywhere they arrived," motorized formations found the French engaged with the enemy, if indeed the Resistance forces "had not already cleared the terrain."[60] A G-3 report to Supreme Headquarters on operations in the Breton peninsula acknowledged that the French had offered "considerable assistance."[61] Patton went further, saying that "the support of Resistance has been invaluable."[62] Clandestine forces played a large part in operations in southern France as well. By taking control of the Alps and the Rhône

Valley, they prepared the way for the Franco-American troops that had landed in Provence; the southwest they succeeded in liberating by themselves, without Allied intervention.

Already by the end of June the unanticipated scope of underground assistance led Supreme Headquarters to increase its weapon shipments, with the result that 18,883 containers were dropped in July (as compared with 666 in January, 5,197 in May, and 6,261 in June).[63] The danger of allowing Great Britain to claim a monopoly on relations with the Resistance had dawned on the Americans only a few months earlier. General Donovan, head of the OSS, complained in late February to the commander of the U.S. Army Air Forces, General Henry H. Arnold, that until quite recently Arnold's service had not been willing to "make planes available to us, and the British would from time to time give us reluctant use of a few planes." Donovan added, "The refusal . . . has resulted in the dominant control of the British and their delivery of American supplies as if they were a British gift to the French. . . . In all these months America as represented by OSS with the French Groups has been placed in a very secondary and humiliating position. I must appeal to you for help, not to OSS, but to the improvement of America's moral position which has a direct effect on our military effort."[64]

The Joint Chiefs of Staff drew the same conclusion in a message sent to Eisenhower on 17 April. "We have been advised by the State Department that the French have made an important political issue out of the problem of furnishing resistance groups with weapons and the impression is abroad that America is against arming these groups for political reasons while the British are doing everything that is being done in the matter. It is desired that you take such action as is in your jurisdiction, insofar as it jibes with the need for military operations, to bring about a balance between the endeavors made by Britain and America in supplying and delivering material to resistance groups in France."[65] These instructions had an almost immediate effect. Whereas until May 1944 the OSS had dropped at most a third of the supplies intended for the Resistance, this rose to almost two-thirds in June, and nearly a half through the first three weeks of July.[66] Assisting the French underground had now become an urgent obligation that the United States moved quickly to meet by assigning overall responsibility to Supreme Headquarters, in the hope that the control the British had exerted until then through the SOE and the RAF might be reduced, if not altogether eliminated.

At Eisenhower's suggestion the Combined Chiefs of Staff agreed in early July to equip as many as 140,000 Resistance fighters. "Our reports show," General Marshall wrote in confirming the commitment, "that the French Resistance troops are fighting well even against regular German Forces, and I believe we should make every reasonable effort to get more supplies and equipment to them."[67] In a further sign of support for the new policy, the CCS authorized Eisenhower on 16 August to provide the *résistants* with weapons captured from the enemy.[68] The excellent results already obtained in the first month of operations had also led General Donovan to argue in early July in favor of enlarging the range of missions assigned to the FFI.

> Thus far, resistance has been effectively used to harry and dis-
> rupt the enemy's communications. It is now considered feasible
> to build up and expand resistances forces to the point where we
> can keep the enemy fighting. . . . By arming and directing the
> steadily expanding Maquis the enemy can be faced with the alter-
> native of diverting divisions, critically needed elsewhere, to com-
> bat resistance or of losing control of a large part of central and
> southern France. . . . There are 7 major areas in France which are
> now substantially controlled by resistance. Some of these areas
> can be expanded and combined to form very large areas which
> would represent a substantial threat to German communications
> and which could not be liquidated by less than 8 German divi-
> sions.[69]

Allied Force Headquarters (AFH) in Algiers, charged with preparing operational plans for ANVIL/DRAGOON, confirmed this analysis. Empha-sizing the advantages of employing French underground forces on a large scale, AFH called for a sizable increase in weapons drops with a view to establishing control over whole areas in the center and south of the country. The alternative—abandoning support for the Resistance—would have serious political repercussions, General Wilson's staff concluded.[70] Just the same, Donovan himself cautioned against expecting too much: "Although much assistance may be expected from resistance groups in direct support of military operations, it is nonetheless dangerous to rely for the success of the operation upon such aid. The value to be derived from resistance must be carefully assessed and never relied upon. In assessing the value of resistance to future military operations, it must be considered only as a bonus."[71] In the event, the Allies' rapid advance eastward, in the wake of the breakthrough to Avranches, and northward, after the landing in Provence on 15 August, rendered the question moot, but it had been raised in the first place only because the unexpectedly impressive performance of Resistance networks had removed any lingering doubts in London and Washington about their effectiveness. Indeed, even the increased quantities of arms sent to them were insufficient to equip all the volunteers who had come forward. The SOE, having based its planning on the assumption of exclusively clandestine activity, had neglected the prospects for open warfare that were to open up during the course of the campaign, and the Allied high command had similarly underestimated the potential scope for recruitment to the ranks of the FFI.[72]

Following the call for a general uprising that went out on the eve of D-Day a great many different groups threw themselves into action—so many, in fact, that the Resistance found itself unable either to train or to arm all its fresh recruits. As a result, General Koenig issued an order on 10 June that guerrilla actions were to be curbed to the fullest extent possible. Disappointed volunteers were told to go back to their homes; and tragic reprisals occurred when premature assaults by poorly trained Resistance forces were turned back. The town of Tulle, in the Corrèze department in Limousin, was liberated on 7–8 June by the Communist FTP and immediately retaken by elements of the Second SS Panzer (Das Reich) Division, which by way of retaliation hanged 99 inhabitants the following day and deported 162 civilians. In the Morbihan department in Brittany, despite the support of the crack troops of the Special Air Service (SAS) battalion commanded by Pierre Bourgoin, the maquis of Saint-Marcel was forced to retreat under attack by German forces in mid-June, leaving behind 200 dead. On hearing the announcement of the invasion of Normandy, hundreds of volunteers scaled the Vercors plateau west of Grenoble and the high Alps, where they established a short-lived republic. It was crushed by Major General Karl Pflaum's Waffen SS parachute and mountain troops, landing by glider, in bloody fighting during the last two weeks of July.[73]

A lack of weapons, insufficient combat training, poor coordination among units, reckless daring on the part of young men elated at the prospect of liberation—all these prevented the Resistance from realizing its full promise, although its achievements, as we have seen, did greatly impress the Allies. In his report on the campaign in France, Eisenhower gratefully acknowledged "the great assistance given us by the FFI," without which the defeat of the enemy would have taken much longer and cost many more lives.[74] This is no doubt true—but it is no less apparent that except in the southwest, French clandestine forces could not have succeeded in liberating territory on their own. Just the same, they helped accelerate the progress of the Anglo-American armies, both by supplying valuable information and by providing tactical support. Most important, the French underground created a climate of confidence that emboldened the regular Allied forces, secure in the knowledge that they were advancing through friendly rather than hostile territory. On the political level, the FFI helped the Gaullist delegates to establish their authority, and so avoid a power vacuum that might have favored the outbreak of civil war. Finally, from the moral point of view, the Resistance proved to the world that France, far from having passively witnessed its liberation, did everything it could to contribute to it. And yet the very determination to resist exacted a heavy toll, for it prompted the Germans to engage in a campaign of retribution, sometimes blind and often savage, whose cost was borne in large part by civilians.

## War Crimes

The landing and subsequent Allied offensive in Normandy hardened the occupying forces in ways that affected France as a whole. Faced with determined and well-equipped armies on the ground, pummeled by unrelenting aerial attacks, harassed by tenacious Resistance fighters, and grimly anticipating if not defeat, then at least the inevitability of retreat, the Germans gave themselves over to horrible acts of violence.[75] Retaliation extended beyond its usual civilian targets (Jews, Communists, and members of the Resistance), to the point that victims came to be selected almost arbitrarily; and whereas until then atrocities had been confined to a few gruesome and exceptional incidents (such as the massacre at Ascq in April 1944), now the German command did nothing to prevent troops from committing the worst atrocities. Although the SS stood out for its extreme barbarism, the cruelty inflicted by the regular army, and particularly by its auxiliary Russian and Georgian troops, was no less terrible.

Three main forms of violence can be distinguished, illustrated by reference to the situation in Brittany.[76] In the first case, a massacre took place simply because civilians had the misfortune to be present, whether or not they had given logistical support to the maquis. At Pommerit-Landy, in the department of Côtes-du-Nord, an underground unit of 120 men was attacked on 9 July not far from a farm. Some of the *maquisards* managed to flee; those who did not were taken into custody along with the owner and three young persons. The owner was killed and then, after the main building was set on fire, he was thrown into the flames; his companions, kept under arrest for a time, were mistreated and then released. But the next day the Germans burned down the entire farm, having first seized the livestock and the furniture. "When the blaze had died out, the bodies of resistance fighters, bound by their hands and feet, were found in the ruins. . . . The occupiers seem to have deliberately left them to be burned alive."[77]

In the second case, civilians were taken hostage by German soldiers looking to protect themselves against Allied attack, or were killed with the aim of deterring local partisans. During the course of three days, 10–12 June, thirty-one people—for the most part farmers without ties to the Resistance—were arrested, taken to the prison at Callac, and then brought to a place near Plestan, in the Côtes-du-Nord, where they were tortured before being killed.[78] Similarly, the residents of Cléder, in Finistère, were awakened on 8 August at just after three o'clock in the morning. Thinking that the Americans had come, they opened their windows, only to discover a detachment of Germans who had been forced to retreat from Brest; some damage to the town was visible, but no crimes had been committed. Just then, however, another group of soldiers suddenly appeared. "On the pretext that they had been attacked by Resistance forces, [the Germans] began to set fire to the crops, wheat and hay, and to the houses, and then to bomb the home of the Seite family. . . . Five hundred meters from there, five persons were forcibly removed from their homes and taken away as hostages. . . . These men, arms raised, were taken to the edge of the town, on the Plouescat road. There they were lined up in the middle of the road and cut down by machine gun fire. All of them had hideous injuries, having been wounded in the head and the face so that they were unrecognizable and horrible to look at."[79]

The third category of crimes seems to have been motivated by simple vengeance, which led the Germans to terrorize towns that made the mistake of celebrating their deliverance prematurely. Thus, for example, at Huelgoat, which the Americans liberated on 5 August after a certain amount of fighting, a band of retreating Germans managed to make their way back into town after the departure of the enemy troops.

They gained entry to [the Hôtel de France] through the gate in the courtyard, [then] went up to the second floor where they found Madame Le Dilasser caring for her husband, who had just suffered a gunshot wound. They shot down this woman with a burst of machine gun fire in front of her terrified five-year old daughter. This heinous crime accomplished, they crossed the street and first entered the premises of the wine wholesaler, Mademoiselle Querneau, where they savagely killed Madame Lescour, her daughter and her son. Mademoiselle Querneau and her maid managed to survive only by hiding behind wine casks. . . . [The Germans] tried to force their way into the buildings next door and threw grenades inside that caused great damage. Another group of Germans, having the same intentions, went around to the west of the Hôtel de France and gained entry to the Cosquer residence through the garden. These soldiers brought outside Monsieur Cosquer, a retired policeman, his wife, their daughter Madame Le Boulch, a schoolteacher, and her five-year old daughter. Monsieur Cosquer and Madame Le Boulch were killed in a cowardly way with a machine gun. It was only by a miracle that Madame Cosquer, seriously wounded in the arm, and her granddaughter survived. A third group explored other buildings whose occupants had fled. In the street they machine-gunned Monsieur Le Scanff, an elderly man eighty years of age, retired from his job as a postman, and Madame Rouillé, both of them on their way home. These two persons were mortally wounded. At the same moment, on the street leading to the rail-way station, the same scenes of horror were taking place. Monsieur Mouzer, another retired postman, and his neighbor, Mademoiselle Le Gall, were also shot down on the ground floor of the latter's house. Monsieur Sébastien Kermanach, an elderly man retired from the navy, was arrested and forcibly conducted to the basement of [Mademoiselle Le Gall's] house, which on account of its isolated location seemed to have been chosen as the command post for this pack of sadists. According to [M. Kermanach's] statement, the blood of the two poor victims [upstairs] trickled down through the floorboards.[80]

Similar acts of violence struck the whole of France, though not everywhere with the same frequency. In Normandy itself some seventy-five to eighty Resistance fighters were massacred in the prison at Caen on 6 June.[81] Almost six hundred people in all were summarily executed in the region of Lower Normandy between June and August 1944.[82] Shops and homes were plundered, particularly in Coutances, where German soldiers appear to have been under orders to notify their officers when they came across objects of value. "The latter at once saw to [their] removal. Doors and cupboards were ruthlessly smashed. All wine was taken and very few objects of value appear to remain in the town. In buildings that can be entered there is a disorder of effects thrown in all directions in the search for loot."[83] And after the bombing of Caen an Allied reconnaissance report suggested that German soldiers committed rapes.[84]

Other regions experienced a still more ghastly fate, particularly Brittany, the southwest, the Alps, and the center. By a strange paradox, crimes against civilians were concentrated in regions spared during the course of fighting (except in the case of operations mounted by the Resistance). On the periphery, the Germans moved to eliminate threats to the rear of their lines by the most brutal means imaginable, whereas nearer the battleground itself they sought to maintain something like peace. "The German command was perfectly aware that any excessive behavior would throw 'the population into the arms of the terrorists,' that the German soldiers would pay sooner or later 'with their blood.'"[85] They wanted to transport reinforcements and munitions under stable conditions, without adding the risks of local guerrilla warfare to the difficulties created by the Allies. At this stage, notwithstanding the many bloody atrocities that had been committed in Normandy (mainly by the SS Security Police [SiPo] and Security Service [SD], in addition to the Hitler Youth Division), the logic of the German position required not a policy of repression, but rather—so far as such a thing was possible—a policy of appeasement.[86]

Basil Liddell Hart has argued that the German army on the whole showed greater respect for the laws of war during the Second World War than during the First, "whereas it was reasonable to expect that the addition of 'Nazism' to 'Prussianism' would make its behavior worse than before."[87] This is true of the battles the Wehrmacht waged against regular troops in Western Europe; but it fails to describe the experience of civilians in many parts of France during the summer of 1944. And even if the incidence of war crimes was relatively low in the northwest, one may well imagine with what relief Normans and Bretons welcomed the return to French civil administration after long weeks of being caught in the middle of one of the most intense battles of the Second World War.

## APOTHEOSIS

On the eve of D-Day, in spite of growing evidence of popular support for the Gaullist movement in France and pressure from the press on both sides of the Atlantic, the United States nonetheless persisted in its opposition to recognizing the provisional government. Roosevelt had made the first concession on 6 June, however, by extending an invitation to de Gaulle to visit the United States. The president's rather hypocritical claim at a press conference, that de Gaulle had expressed a desire to see him, fooled no one—least of all Henri Hoppenot, the GPRF's representative in Washington. "We are in the presence of a domestic political maneuver aimed at calming public opinion while yielding nothing with regard to fundamental positions, at bringing out the absence of bias on the President's part and possibly throwing back onto the General, if he should decline to act after having supposedly been put forward, the responsibility for refusing in the end."[88] Roosevelt had a clear interest, with a presidential election in the offing, in quieting the uproar in the papers. De Gaulle therefore proceeded deliberately and with caution. After putting off his reply for more than a week and accepting the president's invitation only on 26 June, he finally traveled to Washington on 6 July.[89] In his public statements the general was careful not to add oil to the fire; and showing great tact, he made only a brief trip to New York, where, "in order not to furnish occasions for popular manifestations which, three months away from the Presidential elections, might seem to be directed against what had hitherto been the President's policy, it had been agreed that my public appearances would be very restricted. All the more so since Dewey, the candidate opposing Roosevelt, was the governor of New York State."[90] On his return to Algiers on 13 July de Gaulle reaped the rewards of so many months of patient obstinacy: there he found waiting for him a copy of the declaration issued the day before by the U.S. government, accepting the right of the GPRF "to exercise the administration of France"—and thus granting de facto recognition.[91]

From this the talks already under way between the French and the British gained momentum, and at the end of July the Americans agreed to take part in the discussions. By 8 August the major points had been settled, but further negotiation was needed to produce a final agreement, which was signed on 25 August. In return for the Allies' blessing, the GPRF undertook to give the Allied supreme commander the powers necessary for conducting military operations. Additionally, and by no means least of all, the provisional government obtained the sole right to coin money and thereafter furnished the Allies with legal tender in exchange for payment in dollars. France, finally, would be entitled to lend-lease assistance from the United States and terms of mutual aid from Great Britain.[92] At long last, then, the deadlock was broken—although Allied foot-dragging delayed de jure recognition of the new government until 23 October, almost two months later.

On 25 August, however, the same day on which de Gaulle's diplomatic efforts were crowned with victory, the liberation of Paris consecrated his moral and political triumph. The moment was all the sweeter because he had been obliged to fight for so long on two fronts, against the Allies on the one hand and the French Communists on the other. Paris held no military interest for Eisenhower, as we have seen, for its capture would only slow the Allies' advance to the east while carrying the risk of costly street fighting. Meanwhile, his logisticians feared having to assume responsibility for feeding a metropolitan area of several million inhabitants. "We would point out that the capture of Paris will entail a Civil Affairs supply commitment equivalent to the maintenance of 8 divisions in operations. If captured early, before the necessary railroads have been reconstructed and the Seine ports opened, it is likely to be a serious limitation to our ability to maintain forces in the above operations."[93] It was therefore decided to leave the French capital to the French. The Third U.S. Army was thus free to bypass it to the north and south.

Triggering an insurrection in the capital was nonetheless bound to have profound implications for the country's internal political balance of power.[94] A powerful wave of strikes was unleashed on 11 August, beginning with the railways and spreading to the city's subway system and then the police. On the nineteenth the FFI issued the call for a general uprising and seized control of the prefecture of police and other organs of local government. The Communists played a paramount role in these events. Though few of them could have supposed that revolution was possible, they no doubt hoped to gain control of the city at least for a brief time, before the Allies' arrival—a symbolic victory, potentially one of great consequence.

De Gaulle weighed the matter with the utmost care. In his instructions of 12 August he deliberately refrained from encouraging insurrection. The lack of information counseled caution: the situation was developing from hour to hour, and telegrams sent from Paris reached their destination only after a delay of two to four days, owing to backlogs at the decryption centers.[95] From 18 August onward, BBC broadcasts remained noncommittal—a sign of indecision within the Gaullist ranks. De Gaulle feared, with good reason, that supporting the strikers would paralyze vital sectors of production, particularly energy. Most of all, however, he feared having to assume responsibility for precipitating a brutal crackdown by a desperate occupier. Memories of 1871 haunted the capital. Finally, on 23 August de Gaulle told Leclerc, "Go quickly. We cannot have another Commune."[96] At the same time, he could hardly dissociate himself from a movement that clearly enjoyed sweeping mass support. The silence on the radio was only the most obvious sign of this dilemma. "The absence of instructions for Paris," Georges Boris, a political adviser to the general, had already observed on 11 August, "constitutes a serious gap in view of the fact that they are the most urgent and the only ones [whose absence does] present real difficulties."[97] A report dated 14 August, probably originating with the Commission of the Interior, sounded a note of grave concern: "If the GPRF does not give indications and instructions to Paris, the movement will begin without the authorization of the GPRF."[98] The Gaullist authorities tried to stall for time, moving to arrange for a truce with General Choltitz that was to take effect between 20 and 22 August, but they were overtaken by events. "The French National Committee had done everything in their power to restrain Paris from rising," René Massigli told Anthony Eden on the Twenty-second, "but, unfortunately, on Saturday morning [19 August], inspired by the Communists, a rising had taken place."[99]

The Communists found it difficult, however, to control the insurrection once it had begun. Although the strikes had succeeded in mobilizing broad popular support for the armed struggle that followed, the French Communist Party (PCF) nonetheless met with some stinging setbacks. It failed, first of all, to take effective control of the Resistance. Although the authority of the Communist-dominated Military Action Commission of the National Resistance Council was indeed recognized on 14 August by the delegates of de Gaulle's provisional government, Alexandre Parodi and Jacques Chaban-Delmas, their acknowledgment counted for little—considering that General Leclerc became military governor of Paris on his arrival in the capital eleven days later, on 25 August, whereupon he immediately handed over the office to General Koenig. In theory, of course, the Communists had powerful advantages at the local level, since Henri Rol-Tanguy directed the FFI's operations in the Paris region, André Tollet presided over the Paris Liberation Committee, and General Alfred Malleret-Joinville held the strategically important office of national chief of staff of the FFI. No matter that all these men displayed unflinching loyalty to the party, they still had to prove their ability to lead, which was not always in evidence. Nor did the Communists wholly manage to integrate local insurgents into their networks. Harnessing the moral and political momentum of the insurrection depended on the capacity to channel volunteers into a small galaxy of satellite organizations secretly controlled by the party—notably the Francs-Tireurs et Partisans and various patriotic youth militias. Here again, reality failed to live up to expectations.

Statistical discrepancies make it difficult to give a reliable estimate of the strength of the insurgents. On 3 July 1944 COMAC counted 1,750 armed men and 60,000 others who could be mobilized more or less immediately in the Paris region (P1); lists drawn up by the several sector commanders before the insurrection yielded a total of 35,523 men; after the war, military authorities accepted a global figure of 28,757 for the FFI in the Seine department, which at the time included a part of suburban Paris in addition to the city itself.[100] The official statistics moreover suggest that of the some 20,000 Parisian fighters, the PCF controlled only 4,000 men—a mere fifth of the total. It may be for this reason that Rol-Tanguy, in a message of 18 August, urgently called for additional volunteers to come forward: "All able-bodied French men and women must consider themselves mobilized. They must immediately join the FFI formations or the patriotic militia of their neighborhood or factory."[101] A fresh appeal was issued on the twenty-fourth, together with an order that department commanders should "immediately make their recruitment centers ready to receive all the volunteers resolved to take part in the struggle against the Boche."[102] But these directives, which assumed that the people of Paris wanted to join forces with the Communists in the first place, came too late to reverse the tendency of the uprising to develop spontaneously along other lines, from a widely shared love of liberty and in a spirit that was both fearful and joyously defiant, grave and at the same time festive. Local combatants seem in fact to have had little desire to enlist in the party's organizations, as Gaullist leaders suspected quite early on. On 11 August Chaban-Delmas told London that he did not see the FTP as a danger: "They know that they do not constitute all the forces of the FFI and the Resistance."[103] At all events, if the party had hoped to welcome Charles de Gaulle to a city that had been liberated by its forces alone, it was to be disabused of that notion fairly quickly.

The provisional government enjoyed considerable advantages of its own. First of all, its men were in place, from general secretaries ready to take control of the ministries to the future prefect of police, Charles Luizet, who had arrived in secrecy from Algiers on 17 August. De Gaulle's trump card, of course, was the Second Armored Division. Arriving in France himself on the twentieth, he went directly to see Eisenhower at his field headquarters near Tournières, southwest of Bayeux, and demanded that Paris be occupied at the earliest possible moment. In a letter delivered to the supreme commander by General Alphonse Juin and General Koenig the following day, he asked Eisenhower to act at once, in view of the outbreak of fighting there and the growing problems in supplying the city. Eisenhower agreed and directed Leclerc's division to prepare to march on the capital together with the U.S. Fourth Infantry Division.

The Second Armored started out at six o'clock on the morning of the twenty-third. After covering some 120 miles in about fifteen hours, Leclerc's spearheads entered the city the following evening, taking up positions in front of the city hall.[104] This spectacular achievement was not unanimously admired, however. General Bradley complained in his memoirs that Leclerc had set off only on the twenty-third, whereas the departure order had been given on the twenty-second, and that his men had dawdled on the way.

> For the next 24 hours the French 2d Armored stumbled reluctantly through a Gallic wall as townsfolk along the line of march slowed the French advance with wine and celebration. Although I did not censure them for responding to this hospitality of their

countrymen, neither could I wait for them to dance their way to Paris. If von Choltitz was to deliver the city, we had a compact to fulfill.

"To hell with prestige," I finally told [Major General Leven C.] Allen, "tell the 4th to slam on in and take the liberation." Learning of these orders and fearing an affront to France, Leclerc's troopers mounted their tanks and burned up their treads on the brick road.[105]

The truth of the matter is that Bradley was angered by Leclerc's prior indiscretion in detaching an advance unit to Paris on 21 August without permission; and having always hoped that the Fourth Infantry would be the first to enter the City of Light, he accepted Eisenhower's decision with ill grace.

Whether or not it had "danced" its way to Paris, the Second Armored arrived in time and provided de Gaulle with a force capable of maintaining order while at the same time disarming German resistance. The city fell on Friday, 25 August. General Leclerc and Colonel Rol-Tanguy received General von Choltitz's formal surrender later the same day. Between 24 and 27 August the Second Armored sustained almost 300 casualties, including seventy-one dead and 225 wounded, while the FFI lost more than 2,000 men, including 901 dead and 1,455 wounded; civilian casualties in the capital were almost as high, with 582 killed and 2,012 injured.[106]

It remained for de Gaulle to make his grand entrance, the successive stages of which he had carefully planned. Arriving by train early in the afternoon of the twenty-fifth at the Gare Montparnasse, the site of Choltitz's surrender, he proceeded to the war ministry on the rue Saint-Dominique, whose halls he knew well from his days as a member of Paul Reynaud's government before the war. Next the general went to the prefecture, on the Île de la Cité, to salute the police. Only then, having symbolically reaffirmed the authority and preeminence of the state, of which he considered himself the head, did de Gaulle condescend to go to the city hall, where the members of the Resistance had been obliged to wait for him. Paying tribute to the capital in a magnificent speech ("Paris outragé! Paris brisé! Paris martyrisé!"[107]), he nonetheless refused (despite the insistence of Georges Bidault, the president of the CNR) to proclaim the Republic, for in de Gaulle's mind the Republic—thanks to him and him alone—had never ceased to exist.

The hour of his triumph sounded the next day. On 26 August Charles de Gaulle marched down the Champs-Élysées to the acclamation of hundreds of thousands of his fellow citizens. In making his way through this flood of humanity, the head of the provisional government must surely have reflected on the outcome of the extraordinary wager he had made on 18 June 1940. For the encounter four years later between the man and his people amounted to both a coronation and a celebration of marriage between the liberated and their liberator—an apotheosis that brilliantly crowned the vast operation launched in the dawn of 6 June on the beaches of Normandy. But the war itself did not come to an end with the cheers of the crowds along the parade route in Paris. For the ringing of the tenor bell in Notre-Dame's south tower marked the end of only the first act of OVERLORD. France was to wait six long months before being completely freed from German occupation; and another nine months were to pass before the Allied forces had crushed the Third Reich once and for all.

# CONCLUSION

## *Farewell to Crusades?*

WITH THE LIBERATION OF PARIS in late August 1944, the first phase of the odyssey begun on 6 June was complete—a titanic enterprise without precedent in the history of warfare, at least in the magnitude of the human and material resources employed. The British and American economies had, albeit with some difficulty, mobilized for war on a scale never before contemplated. Despite their differences, the Allies managed to agree on a simple but effective strategy that was finally adopted, over Churchill's objections, because of Roosevelt's perseverance and Stalin's support. More than a million and a half men were thrown into battle against the armies of the Reich, still a formidable power after almost five years of war. Although the Allies spared no expense in launching the assault on Hitler's "Fortress Europe," they could not be sure they would prevail. Yet they had no choice but to attempt to cross the Channel. If Germany was to be defeated and the westward advance of the Red Army halted, France had to be liberated.

The Allies' gamble—fraught with risk without being foolhardy, bold but not reckless—was in many ways brilliantly judged. The landing itself went more smoothly than the planners at Supreme Headquarters had dared to hope. The Atlantic Wall collapsed in less than twenty-four hours: by the evening of 6 June all five beaches had been taken; and with the notable exception of bloody Omaha casualties were far less numerous than anticipated. In part this was owing to the indisputable courage and professionalism of the Allied soldiers; but it was also a consequence of careful planning and precise execution. The campaign that followed in Normandy, by contrast, disappointed expectations. Far from making slow but steady progress, the troops found themselves bottled up in a narrow lodgment area. So determined was the German resistance that for two months the British forces, charged with taking Caen on the first day and then at once going on the offensive, were stalled outside the Norman capital, which they finally succeeded in capturing only in mid-August. Instead, it was the Americans who managed to break through the enemy lines first; conquering the Cotentin in late July and then rushing into the breach at Avranches, U.S. troops quickly liberated the west of France through a series of forced marches. By the last week in August they had reached Paris—without, however, having succeeded in capturing the majority of the retreating enemy forces. The British, after freeing themselves at last from the quagmire in Calvados, advanced no less rapidly, covering the 240 miles that separated Normandy from Antwerp in one week—a prodigious leap forward, to say the least.

The French Resistance, for its part, acquitted itself honorably, giving invaluable assistance to the Allies while helping bring about the restoration of the republican regime and the establishment of the Gaullist provisional government without a bloodbath. Through its sangfroid, its sense of its responsibilities, and its commitment to the cause of national unity, the Resistance spared France the agony of civil war. Other countries, such as Greece, were not so fortunate. In the face of this surge of patriotic fervor and the terrifying might of the Anglo-American armies, the Germans could bring to bear only the force of their exceptional bravery. Crippled by the Allies' supremacy on the sea and in the air, and fatally handicapped by shortages of men and matériel, they were eventually forced to withdraw, though the enemy's failure to close the gap at Falaise, and thereafter to pursue, allowed them to carry out their retreat across the Seine in an orderly fashion for the most part.

No single factor by itself assured the triumph of the American and British forces. The tactical and strategic bombing campaigns played an important role, but the Transportation Plan enjoyed only limited success, and German coastal defenses were not seriously damaged by the aerial attacks that preceded the landings on D-Day; FORTITUDE SOUTH misled the German intelligence services, but it did not prevent OKW from strengthening its forces in Normandy; the artificial harbors made it unnecessary to conquer a major port, but the great storm in the third week of June severely compromised their usefulness; British and American air forces were able to achieve mastery of the skies, but bad weather prevented them from taking full advantage of it. The Allied victory resulted instead from the combined effect of these various elements. To the great credit of Supreme Headquarters and particularly of Eisenhower himself, no detail, however small, was neglected; nothing was left to chance.

The defeat of the Reich was due to weaknesses that precisely mirrored Allied strengths. Far from justifying the boasts of Goebbels's propaganda, Germany enjoyed no superiority in any regard other than the ability of its fighting men and the quality of its equipment. For months it had hesitated over which strategy to adopt—the consequence of a dispute, still unresolved on 6 June, that divided both OB West and OKW. German coastal defenses on the eve of D-Day remained unfinished. And neither the Kriegsmarine nor the Luftwaffe was robust enough to intervene decisively. Even if the Reich had correctly guessed the site of the landing—something that in view of the impotence of its intelligence services would have bordered on the miraculous—it would nonetheless have had to bring forward to Normandy the balance of its armored divisions positioned along the Channel and North Sea coast. In that case, however, the concentration of troops would have offered a perfect target for the Allied naval and air forces, and the battle might well have been decided in a matter of hours. In either case, the numerical imbalance between the two sides could only have worked against a defensive strategy that lacked the very things—tanks, airplanes, ships, and fuel—that were needed to carry it out.

Even so, a favorable ratio of forces was not in and of itself sufficient to guarantee victory to the Allies. It was still crucial that the troops not succumb to panic once ashore and that the generals exploit their strategic advantages to the fullest, while at the same time adapting their tactics to changing circumstances. The stalemate of June and July revealed serious weaknesses, however. Logistical delays impeded the conduct of operations; and soldiers cracked under the strain of battle, adding psychiatric casualties to the planners' chronic worries about sustaining adequate troop levels. The erosion of the fragile understanding that had existed at the highest levels of command set off a crisis from which the Americans emerged triumphant, at the expense of the British, who found themselves demoted to the status of junior partners. Meanwhile, the problem of devising effective means of coordinating infantry, air support, and armor was solved by General Bradley only during the COBRA offensive of late July, almost two months after D-Day.

All these problems exposed flaws that had temporarily been masked by the brilliant successes of 6 June. The Allies did not in fact enjoy overwhelming advantages with respect to either men or equipment. War production capacity, only partially mobilized by the United States and Britain, was further restricted by bottlenecks (particularly in the manufacture and delivery of landing craft and ships) that for a time threatened the viability of OVERLORD. Moreover, the United States had moved to limit conscription, out of a desire to avoid labor shortages in the factories at home and, so far as possible, to keep families together. This led in turn to overreliance on mechanized warfare, which it was thought would help reduce infantry losses. But the vital task of consolidating territorial gains could be carried out only by foot soldiers, and their ranks had not been carefully selected. Nor were all, or even many, of these soldiers convinced they were fighting for the rights of man, or dedicated to defeating a regime that embodied the essence of barbarism; indeed, some committed acts of plunder and rape themselves. It is quite true, of course, that uncivilized behavior of this sort was hardly common, and commanders in any case did not seek to use it as a way of imposing their will on a population that they regarded as friendly. The vast majority of soldiers carried out their assigned missions with great courage, under conditions of extreme psychological and physical duress. Even so, incidence of criminal behavior, marginal though it may have been, cast a pall over the advance of the Allied armies and showed how weak the motivation of many soldiers was and how undependable their convictions were. Despite the considerable time and effort devoted by the Allied authorities to training and indoctrinating the troops, many of them did not believe in the cause they had been called upon to serve.

All these things invite us to reexamine the familiar mythology of the invasion of Normandy, dispassionately and with an open mind. It was surely an epic event; of that there can be no doubt. But between the reality of the event and the myth yawns a great abyss. The myth recounts the inevitable triumph of a well-oiled war machine manned by impossibly brave soldiers, eager to sacrifice themselves for the cause of liberty in general and the liberation of France in particular. But this view, propagated by an endless series of memoirs and historical narratives, of young men who gladly risked death without batting an eye, misrepresents the actual nature of the campaign, by disregarding the repugnance felt by many of those who fought in Normandy and overlooking the immense suffering that was inflicted, deliberately or otherwise, on innocent civilians. It also discounts the challenges that had to be met to prepare poorly motivated conscripts to go to war. For the majority of the troops Nazism did not embody a universal evil; to a large extent, their ignorance reflected the more general ignorance of the societies from which they came, poorly informed and insufficiently educated on the whole, where both before and during the war governments failed to make their citizens grasp the real consequences of the struggle in which they were engaged.

Similarly, the idealized picture of a war industry working flat-out and at full capacity to bring about the defeat of the enemy obscures the problems that the democracies encountered in mobilizing labor and capital. In the end, though with rather greater difficulty than is usually acknowledged, Great Britain and the United States, resorting to coercion only in the last instance, managed to clear away the obstacles in their path through a combination of incentives, negotiation, and the free play of market mechanisms. Had sterner measures been taken, production levels might have been higher; but then the British and Americans would to some extent have had to sacrifice their fundamental values in the name of efficiency—a slippery slope they refused to venture down, either in the economic or in the military sphere.

The Second World War has often been seen as a war of unprecedented horror. There can be no doubt that it was. The destruction of the

European Jews, the brutal fighting on the Russian front, and the atomic bomb attacks on Japan are all in their different ways proof of it. In Normandy this horror showed itself among the hedgerows, which, by reducing the effectiveness of mechanized formations, brought about a return to archaic forms of warfare—including hand-to-hand combat—that are now once again a familiar feature of armed conflict. Despite the increasing reliance of modern armies on advanced technologies, the central role of infantry in helping control towns and cities, machine guns at the ready, remains unchanged.

At the same time, however, the campaign in Normandy brought real advances. Soldiers wounded on the battlefield were often saved, thanks to penicillin and prompt evacuation by airlift to field hospitals. Surgeons seldom had to resort to amputation, in striking contrast to the situation they faced during the First World War. Men who had broken under the strain of battle were considered victims of illness, rather than malingerers who deserved to be brought before a court-martial, and they were treated humanely. Last but by no means least, commanders were careful on the whole not to sacrifice their men in useless offensives—another sign that the generals had reflected on the experience of the previous war and learned from it.

Stripped of the glorious trappings of a legendary exploit, the invasion of Normandy can now be seen as a supremely human event—human both in the greatness of what it accomplished and in the magnitude of what it left undone. It hastened the defeat of the Reich—though the rout of the Wehrmacht was achieved mainly on the Russian steppes. The landings delivered Western Europe from Nazi tyranny—but they were powerless to prevent the Sovietization of Eastern Europe. They restored liberty to France—while at the same time inflicting terrible suffering on thousands of innocent people. Triumphalism no longer has a place in the telling of this great epic, for the stories of the soldiers themselves tinge it with the subtle but unmistakable shades of tragedy.

# Notes

For detailed listings of individual archival holdings consulted for this work, see Archival Sources. The most common archival names are abbreviated in the notes as follows:

AVP RF   Arkhiv Vneshnei Politiki Rossiskoi Federatsii (Moscow)
BA-MA   Bundesarchiv-Militärarchiv (Freiburg)
EL   Eisenhower Library (Abilene, Kansas)
MAE   Ministère d'Affaires Étrangères (Paris)
NARA   National Archives and Records Administration (College Park, Maryland)
PRO   Public Record Office (Kew, London)

## INTRODUCTION

1. Quoted in Max Hastings, *Overlord: D-Day and the Battle for Normandy* (London: Michael Joseph, 1984), 11.

2. The British historian John Ellis defends this point of view, for example, in *Brute Force: Allied Strategy and Tactics in the Second World War* (London: Deutsch, 1990); see Terry Copp, *Fields of Fire: The Canadians in Normandy* (Toronto: University of Toronto Press, 2003), 255. The epithet "arsenal of democracy" is due to Roosevelt, who first used it in a 29 December 1940 radio address to rally the American people in support of Great Britain.

3. Quoted in Geoffrey Perret, *There's a War to Be Won: The United States Army in World War II* (New York: Random House, 1991), 33.

4. Dwight D. Eisenhower, *Crusade in Europe* (Garden City, N.Y.: Doubleday, 1948).

5. The order of the day is reproduced on the back of the dust jacket.

6. Stephen E. Ambrose, *D-Day, June 6, 1944: The Climactic Battle of World War II* (New York: Simon and Schuster, 1994), 26.

7. Cited in Olivier Pottier, "Les malentendus transatlantiques," *L'Histoire* 287 (May 2004): 60.

8. Omar N. Bradley, *A Soldier's Story* (New York: Holt, 1951), 12–13.

9. Georges-Henri Soutou, *La Guerre de cinquante ans: Les relations Est-Ouest, 1943–1990* (Paris: Fayard, 2001), 26. [All translations are mine unless otherwise indicated.—Trans.]

10. Frederick Morgan, *Overture to Overlord* (London: Hodder and Stoughton, 1950), 109.

11. Paul Fussell, *Wartime: Understanding and Behavior in the Second World War* (New York: Oxford University Press, 1989), ix, 179.

12. Ralph Ingersoll, *Top Secret* (New York: Harcourt, Brace, 1946), 318.

13. Quoted in Fussell, *Wartime*, 79.

14. In using the phrase "rediscovering the war" I adopt the subtitle that Stéphane Audoin-Rouzeau and Annette Becker gave to their recent book on the First World War, *14–18: Retrouver la Guerre* (Paris: Gallimard, 2000); available in English as *14–18: Understanding the Great War*, trans. Catherine Temerson (New York: Hill and Wang, 2002).

15. Eisenhower, *Crusade in Europe*, 451.

16. See Correlli Barnett, *The Audit of War: The Illusion and Reality of Britain as a Great Nation* (London: Macmillan, 1986), 164.

17. It will of course be understood that in observing that eminent historians specializing in the strategic and diplomatic aspects of the war tend to ignore its economic side, whereas equally distinguished social historians scarcely inquire into the strategic and diplomatic issues it raises, I do not mean in the least to call into question the very high quality of their work.

18. See Gabriel Kolko, *The Politics of War: The World and United States Foreign Policy, 1943–1945* (New York: Random House, 1968), 28.

19. Quoted in Friedrich Ruge, *Rommel in Normandy: Reminiscences*, trans. Ursula R. Moessner (San Rafael, Calif.: Presidio, 1979), 205.

20. Many studies, as Max Hastings has rightly argued, do little more than "reflect comfortable chauvinist legends"; see Hastings, *Overlord*, 11.

21. See, for example, the abridged version of Nigel Hamilton's three-volume account of Montgomery's life and career, *Monty: The Battles of Field Marshal Bernard Montgomery* (London: Hodder and Stoughton, 1994). The most damning, but also the strongest, case against Montgomery has been made by Carlo D'Este in *Decision in Normandy: The Unwritten Story of Montgomery and the Allied Campaign* (London: Collins, 1983).

22. See Michel Boivin, Gérard Bourdin, and Jean Quellien, *Villes normandes sous les bombes (juin 1944)* (Caen: Presses Universitaires de Caen / Mémorial de Caen, 1994), 25.

23. Alan Francis Brooke (Field Marshal Sir; later Lord Alanbrooke), *War Diaries, 1939–1945*, ed. Alex Danchev and Daniel Todman (London: Weidenfeld and Nicolson, 1957), 557.

24. André Kaspi, *Les Américains: Les États-Unis de 1607 à nos jours* (Paris: Seuil, 1986), 329.

25. Historical Section, Operational Aspects of Mulberry B, 10 May 1945, Public Records Office (henceforth PRO), prime minister's cabinet (henceforth CAB), 106/966.

26. Eisenhower, *Crusade in Europe*, 508.

27. See Mark A. Stoler, "The United States: The Global Strategy," in David Reynolds et al., *Allies at War: The Soviet, American, and British Experience, 1939–1945* (New York: St. Martin's, 1994), 74–75.

28. See Soutou, *La Guerre de cinquante ans*, 19.

29. On Roosevelt's geopolitical aims with regard to OVERLORD, see Warren F. Kimball, *The Juggler: Franklin Roosevelt as Wartime Statesman* (Princeton, N.J.: Princeton University Press, 1991), 14ff.

## 1. ALLIES, NOT FRIENDS

1. See Alex Danchev, "Great Britain: The Indirect Strategy," in David Reynolds et al., eds., *Allies at War: The Soviet, American, and British Experience, 1939–1945* (New York: St. Martin's, 1994), 3ff.

2. See Trumbull Higgins, *Winston Churchill and the Second Front, 1940–1943* (New York: Oxford University Press, 1957), 125ff.

3. See Mark A. Stoler, *The Politics of the Second Front: American Military Planning and Diplomacy in Coalition Warfare, 1941–1943* (Westport, Conn.: Greenwood, 1977), 125ff.

4. See Higgins, *Winston Churchill and the Second Front*, 191–201.

5. Ibid., 203.

6. On the capture of Soviet soldiers, see Richard J. Overy, *Russia's War: A History of the Soviet War Effort, 1941–1945* (London: Penguin, 1997), 117.

7. See William O'Neill, *A Democracy at War: America's Fight at Home and Abroad in World War II* (New York: Free Press, 1993), 166.

8. See Russell F. Weigley, *Eisenhower's Lieutenants: The Campaign of France and Germany, 1944–1945* (Bloomington: Indiana University Press, 1981), 5–7.

9. See William Hardy McNeill, *America, Britain, and Russia: Their Cooperation and Conflict, 1941–1946* (London: Oxford University Press, 1952), 192ff.

10. See Stoler, *The Politics of the Second Front*, 30.

11. Ibid., 13, 35.

12. Quoted in McNeill, *America, Britain, and Russia*, 8.

13. Ibid., 103.

14. See Higgins, *Winston Churchill and the Second Front*, 134–135.

15. See McNeill, *America, Britain, and Russia*, 104–105.

16. Quoted in François Bédarida, *Churchill* (Paris: Fayard, 1999), 344.

17. See Mikhail N. Narinski et al., "Mutual Perceptions: Image, Ideals, and Illusions," in Reynolds et al., eds., *Allies at War,* 318.

18. See Warren F. Kimball, *The Juggler: Franklin Roosevelt as Wartime Statesman* (Princeton, N.J.: Princeton University Press, 1991), 29–30.

19. Quoted in McNeill, *America, Britain, and Russia,* 189–190.

20. Quoted ibid., 168–169.

21. See Angus Calder, *The People's War: Britain, 1939–1945* (London: Jonathan Cape, 1969), 298.

22. Joseph Goebbels, *Journal: 1943–1945,* ed. and trans. Pierre Ayçoberry, Horst Möller, and Stefan Martens (Paris: Tallandier, 2005), 234.

23. Quoted in Robert E. Sherwood, *Roosevelt and Hopkins: An Intimate History* (New York: Harper and Brothers, 1948), 563.

24. See Stoler, *The Politics of the Second Front,* 36ff.

25. Ibid., 43ff.

26. Georgi Dimitrov, *Journal, 1933–1949,* ed. Gaël Moullec et al. (Paris: Belin, 2005), 668.

27. Chester Wilmot, *The Struggle for Europe* (London: Collins, 1952), 105.

28. Quoted in Narinski et al., "Mutual Perceptions," 310.

29. See Stoler, *The Politics of the Second Front,* 51.

30. Quoted ibid., 49.

31. Quoted in Sherwood, *Roosevelt and Hopkins,* 569.

32. See McNeill, *America, Britain, and Russia,* 192–193.

33. See Stoler, *The Politics of the Second Front,* 55–56.

34. Quoted in Sherwood, *Roosevelt and Hopkins,* 617–618.

35. Quoted ibid., 619.

36. Ibid., 620.

37. Ibid., 621; also McNeill, *America, Britain, and Russia,* 198ff.

38. See Higgins, *Winston Churchill and the Second Front,* 186.

39. See Maurice Matloff and Edwin M. Snell, *Strategic Planning for Coalition Warfare, 1941–1944,* 2 vols. (Washington, D.C.: Office of the Chief of Military History, Department of the Army, 1953–1959), 2:53.

40. Omar N. Bradley, *A Soldier's Story* (New York: Holt, 1951), 190–191.

41. Wilmot, *The Struggle for Europe,* 123.

42. Quoted in Marlis G. Steiner, "L'attitude allemande face à la capitulation inconditionnelle," in Maurice Vaïsse, ed., *8 mai 1945: La victoire en Europe* (Brussels: Complexe, 2005), 15. [Here and elsewhere I follow Martin Blumenson's practice in transposing German military ranks. Thus, for example, *Generaloberst* corresponds to the Anglo-American rank of general, not colonel-general (as Jodl is customarily styled); see the table of equivalences, Martin Blumenson, *Breakout and Pursuit* (Washington, D.C.: Office of the Chief of Military History, Department of the Army, 1961), appendix A—Trans.].

43. Pierre Ayçoberry, *La société allemande sous le IIIe Reich, 1933–1945* (Paris: Seuil, 1998), 369–370.

44. Robert Gellately, *Backing Hitler: Consent and Coercion in Nazi Germany* (New York: Oxford University Press, 2001), 224.

45. Quoted in Matloff and Snell, *Strategic Planning for Coalition Warfare*, 2:106.

46. See McNeill, *America, Britain, and Russia*, 277.

47. Sherwood, *Roosevelt and Hopkins*, 734.

48. See Lionel Fredric Ellis, et al., *The Battle of Normandy* (London: H. M. Stationery Office, 1962), 18.

49. See Quadrant Conference, second meeting of the president and prime minister with the Combined Chiefs of Staff [henceforth CCS], 23 August 1943, Eisenhower Library [henceforth EL], CCS, box 2, vol. 2.

50. CCS, 108th meeting, 15 August 1943, ibid.

51. See Gordon A. Harrison, *Cross-Channel Attack* (Washington, D.C.: U.S. Government Printing Office, 1951), 97.

52. U.S. Joint Chiefs of Staff [henceforth JCS], Memorandum, Strategic Concept for the Defeat of the Axis in Europe, 9 August 1943, EL, CCS, box 2.

53. Dwight D. Eisenhower, *Crusade in Europe* (Garden City, N.Y.: Doubleday, 1948), 167.

54. Alan Francis Brooke, *War Diaries, 1939–1945*, ed. Alex Danchev and Daniel Todman (London: Weidenfeld and Nicolson, 2001), 437.

55. Ralph Ingersoll, *Top Secret* (New York: Harcourt, Brace, 1946), 70.

56. See Geoffrey Perret, *There's a War to Be Won: The United States Army in World War II* (New York: Random House, 1991), 131–132.

57. See Wilmot, *The Struggle for Europe*, 131.

58. See Harrison, *Cross-Channel Attack*, 92ff; and McNeill, *America, Britain, and Russia*, 31.

59. See Matloff and Snell, *Strategic Planning for Coalition Warfare*, 2:109–111; and Stoler, *The Politics of the Second Front*, 79.

60. See Forrest C. Pogue, *The Supreme Command* (Washington, D.C.: Office of the Chief of Military History, Department of the Army, 1954), 37.

61. Ingersoll, *Top Secret*, 72.

62. On the conflict of Allied interests in designing postwar international institutions, see Robert Skidelsky, *John Maynard Keynes: Fighting for Freedom, 1937–1946* (London: Penguin, 2001), 179–372.

63. Georgii Zhukov, *The Memoirs of Marshal Zhukov* (New York: Delacorte, 1971), 493.

64. See Kimball, *The Juggler*, 70.

65. Telegram from Ivan Maisky to the People's Commissariat for Foreign Affairs (NKID), 13 February 1943, in *Soviet-British Relations in the Years of the Great Patriotic War, 1941–1945: Documents and Materials*, 2 vols. (Moscow, 1983), 1:339–340.

66. See Kimball, *The Juggler*, 37–40.

67. Quoted in Sherwood, *Roosevelt and Hopkins,* 641.

68. Quoted in Matloff and Snell, *Strategic Planning for Coalition Warfare,* 2:282.

69. John R. Deane, *The Strange Alliance: The Story of Our Efforts at Wartime Cooperation with Russia* (New York: Viking, 1947), 49.

70. Proposals Regarding the Staff of the British Naval Mission at Arkhangelsk, May 1944, Archive of Foreign Policy of the Russian Federation [henceforth AVP RF], collection 07, inv. 5, box 42, file 64, pp.6–14.

71. See Stoler, *The Politics of the Second Front,* 105.

72. Quoted in Gabriel Kolko, *The Politics of War: The World and United States Foreign Policy, 1943–1945* (New York: Random House, 1968), 29.

73. Stoler, *The Politics of the Second Front,* 122.

74. See Henri Michel, *La Seconde Guerre mondiale,* 2 vols., 2nd ed. (Paris: Presses Universitaires de France, 1977–1980), 537–562, 633–634.

75. See Ellis, et al., *The Battle of Normandy,* 53.

76. See Harrison, *Cross-Channel Attack,* 118.

77. John Ellis, *The World War II Databook: The Essential Facts and Figures for All the Combatants* (London: Aurum, 1993), 162.

78. See Matloff and Snell, *Strategic Planning for Coalition Warfare,* 2:391.

79. See Kolko, *The Politics of War,* 17.

80. Sherwood, *Roosevelt and Hopkins,* 591.

81. See Stoler, *The Politics of the Second Front,* 143.

82. Sherwood, *Roosevelt and Hopkins,* 776.

83. Christopher Andrew and Vasili Mitrokhin, *The Sword and the Shield: The Mitrokhin Archives and the Secret History of the KGB* (New York: Basic Books, 1999), 111.

84. Elliott Roosevelt, *As He Saw It* (New York: Duell, Sloan, and Pearce, 1946), 173.

85. Winston Churchill, *Closing the Ring* (Boston: Houghton Mifflin, 1951), 356.

86. See Andrew and Mitrokhin, *The Sword and the Shield,* 112.

87. Minutes of Plenary Sessions between the United States, Great Britain, and the USSR, 29 November 1943, in *Compendium of Documents* (Moscow, 1978), 128.

88. Eureka Conference, Minutes of Plenary Sessions between the United States, Great Britain, and the USSR, 29 November 1943, EL, CCS, box 2, vol. 3.

89. S. M. Shtemenko, *The Soviet General Staff at War, 1941–1945,* trans. Robert Daglish (Moscow: Progress, 1971), 262.

90. Churchill, *Closing the Ring,* 370.

91. Ibid., 373.

92. Eureka Conference, Minutes of Plenary Sessions between the United States, Great Britain, and the USSR, 29 November 1943, EL, CCS, box 2, vol. 3.

93. Sebastian Hassner, *Churchill,* trans. John Brownjohn (London: Haus, 2003), 133–135. [German edition published 1967.]

94. See Stoler, *The Politics of the Second Front,* 153.

95. Quoted in Roosevelt, *As He Saw It,* 244–245.

96. Ibid., 245.

## 2. Preparing for War

1. See William L. O'Neill, *A Democracy at War: America's Fight at Home and Abroad in World War II* (New York: Free Press, 1993), 215.

2. See André Kaspi, *Les Américains: Les États-Unis de 1607 à nos jours* (Paris: Seuil, 1986), 328.

3. See Theodore A. Wilson, "The United States: Leviathan," in David Reynolds et al., eds., *Allies at War: The Soviet, American, and British Experience, 1939–1945* (New York: St. Martin's, 1994), 173; and David Reynolds, *Rich Relations: The American Occupation of Britain, 1942–1945* (New York: Random House, 1995), 45.

4. See O'Neill, *A Democracy at War,* 75ff.

5. See Reynolds, *Rich Relations,* 53.

6. O'Neill, *A Democracy at War,* 10, 23, 100.

7. See the detailed analysis in Correlli Barnett, *The Audit of War: The Illusion and Reality of Britain as a Great Nation* (London: Macmillan, 1986), 108ff.

8. See Angus Calder, *The People's War: Britain, 1939–1945* (London: Jonathan Cape, 1969), 436–437.

9. Ibid., 455.

10. See Mark Harrison, *Accounting for War: Soviet Production, Employment and the Defence Burden, 1940–1945* (New York: Cambridge University Press, 1996), 132.

11. See Richard J. Overy et al., "Trade, Aid, and Technology," in Reynolds et al., *Allies at War,* 209.

12. See Richard J. Overy, "Great Britain: Cyclops," ibid., 121.

13. See Reynolds, *Rich Relations,* 50.

14. See Roland G. Ruppenthal, *Logistical Support of the Armies,* 2 vols. (Washington, D.C.: Office of the Chief of Military History, Department of the Army, 1953–1959), 1:257, 258.

15. See Overy, "Great Britain," 134.

16. Ralph Ingersoll, *Top Secret* (New York: Harcourt, Brace, 1946), 7–8.

17. See Geoffrey Perret, *There's a War to Be Won: The United States Army in World War II* (New York: Random House, 1991), 26–29.

18. Ibid., 32.

19. See Maurice Matloff and Edwin M. Snell, *Strategic Planning for Coalition Warfare, 1941–1944,* 2 vols. (Washington, D.C.: Office of the Chief of Military History, Department of the Army, 1953–1959), 2:114ff.

20. The number of troops per division varied by country, a German infantry division having on average 12,800 men in 1944, as opposed to 14,000 in the case of an American division; see Robert R. Palmer, "Mobilization of the Ground Army," study no. 4, Historical Section, 1946, Washington, D.C., National Archives and Records Administration (henceforth NARA), Record Group (henceforth RG) 337, entry 84A, box 9.

21. See Russell F. Weigley, *Eisenhower's Lieutenants: The Campaign of France and Germany, 1944–1945* (Bloomington: Indiana University Press, 1981), 16.

22. Ibid., 1–2.

23. Ibid., 17–18.

24. Ibid., 24–25.

25. See Perret, *There's a War to Be Won,* 105–106.

26. See Robert R. Palmer, "Procurement of Enlisted Personnel for the AGF: The Problem of Quality, 1946," NARA, RG 337, entry 84A, box 9.

27. See Army Research Branch, Services of Supply, "Attitudes of the Troops toward the War," 8 September 1942, NARA, RG 330, entry 93, box 989.

28. Ibid., "Attitudes of Troops toward the War and Our Allies," 30 November 1942, box 990.

29. Ibid., "Attitudes of Officers and Enlisted Men in Six Infantry Divisions toward the War and Our Allies," 16 July 1943, box 991.

30. See Army Research Division, "Preliminary Report on Opinions of Infantry and Artillery Officers and Men in a Single Division," 23 March 1943, ibid.

31. See Army Research Branch, "What the Front-Line Infantryman Thinks," 21 December 1943, ibid., box 992.

32. See Army Research Branch, Morale Division, "Comparison of Attitudes of Officers in Two Overseas Theaters," 30 April 1944, ibid.

33. Ibid.

34. See Army Research Branch, "What the Front-Line Infantryman Thinks."

35. See Jean-Louis Margolin, *L'armée de l'Empereur: Violences et crimes du Japon en guerre, 1937–1945* (Paris: Armand Colin, 2007), 168.

36. See Army Research Branch, "What the Front-Line Infantryman Thinks."

37. Lieutenant Colonel John C. Flanagan, Psychological Branch, "Report on Survey of Aircrew Personnel in the Eighth, Ninth, Twelfth, and Fifteenth Air Forces," April 1944, NARA, RG 112, entry 31 ZI, box 1315.

38. Mental Hygiene Consultation Service Conference, 8–10 January 1945, Aberdeen Proving Ground, Maryland (Tuesday A.M., 9 Jan. 1945, topic no. 2, Neuropsychiatric Disqualification Standards for Overseas Service), ibid., 1296. Emphasis in original.

39. Captain Rutherford B. Stevens, "Racial Aspects of Emotional Problems of Negro Soldiers," November 1945, ibid., box 1314.

40. Army Research Branch, Special Service Division, "Questions American Soldiers Say They Would Like to Ask General Eisenhower," May 1944, NARA, RG 330, entry 94, box 1019.

41. See O'Neill, *A Democracy at War,* 139–142.

42. Army Research Branch, Information and Education Division, "Report on Attitudes of Enlisted Men toward Army Talks," January 1944, NARA, RG 330, entry 94, box 1015.

43. Army Research Branch, Special Service Division, "Survey of Combat Crews in Heavy Bombardment Groups in ETO" [European theater of operations], June 1944, ibid.

44. Paul Fussell, *Wartime: Understanding and Behavior in the Second World War* (New York: Oxford University Press, 1989), 129, 137, 132.

45. Army Research Branch, "What Do Soldiers Think of the Home Front?" 18 March 1943, NARA, RG 330, entry 93, box 990.

46. Flanagan, "Report on Survey of Aircrew Personnel in the Eighth, Ninth, Twelfth, and Fifteenth Air Forces."

47. Entry for 4 March 1944 in Joseph Goebbels, *Journal: 1943-1945,* ed. and trans. Pierre Ayçoberry, Horst Möller, and Stefan Martens (Paris: Tallandier, 2005), 419.

48. See Calder, *The People's War,* 54.

49. Ibid., 267-270.

50. Ingersoll, *Top Secret,* 67.

51. War Office Council and Army Council Records, Morale Committee, 1942 August-1943 October, Morale Report, PRO, War Office, 163/161.

52. Ibid., 1943 November-1944 September, Morale Report: August-October 1943, and November 1943-January 1944, 163/162.

53. Ibid., 1942 August-1943 October, Morale Report: May-July 1943, 163/161.

54. War Office, Department of the Secretary of State of War, Private Office Papers (1937-1953), Army Morale: Paper by Adjutant General (10 May 1944), ibid., 259/44.

55. See War Office Council and Army Council Records, Morale Committee, 1943 November-1944 September, Morale Report: February-April 1944, ibid., 163/162.

56. See Summary of Court-Martial Convictions, 1 September 1939-31 August 1945, ibid., 93/53.

57. War Office Council and Army Council Records, Morale Committee, 1942 August-1943 October, Morale Report: May to July 1943, PRO, War Office, 163/161.

58. Ibid., 1943 November-1944 September, Morale Report: November 1943-January 1944, 163/162.

59. See Barnett, *The Audit of War,* 19ff.

60. Quoted in Stephen E. Ambrose, *D-Day, June 6, 1944: The Climactic Battle of World War II* (New York: Simon and Schuster, 1994), 50.

61. See Reynolds, *Rich Relations,* 333.

62. See Calder, *The People's War,* 248.

63. Ibid., 1943 November-1944 September, Morale Report: August 1943-October 1944, 163/162.

64. Ibid., November 1943 to January 1944.

65. See Charles Perry Stacey, *The Canadian Army, 1939-1945: An Official Historical Summary* (Ottawa: Edmond Cloutier, 1948), 1.

66. See Terry Copp, *Fields of Fire: The Canadians in Normandy* (Toronto: University of Toronto Press, 2003), 15.

67. Ibid., 16.

68. See Reynolds, *Rich Relations,* 136.

69. Quoted in Stacey, *The Canadian Army, 1939-1945,* 47.

70. See Reynolds, *Rich Relations,* 131ff.

71. Stacey, *The Canadian Army, 1939-1945,* 94.

## 3. Planning for D-Day

1. See Frederick Morgan, *Overture to Overlord* (London: Hodder and Stoughton, 1950), 64ff.

2. Ibid., 80ff. and 132–136.

3. Quoted in Gordon A. Harrison, *Cross-Channel Attack* (Washington, D.C.: U.S. Government Printing Office, 1951), 51.

4. Ralph Ingersoll, *Top Secret* (New York: Harcourt, Brace, 1946), 5.

5. Morgan, *Overture to Overlord,* 54–55.

6. Ibid., 143ff.

7. See General Morgan, "Operation Overlord, Report and Appreciation," 27 July 1943, EL, microfilm 31.

8. See General Omar Bradley, "Report of Operations," 20 October 1943–August 1944, 1945, PRO CAB, 106/1004.

9. Minutes of the second meeting held at HMS *Warren,* 28 June 1943, EL, SHAEF, secretary, general staff, microfilm 21.

10. General Morgan, "Operation Overlord, Report and Appreciation," 27 July 1943, EL, microfilm 31.

11. Liberation Campaign North-West Europe, 1944–1945, book 3, PRO CAB, 44/245.

12. Bernard Law Montgomery, *The Memoirs of Field-Marshal the Viscount Montgomery of Alamein* (London: Collins, 1958), 197, 230.

13. Lieutenant Colonel H. A. Pollock, Overlord: Plans and Preparations, 1940 to the "Touch-Down," PRO CAB, 44/242.

14. Dwight D. Eisenhower, *Crusade in Europe* (Garden City, N.Y.: Doubleday, 1948), 230.

15. Henry Stimson, Letter of 10 August 1943, quoted in Maurice Matloff and Edwin M. Snell, *Strategic Planning for Coalition Warfare, 1941–1944,* 2 vols. (Washington, D.C.: Office of the Chief of Military History, Department of the Army, 1953–1959), 2:214.

16. See Alan Francis Brooke, *War Diaries, 1939–1945,* ed. Alex Danchev and Daniel Todman (London: Weidenfeld and Nicolson, 1957), 420, 427, 429.

17. See Matloff and Snell, *Strategic Planning for Coalition Warfare,* 2:275.

18. See Robert E. Sherwood, *Roosevelt and Hopkins: An Intimate History* (New York: Harper and Brothers, 1948; rev. ed., 1950), 759–760.

19. See William D. Leahy, *I Was There: The Personal Story of the Chief of Staff to Presidents Roosevelt and Truman Based on His Notes and Diaries Made at the Time* (New York: Whittlesey House, 1950), 192.

20. Quoted in Sherwood, *Roosevelt and Hopkins,* 803.

21. See Stephen E. Ambrose, *The Supreme Commander: The War Years of General Dwight D. Eisenhower* (Garden City, N.Y.: Doubleday, 1970), 308.

22. Eisenhower, *Crusade in Europe,* 220; see also the account in Carlo D'Este, *Ei-*

*senhower: Allied Supreme Commander* (New York: Henry Holt, 2002), 461–465, 473–481.

23. See Ambrose, *The Supreme Commander,* 59, 319–326.

24. Montgomery, *Memoirs,* 484.

25. See Forrest C. Pogue, *The Supreme Command* (Washington, D.C.: Office of the Chief of Military History, Department of the Army, 1954), 96–97.

26. Minutes of Supreme Commander Conference, 21 January 1944, EL, Eisenhower Pre-Presidential Papers [henceforth EPPP] 136.

27. Entry for 3 February 1944 in Captain Harry C. Butcher, *My Three Years with Eisenhower: The Personal Diary of Captain Harry C. Butcher, USNR, Naval Aide to General Eisenhower, 1942–1945* (New York: Simon and Schuster, 1946), 486.

28. See Morgan, *Overture to Overlord,* 258.

29. Planning of Operation Overlord, 9 August 1945, PRO, War Office, 232/15.

30. Montgomery to Dempsey, 4 May 1944, ibid., 285/2.

31. See Ambrose, *The Supreme Commander,* 340.

32. Notes on a speech made by General Montgomery at a staff conference on future operations, 13 January 1944, PRO CAB, 106/1037.

33. See Hastings L. Ismay, *The Memoirs of Lord General Ismay* (London: Heinemann, 1960), 258–259, 263; on Eisenhower's insistence of the importance of teamwork, see Ambrose, *The Supreme Commander,* 338–346.

34. Minutes of Meeting between the President and the Chiefs of Staff, Held on Board Ship in the Admiral's Cabin, on Friday, 19 November 1943, at 1500, NARA, RG 218, JCS Titles, box 197.

35. Brooke, *War Diaries,* 365.

36. Ingersoll, *Top Secret,* 78.

37. Brooke, *War Diaries,* 505.

38. Eisenhower to Marshall, 18 January 1944, in *The Papers of Dwight David Eisenhower,* 21 vols. (Baltimore: Johns Hopkins University Press, 1970–2002), 3:1665.

39. See Max Hastings, *Overlord: D-Day and the Battle for Normandy* (London: Michael Joseph, 1984), 44–45.

40. See David Irving, *The War between the Generals* (London: Allen Lane, 1981), 15.

41. See Carlo D'Este, *Decision in Normandy: The Unwritten Story of Montgomery and the Allied Campaign* (London: Collins, 1994), 79.

42. See Hastings, *Overlord,* 31–32.

43. Geoffrey Perret, *There's a War to Be Won: The United States Army in World War II* (New York: Random House, 1991), 185.

44. Sherwood, *Roosevelt and Hopkins,* 811.

45. Omar N. Bradley, *A Soldier's Story* (New York: Holt, 1951), 209.

46. See Perret, *There's a War to Be Won,* 303.

47. Ibid., 41.

48. Martin Blumenson, *Patton: The Man behind the Legend, 1885–1945* (New York: William Morrow, 1985), 210.

49. Ambrose, *The Supreme Commander,* 342; see also notes to Chapter 5.

50. Bradley, *A Soldier's Story,* 231.

51. Chief of staff, Historical Sub-Section, "History of COSSAC," May 1944, EL, Bedell Smith, microfilm 33.

52. See Pogue, *The Supreme Command,* 52.

53. Directive to the Supreme Commander of the Allied Expeditionary Force, 12 February 1944; quoted in *D-Day and VE Day: General Eisenhower's Report, 1944–1945* (London: H. M. Stationery Office, 2000), 3.

54. Eisenhower, *Crusade in Europe,* 221.

55. See *The Papers of Dwight David Eisenhower,* 3:1784.

56. Pogue, *The Supreme Command,* 125.

57. SHAEF, Directive of 21 March 1944, PRO CAB, 106/1106.

58. Ingersoll, *Top Secret,* 87.

59. Bradley, *A Soldier's Story,* 221.

60. Quoted in Chester Wilmot, *The Struggle for Europe* (London: Collins, 1952), 174.

61. See General Eisenhower to General Marshall, 23 January 1944, EL, EPPP/130.

62. See Harrison, *Cross-Channel Attack,* 165–166.

63. See Matloff and Snell, *Strategic Planning for Coalition Warfare,* 2:378.

64. See Chief of staff, Historical Sub-Section, "History of COSSAC," May 1944.

65. General Eisenhower to General Marshall, 23 January 1944, EL, EPPP, 130.

66. Montgomery, *Memoirs,* 199.

67. See General Montgomery to General Eisenhower, 18 February 1944, EL, EPPP, box 83.

68. See Ambrose, *The Supreme Commander,* 336.

69. Eisenhower, *Crusade in Europe,* 231.

70. Prime minister to Field Marshal Dill for General Marshall, 12 April 1944, EL, SHAEF, secretary, general staff, microfilm 24.

71. Combined Chiefs of Staff Directive, 19 April 1944, EL, SHAEF, secretary, general staff, microfilm 24.

72. Brooke, *War Diaries,* 541.

73. SHAEF, "Neptune Joint Fire Plan," 8 April 1944, PRO CAB, 106/1003.

74. See Harrison, *Cross-Channel Attack,* 194–196.

75. See SHAEF, "Neptune Joint Fire Plan."

76. See Lionel Frederic Ellis et al., *The Battle of Normandy* (London: H. M. Stationery Office, 1962), 34.

77. See Wilmot, *The Struggle for Europe,* 233.

78. Bradley, *A Soldier's Story,* 242.

79. Directive to the Supreme Commander of the Allied Expeditionary Force, 12 February 1944; quoted in *D-Day and VE Day,* 3.

80. Captain P. M. Walter, Brigadier K. G. McLean, Group Captain H. P. Broad, "Post-Neptune Courses of Action after Capture of Lodgment Area," 3 May 1944, NARA, RG 331, entry 35, box 225.

81. Eisenhower, *Crusade in Europe*, 225.

82. Entry for 17 September 1944 in Joseph Goebbels, *Journal: 1943–1945*, ed. and trans. Pierre Ayçoberry, Horst Möller, and Stefan Martens (Paris: Tallandier, 2005), 611.

83. See Harrison, *Cross-Channel Attack*, 184ff.

84. See War Office Staff, College Camberley, 1947 course notes on D-Day landings and ensuing campaigns (1947), Sixth Airborne Division, Report on Operations, 5 June to 3 September 44, PRO, War Office, 223/14.

85. Air Chief Marshal Leigh-Mallory, "Employment of Airborne Forces in Operation Overlord," 23 April 1944, EL, SHAEF, secretary, general staff, microfilm 25.

86. Bradley, *A Soldier's Story*, 234.

87. Air Chief Marshal Leigh-Mallory, "Employment of U.S. Airborne Forces in Operation Overlord," 29 May 1944, EL, SHAEF, secretary, general staff, microfilm 25.

88. Eisenhower, *Crusade in Europe*, 246.

89. General Eisenhower to Leigh-Mallory, Letter, 30 May 1944, EL, SHAEF, secretary, general staff, microfilm 25.

90. Eisenhower, *Crusade in Europe*, 245.

91. Carlo D'Este has argued that "Eisenhower was wholly misled by the Prime Minister's meaning which was, in General Ismay's words, an expression 'you had often used to me and I had taken it to mean that the more you thought about it the more certain you were of success.' . . . Although this incident was in itself relatively minor, it did, unfortunately, reflect the sort of misunderstandings that occurred during the planning and execution of OVERLORD even between Churchill and Eisenhower, who both went to great lengths to ensure each understood the other's views"; see D'Este, *Decision in Normandy*, 87–88.

92. Report of the Meteorological Implications in Selection of D-Day for the Allied Invasion of France, PRO CAB, 106/976.

93. Eisenhower, *Crusade in Europe*, 231.

94. See Harrison, *Cross-Channel Attack*, 189.

95. See Bernard Law Montgomery, *Normandy to the Baltic* (London: Hutchinson, 1947), 25–26.

96. Bradley, *A Soldier's Story*, 260–261.

97. See Russell F. Weigley, *Eisenhower's Lieutenants: The Campaign of France and Germany, 1944–1945* (Bloomington: Indiana University Press, 1981), 32.

98. See entry for 8 May 1943, Joseph Goebbels, *The Goebbels Diaries, 1942–1943*, trans. Louis P. Lochner (New York: Doubleday, 1948), 359.

## 4. Logistics, Training, Rehearsals

1. See Admiral Ramsay, "Official Report to General Eisenhower," October 1944, 1:128, EL, Bedell Smith Papers, box 33.

2. See General Eisenhower to CCS and BCOS, 23 January 1944, in *The Papers of Dwight David Eisenhower*, 21 vols. (Baltimore: Johns Hopkins University Press, 1970–2002), 3:1674.

3. See Gordon A. Harrison, *Cross-Channel Attack* (Washington, D.C.: U.S. Government Printing Office, 1951), 61–63.

4. See Trumbull Higgins, *Winston Churchill and the Second Front, 1940–1943* (New York: Oxford University Press, 1957), 108–109, 183; Russell F. Weigley, *Eisenhower's Lieutenants: The Campaign of France and Germany, 1944–1945* (Bloomington: Indiana University Press, 1981), 41–42.

5. War Cabinet, Chiefs of Staff Committee, memorandum by the first sea lord, "Landing Ships and Craft Requirements for 1944–1945," 14 March 1944, PRO CAB, 119/93.

6. See War Cabinet, Chiefs of Staff Committee, memorandum by the vice chief of naval staff, "Availability of Landing Craft (Tanks) for Overlord," 22 September 1943, PRO, Headquarters and Ministry of Defence, 2/460.

7. See Monk, Office of the War Cabinet, Aide Mémoire for Meeting with Controller, brief to Robert Sinclair, minister of production, 31 March 1944, PRO, War Office, 193/396.

8. See Major O. G. Villiers to S. Stanes, Admiralty, 21 December 1945, PRO, Home Office, 201/36.

9. CCS, Allocation of Landing Ships and Craft—American Production, memorandum from the United States Chiefs of Staff, 19 August 1943, PRO, Ministry of Defence, 2/460.

10. Winston S. Churchill, *Closing the Ring*, vol. 5 of *The Second World War* (Boston: Houghton Mifflin, 1951), 364.

11. Quoted in Carlo D'Este, *Eisenhower: Allied Supreme Commander* (New York: Holt, 2002), 463.

12. See William O'Neill, *A Democracy at War: America's Fight at Home and Abroad in World War II* (New York: Free Press, 1993), 222–224.

13. CCS, 111th Meeting, 18 August 1943, NARA, RG 218, CCS-JCS Titles, box 499.

14. See JCS, note by the secretaries, "Landing Ships and Craft—Means of Increasing U.S. Production," 8 September 1943, NARA, RG 218, JCS 461-2, box 499.

15. See JCS, no. 462, report by the Joint Administrative Committee, "Landing Ships and Craft—Means of Increasing U.S. Production," Reference CCS 329/2, 30 August 1943, NARA, RG 218, JCS 462, box 499.

16. See Lionel Frederic Ellis et al., *The Battle of Normandy* (London: H. M. Stationery Office, 1962), 34–35.

17. Ibid., 36; Eisenhower to CCS and BCOS, 23 January 1944, in *The Papers of Dwight David Eisenhower*, 3:1675.

18. Joint Planning Staff, "Landing Ships and Craft, 1944," 16 May 1943, PRO CAB, 119/63.

19. Joint Planning Staff, "Landing Ships and Craft, American Production," 28 July 1943, ibid.

20. War Cabinet, meeting of 18 May 1944, PRO CAB, 65/42.

21. See Joint Planning Staff, "Landing Ships and Craft," 16 May 1943, PRO, Ministry of Defence, 2/1114.

22. Monk, Office of the War Cabinet, to Major C. J. Malim G.S. (P), 31 March 1944, PRO, War Office, 193/396.

23. See Joint Planning Staff, "Landing Ships and Craft," 16 May 1943.

24. See Chiefs of Staff, meeting of 23 March 1944, NARA, RG 331, entry 1, box 76.

25. Joint Planning Staff, "Landing Ships and Craft, 1944–45," 13 October 1943, PRO CAB, 119/63.

26. See General Eisenhower to General Handy, 26 January 1944, in *The Papers of Dwight David Eisenhower*, 3:1688.

27. See Chiefs of Staff of Allied Expeditionary Forces, 18 February 1944, NARA, RG 331, entry 1, box 76.

28. General Bedell Smith, "Reassessment of Assault Shipping and Craft Required for Overlord," n.d. [February 1944], PRO, Ministry of Defence, 2/460; first sea lord, Landing Crafts and Ships for Overlord, 20 February 1944, ibid.

29. See Chiefs of Staff, Allied Expeditionary Forces, 13 February 1944, NARA, RG 331, entry 1, box 76.

30. Admiral Ramsay, "Report to the Allied Naval Commander in Chief, Expeditionary Forces on Operation Neptune," 16 October 1944, NARA, RG 331, entry 279, box 4.

31. General Bedell Smith to chief of staff and War Cabinet, Note, 10 February 1944, NARA, RG 331, entry 1, box 76.

32. See Harrison, *Cross-Channel Attack*, 127.

33. See General Eisenhower to General Marshall, 21 March 1944, in *The Papers of Dwight David Eisenhower*, 3:1777.

34. Combined Operations Headquarters and Ministry of Defence, Extract of Defence Committee Meeting, 2 November 1943, PRO, Ministry of Defence, 2/460.

35. See Chester Wilmot, *The Struggle for Europe* (London: Collins, 1952), 180.

36. Quoted in Maurice Matloff and Edwin M. Snell, *Strategic Planning for Coalition Warfare, 1941–1944*, 2 vols. (Washington, D.C.: Office of the Chief of Military History, Department of the Army, 1953–1959), 2:422.

37. Ibid., 400–401.

38. For the first set of figures, see Admiral Ramsay, "Report by the Allied Naval Commander in Chief Expeditionary Forces on Operation Neptune," 16 October 1944, NARA, RG 331, entry 279, box 4; for the second, Annex to the Memorandum XF of 29 March 1944, NARA, RG 331, entry 34, box 86.

39. These words, first used in a telegram addressed to General Marshall (see PRO CAB, 101/250), were later employed in Churchill, *Closing the Ring*, 514.

40. See Roland G. Ruppenthal, *Logistical Support of the Armies*, 2 vols. (Washington, D.C.: Office of the Chief of Military History, Department of the Army, 1953–1959), 1:186–187.

41. See Harrison, *Cross-Channel Attack*, 73.

42. See Director of port and inland water transport, Historical Survey, PRO CAB, 106/968.

43. The term "Mulberry harbors" (or simply "Mulberries") derived from the origi-

nal code name for the operation, MULBERRY; the breakwaters and anchorages similarly took their names from companion operations.

44. See Harrison, *Cross-Channel Attack,* 73–74; and Georges Blond, *Le débarquement, 6 juin 1944* (Paris: Livre de Poche, 1951), 68–71 [1st ed., Paris: Fayard, 1951].

45. See Ruppenthal, *Logistical Support of the Armies,* 1:280.

46. See Blond, *Le débarquement,* 73–74.

47. See Major General Sir Harold Wernher, Note, 21 February 1944, NARA, RG 331, entry 56, box 118.

48. See unsigned and undated note (probably February 1944), NARA, RG 331, entry 56, box 118.

49. See Ruppenthal, *Logistical Support of the Armies,* 1:281.

50. Sir Walter Monckton, "The Role Played in Overlord by the Synthetic Harbours," 12 October 1945, PRO, Ministry of Defence, 2/498.

51. See Matloff and Snell, *Strategic Planning for Coalition Warfare,* 2:391.

52. Ibid., 407.

53. See Ruppenthal, *Logistical Support of the Armies,* 1:234.

54. War Cabinet, meeting of 17 January 1944, PRO CAB, 65/41.

55. War Cabinet Minutes, 18 May 1944, PRO CAB, 118/68.

56. See Ruppenthal, *Logistical Support of the Armies,* 1:237–239.

57. In this connection, see David Reynolds, *Rich Relations: The American Occupation of Britain, 1942–1945* (New York: Random House, 1995).

58. Ibid., 112.

59. War Cabinet, meeting of 28 February 1944, cabinet 65/41.

60. See Major John B. Stanley, "Attitude toward England," 11 June 1942, NARA, RG 330, entry 93, box 989.

61. See Army Research Branch, "Attitudes of Troops toward the War and Our Allies," 30 November 1942, NARA, RG 330, entry 93, box 990.

62. See Army Research Branch, "Attitudes of Troops toward the War," 8 September 1942, NARA, RG 330, entry 93, box 989.

63. General Omar Bradley, Report of Operations, 20 October 1943–1 August 1944, 1945, PRO CAB, 106/1004.

64. See Reynolds, *Rich Relations,* 30ff.

65. See, on all these points, ibid., chap. 10, "U.S. and Them," 143ff.

66. Marc Hillel, *Vie et moeurs des GI's en Europe, 1942–1947* (Paris: Balland, 1981), 31–32.

67. See Reynolds, *Rich Relations,* 262ff.

68. Ibid., 81ff.

69. See Army Research Branch, "Attitude of Enlisted Men toward Negroes for Air Force Duty," 30 November 1942, NARA, RG 330, entry 93, box 990.

70. Army Research Branch, "Attitudes of White Enlisted Men toward Sharing Facilities with Negro Troops," 30 July 1942, ibid., box 989.

71. See Army Research Branch, "What the Soldier Thinks," August 1943, ibid., box 990.

72. Reynolds, *Rich Relations,* 84.

73. Quoted in Hillel, *Vie et moeurs des GI's en Europe,* 68. [Translated from the French.—Trans.]

74. Army Research Branch, "What the Soldier Thinks," August 1943.

75. See Reynolds, *Rich Relations,* 232–233.

76. See General Omar Bradley, Report of Operations 20 October–1 August 1944, 1945, PRO CAB, 106/1004.

77. Army Research Branch, "Attitudes toward the British Officers and Enlisted Men in Six Infantry Divisions," 2 June 1943, NARA, RG 330, entry 93, box 991.

78. Army Research Branch, "What the Soldier Thinks: A Monthly Digest of War Department on the Attitudes of American Troops," no. 2, January 1944, NARA, RG 330, entry 93, box 1004.

79. Curtis J. Siats, Capt. Inf., Chief Base Censor, Digest of Morale Reports, 1–15 February 1944, 15 February 1944, NARA, RG 498, Admiralty, 212, box 41.

80. Susie J. Thurman, Capt. (WAC), History Section, Digest of Anglo-American Relations from Censor's Report, 1–15 March 1944, 21 April 1944, ibid.

81. War Office Council and Army Council Records, Morale Committee, report for November 1943–January 1944, PRO, War Office, 163/162.

82. See Reynolds, *Rich Relations,* 331.

83. Ibid., 75–76.

84. See Michael D. Doubler, *Closing with the Enemy: How GIs Fought the War in Europe, 1944–1945* (Lawrence: University Press of Kansas, 1994), 30–31.

85. See Army Research Branch, "Preliminary Report on Opinions of Infantry and Artillery Officers and Men in a Single Division," March 1943, NARA, RG 330, entry 93, box 991.

86. See Army Research Branch, "What the Soldier Thinks," March 1944, NARA, RG 330, entry 93, box 1004.

87. See Army Research Branch, Special Service Division, "A Report on Attitudes and Morale in the 4th Infantry Division," April 1944, NARA, RG 330, entry 94, box 1019.

88. See Army Research Branch, "Attitudes and Morale of Men in Five Divisions in the First Army," February 1944, NARA, RG 330, entry 93, box 1019.

89. See General De Guingand, "Interim Report on Equipment in the Early Stages of Operation Overlord," 10 August 1944, PRO, War Office, 205/901.

90. See General Omar Bradley, Report of Operations, 20 October 1943–1 August 1944, 1945, PRO CAB, 106/1004.

91. See Fabius Exercise, note of 13 April 1944, PRO, War Office, 199/2326.

92. See Ruppenthal, *Logistical Support of the Armies,* 1:351ff.

93. Admiral Ramsay, Official Report to General Eisenhower, October 1944, 1:128, EL, Bedell Smith Papers, box 33. The American military historian Charles B. McDonald has given a still more somber account: the assigned escort consisted only of a corvette and a World War I–era destroyer (which, having been damaged in a prior collision, had put into port and was not replaced), and casualties amounted to 749. McDonald

also disposes of sensational claims that the Exercise Tiger debacle was covered up by the U.S. government. See "Slapton Sands: The Cover-Up that Never Was," *Army* 38, no. 6 (1988): 64–67; see also D'Este, *Eisenhower*, 515–516; and *http://www.history .navy.mil/faqs/faq20-2.htm*.

94. Paul Fussell, *Wartime: Understanding and Behavior in the Second World War* (New York: Oxford University Press, 1989), 25.

95. Unsigned note, "Working of a Beach Group," 26 April 1944, PRO, War Office, 107/169.

96. See Ruppenthal, *Logistical Support of the Armies*, 1:347, 349.

97. Entry of 28 April 1944 in Captain Harry C. Butcher, *My Three Years with Eisenhower: The Personal Diary of Captain Harry C. Butcher, USNR, Naval Aide to General Eisenhower, 1942–1945* (New York: Simon and Schuster, 1946), 531.

98. Ralph Ingersoll, *Top Secret* (New York: Harcourt, Brace, 1946), 101.

99. Omar N. Bradley, *A Soldier's Story* (New York: Holt, 1951), 249.

## 5. STRATEGIES AND STRATAGEMS

1. Patrick Facon, *Le bombardement stratégique* (Monaco: Éditions du Rocher, 1995), 158, 159.

2. Ibid., 161.

3. See Gordon A. Harrison, *Cross-Channel Attack* (Washington, D.C.: U.S. Government Printing Office, 1951), 213–214.

4. See U.S. Strategic Bombing Survey, Military Analysis Division, "The Defeat of the German Air Force," n.d., NARA, RG 243, entry 6, box 476.

5. See Arthur William Tedder, *With Prejudice: The War Memoirs of Marshal of the Air Force, Lord Tedder* (London: Cassell, 1966), 510.

6. Ibid., 513.

7. See Russell F. Weigley, *Eisenhower's Lieutenants: The Campaign of France and Germany, 1944–1945* (Bloomington: Indiana University Press, 1981), 61.

8. See Directive by the SC [Supreme Commander] to USSTAF and BC [Bomber Command] for Support of Overlord, 17 April 1944, NARA, RG 331, entry 12, box 10.

9. See G2 [U.S. Military Intelligence], "Enemy Rail Requirements at the Time of Overlord," 15 March 1944, ibid., box 9.

10. See G2 to A[ssistant] Chief of Staff, 11 April 1944, ibid., box 10.

11. See Harrison, *Cross-Channel Attack*, 222.

12. Lieutenant Colonel J. O. Ewart for Major General A[ssistant] Chief of Staff, G2, 22 April 1944, NARA, RG 331, entry 12, box 10.

13. See Forrest C. Pogue, *The Supreme Command* (Washington, D.C.: Office of the Chief of Military History, Department of the Army, 1954), 127ff.

14. See F. H. Hinsley et al., *British Intelligence in the Second World War*, vol. 3 (London and Cambridge: H. M. Stationery Office / Cambridge University Press, 1988), 112.

15. See Weigley, *Eisenhower's Lieutenants*, 67.

16. See Pogue, *The Supreme Command,* 132.

17. See Basil H. Liddell Hart, *History of the Second World War* (London: Cassell, 1970), 607.

18. Combined Services Intelligence Committee, meeting of 1 June 1944, NARA, RG 331, entry 12, box 13.

19. See Max Hastings, *Overlord: D-Day and the Battle for Normandy* (London: Michael Joseph, 1984), 43.

20. U.S. Strategic Bombing Survey, V Weapons (Crossbow), 1947, NARA, RG 243, entry 6, box 476.

21. See Confidential Annex, 3 April 1944, PRO CAB 65/46.

22. See Confidential Annex, ibid., 27 April 1944.

23. General Eisenhower to Winston Churchill, 5 April 1944, in *The Papers of Dwight David Eisenhower,* 21 vols. (Baltimore: Johns Hopkins University Press, 1970–2002), 3:1809.

24. See Harrison, *Cross-Channel Attack,* 223.

25. General Eisenhower to Winston Churchill, 2 May 1944, in *The Papers of Dwight David Eisenhower,* 3:1844.

26. Annex, 27 April 1944.

27. For quotation see intervention of Admiral Leahy, JCS meeting, 16 May 1944, NARA, RG 218, JCS Titles, box 197.

28. General Eisenhower to Air Commander in Chief AEAF [Leigh-Mallory]; Air Officer Commander in Chief, Bomber Command [Harris]; Commanding General, USSTAF [Spaatz], 2 June 1944, in *The Papers of Dwight David Eisenhower,* 3:1903.

29. See Eddy Florentin, *Quand les Alliés bombardaient la France, 1940-1945* (Paris: Perrin, 2004), 426.

30. See Weigley, *Eisenhower's Lieutenants,* 70.

31. Georgii Zhukov, *The Memoirs of Marshal Zhukov* (New York: Delacorte, 1971), 493.

32. Robert E. Sherwood, *Roosevelt and Hopkins: An Intimate History,* rev. ed. (New York: Harper and Brothers, 1950), 804.

33. See Mark Harrison, *Accounting for War: Soviet Production, Employment and the Defence Burden, 1940-1945* (New York: Cambridge University Press, 1996), 132. A pound sterling at this time was equal to about four American dollars.

34. The figure for Great Britain covers the period from July 1943 to September 1945.

35. See Richard J. Overy, *Russia's War: A History of the Soviet War Effort, 1941-1945* (London: Penguin, 1997), 195.

36. See Harrison, *Accounting for War,* 133, 110, 142.

37. See John R. Deane, *The Strange Alliance: The Story of Our Efforts at Wartime Cooperation with Russia* (New York: Viking, 1947), 94.

38. See Harrison, *Accounting for War,* 153.

39. See William Hardy McNeil, *America, Britain, and Russia: Their Cooperation and Conflict, 1941-1946* (London: Oxford University Press, 1952), 239.

40. See Josef Schröder, "Bestrebungen zur Eliminierung der Ostfront, 1941-1943,"

in Michael Salewski and Josef Schröder, eds., *Dienst für die Geschichte: Gedenkschrift für Walther Hubatsch, 17 Mai 1915–29 Dezember 1984* (Göttingen: Muster-Schmidt, 1985), 226.

41. See Gerhard L. Weinberg, *A World at Arms: A Global History of World War II* (New York: Cambridge University Press, 1994), 609–611.

42. Joseph Goebbels, *Journal: 1943–1945,* ed. and trans. Pierre Ayçoberry, Horst Möller, and Stefan Martens (Paris: Tallandier, 2005), 235.

43. See McNeil, *America, Britain, and Russia,* 326.

44. Ibid., 330ff.

45. See Deane, *The Strange Alliance,* 21–22.

46. Quotation ibid., 20.

47. Ibid., 64–65.

48. Ibid., 118ff.

49. See Military Mission of the United States to Major General Slavin, 29 February 1944, AVP RF, collection 06, box 24, file 249; Second Report on Operation Overlord, ibid.; Report of the British and American Military Missions, ibid. All three reports are in Russian.

50. See War Office, Note for the CCS, 18 May 1944, PRO, War Office, 193/670. General Burrows had argued for the need to do so several days earlier; see War Office, Directorate of Military Operations and Plans, Co-ordination with U.S.S.R. (1943 September–1945 June), Telegram Top Secret from Military Mission, Moscow to the War Office, 4 April 1944, ibid.

51. Quotation in Deane, *The Strange Alliance,* 48.

52. S. M. Shtemenko, *The Soviet General Staff at War, 1941–1945,* trans. Robert Daglish (Moscow: Progress, 1971), 266.

53. Deane, *The Strange Alliance,* 142.

54. War Office, Directorate of Military Operations and Plans, Co-ordination with the U.S.S.R. (1943 September–1945 June), Telegram from Mission to Air Ministry (General Burrows) to Chiefs of Staff, 10 April 1944, PRO, War Office, 193/670.

55. See General Burrows to chief of staff, 19 May 1944, War Office 106/4162.

56. See Overy, *Russia's War,* 240.

57. Deane, *The Strange Alliance,* 84–85.

58. See David M. Glantz and Jonathan M. House, *When Titans Clashed: How the Red Army Stopped Hitler* (Lawrence: University Press of Kansas, 1995), 283.

59. Sir John Dill, Minutes of CCS 150th Meeting, 17 March 1944, NARA, RG 218, CCS-JCS titles, box 172.

60. Deane, *The Strange Alliance,* 143.

61. See Michael Howard, *Strategic Deception* (London and Cambridge: H. M. Stationery Office / Cambridge University Press, 1990), 71–83, 104–105.

62. Quoted ibid., 105.

63. Ibid., 107.

64. See Plan Bodyguard, Report by the Controlling Officer, PRO CAB, 119/6; and

Joint Planning Staff, "Bodyguard Plan," 24 December 1943, NARA, RG 218, CCS-JCS Titles, box 367.

65. Hitler refers in this directive particularly to the Pas de Calais region, where launch facilities were being constructed for pilotless and rocket weapons: "There—unless all indications are misleading—will be fought the decisive invasion battle"; see John Keegan, *Six Armies in Normandy: From D-Day to the Liberation of Paris* (London: Penguin, 1994), 60–61. The full text of the directive can be found at *http://www.feldgrau.com/dir51.html.*

66. See F. H. Hinsley et al., *British Intelligence in the Second World War: Its Influence on Strategy and Operations,* vol. 3, part 2 (London and Cambridge: H. M. Stationery Office / Cambridge University Press, 1988), 32ff.

67. Joint Planning Staff, Bodyguard Plan, n.d. [probably January 1944], NARA, RG 218, CCS-JCS Titles, box 367.

68. See SHAEF, "Fortitude," 23 February 1943, NARA, RG 331, entry 1, box 73.

69. See R. MacLeod, "A Short History of the Deception or 'Cover Plan' for the Normandy Campaign in 1944," 1954, PRO CAB, 106/1122.

70. Anthony Cave Brown, *Bodyguard of Lies* (London: W. H. Allen, 1975), 466.

71. See, on responsibility for deception schemes, ibid., 1–5.

72. See Draft Agreement on the Bodyguard Plan, 12 February 1944, AVP RF, collection 06, inv. 6, box 24, file 244.

73. The Undertakings of the Soviet Side for the Bodyguard Plan, ibid., file 71.

74. Minutes of the Meeting between Molotov and Ambassador Kerr, 5 May 1944, ibid., box 1, file 16.

75. Joint Planning Staff, "Russian Co-operation in Plan 'Bodyguard,'" 18 May 1944, EL, EPPP, microfilm 28.

76. See General Deane to War Department, 19 May 1944, NARA, RG 218, CCS-JCS titles, box 367.

77. See Brown, *Bodyguard of Lies,* 472.

78. See SHAEF, "Fortitude," 23 February 1943, NARA, RG, 331, entry 1, box 73.

79. See Brown, *Bodyguard of Lies,* 477–478. [A local historian, Joan Leach, citing eyewitness accounts, maintains that Patton actually did refer to the Russians, in addition to the British and Americans, but that this mention was deliberately deleted from press reports by an agent of the British Ministry of Information; Cave Brown, without going so far, nonetheless supports Patton's own view that the incident was contrived by LCS and the Allied Supreme Command, in order to draw German attention to him as part of the QUICKSILVER deception scheme.—Trans.]

80. Ibid., 480.

81. See J. F. M. Whiteley (SHAEF) to chief of staff, 11 June 1944, EL, SHAEF, secretary, general staff, microfilm 30; and Jean Quellien, *Le débarquement et la bataille de Normandie: La Normandie au coeur de la guerre* (Caen and Rennes: Mémorial de Caen / Éditions Ouest-France, 1998), 63.

82. On the number of Abwehr agents working for MI5, see Hastings, *Overlord,* 61.

83. Even his name is a matter of some confusion. In his autobiography, *Operation Garbo: The Personal Story of the Most Successful Double Agent of World War II* (New York: Random House, 1985), he claims to have been baptized Juan Pujol García, but in England during the war and in the archives of the U.S. National Counterintelligence Center he was known as Juan Piyol. For a detailed account of the affair, see Christian Destremau, *Opération Garbo: Le dernier secret du Jour J* (Paris: Perrin, 2004); and Brown, *Bodyguard of Lies*, 481–483.

84. See Destremau, *Opération Garbo*, 81.

85. See F. H. Hinsley and C. A. G. Simkins, *Security and Counter-Intelligence* (London and Cambridge: H. M. Stationery Office / Cambridge University Press, 1990), 227.

86. See the account of the Garbo operation in chapter 1 of Frank J. Rafalko, *A Counterintelligence Reader: World War II* (Washington, D.C.: National Counterintelligence Center, 1998).

87. See Destremau, *Opération Garbo*, 80–81. Cave Brown gives still higher figures (400 letters and 2,000 messages) for 1943–1944; see *Bodyguard of Lies*, 482.

88. Howard, *Strategic Deception*, 122 (italics in the original).

89. See Brown, *Bodyguard of Lies*, 487–492.

90. See ibid., 483–485.

91. See Howard, *Strategic Deception*, 121.

92. See Destremau, *Opération Garbo*, 147–148.

93. Ibid., 155.

94. See Brown, *Bodyguard of Lies*, 487–492.

95. See Thaddeus Holt, *The Deceivers: Allied Military Deception in the Second World War* (New York: Simon and Schuster, 2004), 830.

96. See Brigadier Dudley Clarke, Plan Zeppelin, 1st Approved Version, n.d., PRO CAB, 119/06.

97. See General Wilson to Air Ministry for chief of staff, 16 April, ibid.

98. See Chief of staff to Commander in Chief Middle East, 1 June 1944, ibid.

99. See Howard, *Strategic Deception*, 148–149.

100. See Joint Planning Staff, Plan Royal Flush, 11 May 1944, PRO CAB 119/6.

## 6. THE OTHER SIDE OF THE HILL

1. Adolf Hitler, speech of 20 March 1944, quoted in Erwin Rommel, *The Rommel Papers*, ed. B. H. Liddell Hart (New York: Harcourt, Brace, 1953), 466.

2. Personal communication to the author from Richard J. Overy.

3. See Richard J. Overy, *War and Economy in the Third Reich* (Oxford: Clarendon, 1994), 346, 247, 358. [The official rate of exchange for Reichsmarks (RM) into U.S. dollars (USD) in 1940 was 2.499 RM per 1 USD. It jumped the next year by a factor of almost eight, to 19.723 RM. Between December 1941 and the end of 1944, Reichsmarks could not be converted into dollars; subsequently, in areas under Allied control the rate of exchange was fixed at 10 RM per 1 USD.—Trans.]

4. See Michel Hau, *Histoire économique de l'Allemagne, XIXe-XXe siècles* (Paris: Economica, 1994), 143, 145.

5. See Alan S. Milward, "Économie de guerre," in Jean-Pierre Azéma and François Bédarida, eds., *1938–1948: Les années de tourmente: De Munich à Prague* (Paris: Flammarion, 1997), 181.

6. See Patrick Facon, *Le bombardement stratégique* (Monaco: Éditions du Rocher, 1995), 181, 175–176.

7. Ibid., 178.

8. Richard J. Overy, "Air Power in the Second World War: Historical Themes and Theories," in Horst Boog, ed., *The Conduct of the Air War in the Second World War: An International Comparison* (New York: Berg, 1992), 23.

9. Figures from Richard J. Overy, personal communication.

10. See Max Hastings, *Overlord: D-Day and the Battle for Normandy* (London: Michael Joseph, 1984), 42.

11. See Russell F. Weigley, *Eisenhower's Lieutenants: The Campaign of France and Germany, 1944–1945* (Bloomington: Indiana University Press, 1981), 69.

12. Entry for 3 June 1944 in Joseph Goebbels, *Journal: 1943–1945*, ed. and trans. Pierre Ayçoberry, Horst Möller, and Stefan Martens (Paris: Tallandier, 2005), 456.

13. See Hastings, *Overlord*, 43.

14. See Gordon A. Harrison, *Cross-Channel Attack* (Washington, D.C.: U.S. Government Printing Office, 1951), 265–266.

15. This figure includes some 60,000 foreign volunteers and *Osttruppen;* the total number of troops stationed in the Channel sector (France, Belgium, and Holland), including ground units of the Kriegsmarine and the Luftwaffe, was 1.4 million. See Dieter Ose, *Entscheidung im Westen 1944: Der Oberbefehlshaber West und die Abwehr der aliierten Invasion* (Stuttgart: Deutsche Verlags-Anstalt, 1982), 73.

16. See Hastings, *Overlord*, 184.

17. Report of the Activities of Sections IIa/IIb of the Staff of the Seventh Army, 1 January–31 March 1944.

18. See Hastings, *Overlord*, 64.

19. See John Keegan, *Six Armies in Normandy: From D-Day to the Liberation of Paris* (London: Penguin, 1994), 61.

20. See B. H. Liddell Hart, *The Other Side of the Hill: Germany's Generals, Their Rise and Fall, with Their Own Account of Military Events, 1939–1945*, rev. edition (London: Cassell, 1951), 389–390.

21. See Karl Gundelach, "Drohende Gefahr West: Die Deutsche Luftwaffe vor und während der Invasion 1944," *Wehrwissenschaftliche Rundschau* 9 (1959): 306.

22. See Keegan, *Six Armies in Normandy*, 61–62.

23. Quoted in Friedrich Ruge, *Rommel in Normandy: Reminiscences*, trans. Ursula R. Moessner (San Rafael, Calif.: Presidio, 1979), 15.

24. Rommel, *The Rommel Papers*, 455; see also Weigley, *Eisenhower's Lieutenants*, 45–46.

25. See Jean Quellien, *Le débarquement et la bataille de Normandie: La Normandie au coeur de la guerre* (Caen and Rennes: Mémorial de Caen / Éditions Ouest-France, 1998), 81.

26. Hans Speidel, *Invasion 1944: Rommel and the Normandy Campaign*, trans. Theo R. Crevenna (Chicago: Regnery, 1950), 45.

27. Note from the Diary of Army Group B, cited in Rommel, *The Rommel Papers*, 459.

28. Ibid., 460.

29. See Ruge, *Rommel in Normandy*, 70.

30. Ibid., 457–458; quotation, 67.

31. Undated report, quoted in Rommel, *The Rommel Papers*, 458.

32. See Harrison, *Cross-Channel Attack*, 262.

33. Speidel, *Invasion 1944*, 49.

34. See Keegan, *Six Armies in Normandy*, 63.

35. Speidel, *Invasion 1944*, 30.

36. See Janusz Piekalkiewicz, *Invasion Frankreich, 1944* (Munich: Südwest-Verlag, 1979), 31–33.

37. Rommel to Jodl, 23 April 1944, quoted in Rommel, *The Rommel Papers*, 469.

38. Ibid., 470. [Nettuno was the site of the Allied landing in southern Italy in January 1944—Trans.]

39. See Hans Wegmüller, *Die Abwehr der Invasion: Die Konzeption des Oberbefehlshabers West, 1940–1945* (Freiburg: Rombach, 1979), 160.

40. See Report of Activities of Section Ic of OB West, 1 January–31 March 1944, Bundesarchiv [henceforth BA] Militärarchiv [henceforth MA] RH 19 4/130.

41. See F. H. Hinsley and C. A. G. Simkins, *Security and Counter-Intelligence* (London and Cambridge: H. M. Stationery Office / Cambridge University Press, 1990), 41–44, 193–194, 203.

42. See Walter Schellenberg, *Aufzeichnungen: Die Memoiren des letzten Geheimdienstchefs unter Hitler* (Wiesbaden: Limes, 1979), 316–317.

43. See Robin Denniston, *Churchill's Secret War: Diplomatic Decrypts, the Foreign Office and Turkey* (New York: St. Martin's, 1997), 131–134.

44. See Schellenberg, *Aufzeichnungen*, 319.

45. See Horst Boog, Gerhard Krebs, and Detlef Vogel, *Das Deutsche Reich in der Defensive: Strategischer Luftkrieg in Europa, Krieg im Westen und in Ostasien, 1943–1944/5*, vol. 7 of *Das Deutsche Reich und der Zweite Weltkrieg* (Stuttgart: Deutsche Verlags-Anstalt, 2001), 427–428. [An English version of this volume is now available as part of *Germany and the Second World War*, trans. Derry Cook-Radmore et al., 10 vols. (Oxford: Clarendon, 1990– ).—Trans.]

46. See Michael Howard, *Strategic Deception* (London and Cambridge: H. M. Stationery Office / Cambridge University Press, 1990), 129.

47. Goebbels, *Journal*, 454. For an account of the German capture of the French Special Operations Executive (SOE) agent ("Butler") who controlled the Resistance

network that inadvertently received the action message on the eve of D-Day, see Anthony Cave Brown, *Bodyguard of Lies* (London: W. H. Allen, 1975), 559–561.

48. See Hinsley and Simkins, *Security and Counter-Intelligence*, 249ff.

49. See Memorandum from Lester Halpin to Mr. J. H. Ryan, 12 March 1944, NARA, RG 216, entry 1, box 350.

50. See Memorandum from E. H. Bronson to John E. Fetzer, 19 May 1944, ibid.

51. See Harry C. Butcher, *My Three Years with Eisenhower: The Personal Diary of Captain Harry C. Butcher, USNR, Naval Aide to General Eisenhower, 1942–1945* (New York: Simon and Schuster, 1946), 505.

52. See Omar N. Bradley, *A Soldier's Story* (New York: Holt, 1951), 223–224; and Associated Press dispatch, 7 June 1944, NARA, RG 216, entry 1, box 350.

53. Statement by Duncan Sandys, minister of supply, 17 March 1944, PRO, KV 2/2410.

54. See Source 32A, March 1942, ibid.

55. [Author's name illegible], Report on Captain B. Liddell Hart, n.d., ibid.

56. Winston Churchill to General Ismay, 21 and 24 March 1944, PRO CAB, 101/224. Liddell Hart himself did not breathe a word about this incident in his memoirs, which end in 1940; see *The Memoirs of Captain Liddell Hart* (London: Cassell, 1965).

57. Report on Captain B. Liddell Hart.

58. Lieutenant General (later Sir) Frederick Pile was head of the Anti-Aircraft Command.–Trans.

59. E. J. P. Cussen, "Termination of the Present Enquiry," 17 August 1944, PRO, KV 2/2411.

60. See note from Lester Halpin, 3 June 1944, NARA, RG 212, entry 1, box 350; and Butcher, *My Three Years with Eisenhower*, 559.

61. See David Reynolds, *Rich Relations: The American Occupation of Britain, 1942–1945* (New York: Random House, 1995), 352.

62. Entry for 18 April 1944 in Goebbels, *Journal*, 437.

63. See Ruge, *Rommel in Normandy*, 157.

64. Army Staff, Foreign Armies West Section, no. 6648/43, 16 July 1943, "Initial Findings Concerning British and American Tactics in Sicily," BA, MA, RH 20–7/191.

65. See B. H. Liddell Hart, *The German Generals Talk: Startling Revelations from Hitler's High Command* (New York: William Morrow, 1948), 51–52; also Boog et al., *Das Deutsche Reich in der Defensive*, 458–460.

66. Quoted in Howard, *Strategic Deception*, 130.

67. Ibid., 115–117.

68. See ibid., 145.

69. See ibid., 154.

70. See Michel Boivin, "Les Manchois dans la tourmente de la guerre, 1939–1945" (doctoral thesis, 4 vols., University of Caen, 2003) 4:863.

71. See Howard, *Strategic Deception*, 115.

72. See F. H. Hinsley et al., *British Intelligence in the Second World War: Its*

*Influence on Strategy and Operations,* vol. 3, part 2 (London and Cambridge: H. M. Stationery Office / Cambridge University Press, 1988), 51–52.

73. On the whole of this affair see Brown, *Bodyguard of Lies,* 497–499.

74. See Colonel J. H. Bevan to General Morgan, 20 July 1943, EL, SHAEF, secretary, general staff, microfilm 30.

75. See Piekalkiewicz, *Invasion Frankreich 1944,* 121–126.

76. See Hinsley et al., *British Intelligence in the Second World War,* vol. 3, part 2, 125–126.

77. Quoted in Rommel, *The Rommel Papers,* 470.

78. See Forrest C. Pogue, *The Supreme Command* (Washington, D.C.: Office of the Chief of Military History, Department of the Army, 1954), 160.

79. See Hinsley et al., *British Intelligence in the Second World War,* vol. 3, part 2, 18.

80. See Headquarters Twenty-first Army Group, "Note on Manacle Raids in Neptune Area," 3 January 1944, RG 331, entry 12, box 14.

81. See General F. Morgan to General de Guingand, 1 February 1944 NARA, RG 331, entry 12, box 9; and Lieutenant Colonel J. E. Fass to Lieutenant Colonel La Trobe-Bateman, 9 February 1944, ibid—.

82. See Hinsley et al., *British Intelligence in the Second World War,* vol. 3, part 2, 89.

83. See F. W. Winterbotham, *The Ultra Secret* (London: Weidenfeld and Nicolson, 1974).

84. See Hinsley et al., *British Intelligence in the Second World War,* vol. 3, part 2, 33.

85. The actual number was effectively fifty-eight, since two divisions (the Second Parachute and Nineteenth Panzer) did not leave for the western front before D-Day; ibid., 87.

86. General Whiteford to Generals Bull and West, 20 January 1944, NARA, RG 331, entry 12, box 9.

87. Winston Churchill to General Ismay for COS Committee, 21 May 1944, PRO CAB, 101/244.

88. Quoted in Hinsley et al., *British Intelligence in the Second World War,* vol. 3, 580.

89. Daniel I. Man, "Discussion of the Situation concerning Gas in Combat on Utah Beach," n.d., NARA, RG 112, entry 31, box 494.

90. Entry for 18 April 1944 in Goebbels, *Journal,* 437.

91. Quoted in Rommel, *The Rommel Papers,* 462.

92. Walter Warlimont, *Inside Hitler's Headquarters, 1939–1945,* trans. R. H. Barry (London: Weidenfeld and Nicolson, 1964), 424.

93. Retrospective commentary added to entry for 5 June 1944 in Alan Francis Brooke, *War Diaries, 1939–1945,* ed. Alex Danchev and Daniel Todman (London: Weidenfeld and Nicolson, 1957), 554.

94. Entry for 6 June 1944 in Air Marshal Leigh-Mallory, diary, PRO, Air Force, 37/784.

95. Entry for 5 June 1944 in Admiral Ramsay, diary, PRO CAB, 106/1124.

96. Butcher, *My Three Years with Eisenhower,* 544.

97. Bradley, *A Soldier's Story*, 256–257.

98. Butcher, *My Three Years with Eisenhower*, 538.

99. See Terry Copp, *Fields of Fire: The Canadians in Normandy* (Toronto: University of Toronto Press, 2003), 38.


## 7 · D-DAY, H-HOUR

1. See Max Hastings, *Overlord: D-Day and the Battle for Normandy* (London: Michael Joseph, 1984), 46.

2. See General Lord to General Bedell Smith, 11 May 1944, EL, SHAEF, secretary, general staff, microfilm 44.

3. See Operation Overlord, South-Western Zone, 15 May 1944, NARA, RG 331, entry 34, box 37.

4. Angus Calder, *The People's War: Britain, 1939–1945* (London: Jonathan Cape, 1969), 558.

5. Paul Fussell, *Wartime: Understanding and Behavior in the Second World War* (New York: Oxford University Press, 1989), 109.

6. See Graham A. Cosmas and Albert E. Cowdrey, *The Medical Department: Medical Service in the European Theater of Operations* (Washington: Center of Military History, United States Army, 1991), 173; and Joint Administrative Plan for Operation Overlord, 19 April 1944, NARA, RG 331, entry 1, box 79.

7. See Cosmas and Cowdrey, *The Medical Department*, 195.

8. See Hastings, *Overlord*, 69–70.

9. See Lionel Frederic Ellis et al., *The Battle of Normandy* (London: H. M. Stationery Office, 1962), 136.

10. Ralph Ingersoll, *Top Secret* (New York: Harcourt, Brace, 1946), 111.

11. See David Reynolds, *Rich Relations: The American Occupation of Britain, 1942–1945* (New York: Random House, 1995) 369ff.

12. See Roland G. Ruppenthal, *Logistical Support of the Armies*, 2 vols. (Washington, D.C.: Office of the Chief of Military History, Department of the Army, 1953–1959): 1:362–363.

13. See John Keegan, *Six Armies in Normandy: From D-Day to the Liberation of Paris* (London: Penguin Books, 1994), 74–75.

14. Dwight David Eisenhower, *Crusade in Europe* (Garden City, N.Y.: Doubleday, 1948), 249.

15. See Report of the Meteorological Implications in Selection of the D-Day for the Allied Invasion of France, June 1944, PRO CAB, 106/976. Eisenhower's exact words have long been a subject of dispute; see Carlo D'Este, *Eisenhower: Allied Supreme Commander* (New York: Henry Holt, 2002), 782n38.

16. Eisenhower, *Crusade in Europe*, 250.

17. See Admiral Ramsay, "Report by the Allied Commander-in-Chief, Expeditionary Force on Operation Neptune," 16 October 1944, NARA, RG 331, entry 279, box 4.

18. See Ellis et al., *The Battle of Normandy*, 143, 161ff.

19. See Admiral Ramsay, "Report by the Allied Commander-in-Chief."

20. See Ellis et al., *The Battle of Normandy*, 160.

21. See Joint Intelligence Sub-Committee, "German Appreciation of Allied Intentions Regarding 'Overlord,'" 3 June 1944, EL, SHAEF, secretary, general staff, Division, microfilm 22.

22. See [Solly Zuckerman], "Air Support Operation Overlord," 22 September 1944, PRO, Ministry of Defence, 2/487.

23. See Chester Wilmot, *The Struggle for Europe* (London: Collins, 1952), 247.

24. Liberation Campaign North-West Europe 1944–1945, bk. 3, chap. 8, PRO CAB, 44/245.

25. See Wilmot, *The Struggle for Europe*, 244.

26. See Keegan, *Six Armies in Normandy*, 110–114.

27. See Liberation Campaign North-West Europe 1944–1945.

28. See Lieutenant Colonel Shephard, Immediate Report no. 19, 18 June 1944, PRO CAB, 106/963.

29. See Sixth Airborne Division, Report on Operations in Normandy, ibid., 970.

30. Omar N. Bradley, *A Soldier's Story* (New York: Holt, 1951), 268.

31. See Liberation Campaign North-West Europe 1944–1945.

32. From AMSSO [Air Ministry Special Signals Office] to SACMED [Commander in Chief, Mediterranean Theater], 28 July 1944, NARA, RG 331, entry 1, box 79.

33. Royal Navy report, quoted in Terry Copp, *Fields of Fire: The Canadians in Normandy* (Toronto: University of Toronto Press, 2003), 43–44.

34. See J. C. Dordward, I. Evans, and F. C. Liston, "Casualties and Effects of Fire Support on the British Beaches in Normandy" (Army Operational Research Group, Report no. 261), 21 April 1945, PRO CAB, 106/967.

35. See I. Evans, "Comparison of British and American Areas in Normandy," 14 August 1945, PRO, War Office, 291/270.

36. See Ruppenthal, *Logistical Support of the Armies*, 1:378.

37. See Russell F. Weigley, *Eisenhower's Lieutenants: The Campaign of France and Germany, 1944–1945* (Bloomington: Indiana University Press, 1981), 80.

38. Fussell, *Wartime*, 23–24.

39. See Hastings, *Overlord*, 96, 91–92.

40. Bradley, *A Soldier's Story*, 271.

41. See Stephen E. Ambrose, *D-Day, June 6, 1944: The Climactic Battle of World War II* (New York: Simon and Schuster, 1994), 450.

42. See Ruppenthal, *Logistical Support of the Armies*, 1:383.

43. See Ambrose, *D-Day, June 6, 1944*, 407–417.

44. See Liberation Campaign North-West Europe 1944–1945.

45. See ibid.

46. Ingersoll, *Top Secret*, 134. [Ingersoll landed on Utah as part of Task Force Raff, an American unit composed of tanks, gliders, and glider infantrymen led by Colonel Edson Raff, whose mission was to penetrate enemy lines and join up with the Eighty-

second Airborne, which was dropping inland beyond the German coastal defenses: ibid., 109.—Trans.]

47. See Evans, "Comparison of British and American Areas."

48. See Ellis et al., *The Battle of Normandy,* 170.

49. See Evans, "Comparison of British and American Areas."

50. See Hastings, *Overlord,* 105.

51. See Evans, "Comparison of British and American Areas."

52. See Hastings, *Overlord,* 102–103.

53. One of the most famous and decorated figures of the French Resistance, Kieffer held the naval rank of *capitaine de corvette* at the time of D-Day, equivalent to commandant in the French army and major in the British Army.—Trans.

54. See Evans, "Comparison of British and American Areas."

55. Ibid.

56. See Ellis et al., *The Battle of Normandy,* 187.

57. See Ambrose, *D-Day, June 6, 1944,* 522.

58. See Geoffrey Perret, *There's a War to Be Won: The United States Army in World War II* (New York: Random House, 1991), 323.

59. See Dordward, Evans, and Liston, "Casualties and Effects of Fire Support."

## 8. To Win a Battle

1. See Friedrich Ruge, *Rommel in Normandy: Reminiscences,* trans. Ursula R. Moessner (San Rafael, Calif.: Presidio, 1979), 183.

2. Walter Warlimont, *Inside Hitler's Headquarters, 1939–45,* trans. R. H. Barry (London: Weidenfeld and Nicolson, 1964), 425. Warlimont refers here to General Speidel's memoir of the Normandy campaign, *Invasion 1944: Ein Beitrag zu Rommels und des Reiches Schicksal* (Tübingen: Wunderlich, 1949); Speidel, however, claims that he spoke by telephone with Rommel shortly after 6:00 A.M. OKW's official reserve also included the headquarters of First SS Panzer Corps, which had general responsibility for the Caen sector. On the "Panzerkontroverse," see Dieter Ose, *Entscheidung im Westen, 1944: Der Oberbefehlshaber West und die Abwehr der aliierten Invasion* (Stuttgart: Deutsche Verlags-Anstalt, 1982), 56–59; also F. W. Winterbotham, *The Ultra Secret: The Inside Story of Operation Ultra, Bletchley Park and Enigma* (London: Weidenfeld and Nicolson, 1974), 125–128.

3. Max Hastings, *Overlord: D-Day and the Battle for Normandy* (London: Michael Joseph, 1984), 111. "The news couldn't be better," Hitler went on to say. "As long as they were in Britain we couldn't get at them. Now we have them where we can destroy them." See John Keegan, *Six Armies in Normandy: From D-Day to the Liberation of Paris* (London: Penguin, 1994), 146; also Carlo D'Este, *Eisenhower: Allied Supreme Commander* (New York: Henry Holt, 2002), 531.

4. See Hans Speidel, *Invasion 1944,* trans. Theo R. Crevenna (Chicago: Regnery, 1950), 82.

5. Second Army Intelligence Summary no. 3, 6 June 1944, PRO, War Office, 285/3.

6. Quoted in Erwin Rommel, *The Rommel Papers*, ed. B. H. Liddell Hart (New York: Harcourt, Brace, 1953), 471.

7. See Army Operational Research Group, "Opposition Encountered on the British Beaches on D-Day," PRO CAB, 106/975.

8. Rommel, *The Rommel Papers*, 484.

9. See War Diary of the Division of Naval Operations, 15 June 1944, S. 397.

10. See Admiral Ramsay, "Report by the Allied Commander-in-Chief, Expeditionary Force on Operation Neptune," October 1944, EL, Bedell Smith Papers, box 33.

11. See Admiral Ramsay, "Report by the Allied Commander-in-Chief, Expeditionary Force on Operation Neptune," 16 October 1944, NARA, RG 331, entry 279, box 4.

12. See Horst Boog, Gerhard Krebs, and Detlef Vogel, *Das Deutsche Reich in der Defensive: Strategischer Luftkrieg in Europa, Krieg im Westen und in Ostasien, 1943–1944/5* (Stuttgart: Deutsche Verlags-Anstalt, 2001), 294–295.

13. See Karl Gundelach, "Drohende Gefahr West: Die Deutsche Luftwaffe vor und während der Invasion 1944," *Wehrwissenschaftliche Rundschau* 9 (1959): 306.

14. See Informal Notes of the CCS, 162nd Meeting, 10 June 1944, NARA, RG 218, CCS-JCS Titles, box 172.

15. Rommel, *The Rommel Papers*, 483–484.

16. See US Strategic Bombing Survey, "The Impact of the Allied Air Effort on German Logistics," 1945, NARA, RG 243, entry 6, box 480.

17. Air Marshall Leigh-Mallory, diary, 13 June 1944, PRO, Air Force, 37/784.

18. See Carlo D'Este, *Decision in Normandy: The Unwritten Story of Montgomery and the Allied Campaign* (London: Collins, 1994), 152.

19. Extract from Ministry of Information Home Intelligence Weekly Report (20–27 June 1944), PRO, Home Office, 199/410.

20. See Keegan, *Six Armies in Normandy*, 164–165.

21. See Hastings, *Overlord*, 113–114.

22. See D'Este, *Decision in Normandy*, 144–145.

23. See Stephen Ambrose, *D-Day, June 6, 1944: The Climactic Battle of World War II* (New York: Simon and Schuster, 1994), 525.

24. See Hastings, *Overlord*, 135.

25. Notes on the Normandy campaign by Brigadier James Hargest, New Zealand Army Observer with XXX Corps, 6 June–10 July 1944, PRO CAB, 106/1060; quoted by D'Este, *Decision in Normandy*, 280.

26. Notes on the Normandy campaign.

27. "Report on Operations of 6th Airborne Division in Normandy 1944 June 6–Aug 27," PRO CAB, 106/970.

28. Allied Air Commanders' Conference Held at H.Q. [Headquarters], A.E.A.F. [Allied Expeditionary Air Force], [date not indicated, probably 13 June 1944], PRO, Air Force, 37/1057.

29. Quoted in Dwight D. Eisenhower, *Crusade in Europe* (Garden City, N.Y.: Doubleday, 1948), 260.

30. See General Miles Dempsey, diary, 19 June 1944, PRO, War Office, 285/9.

31. See Terry Copp, *Fields of Fire: The Canadians in Normandy* (Toronto: University of Toronto Press, 2003), 79–87, and Keegan, *Six Armies in Normandy*, 166–181.

32. Bernard Law Montgomery, *The Memoirs of Field-Marshal the Viscount Montgomery of Alamein* (London: Collins, 1958), 228.

33. Eisenhower, *Crusade in Europe*, 258.

34. General Montgomery to Generals Bradley and Dempsey, 18 June 1944, PRO, War Office, 285/2.

35. Air Marshal Leigh-Mallory, diary, 19 June 1944, PRO, Air Force, 37/784.

36. Basil H. Liddell Hart, *History of the Second World War* (London: Cassell, 1970), 546.

37. General Miles Dempsey, diary, 30 June 1944, PRO, War Office, 285/9.

38. See Forrest C. Pogue, *The Supreme Command* (Washington, D.C.: Office of the Chief of Military History, Department of the Army, 1954), 182.

39. Keegan, *Six Armies in Normandy*, 181.

40. See Michael D. Doubler, *Closing with the Enemy: How GIs Fought the War in Europe, 1944–1945* (Lawrence: University Press of Kansas, 1994), 40.

41. Ibid., 37–38.

42. Ibid., 42.

43. Ibid., 44–45, 48.

44. General Bradley, Report of Operations of First United States Army (20 October 1943–1 August 1944), 1945, PRO CAB, 106/1004.

45. Brigadier Charles Richardson, "Appreciation on Possible Developments of Operations to Secure a Lodgment Area/Operation Overlord," 7 May 1944, PRO, War Office, 205/118.

46. With regard to the effect on German morale, see Rémy Desquesnes, *Normandie, 1944* (Caen and Rennes: Mémorial de Caen / Éditions Ouest-France, 1993), 170ff.

47. Omar N. Bradley, *A Soldier's Story* (New York: Holt, 1951), 313, 314.

48. Draft Minute from Chiefs of Staff to Prime Minister, "'Overlord'—Shipping Requirements," 11 May 1944, EL, SHAEF, secretary, general staff, microfilm 44.

49. See Direction of Ports and Inland Water Transport, Mulberry, 23 May 1945, PRO CAB, 106/968; Sir Walter Monckton, "The Part Played in 'Overlord' by the Synthetic Harbours," 12 October 1945, PRO, Ministry of Defence, 2/498.

50. See Build Up Control [BUCO] West, Report, 30 June 1944, NARA, RG 331, entry 34, box 10.

51. See "Liberation Campaign North-West Europe 1944–1945, Phase 4: The Break-Out and the Advance to the Crossing of the Seine," n.d., PRO CAB, 44/251; Historical Section, Operational Aspects of Mulberry B, 10 May 1945, ibid., 106/966.

52. Historical Section, "Notes on the Operation of 21st A[rmy] G[roup]," PRO CAB 106/973.

53. Bradley, *A Soldier's Story*, 304, 306.

54. See Sir Walter Monckton, "The Part Played in 'Overlord' by the Synthetic Harbours," 12 October 1945, PRO, Ministry of Defence, 2/498.

55. "See Liberation Campaign North-West Europe 1944–1945, Phase 4."

56. Monckton, "The Part Played in 'Overlord' by the Synthetic Harbours."

57. See Interviews with High-Ranking German Officers Keitel and Jodl, 23 July 1945, EL, Bedell Smith Papers, box 41.

58. See Vice-Marshal S. C. Strafford, diary, 9 June 1944, PRO, Air Force, 37/574.

59. See "Liberation Campaign North-West Europe 1944–1945, Phase 4."

60. SHAEF G3, Daily Summary no. 26, 2 July 1944, EL, Bedell Smith Papers, box 32.

61. Headquarters 101st Airborne Division, Casualties 101st Airborne Division, June 6–July 10, 1944, 4 July 1944, EL, SHAEF, secretary, general staff, Division, microfilm 25.

## 9. Stalemate

1. Supreme Allied Command Dispatch, [July 1944], PRO CAB, 106/978.

2. See Air Commodore E. J. Kingston-McGloughry and Professor S. Zuckerman, Allied Expeditionary Air Force Headquarters, "Observations on RAF Bomber Command's Attack on Caen July 7, 1944," n.d., PRO, Air Force, 37/361.

3. Twelfth Army Group, Publicity and Psychological Section, Report of Operations, vol. 14, p. 49, NARA, RG 331, entry 200A, box 268.

4. See Nigel Hamilton, *Monty: The Battles of Field Marshal Bernard Montgomery* (London: Hodder and Stoughton, 1994), 328–330.

5. See Lionel Frederic Ellis et al., *The Battle of Normandy* (London: H. M. Stationery Office, 1962), 329–330.

6. Field Marshal Montgomery, "Notes on Second Army Operations 16–18 July," 15 July 1944, PRO, War Office, 205/5G.

7. Bernard Law Montgomery, *The Memoirs of Field-Marshal the Viscount Montgomery of Alamein* (London: Collins, 1958), 200. Italics in the original.

8. Entry for 3 August 1944 in Joseph Goebbels, *Journal: 1943–1945*, ed. and trans. Pierre Ayçoberry, Horst Möller, and Stefan Martens (Paris: Tallandier, 2005), 569.

9. Quoted in Stephen E. Ambrose, *The Supreme Commander: The War Years of General Dwight D. Eisenhower* (Jackson: University Press of Mississippi, 1999), 435.

10. On Troarn, see S. Zuckerman, "Preliminary Analysis of Air Operation Goodwood," 4 August 1944, PRO, Air Force, 37/762.

11. See Carlo D'Este, *Decision in Normandy: The Unwritten Story of Montgomery and the Allied Campaign* (London: Collins, 1994), 360.

12. Ibid.; see also Ellis et al., *The Battle of Normandy*, 336.

13. See Ambrose, *The Supreme Commander*, 439.

14. Terry Copp, *Fields of Fire: The Canadians in Normandy* (Toronto: University of Toronto Press, 2003), 148.

15. Ibid., 153.

16. Ellis et al., *The Battle of Normandy*, 346, 350–351.

17. See Martin Blumenson, *Breakout and Pursuit* (Washington, D.C.: Office of the Chief of Military History, Department of the Army, 1961), 15.

18. Air Commodore A. J. W. Geddes, "Examination of Operation 'Goodwood,'" 26 July 1944, PRO, Air Force, 37/362.

19. See D'Este, *Decision in Normandy*, 255.

20. Harry C. Butcher, *My Three Years with Eisenhower: The Personal Diary of Captain Harry C. Butcher, USNR, Naval Aide to General Eisenhower, 1942–1945* (New York: Simon and Schuster, 1946), 605.

21. Alan Francis Brooke, *War Diaries, 1939–1945*, ed. Alex Danchev and Daniel Todman (London: Weidenfeld and Nicolson, 1957), 564, 566.

22. Butcher, *My Three Years with Eisenhower*, 616–617.

23. See John Keegan, *Six Armies in Normandy: From D-Day to the Liberation of Paris* (London: Penguin, 1994), 217.

24. Quoted in Arthur William Tedder, *With Prejudice: The War Memoirs of Marshal of the Air Force, Lord Tedder* (London: Cassell, 1966), 571.

25. See D'Este, *Decision in Normandy*, 325.

26. Ibid., 302.

27. Directive from General Montgomery to General Bradley, General Dempsey, General Patton, General Crerar, 21 July 1944, PRO, War Office, 205/5 G.

28. Directive from General Montgomery to General Bradley, General Dempsey, General Patton, General Crerar, 27 July 1944, PRO, War Office, 205/5 G.

29. See Jean Quellien, *Le débarquement et la bataille de Normandie: La Normandie au coeur de la guerre* (Caen and Rennes: Mémorial de Caen / Éditions Ouest-France, 1998), 192.

30. See Russell F. Weigley, *Eisenhower's Lieutenants: The Campaign of France and Germany, 1944–1945* (Bloomington: Indiana University Press, 1981), 128–129.

31. Blumenson, *Breakout and Pursuit*, 85.

32. On the role of the Twenty-ninth Division in pioneering these tactics, see Michael D. Doubler, *Closing with the Enemy: How GIs Fought the War in Europe, 1944–1945* (Lawrence: University Press of Kansas, 1994), 54–56. Further refinements were due to the Third Armored Division: ibid., 60–62.

33. See Blumenson, *Breakout and Pursuit*, 175.

34. See Roland G. Ruppenthal, *Logistical Support of the Armies*, 2 vols. (Washington, D.C.: Office of the Chief of Military History, Department of the Army, 1953–1959), 1:457.

35. See D'Este, *Decision in Normandy*, 259–260.

36. Brigadier DAG to Brigadier General of Staff, 28 July 1944, PRO, War Office, 171/139.

37. Major General Chief of Staff de Guingand to First Canadian Army and Second Army (Headquarters), 18 August 1944, PRO, War Office, 171/115.

38. See Ruppenthal, *Logistical Support of the Armies*, 1:458.

39. Ibid., 1:460.

40. Ibid., 1:300.

41. See Colonel Edwin N. Clark, "Service and Combat Troops Landed," 29 June 1944, NARA, RG 331, entry 35, box 227.

42. See Major General H. R. Bull, Memorandum to the Supreme Commander, 29 June 1944, NARA, RG 331, entry 23, box 52.

43. See Ruppenthal, *Logistical Support of the Armies,* 1:447.

44. Twelfth Army Group, Report of Operations, 1944, NARA, RG 331, entry 200, box 268.

45. See Ruppenthal, *Logistical Support of the Armies,* 1:465.

46. See ANCXF [Allied Naval Command Expeditionary Force] to SHAEF, 31 August 1944, NARA, RG 331, entry 34, box 87.

47. See AGWAR [United States War Department] from Marshall to ETOUSA for Eisenhower, 5 August 1944, NARA, RG 331, entry 34, box 87.

48. See Ruppenthal, *Logistical Support of the Armies,* 1:502.

49. See Jean-Luc Leleu, "Soldats politiques en guerre: Sociologie, organisation, rôle et comportements des formations de la Waffen SS en considération particulière de leur présence en Europe de l'Ouest, 1940–1945" (doctoral thesis, Université de Caen, 2005), 762.

50. Ibid., 712–713.

51. See F. H. Hinsley et al., *British Intelligence in the Second World War: Its Influence on Strategy and Operations,* vol. 3 (London and Cambridge: H. M. Stationery Office / Cambridge University Press, 1988), 114.

52. See Weigley, *Eisenhower's Lieutenants,* 63.

53. See Leleu, "Soldats politiques en guerre," 959.

54. See Hinsley et al., *British Intelligence in the Second World War,* vol. 3, 167.

55. See "Allied Shipping Losses in Operation Neptune, 6th to 30th June (Excluding Landing Craft and Other Miscellaneous Small Craft)," n.d., PRO CAB, 106/1126.

56. See General Miles Dempsey, Diary, 25 June 1944, PRO, War Office, 285/9.

57. See Allied Naval Commander in Chief Expeditionary Forces, War Diary, 30 June 1944, NARA, RG 331, entry 277, box 1.

58. See Copp, *Fields of Fire,* 123.

59. See Blumenson, *Breakout and Pursuit,* 178.

60. See Leleu, "Soldats politiques en guerre," 755–756.

61. See Blumenson, *Breakout and Pursuit,* 181.

62. Erwin Rommel, *The Rommel Papers,* ed. B. H. Liddell Hart, trans. Paul Findlay (New York: Harcourt, Brace, 1953), 486.

63. See Ambrose, *The Supreme Commander,* 460; see also Weigley, *Eisenhower's Lieutenants,* 163–164.

64. Government Code and Cypher School, Signals Intelligence Passed to the Prime Minister, Messages and Correspondence, Japanese Ambassador, Berlin to Foreign Minister, 22 June 1944, PRO, HW 1/2993.

65. Colonel H. N. H. Wil, "Resources Allotted to 'FORTITUDE,'" 4 August 1944, NARA, RG 331, entry 1, box 73.

66. See Michael Howard, *Strategic Deception* (London and Cambridge: H. M. Stationery Office / Cambridge University Press, 1990), 193.

67. See Blumenson, *Breakout and Pursuit,* 33.

68. See U.S. Strategic Bombing Survey, "The Impact of the Allied Air Effort on German Logistics," 1945 [day and month not indicated], NARA, RG 243, entry 6, box 480.

69. From Transcript of Intercepted Traffic, Telephone Journal of Seventh Army, 29 June 1944, PRO CAB, 106/978.

70. See Max Hastings, *Overlord: D-Day and the Battle for Normandy* (London: Michael Joseph, 1984), 43.

71. See U.S. Strategic Bombing Survey, "The Impact of the Allied Air Effort on German Logistics."

72. See Assistant to the Chief of Staff [G2], "Views of an Officer on the Results of Attacks against Railroads," 24 April 1945, NARA, RG 331, entry 226, box 56.

73. Inspector General of Tank Troops, Immediate Report to the Führer, 20 June 1944, §5, no. 1718/44 g.Kdos., Bundesarchiv–Militärarchiv [henceforth BA-MA], Reich-Heer [henceforth RH] 10/90 (fol. 163).

74. See Chester Wilmot, *The Struggle for Europe* (London: Collins, 1952), 341–342.

75. Telex from Kluge to Hitler, 21 July 1944, BA-MA, RH 19 9/8 (fol. 21–23), quoted in Keegan, *Six Armies in Normandy,* 219.

76. Dr. Hans H. Reese and Professor Mark A. May, "Tactical Effects of Bombardment Committee Reports / The Psychological Effects of Weapons," 25 October 1944, NARA, RG 112, entry 31 ZI, box 1294.

77. See Psychological Warfare Division, "Background for PWE/OWI Direction Meeting," 1 August 1944, NARA, RG 331, entry 23, box 51.

78. See Major Gurfein, acting chief, Intelligence Section, "Some Observations on the Morale of the Wehrmacht," 19 July 1944, PRO, War Office, 219/4717 A.

79. Twelfth Army Group, Publicity and Psychological Warfare Section, Report of Operations, vol. 14, NARA, RG 331, entry 200A, box 268.

80. See Colonel Chas. E. Hart, Artillery Report no. 16, 29 June 1944, NARA, RG 337, entry 15A, box 54.

81. See Lieutenant Colonel Calvin A. L. Dickey, After Action Report, n.d., NARA, RG 337, entry 15A, box 57.

82. See Captain Holman Hamilton, extracts from various observer reports, 18 November 1944, NARA, RG 337, entry 15A, box 57. '

83. See Lieutenant Colonel P. H. "Bethune, Report on Observations of Normandy Operations," 7 September 1944, NARA, RG 337, entry 15A, box 56.

84. See Graham A. Cosmas and Albert E. Cowdrey, *The Medical Department: Medical Service in the European Theater of Operations* (Washington, D.C.: Center of Military History, United States Army, 1991), 229.

85. See Hastings, *Overlord,* 209.

86. Quoted in Leleu, "Soldats politiques en guerre," 1237.

87. See "Report of the Court of Inquiry Re: Shooting of POWs by German Army Forces at Château d'Audrieu, Normandy," 8-6-1944, 1944 [day and month not indicated], NARA, RG 331, entry 56, box 2.

88. See Leleu, "Soldats politiques en guerre," 1245.

89. See Colonel Charles L. Decker, Colonel, JAGD [Judge Advocate Group Detachment], acting deputy theater judge advocate, "Report on Results of Investigations into Mistreatment of Prisoners of War by U.S. Forces, Memorandum for General Betts," 31 December 1945, NARA, RG 498, entry 19, box 51.

90. See Leleu, "Soldats politiques en guerre," 1233.

91. Decker, "Report on Results of Investigations into Mistreatment of Prisoners of War by U.S. Forces."

92. Quoted in Friedrich Ruge, *Rommel in Normandy: Reminiscences,* trans. Ursula R. Moessner (San Rafael, Calif.: Presidio, 1979), 150.

93. Generalleutnant Viktor von Drabich-Wächter, 8 June 1944, quoted in "Nazi Commissars Give Directive for Atrocity Propaganda to German Soldiers about Allied Measures against German Prisoners of War and German Civilian Population," Psychological Warfare Division, Records, 30 August 1944, PRO, War Office, 219/4730.

94. Copp, *Fields of Fire,* 158.

95. See Hastings, *Overlord,* 247.

96. See Leleu, "Soldats politiques en guerre," 1178.

97. Ibid., 1217, 1218, 1222, 1226.

98. Quoted in Blumenson, *Breakout and Pursuit,* 27.

99. On making the most of the terrain, see Doubler, *Closing with the Enemy,* 35.

100. Quoted in Wilmot, *The Struggle for Europe,* 347.

101. Quoted in Hans Speidel, *Invasion 1944: Rommel and the Normandy Campaign,* trans. Theo R. Crevenna (Chicago: Regnery, 1950), 110.

102. Quoted in Blumenson, *Breakout and Pursuit,* 213.

103. Klaus-Jürgen Müller, "Le débarquement allié en Normandie et l'opposition à Hitler," in François Bédarida, ed., *Normandie 1944: Du débarquement à la libération* (Paris: Albin Michel, 1987), 262–264.

104. Speidel, *Invasion 1944,* 74.

105. Quoted in Ruge, *Rommel in Normandy,* 205.

## 10. Psychoneuroses

1. Lloyd J. Thompson, "History of Neuropsychiatric Services in the European Theater of Operations," n.d., NARA, RG 112, entry 31, AH, box 311.

2. Personal reminiscence of soldier of the 314th Regiment, quoted in Martin Blumenson, *Breakout and Pursuit* (Washington, D.C.: Office of the Chief of Military History, Department of the Army, 1961), 176.

3. See Roland G. Ruppenthal, *Logistical Support of the Armies,* 2 vols. (Washington, D.C.: Office of the Chief of Military History, Department of the Army, 1953–1959), 1:520.

4. See "Impression of Fighting in Normandy," 17 June 1944, PRO CAB 106/963.

5. See Michael D. Doubler, *Closing with the Enemy: How GIs Fought the War in Europe, 1944–1945* (Lawrence: University Press of Kansas, 1994), 262.

6. See Lieutenant General H. D. G. Crerar, [war] diary, 24 July 1944, PRO CAB, 106/1064.

7. Quoted in Terry Copp, *Fields of Fire: The Canadians in Normandy* (Toronto: University of Toronto Press, 2003), 118.

8. See Headquarters FWD ECH COM [forward echelon commander] Z, Communications Postal Plan, n.d., NARA, RG 331, entry 23, box 48.

9. See Geoffrey Perret, *There's a War to Be Won: The United States Army in World War II* (New York: Random House, 1991), 471.

10. See After Action Report, HQ Nineteenth Corps [undated], NARA, RG 337, entry 15A, box 56.

11. See Lieutenant Colonel Johnson and Lieutenant Colonel Renshaw, Memorandum for the Commanding General, Army Ground Forces, 2 August 1944, NARA, RG 337, entry 15A, box 56.

12. See Medical Historian Papers, Campaign in North West Europe, 1944 June–1945 May, n.d., PRO, War Office 221/1496.

13. See JAG [Judge Advocate General], Return of Convictions by Court Martial upon Other Ranks, n.d., PRO, War Office 171/182. These figures do not include officers.

14. See Twelfth Army Group, Report of Operations (Final After Action Report), vol. II [1945], NARA, RG 331, entry 200A, box 266.

15. See Doubler, *Closing with the Enemy*, 285.

16. See Lieutenant Colonel William G. Srodes, "Neuropsychiatry in First United States Army," January 1945, NARA, RG 112, entry 31 ZI, box 1313.

17. Blumenson, *Breakout and Pursuit*, 175.

18. See Lieutenant Williams, "Report on the Medical Facilities of the First Army," 21 November 1944, NARA, RG 112, entry 31, box 430.

19. See Twelfth Army Group, Report of Operations (Final After Action Report), vol. 2 [1945], NARA, RG 331, entry 200A, box 266.

20. See Copp, *Fields of Fire*, 213.

21. See Second Army Quarterly Medical Report for Quarter Ending 31 Dec[ember] 1944, PRO, War Office 222/275.

22. See Thompson, "History of Neuropsychiatric Services in the European Theater of Operations."

23. See Report by Psychiatrist Attached to Second Army (Major R.A.M.C. Watterson) for month of July [19]44, 5 August 1944, PRO, War Office 177/321.

24. See Colonel Holmes Ginn, Colonel W. E. Wilkinson, and Lieutenant Colonel Edward Whitely, General Board, ETO, Combat Exhaustion, n.d., NARA, RG 319, entry 47, box 1622; see also Doubler, *Closing with the Enemy*, 270–272.

25. "What the Soldier Thinks," no. 2, NARA, RG 330, entry 93, box 1004.

26. See Medical Historian Papers, Campaign in North West Europe, 1944 June–1945 May.

27. Lieutenant Colonel Robert J. Carpenter, circular letter no. 176, 20 October 1943, NARA, RG 330, entry 31 ZI, box 1293.

28. Louis Crocq, *Les traumatismes psychiques de la guerre* (Paris: Odile Jacob, 1999), 44.

29. Major General Paul R. Hawley, Memorandum for G1, 4 August 1944, quoted in Thompson, "History of the Neuropsychiatric Services in the European Theater of Operations."

30. See Crocq, *Les traumatismes psychiques de la guerre*, 45. For a graphic example of the syndrome, see Doubler, *Closing with the Enemy*, 271–272.

31. See Lieutenant Colonel Robert J. Carpenter, circular letter no. 176, 20 October 1943, NARA, RG 330, entry 31 ZI, box 1293.

32. Captain Harry C. Butcher, *My Three Years with Eisenhower: The Personal Diary of Captain Harry C. Butcher, USNR, Naval Aide to General Eisenhower, 1942–1945* (New York: Simon and Schuster, 1946), 645.

33. Report on State of 6 DWR (49 DIV) [Sixth Battalion, Duke of Wellington's Regiment, Forty-ninth (West Riding) Division] as of 30 June by Lieutenant A. J. Turner, commanding, 6 DWR, 30 June 1944, PRO, War Office 205/5 G.

34. Major Theodore P. Suratt, "Combat Psychiatry in an Infantry Division," n.d., probably 1945 or 1946, NARA RG 112, entry 31 ZI, box 1295.

35. Quoted in Robert H. Ahrenfeldt, *Psychiatry in the British Army in the Second World War* (London: Routledge and Kegan Paul, 1958), 26.

36. See Crocq, *Les traumatismes psychiques de la guerre*, 41.

37. See Medical Historian Papers / Notes on Administration of Army Psychiatry for the Period September 1939–May 1943, n.d., PRO, War Office 222/8.

38. See Terry Copp and Bill McAndrew, *Battle Exhaustion: Soldiers and Psychiatrists in the Canadian Army, 1939–1945* (Montreal: McGill-Queen's University Press, 1990), 28ff.

39. Ibid., 35–36; see also Crocq, *Les traumatismes psychiques de la guerre*, 43.

40. See Copp and McAndrew, *Battle Exhaustion*, 37.

41. Ibid., 20.

42. Ibid., 110.

43. See Deputy director of medical services, Second Army, "Psychiatric Summary for Week Ending Sunday 19 June [19]44 by Major J. Watterson," RAMC, PRO, War Office, 177/321.

44. See Copp and McAndrew, *Battle Exhaustion*, 115.

45. Major General Paul R. Hawley, Memorandum for G1, 4 August 1944, quoted in Thompson, "History of the Neuropsychiatric Services in the European Theater of Operations." Italics in the original.

46. "What the Soldier Thinks," no. 5, April 1944, NARA, RG 330, entry 93, box 1004.

47. European Theater of Operations, Manual of Therapy, 5 May 1944, NARA, RG 112, entry 31, box 427.

48. Ibid.

49. See Lieutenant Colonel Johnson and Lieutenant Colonel Renshaw, Memoran-

dum for the Commanding General, Army Ground Forces, 2 August 1944, NARA, RG 337, entry 15A, box 56.

50. See Lieutenant Colonel William G. Srodes, Annual Report of Consultant in Neuropsychiatry [to the First Army] for the Year 1944, n.d., NARA, RG 112, entry 31 ZI, box 311; see also Albert E. Cowdrey, *Fighting for Life: American Military Medicine in World War II* (New York: Free Press, 1994), 256.

51. See Copp and McAndrew, *Battle Exhaustion,* 129.

52. See Graham A. Cosmas and Albert E. Cowdrey, *The Medical Department: Medical Service in the European Theater of Operations* (Washington, D.C.: Center of Military History, United States Army, 1991), 236.

53. See Lieutenant Williams, Report on the Medical Facilities of the First Army, 21 November 1944, NARA, RG 112, 31, box 430.

54. See Thompson, "History of Neuropsychiatric Services in the European Theater of Operations."

55. See Report by Psychiatrist Attached to Second Army (Major R.A.M.C. Watterson) for month of June [19]44, 7 July 1944, PRO, War Office 177/321.

56. Ibid.

57. See Copp and McAndrew, *Battle Exhaustion,* 132.

58. See Medical Historian Papers, Campaign in North West Europe, 1944 June–1945 May.

59. See Report by Psychiatrist.

60. George S. Patton, *War As I Knew It* (New York: Bantam, 2004), 105.

61. See Second Army Quarterly Medical Report for Quarter Ending 31 Dec[ember] 1944.

62. See Medical Historian Papers, Campaign in North West Europe, 1944 June–1945 May.

63. See JAG, Return of Convictions by Court Martial.

64. See Twelfth Army Group, Medical Section, Report of Operations (Final After Action Report), 11 October 1944, NARA, RG 331, entry 200A, box 268.

65. See Headquarters Third U.S. Army, Office of the Surgeon, Report, 11 September 1944, NARA, RG 112, 31 ZI, box 1293.

66. See Information and Education Division, Morale Problems of 5,000 Returnees in the U.S., 31 January 1945, NARA, RG 330, entry 93, box 993.

## 11. From Avranches to Paris

1. Omar N. Bradley, *A Soldier's Story* (New York: Holt, 1951), 318.

2. Ralph Ingersoll, *Top Secret* (New York: Harcourt, Brace, 1946), 168.

3. See First Army Headquarters, Intelligence Annex to Operation Plan Cobra, 16 July 1944, PRO, War Office, 205/228.

4. See Michael D. Doubler, *Closing with the Enemy: How GIs Fought the War in Europe, 1944–1945* (Lawrence: University Press of Kansas, 1994), 50–51.

5. See Martin Blumenson, *Breakout and Pursuit* (Washington, D.C.: Office of the Chief of Military History, Department of the Army, 1961), 207–208.

6. See Doubler, *Closing with the Enemy,* 83.

7. Ingersoll, *Top Secret,* 167–168.

8. These figures are given by Eisenhower; see Desmond Hawkins, ed., *From D-Day to VE Day: Radio Reports from the Western Front, 1944–45* (London: BBC Books, 1994), 136.

9. See "Notes of a Conference Held in the Air C-in-C's Office at HQ AEAF on Saturday July 15th at 12.15 Hours to Discuss Plans for Air Support to a 1st U.S. Army Attack in the St. Lo Area," PRO, Air Force, 37/1057.

10. See Blumenson, *Breakout and Pursuit,* 236.

11. See Russell F. Weigley, *Eisenhower's Lieutenants: The Campaign of France and Germany, 1944–1945* (Bloomington: Indiana University Press, 1981), 153.

12. Twelfth Army Group, Publicity and Psychological Warfare Section, Report of Operations, vol. 14, n.d., NARA, RG 331, entry 200A, box 268.

13. Blumenson, *Breakout and Pursuit,* 245.

14. Ibid., 329.

15. Quoted in Erwin Rommel, *The Rommel Papers,* ed. B. H. Liddell Hart, trans. Paul Findlay (New York: Harcourt, Brace, 1953), 489.

16. Extracts from Telephone Conversation of Field Marshal von Kluge, C-in-C West, with Chief of Staff Seventh Army, Colonel von Gersdorff, 31 July 1944, in First United States Army, Report of Operations (20 October 1943–1 August 1944), PRO CAB, 106/1004.

17. See Carlo D'Este, *Decision in Normandy: The Unwritten Story of Montgomery and the Allied Campaign* (London: Collins, 1994), 404.

18. See Blumenson, *Breakout and Pursuit,* 207, 333.

19. Ingersoll, *Top Secret,* 178.

20. Blumenson, *Breakout and Pursuit,* 271.

21. Eisenhower to Montgomery, 21 July 1944, EL, EPPP, box 83.

22. General Dempsey, diary, 25 July 1944, PRO, War Office, 285/9.

23. Prime Minister's Personal Minute, To General Ismay and Mr. Peck, 16 July 1944, PRO CAB, 120/421.

24. Telegram from Winston Churchill to General Montgomery (Normandy), 27 July 1944, PRO CAB, 101/250.

25. On the implications of this maneuver for the Allied forces, see Bernard Law Montgomery, *Normandy to the Baltic* (London: Hutchinson, 1947), 87–88.

26. On the lack of precise intelligence, see Major X, "Operation Bluecoat," 2 August 1944, PRO, War Office, 205/232.

27. See telegram from General Eisenhower to General Montgomery, 31 July 1944, PRO CAB, 106/1091.

28. Quotation in Admiral Ramsay, diary, 29 July [1944], PRO CAB, 106/1124 and cable from General Montgomery to General Eisenhower, 28 July 1944, PRO CAB, 106/979.

29. See H. G. Gee, "A Survey of Tank Warfare in Europe from D-Day to 12 August 1944," 1952, PRO, War Office, 291/1218.

30. See "Liberation Campaign North-West Europe 1944–1945, Phase 4: The Break-Out and the Advance to the Crossing of the Seine (16 June–29 August 1944)," PRO CAB, 44/251.

31. See War Diary: Progress Report (Chaplains) for Week Ending on 7 August 1944, PRO, War Office, 171/140.

32. Adolf Hitler, *Speeches and Proclamations, 1932–1945: The Chronicle of a Dictatorship,* ed. Max Domarus, trans. Mary Fran Gilbert et al., 4 vols. (Wauconda, Ill.: Bolchazy-Carducci, 1990–2004), 4:2931.

33. See F. W. Winterbotham, *The Ultra Secret* (London: Weidenfeld and Nicolson, 1974), 148–152.

34. See Operation Totalize, Ground Plan, 4 August 1944, PRO, Air Force, 37/763.

35. See note from Marshal Leigh-Mallory, 23 August 1944, ibid.

36. See Marshal Leigh-Mallory, diary, 7–9 August, ibid., 784.

37. See Memorandum, Main HQ First Canadian Army, 14 August 1944, PRO, War Office, 179/2596.

38. See P. J. Montagu, "Canadian Operations, North-West Europe," 20 December 1944, NARA, RG 331, entry 23, box 13.

39. Bradley, *A Soldier's Story,* 377.

40. Ibid.

41. CCS for General Wilson, 2 July 1944, EL, secretary, general staff, microfilm 23.

42. Forrest C. Pogue, *The Supreme Command* (Washington, D.C.: Office of the Chief of Military History, Department of the Army, 1954), 224.

43. See Robert E. Sherwood, *Roosevelt and Hopkins: An Intimate History* (New York: Harper Brothers, 1948), 810.

44. Harry C. Butcher, *My Three Years with Eisenhower: The Personal Diary of Captain Harry C. Butcher, USNR, Naval Aide to General Eisenhower, 1942–1945* (New York: Simon and Schuster, 1946), 635.

45. See editor's note, Message from Eisenhower to Marshall, 5 August 1944, in *The Papers of Dwight David Eisenhower,* 21 vols., ed. Alfred D. Chandler, Jr. (Baltimore: Johns Hopkins University Press, 1970), 4:2056.

46. SHAEF, Planning Staff, Post-Neptune Operation: Section III: Crossing of the Seine and Capture of Paris, 17 August 1944, NARA, RG 331, entry 23, box 52.

47. See Weigley, *Eisenhower's Lieutenants,* 237; and Stephen E. Ambrose, *The Supreme Commander: The War Years of General Dwight D. Eisenhower* (Garden City, N.Y.: Doubleday, 1970), 458. Ninety percent of the Mediterranean cargo went through Marseille; see Roland G. Ruppenthal, *Logistical Support of the Armies,* 2 vols. (Washington, D.C.: Office of the Chief of Military History, Department of the Army, 1953–1959), 2:124.

48. Winston S. Churchill, *Triumph and Tragedy* (Boston: Houghton Mifflin, 1953), 100. On American and British differences over Berlin, see Carlo D'Este, *Eisenhower: Allied Supreme Commander* (New York: Holt, 2002), 690–694.

49. See General Eisenhower to CCS, General Marshall, and General Wilson, 23 June 1944, in Eisenhower, *Papers of Dwight David Eisenhower,* 3:1943.

50. See General Marshall to General Eisenhower, 29 June 1944, EL, EPPP, box 133.

51. See David M. Glantz and Jonathan House, *When Titans Clashed: How the Red Army Stopped Hitler* (Lawrence: University Press of Kansas, 1995), 201 ff.

52. See Richard Overy, *Russia's War: A History of the Soviet War Effort, 1941–1945* (London: Penguin, 1997), 243.

53. *Pravda,* 14 June 1944. [Translated from the French version provided by Mikhail Narinski.—Trans.]

54. John R. Deane, *The Strange Alliance: The Story of Our Efforts at Wartime Cooperation with Russia* (New York: Viking, 1947), 151.

55. General Burrows to COS, 7 June 1944, PRO, War Office, 106/4162.

56. See War Office to British Military Mission (Moscow), 13 June 1944, PRO, War Office, 106/4162.

57. See Note from Joint Chiefs of Staff, Appendix, [early September 1944], NARA, RG 218, JCS, box 213.

58. See Notes on the Operations of 21st Army Group, 6 June 1944–5 May 1945, n.d., PRO CAB, 106/973.

59. The figures of ten thousand dead and fifty thousand prisoners are now generally accepted; see D'Este, *Decision in Normandy,* 437–438.

60. Quoted in Blumenson, *Breakout and Pursuit,* 558.

61. Estimates can be found ibid., 555; in Martin Blumenson, *Patton: The Man behind the Legend, 1885–1945* (New York: Morrow, 1985), 236; and in Weigley, *Eisenhower's Lieutenants,* 215.

62. See Max Hastings, *Overlord: D-Day and the Battle for Normandy* (London: Michael Joseph, 1984), 305.

63. See Air Vice-Marshal S. C. Strafford, War Diary (May–September 1944), 15 August 1944, PRO, Air Force, 37/354; and Terry Copp, *Fields of Fire: The Canadians in Normandy* (Toronto: University of Toronto Press, 2003), 252.

64. On the number of vehicles, see Operational Research Section, Twenty-first Army Group, "Enemy Casualties in Vehicles and Equipment during the Retreat from Normandy to the Seine," n.d., NARA, RG 331, entry 23, box 13; on the number of men, see John Keegan, *Six Armies in Normandy: From D-Day to the Liberation of Paris* (London: Penguin, 1994), 285.

65. See Operational Research Section, Twenty-first Army Group, "Enemy Casualties in Vehicles and Equipment," 13.

66. Blumenson, *Patton,* 236.

67. See U.S. Strategic Bombing Survey, "The Impact of the Allied Air Effort on German Logistics," 1945, NARA, RG 243, entry 6, box 480.

68. See General Eisenhower to General Marshall, 7 August 1944, PRO CAB, 106/979.

69. See General Bedell Smith, "Command and Organization after D-Day Overlord," 1 June 1944, NARA, RG 331, entry 12, box 9.

70. See editor's note, General Eisenhower to General Marshall, 19 August 1944, *The Papers of Dwight David Eisenhower*, 4:2077.

71. Bradley, *A Soldier's Story*, 353.

72. Bernard Law Montgomery, *The Memoirs of Field-Marshal the Viscount Montgomery of Alamein* (London: Collins, 1958), 234.

73. See Home Intelligence Division, "Weekly Interest Index, Prepared by the British Institute of Public Opinion, Based on Interviews Made September 1–3 [1944] Inclusive," PRO, Home Office, 262/16.

74. Dwight D. Eisenhower, *Crusade in Europe* (Garden City, N.Y.: Doubleday, 1948), 299.

75. See E. G. Smiths, Army Operational Research Group, "Some Statistics of the North-West European Campaign—June 1944 to May 1945," October 1954, PRO CAB, 106/1580.

76. Personal for CIGS [chief of Imperial General Staff] from General Montgomery, 18 August 1944, PRO CAB, 44/252.

77. See Personal for C.I.G.S. from General Montgomery, 23 August 1944, ibid.

78. See Basil H. Liddell Hart, *History of the Second World War* (London: Cassell, 1970), 564–565.

79. Montgomery, *Memoirs*, 243.

80. Ibid., 255–256.

81. Eisenhower, *Crusade in Europe*, 306.

82. See Clement Attlee's interventions in "Conclusions of a Meeting of the War Cabinet Held in the Cabinet War Room," 14 August 1944, PRO CAB, 65/43.

83. See Ruppenthal, *Logistical Support of the Armies*, 1:504–505.

84. See Smiths, "Some Statistics of the North-West European Campaign."

85. See Ruppenthal, *Logistical Support of the Armies*, 1:491.

86. See "Planning of Operation Overlord," 9 August 1945, PRO, War Office, 232/15.

87. See Ruppenthal, *Logistical Support of the Armies*, 1:560.

88. Ibid., 1:509–513.

89. Ibid., 1:582.

## 12. The Battle of France—and France's Battle

1. Quoted by François Kersaudy, *Churchill and De Gaulle* (London: Collins, 1981), 284.

2. Quoted in Jean-Baptiste Duroselle, *L'Abîme, 1939–1945* (Paris: Imprimerie Nationale, 1982), 477. [This extract and others following are translated from the versions contained in Free French cipher traffic to and from de Gaulle's headquarters, designated by the code name Diplofrance.—Trans.]

3. Quotations ibid., 478.

4. Note of 7 September 1943, Ministry of Foreign Affairs [henceforth MAE], Political and Commercial Correspondence, 1939–1945 War, London and Algiers [henceforth CPCLA],698.

5. Pierre Viénot to Diplofrance, 23 November 1943, MAE, CPCLA, 698.

6. René Massigli to Pierre Viénot, 9 February 1944, ibid., 697.

7. Hervé Alphand, "Note on Conversations concerning the Recognition of the Committee of Liberation," 21 March 1944, MAE, CPCLA, Papiers Massigli (Massigli Papers) [henceforth PM], 1466.

8. Winston Churchill to foreign secretary, 10 May 1944, PRO CAB, 101/244.

9. See Europe/America Department to Moscow Embassy, 24 March 1944, MAE, CPCLA, PM, 1612.

10. Diplofrance to the Moscow Embassy, 8 June 1944, ibid., 1465.

11. See François Lévêque, "Les relations franco-soviétiques pendant la Seconde Guerre mondiale: De la Défaite à l'Alliance, 1939–1945" (Doctoral thesis, University of Paris I, 1992), 861.

12. Maurice Dejean, note of 13 January 1944, MAE, CPCLA, 1263; Dejean, telegram of 5 February 1944, ibid.

13. From an article published in *Voina i rabochii klass* [War and the Working Class], with commentary by Roger Garreau, telegram of 17 June 1944, MAE, CPCLA, 1264.

14. Department of Economic Affairs to René Massigli, 5 April 1944, MAE, CPCLA, 698.

15. Winston Churchill to foreign secretary, 23 May 1944, PRO CAB, 101/244.

16. Lévêque, "Les relations franco-soviétiques pendant la Seconde Guerre mondiale," 909 (quotation), 911.

17. See Roger Garreau, telegram of 10 June 1944, MAE, CPCLA, PM, 1465.

18. Quoted in Roger Garreau, telegram of 26 June 1944, ibid., 1611.

19. Quoted in Roger Garreau, telegram of 26 June 1944, ibid., 1264.

20. Lieutenant General F. E. Morgan, "Operation Overlord, Report and Appreciation," 15 July 1943, NARA, RG 331, entry 35, box 226.

21. Third United States Army Outline Plan, Operation Overlord, SOE/SO Plan, 12 May 1944, NARA, RG 331, entry 35, box 228.

22. War Cabinet and Cabinet Office: Historical Section, "The Sabotage Campaign in France Prior to 1944 June," 1955, PRO CAB, 106/1118.

23. Hervé Alphand, "Note on the Conversations concerning the Recognition of the Committee of Liberation," 21 March 1944, MAE, CPCLA, PM, 1466.

24. Hervé Alphand to René Massigli and Maurice Couve de Murville, 5 November 1943, MAE, CPCLA, 698.

25. Henri Hoppenot to Diplofrance, 2 December 1943, ibid., 697.

26. Lieutenant General Bedell Smith, untitled message, 28 March 1944, NARA, RG 331, entry 34, box 38.

27. Charles de Gaulle, *The Complete War Memoirs of Charles de Gaulle,* trans. Jonathan Griffin and Richard Howard (New York: Carroll and Graf, 1998), 553.

28. General Koenig to Lieutenant General Grasset, 16 May 1944, NARA, RG 331, entry 2, box 108.

29. Franklin D. Roosevelt, Directive to the Supreme Commander, 15 March 1944, NARA, RG 331, entry 2, box 108.

30. Quoted in François Kersaudy, *De Gaulle et Roosevelt: Le duel au sommet* (Paris: Perrin, 2004), 373.

31. Franklin Roosevelt to General Eisenhower, 13 May 1944, EL, EPPP, box 133.

32. See Lieutenant General Bedell Smith to CCS, 19 April 1944, NARA, RG 331, entry 2, box 108.

33. Major General Hilldring to the commanding general, European Theater of Operations, 11 October 1943, EL, Ray Barker Papers, 1.

34. Quoted in Jean Quellien, "Les Normands au coeur de la guerre," in Bernard Garnier, Jean-Luc Leleu, Françoise Passera, and Jean Quellien, eds., *Les populations civiles face au débarquement et à la bataille de Normandie* (Caen: Mémorial de Caen, 2005), 16.

35. Third United States Army, Outline Plan, Annex 10 G-5 Plan, 10 June 1944, NARA, RG 331, entry 35, box 228.

36. De Gaulle, *Complete War Memoirs,* 599.

37. Note from G3, Implication of Injection of a French Division Early in Neptune or in Rankin C, 18 January 1944, NARA, RG 331, entry 2, box 110.

38. Major General Bull to Chief, Plans and Operations Section, "Employment of a French Division in 'OVERLORD' and 'RANKIN' 'C' from the Northwest," 15 January 1944, NARA, RG 331, entry 35, box 226.

39. Lieutenant General Bedell Smith to COS, 28 January 1944, ibid., entry 2, box 110.

40. Lieutenant General Morgan to Assistant COS G3, 14 January 1944, ibid., box 10.

41. Ibid.

42. Charles de Gaulle, *Mémoires de guerre, L'unité: 1942–1944* (Paris: Plon, 1956), 675.

43. See H. R. Bull to Lieutenant General Morgan, 19 January 1944, NARA, RG 331, entry 2, box 110.

44. In the event, Leclerc's division was cobbled together from "not only the two opposed camps of Pétainism and Gaullism, but the three unmingling streams of which the old army was composed, *métropolitain, colonial, Africain.*" In addition to two tank regiments and two regiments of artillery from North Africa, an antitank regiment formed by a pro-Vichy naval battalion of Fusiliers-Marins, and a Gaullist reconnaissance regiment, the First Spahis Marocains, "the infantry, Gaullist from the start, had reluctantly to be remade. The Senagalese would not do as liberators and so, against their will and their officers'—had they not been good enough to march in the front rank of Nivelle's 'victory' offensive of 1917?—were sent home, to be replaced by Frenchmen. The Régiment de marche du Tchad would return to France as a white regiment. Christian Arabs from the Lebanon, who had 'rallied' after the defeat of the Army of the Levant in 1941, provided the engineers." See John Keegan, *Six Armies in Normandy: From D-Day to the Liberation of Paris* (London: Penguin, 1994), 303–304.

45. Conclusions of a Meeting of the War Cabinet Held at 10 Downing Street, 19 May 1944, PRO CAB, 65/42.

46. Quoted in Kersaudy, *Churchill and De Gaulle,* 336.

47. Quotation ibid., 342. [Kersaudy's English version slightly modified.—Trans.]

48. De Gaulle, *Complete War Memoirs,* 559.

49. Ibid.

50. Ibid., 560.

51. Charles de Gaulle, *Discours et messages, 1940–1969,* 5 vols. (Paris: Plon, 1970), 1:407–408.

52. See Winston Churchill to Franklin D. Roosevelt, 8 June 1944, PRO CAB, 101/250.

53. De Gaulle, *Discours et messages,* 1:408.

54. De Gaulle, *Complete War Memoirs,* 552.

55. Winston Churchill to Franklin D. Roosevelt, 9 June 1944, PRO CAB, 66/51.

56. Winston Churchill to foreign secretary and chancellor of the Exchequer, 9 June 1944, ibid., 101/244.

57. See Franklin Roosevelt to Winston Churchill, 13 June 1944, ibid., 66/51.

58. Winston Churchill to Franklin D. Roosevelt, 10 June 1944, ibid., 101/250.

59. Cabinet, Annex, 13 June 1944, ibid., 65/46.

60. Winston Churchill to Franklin D. Roosevelt, 21 June 1944, ibid., 101/250.

61. See Conclusions of a Meeting of the War Cabinet Held at 10 Downing Street, 7 June 1944, ibid., 65/42.

62. See Telegram from Franklin D. Roosevelt to Winston Churchill, 13 June 1944, quoted in Conclusions of a Meeting of the War Cabinet Held at 10 Downing Street, 13 June 1944, ibid. For a fuller account of the course of developments during de Gaulle's stay in London in June 1944, see Kersaudy, *Churchill and De Gaulle,* 337–359.

### 13. Liberators and Liberated

1. See Michel Boivin, Gérard Bourdin, and Jean Quellien, *Villes normandes sous les bombes, juin 1944* (Caen: Presses Universitaires de Caen / Mémorial de Caen, 1994), 19.

2. Ibid., 25.

3. C. D. Jackson to [Major General Robert] McClure, 5 May 1944, EL, Bedell Smith Papers, box 6.

4. Civil Affairs, Twenty-first Army Group, "Preliminary Report on Recce of British Beach-head by Lt. Col. D. R. Ellias," 9–12 June 1944, PRO, War Office, 219/3727.

5. Civil Affairs, Rear Headquarters, Twenty-first Army Group, "Operation Overlord, First General Report (Period D-Day to Capture of Caen)," 15 August 1944, NARA RG 331, entry 54, box 290.

6. Marc Hillel, *Vie et moeurs des GI's en Europe, 1942–1947* (Paris: Balland, 1981), 139.

7. See Captain E. G. de Pury, "First Report on U.S. Zone of Operations in France," 25 June 1944, PRO, War Office, 219/3727.

8. Captain de Pury to DCCAO HQ [deputy chief civil affairs officer, headquarters], Reconnaissance Report on Caen, 12 July 1944, NARA RG 331, entry 54, box 290. [British translation slightly modified.—Trans.]

9. Captain de Pury, First Army, Intelligence Report on Cherbourg, 7 July 1944, NARA RG 331, entry 54, box 282.

10. Notes on the Normandy campaign by Brigadier James Hargest, New Zealand Army Observer with Thirtieth Corps, 6 June–10 July 1944, PRO CAB 106/1060.

11. Ibid.

12. Rex North, "These People Terrify Me," *Sunday Pictorial*, 18 June 1944, PRO, Foreign Office, 371/41 863.

13. See Foreign Office, "Attitude of the Civil Population in Liberated Normandy," 26 June 1944, PRO CAB 66/51.

14. Quoted in Michael J. Gunton, "Les Normands et la presse populaire britannique," in Bernard Garnier et al., eds., *Les populations civiles face au débarquement et à la bataille de Normandie* (Caen: Mémorial de Caen, 2005), 200.

15. Foreign Office, "Attitude of the Civil Population in Liberated Normandy," 26 June 1944, PRO CAB 66/51.

16. General Lewis, Second Army, letter to DCCAO, 14 June 1944, NARA RG 331, entry 54, box 292.

17. See Civil Affairs Summary, 20 June 1944, ibid., box 281.

18. See Michel Boivin, "Les Manchois dans la tourmente de la guerre, 1939–1945" (Doctoral thesis, Université de Caen, 2003), 4:919; also ibid., 4:1100.

19. General court-martial, verdict of 1 September 1944, NARA RG 331, entry 237, box 13.

20. See Boivin, "Les Manchois dans la tourmente," 4:1096.

21. Prefect of the Manche, letter to the regional commissioner of the Republic in Bayeux, 19 August 1944, quoted ibid., 4:919.

22. See Twelfth Army Group, Report of Operations (Final After-Action Report), NARA RG 331, entry 200A, box 267.

23. Colonel Julian C. Hyer and Lieutenant Colonels Burton S. Hill, Charles T. Shanner, and William H. Moroney, "Report of the General Board, United States Forces, European Theater, November 1945," NARA RG 319, entry 47, box 162.

24. See J. Robert Lilly, *La face cachée des GI's: Les viols commis par des soldats américains en France, en Angleterre et en Allemagne pendant la Seconde Guerre mondiale* (Paris: Payot, 2003), 155.

25. See Boivin, "Les Manchois dans la tourmente," 4:1094–1096.

26. See Comprehensive Summary of Court-Martial Convictions (British Other Ranks, Home and Overseas), PRO, War Office, 93/53.

27. Hillel, *Vie et moeurs des GI's en Europe, 1942–1947*, 7.

28. J. Robert Lilly and François Le Roy, "L'armée américaine et les viols en France, juin 1944–mai 1945," *Vingtième Siècle: Revue d'Histoire* 75 (July–September 2002): 116.

29. Colonel Julian C. Hyer and Lieutenant Colonel Andre B. Moore, "Military Offenders in Theater of Operations," study no. 84, n.d. [probably 1945 or 1946], NARA RG 319, entry 47, box 162.

30. See Lilly and Le Roy, "L'armée américaine et les viols en France," 116.

31. Ibid., 118.

32. General court-martial, verdict of 1 September 1944, NARA RG 331, entry 237, box 13.

33. Colonel Julian C. Hyer and Lieutenant Colonels Burton S. Hill, Charles T. Shanner, and William H. Moroney, "Report of the General Board, United States Forces, European Theater," November 1945, NARA RG 319, entry 47, box 162.

34. See Hillel, *Vie et moeurs des GI's en Europe, 1942–1947,* 148.

35. R. W. Hartman and Charles A. Copp, Third headquarters, European Civil Affairs Division, "Police in Normandy," bulletin no. 10, 11 July 1944, NARA RG 331, entry 54, box 282.

36. See Civil Affairs Operations in XV Corps Historical, 1 April 1944–31 August 1944, ibid., box 285.

37. Major General R. B. Lord, Instruction to Commanding General, 13 December 1944, NARA RG 331, entry 100, box 13.

38. See Boivin, "Les Manchois dans la tourmente," 4:1207.

39. Telegram from Franklin Roosevelt to Winston Churchill, 13 June 1944, PRO CAB 65/42.

40. Telegram from Winston Churchill to General Montgomery, 13 June 1944, PRO CAB 120/867.

41. Telegram from General Montgomery to Winston Churchill, 15 June 1944, ibid.

42. Captain E. G. de Pury, "Report on CA [Civil Affairs] Recce of Second Army Area from 12 June to 18 June 1944," NARA RG 331, entry 54, box 292.

43. Telegram from General Montgomery to Winston Churchill, 15 June 1944.

44. SCAO [senior civil affairs officer] to DCCAO, 16 June 1944, NARA RG 331, entry 54, box 292.

45. Second British Army, Establishment of Cordial Relationship with the French, D-Day to 17 July 1944, n.d., ibid.

46. Civil Affairs Main Headquarters, Twenty-first Army Group, Political Development in Normandy: Week Ending 18 June 1944, 19 June 1944, NARA RG 331, entry 54, box 290.

47. Colonel W. F. Durbin, "Report on Field Trip Made from 1–10 July 1944," Special Intelligence Bulletin no. 10, 26 July 1944, ibid., box 282.

48. Lieutenant Colonel Charles A. Copp, headquarters, European Civil Affairs Division, G2 Section, [untitled report], Special Intelligence Bulletin no. 4, 10 July 1944, ibid.

49. See Captain E. G. de Pury, "Recce Report on St. Lô, Coutances and Coutances Coastal Areas," 31 July 1944, PRO, War Office, 219/3727.

50. See Boivin, "Les Manchois dans la tourmente," 4:901–902.

51. See SHAEF G5, Twelfth Army Group, Daily Civil Summary, n.d., NARA RG 331, entry 54, box 281.

52. Lieutenant Charles A. Copp, Third headquarters, European Civil Affairs Division, G2 Section, Special Intelligence Bulletin no. 4.

53. See Jean Quellien, "Les Normands au coeur de la guerre," in Bernard Garnier, Jean-Luc Leleu, Françoise Passera, and Jean Quellien, eds., *Les populations civiles face au débarquement et à la bataille de Normandie* (Caen: Mémorial de Caen, 2005), 16.

54. See Medical Historian Papers, Campaign in North West Europe (1944 June–1945 May), n.d., PRO 222/1496.

55. See Political Warfare Division, directive no. 3 (for the Week Beginning 29 June 1944), n.d., NARA RG 331, entry 23, box 51.

56. SHAEF, Office of the Chief of Staff, Minutes of Meeting Held in the Office of the Chief of Staff, 17 June 1944, NARA RG 331, entry 34, box 25.

57. For an overview see Jean-Louis Crémieux-Brilhac, *La France libre: De l'appel du 18 juin à la libération* (Paris: Gallimard, 1996), 856ff.

58. French Resistance during the First Ten Days of the Operations in Normandy, n.d., NARA RG 226, microfilm 1642, roll 103, frame 826.

59. See SHAEF G3 Division, Special Report on Resistance Operation in Brittany no. 5, 7–8 August 1944, NARA RG 331, entry 30A, box 145.

60. National staff of the FFI, 2nd Bureau, summary no. 6, 12 August, PRO CAB 106/989.

61. SHAEF G3 Division, Special Report on Resistance Operation in Brittany, no. 2, 4–5 August 1944, NARA RG 331, entry 30A, box 145.

62. SHAEF G3 Division, Special Report on Resistance Operation in Brittany, no. 6, 8–9 August 1944, ibid.

63. See William J. Donovan, memorandum for JCS, 22 July 1944, NARA RG 226, microfilm 1642, roll 1, frame 103.

64. W. J. Donovan to General H. H. Arnold, 25 February 1944, ibid., roll 103, frame 1108.

65. Wire addressed to G2, ETOUSA, for General Eisenhower from the Joint Chiefs of Staff, 19 April 1944, NARA RG 226, ibid., roll 104, frame 154.

66. The actual figures for June and 1–21 July were 64 percent and 47 percent, respectively. See William J. Donovan, memorandum for JCS, 22 July 1944, , ibid., roll 1, frame 103.

67. From General Marshall to SHAEF for General Eisenhower, 9 July, NARA RG 331, entry 35, box 227.

68. See CCS to General Eisenhower, 16 August 1944, PRO CAB 106/982.

69. Memorandum from W. J. Donovan for General Marshall, 9 July 1944, NARA RG 226, microfilm 1642, roll 103, frame 884.

70. See [Allied Force Headquarters], Report on the Potential of the Resistance in Eastern, Southern, and Central France, 13 July 1944, ibid., roll 1, frame 103.

71. W. J. Donovan, memorandum for General Marshall, 12 July 1944, ibid., roll 103, frame 826.

72. See Lieutenant Colonel [Broad?] to General Ismay, General Koenig's Command, 31 July 1944, PRO, Defence Ministry, 2/1151.

73. See Philippe Buton, *La joie douloureuse: La libération de la France* (Brussels: Complexe, 2004), 63–66, 85–91; also Robert Aron, *Histoire de la libération de la France, juin 1944–mai 1945* (Brussels: Marabout, 1984), 184–186, 282–316, 559–562.

74. Quoted in Desmond Hawkins, ed., *From D-Day to VE Day: Radio Reports from the Western Front, 1944–45* (London: BBC Books, 1994), 136.

75. On the situation in Brittany, see Luc Capdevilla, *Les Bretons au lendemain de l'Occupation: Imaginaire et comportement d'une sortie de guerre, 1944–1945* (Rennes: Presses Universitaires de Rennes, 1999), 28ff.

76. This classification is inspired in part by the discussion found ibid., 33ff.

77. See Judge Advocate General, War Crimes in France, n.d., NARA RG 153, JAG, entry 151, box 1. Text of original document is in French.—Trans.

78. Ibid.

79. Report of the mayor of Cléder to the subprefect of Morlaix, n.d. [probably September 1944], NARA RG 153, JAG, entry 151, box 2.

80. Captain Hemery, military commander for Huelgoat, report of 29 September 1944, ibid.

81. See Jean Quellien and Jacques Vico, *Massacres nazis en Normandie: Les fusillés de la prison de Caen* (Condé-sur-Noireau: Éditions Charles Corlet, 2004).

82. See Quellien, "Les Normands au coeur de la guerre," 14.

83. Captain E. G. de Pury, "Recce Report on St. Lô, Coutances and Coutances Coastal Areas," 31 July 1944, PRO, War Office, 219/3727.

84. See Captain E. G. de Pury, "Reconnaissance Report on Caen," 12 July 1944, NARA RG 331, entry 54, box 290. It should be noted, however, that Jean Quellien, a leading authority on Normandy under the occupation, is skeptical of this conclusion.

85. Jean-Luc Leleu, "Les troupes allemandes face à la population normande au cours des combats de l'été 1944," in Garnier et al., *Les populations civiles face au débarquement*, 124. Leleu quotes a 16 July 1944 OKW directive to the Tenth SS Panzer Division.

86. See Leleu, "Les troupes allemandes face à la population normande," 127.

87. Basil H. Liddell Hart, *The Other Side of the Hill: Germany's Generals, Their Rise and Fall, with Their Own Account of Military Events, 1939–1945* (London: Cassell, 1951), 35.

88. Henri Hoppenot to Diplofrance, 9 June 1944, MAE CPCLA, PM, 1466.

89. See François Kersaudy, *Churchill and De Gaulle* (London: Collins, 1981), 360–361.

90. Charles de Gaulle, *The Complete War Memoirs of Charles de Gaulle*, trans. Jonathan Griffin and Richard Howard (New York: Carroll and Graf, 1998), 576.

91. Ibid, 579.

92. See Instructions Retracing the General Lines of the Accords Concluded on 25 August 1944, MAE CPCLA, PM, 1466.

93. SHAEF, planning staff, Post-Neptune Operation, Section 3: Crossing of the Seine and Capture of Paris, 17 August 1944, NARA RG 331, entry 23, box 52.

94. On the Paris uprising as a whole, see the proceedings of a conference marking the fiftieth anniversary of the event, ed. Christine Levisse-Touzé, *Paris 1944: Les enjeux de la libération* (Paris: Albin Michel, 1994).

95. See Crémieux-Brilhac, *La France libre*, 890–891.

96. Quoted in John Keegan, *Six Armies in Normandy: From D-Day to the Liberation of Paris* (London: Penguin, 1994), 306.

97. Georges Boris, telegram to [Emmanuel] d'Astier, National Archives [henceforth AN] F1 A 3717.

98. [Ministry of the Interior], "Thoughts on the National Uprising in Paris," 14 August 1944, AN 72 AJ 1901.

99. Quoted in Anthony Eden to Duff Cooper, 22 August 1944, PRO, Foreign Office, 371/41 863.

100. See [COMAC], Summary of the Meeting of 3 July 1944, AN 72 AJ 3; Adrien Dansette, *Histoire de la libération de Paris* (Paris: Fayard, 1947), 50; and Service Historique de l'Armée de Terre (Army Historical Department) [henceforth SHAT], 13, P 43.

101. Quoted in Colonel Rol-Tanguy and Roger Bourderon, *La libération de Paris: Les cent documents* (Paris: Hachette, 1994), 158 bis.

102. Henri Rol-Tanguy, directive of 24 August 1944, SHAT 13 P 42.

103. Summary of Meeting with Chaban, telegram from the Ministry of the Interior (London) to the Ministry of the Interior (Algiers), received 11 August 1944, AN 72 AJ 1901.

104. See Crémieux-Brilhac, *La France libre,* 898ff.

105. Omar N. Bradley, *A Soldier's Story* (New York: Holt, 1951), 392.

106. See Buton, *La joie douloureuse,* 90–91.

107. "Paris desecrated! Paris broken! Paris martyred!"—Trans.

# Acknowledgments

Once my research was complete, I was naturally eager to thank all those who made it possible. In each of the archives where I worked, in Abilene, London, Paris, and Washington, I was fortunate to be able to count on the friendly and expert assistance of the staff. In Freiburg Hans Umbreit, who has unfortunately since passed away, generously agreed to act as an adviser on the German side, locating and translating from primary and secondary sources; Mikhail Narinski, in Moscow, performed the same service on the Russian side. My stays abroad were greatly assisted by the financial support offered by the Institut d'Histoire du Temps Présent (IHTP) in Paris, then directed by Henry Rousso. For the hospitality shown me in London by Emmanuelle Ertel and David Strasavage, and for that of Christine Mengin and Pierre Duquesne in Washington, I am particularly grateful. Back in Paris, thanks to the legendary courtesy of Jean Astruc and Anne-Marie Pathé, I was able to take advantage of the resources of the IHTP library. Stefan Martens, at the Institut Historique Allemand, kindly consented to clarify a number of points that remained obscure. Last, but not least, Patrice Duran, director of the Department of Social Sciences at the École Normale Supérieure de Cachan, followed the project with enthusiasm.

The French manuscript benefited from the critical and constructive reading of Annie François at Éditions du Seuil, who gave generously of both her time and her talent. Among my colleagues in France, I am indebted to François Besse, Jean-Louis Crémieux-Brilhac, Jean-Luc Leleu,

Jean Quellien, and Maurice Vaïsse, as well as to my sister, Sylvie Wieviorka, and my mother, Rachel Wieviorka, whose advice and comments substantially improved the text. I owe thanks, finally, to Michel Winock, who, before he left Seuil, welcomed the project and encouraged it as both a scholar and friend.

A number of people helped bring the American edition into the world. My heartfelt thanks are due to Patrice Higonnet, who eloquently argued in favor of the book's publication in English at Harvard University Press. My editor there, Kathleen McDermott, skillfully supervised the project with the cheerful efficiency that only an author can appreciate. The manuscript profited most of all from the careful scrutiny of my translator, Malcolm DeBevoise, who queried a great many details and made a number of helpful editorial suggestions. A final round of documentary checking was carried out with infinite patience by Hélène Mercier at the National Archives and Records Administration in College Park, Maryland, and by Julie Le Gac at the Public Records Office in Kew, London. Finally, the support and suggestions of colleagues in North America, particularly Eric Jennings, Alice Kaplan, Richard Kuisel, and Venita Datta, were invaluable to me.

To all these people, once again, I express my gratitude.

# Archival Sources

PUBLIC RECORD OFFICE (LONDON)

AIR 37 Air Ministry: Allied Expeditionary Air Force and Second Tactical Air Force
574, 761, 762, 763, 766, 784, 1057
CAB 44 War Cabinet: Historical Section
242, 243, 244, 245, 251, 252, 265
CAB 65 War Cabinet and Cabinet: Minutes
41, 42, 43, 44, 45, 46, 47
CAB 66 War Cabinet and Cabinet: Memoranda
45, 46, 47, 48, 49, 50, 51, 52, 53, 54
CAB 101 War Cabinet
244, 250
CAB 105 War Cabinet and Cabinet Office: Telegrams
157
CAB 106 War Cabinet: Historical Section
963, 966, 967, 968, 970, 973, 975, 976, 977, 978, 979, 981, 982, 989, 999, 1001,
1003, 1004, 1037, 1041, 1060, 1064, 1091, 1106, 1116, 1117, 1118, 1122, 1126, 1212, 1580
CAB 118 War Cabinet and Cabinet: Various Ministers, Private Office Files
68
CAB 119 War Cabinet and Cabinet Office: Joint Planning Staff, Correspondence and
Papers
6, 62, 63, 93
CAB 120 Cabinet Office: Ministry of Defence Secretariat, Records
421, 867
CAB 139 War Cabinet and Cabinet Office: Central Statistical Office, Correspondence
and Papers
52, 61, 133
DEFE 2 Combined Operations Headquarters and Ministry of Defence
426, 427, 460, 487, 498, 499, 501, 1114, 1151

FO 371 Foreign Office: Political Departments, General Correspondence, 1906–1966
40361, 41863, 41871

HO 199 Ministry of Home Security: Intelligence Branch, Registered Files, 1939–1950
394 A, 410

HO 201 Ministry of Home Security: Key Points Intelligence Directorate, Reports and Papers
22, 36

HO 203 Ministry of Home Security: Home Security Daily Intelligence Reports
14

HO 262 Ministry of Information: Home Intelligence Division (HI) Files
15, 16

HS 8 Ministry of Economic Warfare: Special Operations Executive and Successors; Headquarters, Records
899

HW 1 Government Code and Cipher School, Ultra
2890, 2903, 2907, 2939, 2985, 2993, 3056, 3058, 3143, 3152, 3174

INF 1 Ministry of Information: Mass-Survey Observations
282, 291, 293, 970, 972, 973

KV 2 The Security Service, Personal (PF Series)
2410, 2411

PREM 3 Prime Minister's Office: Operational Correspondence and Papers, 1937–1946
177/4

WO 93 Judge Advocate General's Office: Miscellaneous Correspondence and Papers, 1650–1969
53, 55

WO 106 War Office: Directorate of Military Operations and Military Intelligence; Correspondence and Papers, 1837–1962
4162

WO 107 Office of the Commander in Chief and War Office: Quartermaster General's Department
169, 243

WO 163 War Office, Morale Committee
161, 162, 163

WO 171 War Office: Allied Expeditionary Force, North West Europe (British Element); War Diaries, Second World War, 1943–1946
115, 138, 139, 140, 182, 190

WO 177 War Office: Army Medical Services; War Diaries, Second World War, 1939–1946
316, 321

WO 179 War Office: Canadian, South African, New Zealand, and Indian (United Kingdom) Forces (Dominion Forces); War Diaries, Second World War, 1939–1946
2596

WO 193 War Office: Directorate of Military Operations and Plans, later Directorate of Military Operations; Files concerning Military Planning, Intelligence, and Statistics, 1934–1958
  396, 489, 670, 821, 822
WO 201 War Office: Middle East Forces; Military Headquarters Papers, Second World War, 1936–1946
  2374
WO 205 War Office: Twenty-first Army Group; Military Headquarters Papers, Second World War, 1942–1947
  5 D, 5 G, 19 B, 39, 56, 118, 172, 228, 232, 644, 901
WO 213 Judge Advocate General's Office: Field Marshal Courts Martial and Military Courts; Registers, 1909–1963
  55
WO 216 War Office: Office of the Chief of the Imperial General Staff; Papers, 1935–1964
  101
WO 219 War Office: Supreme Headquarters Allied Expeditionary Force; Military Headquarters Papers, Second World War, 1939–1947
  3727, 4717 A, 4730
WO 222 War Office: Medical Historians' Papers, First and Second World Wars, 1914–1949
  8, 158, 275, 1496
WO 223 War Office: Staff College Camberley; Course Notes on D-Day Landings and Ensuing Campaigns, 1947
  14
WO 232 War Office: Directorate of Tactical Investigations; Papers, 1939–1950
  15
WO 259 War Office: Department of the Secretary of State for War; Private Office Papers, 1937–1953
  44
WO 285 War Office: General Miles Christopher Dempsey; Papers, 1944–1969
  2, 13, 39
WO 291 Ministry of Supply and War Office: Military Operational Research Unit; Reports and Papers, 1941–1979
  243, 246, 262, 270, 848, 1141, 1218

## EISENHOWER LIBRARY, ABILENE, KANSAS

Pre-Presidential Papers
  80, 83, 130, 132, 133, 136
Archives of the Secretary General Staff (SGS) Division of SHAEF, Microfilms
  MC 2, 4, 5, 9, 12, 13, 14, 21, 22, 23, 24, 25, 28, 30, 31, 32, 44, 45, 45, 51

Walter Bedell Smith Papers

  1, 28, 32, 33, 34, 37, 41, 49

Ray W. Barker Papers

  1, 2


# NATIONAL ARCHIVES AND RECORDS ADMINISTRATION, WASHINGTON, D.C.

RG 112 Records of the Office of the Surgeon General (Army)

  Entry 31: boxes 311, 427, 430, 494, 1293, 1294, 1295, 1296, 1313, 1314, 1315, 1323, 1339

RG 153 Records of the Office of the Judge Advocate General (Army)

  Entry 151: boxes 1–2

RG 216 Entry 1, Office of Censorship, Service Section

  9, 30, 350, 502, 503, 504

RG 218 Records of the United States Joint Chiefs of Staff

  CCS-JCS files: boxes 171, 172, 173, 194–198, 213, 214, 366, 499, 500, 501, 502

  Leahy Papers: box 5

RG 243 Records of the United States Strategic Bombing Survey

  Entry 6: boxes 476, 479, 480, 482, 483

RG 319 Records of the Army Staff

  Entry 1: boxes 30, 350, 502–504

  Entry 47: box 162

RG 330 Records of the Office of the Secretary of Defense

  Entry 74: boxes 1014, 1015, 1016, 1017, 1018, 1019

  Entry 93: boxes 989–993, 1003–1004

RG 331 Records of Allied Operational and Occupation Headquarters, World War II

  Entry 1: boxes 69, 73, 76–79

  Entry 2: boxes 108–110

  Entry 6: box 13

  Entry 12: boxes 9–11, 13–14

  Entry 23: boxes 13, 14, 47–52, 55

  Entry 29A: boxes 119–120

  Entry 30A: boxes 145–148

  Entry 34: boxes 9, 10, 25, 26, 35–39, 86–89

  Entry 35: boxes 225–229

  Entry 45: box 280

  Entry 54: boxes 276, 277, 281–283, 285, 290, 292, 294

  Entry 56: boxes 2, 118–120

  Entry 93A: box 102

  Entry 100: boxes 12–14

  Entry 200A: boxes 266–268

  Entry 237: box 13

  Entry 266: box 56

Entry 270: boxes 101–103

Entry 277: box 1

Entry 279: box 4

RG 337 Records of Headquarters Army Ground Forces

Entry 15A: boxes 54–58

Entry 84A: box 9

RG 498 Records of Headquarters, European Theater of Operations, U.S. Army (ETOUSA), World War II

USFET SGS File: box 51

ETOUSA Historical Division, Morale Branch: box 41

SGS: box 142

OSS MI 642 R1 Records of the Office of Strategic Services (OSS)

Microfilm reels 103–104

Ministry of Foreign Affairs (MAE)(Paris)

Political and Commercial Correspondence, 1939–1945 war: London and Algiers

French Government, Normandy landing, Negotiations with the Allies: 697, 698, 699, 700

Relations with the USSR: 1263, 1264, 1268

Massigli Papers: 1465, 1466, 1610, 1611, 1612

# Select Bibliography

## Archival Documents

Cantwell, John D. *The Second World War: A Guide to Documents in the PRO.* London: Public Record Office Handbooks, 1993.

*Foreign Relations of the United States; Diplomatic Papers: The Conferences at Cairo and Tehran, 1943.* Washington, D.C.: U.S. Government Printing Office, 1961.

Mulligan, Timothy P. *Guide to Records Relating to U.S. Military Participation in World War II.* Vol. 1, *Policy, Planning, Administration;* vol. 2, *Supply and Support.* Washington, D.C.: National Archives and Records Administration, 1996–1998.

*The Papers of Dwight David Eisenhower.* 21 vols. Vols. 1–5, *The War Years,* ed. Alfred D. Chandler, Jr. Baltimore: Johns Hopkins University Press, 1970.

## Diaries and Memoirs

Brooke, Alan Francis (Field Marshal Lord Alanbrooke). *War Diaries, 1939–1945.* Ed. Alex Danchev and Daniel Todman. London: Weidenfeld and Nicolson, 1957.

Bradley, Omar N. *A Soldier's Story.* New York: Holt, 1951.

Butcher, Harry C. *My Three Years with Eisenhower: The Personal Diary of Captain Harry C. Butcher, USNR, Naval Aide to General Eisenhower, 1942–1945.* New York: Simon and Schuster, 1946.

Churchill, Winston S. *Closing the Ring.* Vol. 5 of *The Second World War.* Boston: Houghton Mifflin, 1951.

———. *Triumph and Tragedy.* Vol. 6 of *The Second World War.* Boston: Houghton Mifflin, 1953.

Deane, John R. *The Strange Alliance: The Story of Our Efforts at Wartime Cooperation with Russia.* New York: Viking, 1947.

De Gaulle, Charles. *Mémoires de guerre: L'unité, 1942–1944.* Paris: Plon, 1956.

———. *The Complete War Memoirs of Charles de Gaulle.* Trans. Jonathan Griffin and Richard Howard. New York: Carroll and Graf, 1998.

Eisenhower, Dwight D. *Crusade in Europe.* Garden City, N.Y.: Doubleday, 1948.

Goebbels, Joseph. *The Goebbels Diaries, 1942–1943.* Ed. and trans. Louis P. Lochner. New York: Doubleday, 1948.

———. *Journal: 1943–1945.* Ed. and trans. Pierre Ayçoberry, Horst Möller, and Stefan Martens. Paris: Tallandier, 2005.

Ingersoll, Ralph. *Top Secret.* New York: Harcourt, Brace, 1946.

Ismay, Hastings L. *The Memoirs of Lord General Ismay.* London: Heinemann, 1960.

Leahy, William D. *I Was There: The Personal Story of the Chief of Staff to Presidents Roosevelt and Truman Based on His Notes and Diaries Made at the Time.* New York: Whittlesey House, 1950.

Montgomery, Bernard Law. *The Memoirs of Field-Marshal the Viscount Montgomery of Alamein.* London: Collins, 1958.

Morgan, Frederick E. *Overture to Overlord.* London: Hodder and Stoughton, 1950.

Patton, George S. *War as I Knew It.* Boston: Houghton Mifflin, 1947; paperback reprint, New York: Bantam, 2004.

Rommel, Erwin. *The Rommel Papers.* Ed. B. H. Liddell Hart, trans. Paul Findlay. New York: Harcourt, Brace, 1953.

Roosevelt, Elliott. *As He Saw It.* New York: Duell, Sloan, and Pearce, 1946.

Ruge, Friedrich. *Rommel in Normandy: Reminiscences.* Trans. Ursula R. Moessner. San Rafael, Calif.: Presidio, 1979.

Shtemenko, S. M. *The Soviet General Staff at War, 1941–1945.* Trans. Robert Daglish. Moscow: Progress, 1971.

Tedder, Arthur William. *With Prejudice: The War Memoirs of Marshal of the Air Force, Lord Tedder.* London: Cassell, 1966.

Warlimont, Walter. *Inside Hitler's Headquarters, 1939–45.* Trans. R. H. Barry. London: Weidenfeld and Nicolson, 1964.

Winterbotham, Frederick. *The Ultra Secret.* London: Weidenfeld and Nicolson, 1974.

Zhukov, Georgii. *The Memoirs of Marshal Zhukov.* New York: Delacorte, 1971.

## SECONDARY PUBLISHED SOURCES

### General Studies

Ambrose, Stephen E. *D-Day, June 6, 1944: The Climactic Battle of World War II.* New York: Simon and Schuster, 1994.

Blumenson, Martin. *Breakout and Pursuit.* Washington, D.C.: Office of the Chief of Military History, Department of the Army, 1961.

Copp, Terry. *Fields of Fire: The Canadians in Normandy.* Toronto: University of Toronto Press, 2003.

D'Este, Carlo. *Decision in Normandy: The Unwritten Story of Montgomery and the Allied Campaign.* 50th anniversary ed. London: Collins, 1994 (1983).

Doubler, Michael D. *Closing with the Enemy: How GIs Fought the War in Europe, 1944–1945.* Lawrence: University Press of Kansas, 1994.

Eisenhower, Dwight D. *Report by the Supreme Commander to the Combined Chiefs of*

*Staff on Operations in Europe of the Allied Expeditionary Forces, 6 June 1944–8 May 1945.* Washington, D.C.: U.S. Government Printing Office, 1946.

Ellis, Lionel Frederic, et al. *The Battle of Normandy.* Vol. 1 of *Victory in the West.* London: H. M. Stationery Office, 1962.

Harrison, Gordon A. *Cross-Channel Attack.* Washington, D.C.: Office of the Chief of Military History, Department of the Army, 1951.

Hastings, Max. *Overlord: D-Day and the Battle for Normandy.* London: Michael Joseph, 1984.

Keegan, John. *Six Armies in Normandy: From D-Day to the Liberation of Paris.* London: Penguin, 1994.

Liddell Hart, Basil H. *History of the Second World War.* London: Cassell, 1970.

Michel, Henri. *La Seconde Guerre mondiale.* 2 vols., 2nd ed. Paris: Presses Universitaires de France, 1977–1980.

Montgomery, Bernard Law. *Normandy to the Baltic.* London: Hutchinson, 1947.

Reynolds, David, Warren F. Kimball, and Alexander O. Chubarian, eds. *Allies at War: The Soviet, American, and British Experience, 1939–1945.* New York: St. Martin's, 1994.

Stacey, Charles Perry. *The Canadian Army, 1939–1945: An Official Historical Summary.* Ottawa: Cloutier, 1948.

Weigley, Russell F. *Eisenhower's Lieutenants: The Campaign of France and Germany, 1944–1945.* Bloomington: Indiana University Press, 1981.

Wilmot, Chester. *The Struggle for Europe.* London: Collins, 1952.

## Economic, Logistical, and Strategic Aspects

Barnett, Correlli. *The Audit of War: The Illusion and Reality of Britain as a Great Nation.* London: Macmillan, 1986.

Facon, Patrick. *Le bombardement stratégique.* Monaco: Éditions du Rocher, 1995.

Matloff, Maurice, and Edwin M. Snell. *Strategic Planning for Coalition Warfare, 1941–1944.* 2 vols. Washington, D.C.: Office of the Chief of Military History, Department of the Army, 1953–1959.

Ruppenthal, Roland G. *Logistical Support of the Armies.* 2 vols. Vol. 1: *May 1941–September 1944;* Vol. 2: *September 1944–May 1945.* Washington, D.C.: Office of the Chief of Military History, Department of the Army, 1953–1959.

## International Relations

Coles, Harry L., and Albert K. Weinberg. *Civil Affairs: Soldiers Become Governors.* Washington, D.C.: Office of the Chief of Military History, Department of the Army, 1964.

Higgins, Trumbull. *Winston Churchill and the Second Front, 1940–1943.* New York: Oxford University Press, 1957.

Kersaudy, François. *Churchill and De Gaulle.* London: Collins, 1981; subsequently published in French as *De Gaulle et Churchill: La mésentente cordiale* (Paris: Plon, 1982).

————. *De Gaulle et Roosevelt: Le duel au sommet.* Paris: Perrin, 2004.

Kimball, Warren F. *The Juggler: Franklin Roosevelt as Wartime Statesman.* Princeton, N.J.: Princeton University Press, 1991.

Kolko, Gabriel. *The Politics of War: The World and United States Foreign Policy, 1943–1945.* New York: Random House, 1968.

McNeill, William Hardy. *America, Britain, and Russia: Their Cooperation and Conflict, 1941–1946.* London: Oxford University Press, 1952.

Soutou, Georges-Henri. *La Guerre de cinquante ans: Les relations Est-Ouest, 1943–1990.* Paris: Fayard, 2001.

Stoler, Mark A. *The Politics of the Second Front: American Military Planning and Diplomacy in Coalition Warfare, 1941–1943.* Westport, Conn.: Greenwood, 1977.

## The Commanders

Ambrose, Stephen E. *The Supreme Commander: The War Years of General Dwight D. Eisenhower.* Garden City, N.Y.: Doubleday, 1970.

Blumenson, Martin. *Patton: The Man behind the Legend, 1885–1945.* New York: William Morrow, 1985.

D'Este, Carlo. *Eisenhower: Allied Supreme Commander.* New York: Holt, 2002.

Hamilton, Nigel. *Monty: The Battles of Field Marshal Bernard Montgomery.* London: Hodder and Stoughton, 1994.

Irving, David. *The War between the Generals.* London: Allen Lane, 1981.

Pogue, Forrest C. *The Supreme Command.* Washington, D.C.: Office of the Chief of Military History, Department of the Army, 1954.

Sherwood, Robert E. *Roosevelt and Hopkins: An Intimate History.* New York: Harper and Brothers, 1948; rev. ed., 1950.

## The German Side

Liddell Hart, Basil H. *The Other Side of the Hill: Germany's Generals, Their Rise and Fall, with Their Own Account of Military Events, 1939–1945.* Rev. ed. London: Cassell, 1951; originally published in 1948 as *The German Generals Talk.*

Speidel, Hans. *Invasion 1944: Rommel and the Normandy Campaign.* Trans. Theo R. Crevenna. Chicago: Regnery, 1950.

## The Soviet Side

Glantz, David M., and Jonathan M. House. *When Titans Clashed: How the Red Army Stopped Hitler.* Lawrence: University Press of Kansas, 1995.

Harrison, Mark. *Accounting for War: Soviet Production, Employment and the Defence Burden, 1940–1945.* Cambridge: Cambridge University Press, 1996.

Lévêque, François. "Les relations franco-soviétiques pendant la Second Guerre mondiale: De la défaite à l'alliance (1939–1945)." 4 vols. Doctoral thesis, Université de Paris-I, 1992.

Overy, Richard. *Russia's War: A History of the Soviet War Effort, 1941–1945.* London: Penguin, 1998.

## The Combatants

Bartov, Omer. *Hitler's Army: Soldiers, Nazis, and War in the Third Reich.* New York: Oxford University Press, 1991.

Copp, Terry, and Bill McAndrew. *Battle Exhaustion: Soldiers and Psychiatrists in the Canadian Army, 1939–1945.* Montreal and Kingston: McGill–Queen's University Press, 1990.

Cosmas, Graham A., and Albert E. Cowdrey. *The Medical Department: Medical Service in the European Theater of Operations.* Washington, D.C.: Center of Military History, United States Army, 1991.

Crocq, Louis. *Les traumatismes psychiques de guerre.* Paris: Odile Jacob, 1999.

Fussell, Paul. *Wartime: Understanding and Behavior in the Second World War.* New York: Oxford University Press, 1989.

Hillel, Marc. *Vie et mœurs des GI's en Europe, 1942–1947.* Paris: Balland, 1981.

Leleu, Jean-Luc. "Soldats politiques en guerre: Sociologie, organisation, rôle et comportements des formations de la Waffen SS en considération particulière de leur présence en Europe de l'Ouest, 1940–1945." Thesis, Université de Caen, 2005.

Lilly, J. Robert. *La face cachée des GI's: Les viols commis par des soldats américains en France, en Angleterre et en Allemagne pendant la Seconde Guerre mondiale.* Paris: Payot, 2003.

Lilly, J. Robert, and François Le Roy. "L'armée américaine et les viols en France, juin 1944–mai 1945." *Vingtième Siècle: Revue d'Histoire* 75 (July–September 2002): 109–121.

Perret, Geoffrey. *There's a War to Be Won: The United States Army in World War II.* New York: Random House, 1991.

## Civilians

Calder, Angus. *The People's War: Britain, 1939–1945.* London: Jonathan Cape, 1969.

O'Neill, William L. *A Democracy at War: America's Fight at Home and Abroad in World War II.* New York: Free Press, 1993.

Reynolds, David. *Rich Relations: The American Occupation of Britain, 1942–1945.* New York: Random House, 1995.

## Spies

Brown, Anthony Cave. *Bodyguard of Lies.* London: W. H. Allen, 1975.

Destremau, Christian. *Opération Garbo: Le dernier secret du Jour J.* Paris: Perrin, 2004.

Foot, M.R.D. *SOE in France: An Account of the Work of the British Special Operations Executive in France, 1940–1944.* London: H.M. Stationery Office, 1966.

Hinsley, F. H., et al. *British Intelligence in the Second World War: Its Influence on Strategy and Operations.* Vols. 1–3 of *British Intelligence in the Second World War.* London and Cambridge: H. M. Stationery Office / Cambridge University Press, 1979–1988.

Hinsley, F. H., and C. A. G. Simkins. *Security and Counter-Intelligence.* Vol. 4 of *British*

*Intelligence in the Second World War.* London and Cambridge: H. M. Stationery Office / Cambridge University Press, 1990.

Holt, Thaddeus. *The Deceivers: Allied Military Deception in the Second World War.* New York: Simon and Schuster, 2004.

Howard, Michael. *Strategic Deception.* Vol. 5 of *British Intelligence in the Second World War.* London and Cambridge: H. M. Stationery Office / Cambridge University Press, 1990.

### France, Brittany, and Normandy

Boivin, Michel. "Les Manchois de la libération à ses lendemains." Vol. 4 of "Les Manchois dans la tourmente de la guerre, 1939–1945." Doctoral thesis, Université de Caen, 2003.

Boivin, Michel, Gérard Bourdin, and Jean Quellien. *Villes normandes sous les bombes, juin 1944.* Caen: Presses Universitaires de Caen / Mémorial de Caen, 1994.

Buton, Philippe. *La joie douloureuse: La libération de la France.* Brussels: Complexe, 2004.

Capdevilla, Luc. *Les Bretons au lendemain de l'Occupation: Imaginaire et comportement d'une sortie de guerre, 1944–1945.* Rennes: Presses Universitaires de Rennes, 1999.

Comité d'histoire de la Seconde Guerre mondiale. *La libération de la France.* Paris: CNRS Éditions, 1976.

Crémieux-Brilhac, Jean-Louis. *La France libre: De l'appel du 18 juin à la libération.* Paris: Gallimard, 1996.

Garnier, Bernard, Jean-Luc Leleu, Françoise Passera, and Jean Quellien, eds. *Les populations civiles face au débarquement et à la bataille de Normandie.* Caen: Mémorial de Caen, 2005.

Levisse-Touzé, Christine, ed. Paris, 1944: *Les enjeux de la libération.* Paris: Albin Michel, 1994.

Quellien, Jean. *Le Débarquement et la Bataille de Normandie: La Normandie au coeur de la guerre.* Caen and Rennes: Mémorial de Caen / Éditions Ouest-France, 1998.

# Index